OXFORD CLASSIC

Published under the superv...
Faculty of Literae Humaniores in the University of Oxford

THE LIBRARY

ISBN 814090-8 FLEX CAT. IJQ

DATE RIP ~~PUBLISHED~~ APRIL 1998

RIP ~~PUBLISHED~~ PRICE £19.99

DATE O/P

O/P NUMBER

OXFORD CLASSICAL MONOGRAPHS

The aim of the Oxford Classical Monographs series (which replaces the Oxford Classical and Philosophical Monographs) is to publish outstanding theses on Greek and Latin literature, ancient history, and ancient philosophy examined by the faculty board of Literae Humaniores.

METAMORPHOSIS IN GREEK MYTHS

P. M. C. FORBES IRVING

CLARENDON PRESS · OXFORD

Oxford University Press, Great Clarendon Street, Oxford OX2 6DP
Oxford New York
Athens Auckland Bangkok Bogota Bombay Buenos Aires
Calcutta Cape Town Dar es Salaam Delhi Florence Hong Kong Istanbul
Karachi Kuala Lumpur Madras Madrid Melbourne Mexico City
Nairobi Paris Singapore Taipei Tokyo Toronto Warsaw
and associated companies in
Berlin Ibadan

Oxford is a registered trade mark of Oxford University Press

Published in the United States
by Oxford University Press Inc., New York

Reprinted 1998

ISBN 0-19-814090-8

Printed in Great Britain
by Biddles Short Run Books
King's Lynn

Preface

I am very grateful for the advice I received from Professor J. R. Baines and Dr J. Black on those parts of this book which deal with Egyptian and with Mesopotamian myth and religion. I should also like to thank Professor Hugh Lloyd-Jones for a very large number of helpful comments on the dissertation which was the original form of this book, Professor J. Boardman, all the examiners of the dissertation, and, most of all, Robert Parker, for his advice and assistance over many years, first in supervising the dissertation and then in helping me to revise it for publication.

P. M. C. F. I.

London
November 1989

Contents

List of Abbreviations

For the most part the abbreviations in N. G. L. Hammond and H. H. Scullard, *The Oxford Classical Dictionary*[2] (Oxford, 1970), ix–xxii, have been followed where available. For other cases those in H. G. Liddell, R. Scott, and H. Stuart Jones, *A Greek–English Lexicon*[9] (Oxford, 1940), and C. T. Lewis and C. Short, *A Latin Dictionary* (Oxford, 1879), have normally been used. Exceptions and additions to these lists are given below.

Where specific editors are not named *fragments* are cited according to the numerations of the following collections: Hesiod, R. Merkelbach and M. L. West (Oxford, 1967); epic poets, *PEG*; lyric poets, *PMG* or E. Lobel and D. L. Page, *Poetarum Lesbiorum Fragmenta* (Oxford, 1955); iambic and elegaic poets, M. L. West, *Iambi et Elegi Graeci ante Alexandrum cantati* (Oxford, 1971–2); historians, *FGH*; Pindar, B. Snell and H. Maehler[4] (Leipzig, 1975); Euripides, A. Nauck, with supplement of B. Snell (Hildesheim, 1964); other tragic poets, *TGF*; Attic comic poets, Kock, *CAF*, except where a reference to *PCG* is indicated; Dorian comedy, G. Kaibel (Berlin, 1899); Callimachus, R. Pfeiffer (Oxford, 1949); Nicander, O. Schneider (Leipzig, 1856); other Hellenistic poets, J. U. Powell, *Collectanea Alexandrina* (Oxford, 1925), except where a reference to *SH* is indicated.

I. ANCIENT AUTHORS, PERIODICALS, COLLECTIONS OF TEXTS, SERIES AND GENERAL REFERENCE WORKS:

AJA	*American Journal of Archaeology*
AJP	*American Journal of Philology*
AK	*Antike Kunst*
AL	Antoninus Liberalis

ANET[3]	J. B. Pritchard, *Ancient Near Eastern Texts Relating to the Old Testament* (Princeton, 1969)
AP	*Anthologia Palatina*
AR	Apollonius Rhodius
Bacch.	Bacchylides
CAF	T. Kock, *Comicorum Atticorum Fragmenta* (Leipzig, 1880–8)
CGCBM	*Catalogue of Greek Coins in the British Museum* (1873–1927)
CPCP	*California Publications in Classical Philology*
CSCA	*California Studies in Classical Antiquity*
DS	Diodorus Siculus
EAA	*Enciclopedia dell'arte antica classica e orientale* (Rome, 1958–66)
EM	*Etymologicum Magnum*
FGH	F. Jacoby, *Fragmente der griechischen Historiker* (Berlin, 1923–)
FPL	W. Morel, *Fragmenta Poetarum Latinorum* (Leipzig, 1927)
Geop.	*Geoponica*
GLP	D. L. Page, *Greek Literary Papyri* (London, 1941)
HSCP	*Harvard Studies in Classical Philology*
HTR	*Harvard Theological Review*
Hyg. *PA*	Hyginus, *Poetica Astronomica*
LIMC	L. Kahil, *Lexicon Iconographicum Mythologiae Classicae* (1981–)
LSCG	F. Sokolowski, *Lois sacrées des cités grecques* (Paris, 1969)
LSS	—— *Lois sacrées des cités grecques*, supplement (Paris, 1962)
Lact. Plac. *Narr.*	Lactantius Placidus, *Narrationes Fabularum Ovidianarum*
Lyc.	Lycophron
Myth. Vat.	G. H. Bode, *Mythographi Vaticani* (Celle, 1834)

PCG	R. Kassel and C. Austin, *Poetae Comici Graeci* (Berlin, 1983–)
PEG	A. Bernabé, *Poetae Epici Graeci* (Leipzig, 1987)
PMG	D. L. Page, *Poetae Melici Graeci* (Oxford, 1962)
Peek	W. Peek, *Griechische Vers-Inschriften* i, Grab-Epigramme (Berlin, 1955)
Pliny, *NH*	Pliny, *Naturalis Historia*
Plut. *GQ*	Plutarch, *Greek Questions*
Plut. *RQ*	Plutarch, *Roman Questions*
QS	Quintus Smyrnaeus
RE	A. Pauly, G. Wissowa, and others, *Real-Encyclopädie der classischen Altertumswissenschaft* (Stuttgart, 1893–)
REA	*Revue des études anciennes*
REG	*Revue des études grecques*
RHR	*Revue de l'histoire des religions*
RhM	*Rheinisches Museum für klassische Philologie*
RML	W. H. Roscher, *Ausführliches Lexikon der griechischen und römischen Mythologie* (Leipzig, 1884–1937)
SH	P. J. Parsons and H. Lloyd-Jones, *Supplementum Hellenisticum* (Berlin, 1983)
TGF	R. Kannicht, S. Radt, B. Snell, *Tragicorum Graecorum Fragmenta* (Göttingen, 1971–)
Virgil, *A*, *E*, and *G*	Virgil, *Aeneid*, *Eclogues*, and *Georgics*
Westermann, *Myth.*	A. Westermann, *Mythographi* (Brunswick, 1843)
ZA	*Zeitschrift für Assyriologie*

In addition when one of the following authors is cited without a work being named, the following works are being referred to: Aelian, *De Natura Animalium*; Apollonius Rhodius, *Argonautica*; Nonnus, *Dionysiaca*; Ovid, *Metamorphoses*; Pliny, *Naturalis Historia*.

Note: References to the sources for transformation stories are given in the Catalogue and are not usually cited every time such a story is mentioned anywhere else.

2. OTHER WORKS

Atallah, *Adonis*	W. Atallah, *Adonis dans la littérature et l'art grec* (Paris, 1966)
Bodson	L. Bodson, ΙΕΡΑ ΖΩΙΑ (Brussels, 1978)
Boetticher	C. Boetticher, *Der Baumcultus der Hellenen* (Berlin, 1856)
Bömer	Ovid, *Metamorphosen*, ed. F. Bömer (Heidelberg, 1969–)
Borgeaud	P. Borgeaud, *Recherches sur le dieu Pan* (Rome, 1979)
Brelich, *Paides*	A. Brelich, *Paides e Parthenoi* (Rome, 1969)
Bremmer	J. Bremmer (ed.), *Interpretations of Greek Mythology* (London, 1987)
Brisson	L. Brisson, *Le Mythe de Tirésias* (Leiden, 1976)
Brommer, *Vasenlisten*[3]	F. Brommer, *Vasenlisten zur griechischen Heldensage* (Marburg, 1973)
Bubbe	W. Bubbe, *De Metamorphosibus Graecorum Capita Selecta* (diss. Halle, 1913)
Burkert, *HN*	W. Burkert, *Homo Necans: Interpretationen altgriechischer Opferriten und Mythen* (Berlin, 1972)
—— *GR*	—— *Greek Religion* (Eng. tr. Oxford, 1985)
—— *SH*	—— *Structure and History in Greek Mythology and Ritual* (Berkeley, 1979)
Calame	C. Calame, *Les Chœurs de jeunes filles en Grèce archaïque* (Rome, 1977)
Cook, *Zeus*	A. B. Cook, *Zeus: A Study in Ancient Religion* (Cambridge, 1914–40)
Davies and Kathiramby	M. Davies and J. Kathiramby, *Greek Insects* (London, 1986)

Delcourt, *Hermaphrodite*	M. Delcourt, *Hermaphrodite: Myths and Rites of the Bisexual Figure in Classical Antiquity* (Eng. tr. London, 1961)
Detienne, *Dionysos Slain*	M. Detienne, *Dionysos Slain* (Eng. tr. Baltimore, 1979)
—— *Gardens of Adonis*	—— *The Gardens of Adonis* (Eng. tr. Hassocks, 1977)
Detienne–Vernant	M. Detienne and J. P. Vernant, *Cunning Intelligence in Greek Culture and Society* (Eng. tr. Hassocks, 1978)
Deubner	L. Deubner, *Attische Feste* (Berlin, 1932)
Diggle, *Phaethon*	Euripides, *Phaethon*, ed. J. Diggle (Cambridge, 1970)
Dodds	Euripides, *Bacchae*², ed. E. R. Dodds (Oxford, 1960)
Farnell, *Cults*	L. R. Farnell, *The Cults of the Greek States* (Oxford, 1896–1909)
Fontenrose, *Orion*	J. Fontenrose, *Orion: The Myth of the Hunter and the Huntress* (Berkeley, 1981)
—— *Python*	—— *Python: A Study of the Delphic Myth and its Origins* (Berkeley, 1959)
Frazer, *GB*	J. G. Frazer, *The Golden Bough: A Study in Comparative Religion*³ (London, 1911–12)
—— *Apollodorus*	Apollodorus, *The Library*, ed. J. G. Frazer (London, 1921)
Gordon	R. L. Gordon (ed.), *Myth, Religion and Society: Structuralist Essays by M. Detienne, L. Gernet, J. P. Vernant and P. Vidal-Naquet* (Cambridge, 1981)
Halliday	Plutarch, *The Greek Questions*, ed. W. Halliday (Oxford, 1928)
Hollis	Ovid, *Metamorphoses* VIII, ed. A. S. Hollis (Oxford, 1970)
Jeanmaire, *Couroi*	H. Jeanmaire, *Couroi et Courètes: Essai sur l'éducation spartiate et sur les rites d'adolescence dans l'antiquité hellénique* (Lille, 1939)

Keller	O. Keller, *Die antike Tierwelt* (Berlin, 1909–13)
Kirk, *Myth*	G. S. Kirk, *Myth: Its Meaning and Function in Ancient and Other Cultures* (Cambridge, 1970)
Lafaye	G. Lafaye, *Études sur les Métamorphoses d'Ovide et leurs modèles grecs* (Paris, 1904)
Lyne	*Ciris*, ed. R. O. A. M. Lyne (Cambridge, 1978)
Murr	J. Murr, *Die Pflanzenwelt in der griechischen Mythologie* (Innsbruck, 1890)
Nilsson, *GF*	M. P. Nilsson, *Griechische Feste von religiöser Bedeutung mit Ausschluß der attischen* (Leipzig, 1906)
—— *MOGM*	—— *The Mycenaean Origin of Greek Mythology* (Cambridge, 1932)
—— *MMR*	—— *The Minoan-Mycenaean Religion and its Survival in Greek Religion*^{2} (Lund, 1950)
—— *GGR*	—— *Geschichte der griechischen Religion*^{3}, vol. i (Munich, 1967)
Ninck	M. Ninck, *Die Bedeutung des Wassers* (*Philologus* Suppl. 14 (2), 1921)
Otis	B. Otis, *Ovid as an Epic Poet* (Cambridge, 1966)
Papathomopoulos	Antoninus Liberalis, *Les Métamorphoses*, ed. M. Papathomopoulos (Paris, 1968)
Piccaluga	G. Piccaluga, *Lykaon: Un tema mitico* (Rome, 1968)
Preller	L. Preller, *Griechische Mythologie*^{4}, ed. C. Robert, vol. i, *Theogonie und Götter* (Berlin, 1887–94)
Renner	T. Renner, 'A Papyrus Dictionary of Metamorphoses', *HSCP* 82 (1978), 277–95
Richardson	*The Homeric Hymn to Demeter*, ed. N. J. Richardson (Oxford, 1974)
Robert, *Heldensage*	C. Robert, *Die griechische Heldensage* (Berlin, 1920–6)

—— *Eratosth.*	*Eratosthenis Catasterismorum Reliquiae*, ed. C. Robert (Berlin, 1878)
Rohde, *Psyche*	E. Rohde, *Psyche*[4] (Tübingen, 1907)
Rose, *Handbook*	H. J. Rose, *A Handbook of Greek Mythology*[6] (Oxford, 1958)
Thompson	W. D. Thompson, *A Glossary of Greek Birds*[2] (Oxford, 1936)
Vernant, *Myth and Society*	J. P. Vernant, *Myth and Society in Ancient Greece* (Eng. tr. Brighton, 1980)
Weicker, *Seelenvogel*	G. Weicker, *Der Seelenvogel in der alten Literatur und Kunst* (Leipzig, 1902)
West	Hesiod, *Theogony*, ed. M. L. West (Oxford, 1966)

Introduction

METAMORPHOSIS has always been considered one of the most fantastic of mythical motifs, and there were attempts to explain it even in ancient writers. Transformation stories figure prominently in the works of the rationalizers Palaephatus and Heraclitus, where they were seen as misunderstandings of everyday events, or as springing from metaphors or exaggerations. Sometimes the stories are taken more seriously; in particular those stories which were recounted in the Homeric poems were seen as examples of philosophical allegory. Proteus, for instance, was explained as the original undifferentiated substance which contained all the forms.[1] For Augustine stories of metamorphosis presented special theological problems: these changes could not have been worked by a god, and yet devils have no power to change or create physical substance.[2] Transformations are therefore illusions caused by devils.

These ancient approaches considered the stories as historical reports that had to be explained away, whereas modern studies have looked at them as products of the human imagination. Nevertheless, earlier modern explanations of these stories come very close to those of the ancient rationalists. In 1786 Mellman's[3] list of categories of transformations included those originating in ambiguity of speech, in actions poetically elaborated, in metaphors and symbols, or in philosophical allegory (e.g. Proteus). It is in the second half of the nineteenth century that we first find a radically different approach. The comparative study of primitive societies and the birth of anthropology had given rise to a range of new concepts including totemism, animism, and fetishism, which threw a new light on Greek gods and their myths. Works such as Visser's *Die nichtmenschengestaltigen Götter der Griechen*[4] ('The Non-anthropomorphic Gods of the Greeks') set out to uncover a primitive stage in

[1] See schol. *Od.* 4. 384, 456.

[2] *De Civ. D.* 18. 18.

[3] J. G. L. Mellman, *Commentatio de causis et auctoribus narrationum de mutatis formis* (Leipzig, 1786).

[4] M. W. Visser (Leiden, 1903).

Greek religion in which the Greeks had worshipped animal-gods and believed that animals and objects around them possessed souls. Transformation stories were regarded as survivals of such beliefs and an important source of evidence for them.

Such views were an important influence on Bubbe's thesis *De Metamorphosibus Graecorum Capita Selecta*,[5] the only full work so far written on Greek metamorphoses. For Kern[6] a belief in animal-gods was the origin of the transformation story. Weicker's[7] influential book, *Der Seelenvogel*, cited transformation stories as evidence for a general Greek belief that the souls of the dead took the form of birds. In the sphere of plants Boetticher[8] argued that trees were the home of the gods and the souls of the dead, and Mannhardt[9] that stories of transformations into trees were evidence of an earlier belief in tree spirits and dryads. This approach to transformation stories became standard. The *RML* article on *Verwandlungen* ('transformations') published in 1937 declares that the origin of transformations is closely tied to totemism and animism. The *RE* article on transformations is actually a sub-section of the article on animal-gods.[10] Some of these theories, for instance that of the soul bird, have now been generally rejected; nevertheless, the general approach has had enormous influence, and it has been the only systematic attempt to explain the origins of transformations.

Although some scholars were sceptical of these theories, there was not much attempt to offer an alternative explanation of the origin of the stories. Some scholars[11] attempted to find folk-tale parallels for them; some concerned themselves simply with literary history.[12] Often these approaches were combined and the standard analysis of a myth consisted in following the literary sources back to a supposed folk-tale origin of the story; where, as in the case of

5 W. Bubbe (1913).

6 O. Kern, 'Metamorphose in Religion und Dichtung der Antike', in J. Walther (ed.), *Goethe als Seher und Erforscher* (Leipzig, 1930), 185–204.

7 G. Weicker (Leipzig, 1902).

8 C. Boetticher, *Der Baumcultus der Hellenen* (Berlin, 1856).

9 W. Mannhardt, *Wald- und Feldkulte*, ii (Berlin, 1875–7).

10 *RE* VI A 1 (1936), col. 893.

11 See e.g. M. Ninck, *Die Bedeutung des Wassers* (*Philologus* Suppl. 14 (2), 1921).

12 See e.g. the very full treatments of the nightingale legend in I. Cazzaniga, *La Saga di Itys* (Varese, 1950–1) and G. Mihaelov, *Annuaire de l'Université de Sofia* L 2 (1955), 77–208.

many of the transformation stories, no pre-Alexandrian sources could be produced, the story could be dismissed as a literary invention. The most important work exploring the literary origins and development of transformation stories is Lafaye's study of Ovid's sources,[13] in which he traced the evolution of the metamorphosis story from the Homeric myths, which he saw as examples of the primitive folk-tale type, to the elaborate inventions of the Alexandrians. The literary survey and the search for religious origins were in one important respect complementary: they both supposed that the myth-making of the folk-tradition was an entirely different activity from that of the poets. Kern wrote that it was necessary in a work on metamorphosis to distinguish religion, saga, legend, and poetry; Bubbe divided the transformation stories, sometimes quite arbitrarily, into genuine myths (which very often have a religious origin) and inventions of the poets. This is a general distinction that is still made by many modern writers. Kirk,[14] noting the difference between the Greek myths and the more fantastic myths of other cultures, has argued that there was a proper myth-making period in Greek history and that surviving Greek myths are distorted echoes of these original ones. Other scholars carry this sort of approach to an opposite extreme and argue that there is no such thing as a myth, but only individual tellings of it:[15] one should therefore study the particular literary versions that have survived and not attempt to discover the underlying meaning of the myth.

In the last fifty years transformation stories have been a neglected area of Greek myths. The animal-god theories have not been systematically rejected, and in fact are sometimes referred to as the standard view,[16] but they are no longer an important basis of new research. Ritual explanations are still popular, but these are more usually concerned with rites of passage than totemism, and the stories of sex change have received more attention recently than the stories of animals or birds.[17]

[13] G. Lafaye, *Études sur les Métamorphoses d'Ovide et leurs modèles grecs* (Paris, 1904).

[14] G. S. Kirk, *Myth: Its Meaning and Function in Ancient and Other Cultures* (Cambridge, 1970), 244–5.

[15] See e.g. N. J. Richardson, *CR* 31 (1981), 64.

[16] See below, ch. 2.

[17] See below, ch. 7.

The most important new approach in the study of Greek myths in general has been that of the structuralists.[18] The structuralists reject two major assumptions of many previous studies of Greek myths. First of all, they think that all the variations of a story are important; myth-making, they argue, is to some extent an autonomous activity which can be performed by the Alexandrian poet as well as by the oral story-teller. Secondly, structuralists have emphasized that explaining a myth's history and the origins of its different parts can only take us a certain way. One valuable feature of this approach is the attention they pay to the story as a whole structure, not merely as a collection of independent motifs. An animal in a transformation story has to be seen not merely as something that points to an external historical ritual, but as something that has significance within the structure of the story.

In this book I have set out to explore both the history of these stories and their structure. Greek myths are not completely timeless entities as structuralists sometimes argue; they undergo a development, and in the case of any one version of a myth there will always be questions to ask about the particular context of its telling. This does not mean that one should only be concerned with discovering the original myth or folk-tale. Greek myths as we know them are the products of poets as much as of any folk-tale tradition; distinctions such as literate and non-literate inevitably seem artificial when we remember that the Greek epic tradition is in origin an oral one, and it is anyway implausible to imagine that the oral story-teller is a mere mouthpiece of the myth incapable of innovation and immune to external influence. In the first chapter I have tried to draw some general conclusions about the way that different periods of Greek literature have a different emphasis in their treatment of the myths: motifs drop out, or are brought in from other stories, and sometimes new myths may be invented. In the catalogue I have set out the variants of the individual myths in some detail, trying to show how the myths developed in response to such influences and what par-

[18] For the place of structuralism in the history of the study of Greek myths see J. P. Vernant, *Myth and Society in Ancient Greece* (Eng. tr. Brighton, 1980), 186–242, M. Detienne, *Dionysos Slain* (Eng. tr. Baltimore, 1979), ch. 1.

ticular external historical and religious factors may be relevant in each case.

In the main part of the book I have been more concerned with the structure of the stories. In spite of the change of taste in different periods the basic structure and themes of the traditional stories remain virtually unchanged. The story of Io in Ovid, for instance, is in important respects the same story as that of Pseudo-Hesiod or Aeschylus. This continuity applies not only on the level of single stories: Greek myths as a whole form a coherent body of stories in which, to some extent at least, common themes and attitudes and even rules of development may be traced. While therefore it is in a sense true that myths do not exist independently of individual tellings of them, no analysis of a treatment of a myth will be complete which does not explore the myth's part in the wider system of Greek mythology. Myth-tellers, whether literate or oral, will have been brought up on and made familiar with a large body of these myths, and their own accounts will neither be the products of an entirely individual creative spirit, nor a direct reflection of their social background and attitudes, but may be expected to be influenced by the structures of Greek mythology as a whole.

My method is not a strictly structuralist one. I do think that the sort of polarizations and antitheses to which the structuralists draw attention are important, and in particular their favourite opposition of nature and culture has a very important role in these stories of transformation from men to animals. But the structuralists have a tendency to see these oppositions as purely formal ones, which have an interest in themselves. I am less inclined to accept that the only meaning of a mythical motif lies in its relation with another one, and that the stories have no direct relevance to general human concerns (even though this relevance may be a metaphorical rather than a literal one). In the discussion of sex changes, for instance, I have argued that the stories are concerned, to some extent at least, with the relation of the sexes, and that the sex change is not merely a formal mediation.

Secondly, structuralists have a tendency to suppose that myths are problem-solving, and, sometimes, that the function of myths is to resolve contradictions.[19] In this respect they are typical of a more widespread approach. Kirk, for instance, continually draws a distinction between what he describes as the speculative and explanatory function of myths and their narrative function. It is the former that he regards as the more properly mythical element in the stories. My approach is rather to suppose that the myths are primarily stories, and that the imaginative and emotional response they evoke is not something to be distinguished from their narrative function but a central part of it. I have argued that the meaning of these myths—and I am excluding here certain very simple aetiological stories—lies not so much in the answers they provide to basic questions, or the morals that can be derived from them, as in the way that they play upon basic themes to create an exciting, moving, or amusing story. There are times when it is useful to distinguish a narrative device from what may be described as an underlying theme. But this is in a sense a shorthand; what one may be really distinguishing is a more important narrative element from a less important one.

[19] The view that the function of myths is to resolve contradictions is seen as a misinterpretation of structuralism by Detienne, *Dionysos Slain*, 3, but it is assumed in the structuralist interpretations of Kirk (*Myth*, ch. 2), and E. Leach (*Lévi-Strauss* (London, 1970), ch. 4).

I

The Sources

BEFORE attempting to classify and interpret the myths themselves I shall consider the literary sources in which they appear.[1] This will serve two functions. First, it seems helpful for the understanding of the myths to have some general idea of the contexts in which they appear and the sort of literary uses to which they are put. Secondly, there is the more specific question of their date of origin. It is often suggested that the stories of metamorphosis, most of which do not appear before the Alexandrian period, are largely the invention of the Hellenistic poets. As we have little evidence for the metamorphosis myths apart from the literary sources it is difficult to draw any conclusions on external grounds, and one can only attempt to answer the question by examining the nature and purpose of these poems and of the earlier works that neglected these stories. It is necessary to consider both whether these stories are late inventions and whether this means they are myths of a different status from the earlier ones.

One can recognize three fairly distinct stages in our sources for transformation stories: there is first Homer; secondly, the period of the earlier Greek poets and mythographers from Hesiod to the tragedians; and thirdly, the Hellenistic period and after.

It is perhaps inevitable that my discussion of Nicander and Boios will be much fuller than that of the earlier sources. They are the main source for a very large number of our metamorphoses, and metamorphoses form the main theme of their work, or of one of their works. My discussion of Homer and the tragedians will necessarily be more selective; transformation is only a minor theme

[1] For the literary treatment of metamorphosis before Ovid see Lafaye; Kern (art. cit. Introduction, n. 6); S. Jannacone, *La letteratura greco-latina delle metamorphosi* (Messina, 1953); W. Fauth, *Poetica* 7 (1975), 235–68.

among their myths, and I can assume a greater familiarity with their general themes and purpose.

HOMER

In neither the *Iliad* nor the *Odyssey* do we find any transformation stories of the type that became popular in the later poets, in which the gods transform a man in pity or as a punishment. There are basically two types of transformation in Homer. One is the transformations worked by magicians. Circe turns the sailors of Odysseus into pigs, and Proteus undergoes a series of transformations to avoid being captured by Menelaus.[2] Although Circe and Proteus are technically gods they are sinister amoral beings who live on magical islands far away from the normal heroic and divine world: the changes they work lack the religious or moral motivation that is a basic feature of the later pattern.

The other is a petrification by the gods as a sign to men: thus in Book 2 of the *Iliad* we are told how Zeus changed a snake to stone in a portent about the capture of Troy, and in Book 13 of the *Odyssey* Poseidon turns the ship of the Phaeacians to stone as a warning not to carry any more travellers across the sea.[3] In neither case is there any reference to men being transformed. In the *Odyssey* passage it is the Phaeacian ship that is of interest, not the sailors on board; if they were transformed too this is not mentioned and is only incidental. In each case, therefore, metamorphosis is a miraculous sign revealing the will of the gods and not a mysterious experience for the human sufferer. What is crucial is the effect on the beholder and we are immediately informed of this:

> For the son of Kronos of the crooked counsels turned it [the snake] to stone; and we stood marvelling at what had happened. . . . But Calchas there and then spoke in prophecy . . .[4]

[2] Circe: *Od.* 10. 238 f.; Proteus: *Od.* 4. 355 ff.

[3] Phaeacian ship: *Od.* 13. 163 f.; snake: *Il.* 2. 319.

[4] *Il.* 2. 319 ff.

The subsequent role of the petrified object is of little importance. We may contrast with this the later story of the metamorphosis of the nightingale, where the logic of the story and the function of the change depend on the nature and experiences of the character involved; there is no question of Aedon's change being a sign to anyone, and no reports speak of witnesses.

The other transformation story told in the *Iliad*, the petrification of Niobe's neighbours after her children are killed by the gods, is a variation on this latter type. Although the transformation is not a sign and is of human beings it is still entirely a device in some further purpose of the Olympians (in this case to prevent the burial of Niobe's children); there is no question of the neighbours deserving their fate or of being of any interest in themselves at all. Like the Phaeacian sailors they are incidental.

The type of transformation as a sign has a similar function to other miracles of the gods and in particular the transformations of the gods themselves into birds. These are almost always connected with a miraculous appearance or disappearance of the god and are sometimes followed by a recognition speech from a human character corresponding to the speech of Calchas after the petrification of the snake.[5] Again what is important is the demonstration to men of the will or the support of the Olympians.

However, if Homer is reticent about actually recounting the familiar transformation stories or even recounting human as opposed to divine transformations at all, it is clear that he was aware of them. The transformations of Aedon, the halcyon, and Niobe are all hinted at.[6] The case of Niobe is particularly interesting since here we can probably see Homer replacing a familiar transformation with a new one invented to suit its particular context.[7] The story of Niobe is told as an *exemplum* by Achilles, who is urging Priam to eat; every feature of his story corresponds to a feature of Priam's own situation, and the petrification of Niobe's neighbours is introduced to explain why her children's bodies, like that of Priam's son, were unburied. It does not occur in any other source.

[5] See e.g. the speech of Nestor after Athene flies away as a sea eagle: *Od.* 3. 372 ff.

[6] Aedon: *Od.* 19. 518 ff.; Niobe: *Il.* 24. 610 ff.; halcyon: *Il.* 9. 563.

[7] See J. T. Kakridis, *RhM* 79 (1930), 113–22; M. Willcock, *CQ* 14 (1964), 141–54.

There is no reason, therefore, to believe that Homer's favoured type of transformation is in fact the oldest or that his reticence with regard to the transformation of human beings reflects an ignorance of these stories. So how is this reticence to be explained?

One possible explanation might be found in Homer's subject matter. War and voyages allow little scope for metamorphosis; later transformations tend to be connected with women, love, and family intrigue. However, there are a number of transformations in episodes of the Trojan war related by other poets (e.g. those of Kyknos, Memnon, and Hecuba), while in the context of a voyage the *Argonautica* of Apollonius makes much more use of metamorphosis than the *Odyssey*. We need to look further.

The rarity of transformations in Homer must be seen in the wider context of Homeric selectivity. The differences between Homer and the other epic poets in their choice of material have been discussed by Griffin,[8] who cites transformation stories as just one of the fantastic or magical themes that are neglected by Homer; he contrasts in the *Cypria* the fabulous eyesight of Lynceus, the magical daughters of Anius who feed the Greek army, the swan-white Kyknos, and in the *Ilias Parva* the magic bow of Philoctetes.

The Homeric world is characterized by a rigid distinction between the main categories of existence that offers little room for compromise or ambiguity. This applies both to the distinction between man and animal and, more particularly, to that between man and god; at the heart of this latter distinction is the inevitability of death, and this is incompatible with the compromise represented by transformation. The heroes of the Trojan war are not generally translated after death in Homer, as they nearly all are in the later poets; neither is there yet any suggestion of the invulnerability of Achilles or Ajax. Mysterious afterlife and invulnerability are, like metamorphosis, a compromise of mortal status and therefore excluded. Homer describes a miraculous disappearance of Sarpedon's body that recalls the spiriting away of Memnon, but this is now a preparation for burial, not immortality.[9]

[8] *JHS* 97 (1977), 39–53.

[9] Sarpedon: *Il.* 16. 666 ff. The death and translation of Memnon was recounted in the *Aethiopis*.

The changes in the Niobe story illustrate this point. The new moral that one must give up mourning and return to normal life is in direct conflict with the desire for eternal mourning that is so common in metamorphosis stories. Metamorphosis represents a way out of the natural order; at the expense of normal human status one may continue in a state of obsessive mourning and identification with the dead, but this halfway stage and isolation are something alien to the spirit of the *Iliad*. The petrification of the neighbours, by contrast, is an extinction that allows no scope for ambiguity.

Where fantastic events or creatures are referred to which appear to blur the boundaries of men, gods, and the animal world, they tend, like the translation to heaven of Ganymede and Kleitos and the apotheosis of Leocothea,[10] to be set in the remote past outside the main story or, like the pigs with human minds on Circe's island, to be located on the geographical fringes of the world. The few fantastic events that are recounted in the main narrative and take place on the central stage of the heroic world, such as the speaking of Achilles' horse,[11] or the spiriting away of Sarpedon, tend to be miraculous rather than magical, in that they serve only to reinforce the difference between men and gods. Human and animal generally touch only in a metaphorical sense, in the form of comparisons. Hecuba desires to eat her enemy, in an implied comparison, like a dog;[12] it is at least possible that there is a hint here of the story that she eventually became a dog in her bitterness. Old men are compared to crickets; later writers tell how the impossibly old Tithonus eventually became a cricket.[13] Marpessa cries like a halcyon, but does not become one.[14]

In conclusion, therefore, the distinct bias in Homer towards a special conception of metamorphosis as a public miracle, and a lack of interest in the later popular theme of the continuing ambiguous status of the transformed individual, are in keeping with the

[10] Ganymede: *Il.* 20. 232 ff.; Kleitos: *Od.* 15. 250 f.; Leukothea: *Od.* 5. 334 f.

[11] *Il.* 19. 418. This is anyway immediately silenced by the Erinyes.

[12] *Il.* 24. 212–13.

[13] See Cat. 5*c*. iv s.v.

[14] *Il.* 9. 563.

censorship of other elements that conflict with his notion of heroic mortality: since we have hints that he was at least aware of some stories of this other kind, though he does not recount them, we may suppose that others are omitted as a result of deliberate suppression rather than ignorance.

THE HESIODIC POEMS

In the second period, from Hesiod to the tragedians,[15] transformation stories become more popular: we know of at least thirteen that are mentioned in Hesiod[16] and fifteen in tragedy. None of the transformations recounted in Homer recur in this period, and the basic type becomes the man transformed by the god in punishment or pity for his own behaviour or sufferings.

It is very difficult to generalize about the Hesiodic treatment of the transformations since they all come in the lost works and in most cases we have only citations rather than the actual words of the poet. I shall therefore merely make a number of brief and fairly speculative points.

The Hesiodic magical shape-shifter corresponding to the Homeric Proteus is not a mysterious magician but a human hero, Periclymenus, whose transformations take place within the heroic context of a battle. We may compare Kyknos, again a human warrior, whose magical invulnerability and swan-like nature put him on the edge of the divine and animal worlds. It seems that the increased fondness for transformation stories may coincide with the loosening of the boundaries between men and the gods and animals.[17]

Secondly, in spite of the fragmentary state of the evidence, one can deduce a characteristic Hesiodic pattern in the transformation

[15] Here as elsewhere, for the sake of convenience, I have used the name Hesiod to include the authors of the *Catalogue of Women*, the *Melampodia*, and the other pseudo-Hesiodic poems. There are no transformations at all in the *Theogony* and the *Works and Days*.

[16] Periclymenus (fr. 33), Io, Callisto, Actaeon, Battos, Lycaon, Ceyx and Alcyone, the Proitides (see below, ch. 3 n. 34), Mestra (fr. 43). For other references see below, Catalogue.

[17] See frs. 237, 33. Cf. frs. 205, 234.

stories. Of the non-magical human transformations, those of Actaeon, Io, Callisto, Battos, Lycaon, Ceyx and Alcyone, Niobe and the Proitides (a transformation of a sort if not to an animal) are nearly all examples of a pattern of insult to a god, usually one of the major gods, followed by punishment in the form of a degrading transformation. Here we can speak of the transformation story as a punishment pattern rather than as a mysterious sign or dangerous encounter with a magician as in Homer.

In two cases the clear pattern of crime and punishment, and the predominant role of Zeus, conflict with the later Hellenistic version of the story. In later versions Ceyx becomes the tragic victim of a shipwreck, and his wife becomes a bird in mourning; in Hesiod they call themselves Zeus and Hera and are punished by transformation. In later accounts Actaeon accidentally comes across Artemis bathing; in Hesiod he is a rival of Zeus in incestuous pursuit of his aunt. There are reasons in each case to reject the obvious assumption that Hesiod's is the original version which has been distorted by the Hellenistic poets. In that of Ceyx and Alcyone the Hesiodic story offers no account of why the birds should be sea-birds, the aetiological function of the story is suited much better by the story that Ceyx was lost at sea.[18] In that of Actaeon the Semele–Zeus motif is a complication that does not really explain the predominant role of Artemis in the myth[19] (from our earliest representations in art or reports in literature she is the central figure in carrying out the punishment).

TRAGEDY

In surviving tragedies or fragments Aeschylus refers to or recounts six transformation stories, Sophocles five, and Euripides eleven.[20] Aeschylus wrote plays based upon the transformation stories of

[18] See further Cat. 2 (halcyons: Alcyone and Ceyx).

[19] See further Cat. 1*a* (Actaeon).

[20] Aeschylus: Io, Actaeon, Aedon, Niobe, Callisto, the sisters of Phaethon. Sophocles: Io, Procne, Achelous, Thetis, Niobe, and possibly the Meleagrides. Euripides: Io, Actaeon, Procne, Callisto, Hecuba, Taygete, Cadmus, Hippo, the sisters of Phaethon, Ceyx, and possibly Erechtheus or Cecrops (see fr. 930). For other references see Catalogue.

Niobe, Actaeon, and Callisto, while the *Prometheus* features the transformed Io as a character. Sophocles wrote an *Inachus* concerned with Io's transformation, a *Tereus*, and a *Niobe*. Euripides apparently used no transformation stories as his main theme, but very frequently refers to them in comparisons or final prophecies. Among the lost work of other tragedians we know of three *Actaeon*s, two *Lycaon*s, an *Io*, and a *Tereus*.[21] There are two questions we have to consider. First, can we draw any general conclusions about what the tragedians saw in these stories, or recognize distinctive tragic treatments of the myths? Secondly, do these conclusions tell us anything about the date of the stories?

Let us begin with the story of Io, since this, in the *Prometheus* and the *Supplices* of Aeschylus, receives a more extended treatment than is given to any other transformation story in surviving tragedy.

We have very few traces of the story of Io in Hesiod, but it appears to have received a sort of burlesque treatment as a competition in cunning between the gods.[22] We can see some of the rhythm of the plot and even the spirit of the Hesiodic treatment in the brief summary of the story in lines 290 ff. of the *Supplices*, but the tone of the play as a whole is different, and both the *Supplices* and the *Prometheus* use the story of Io as an episode or illustration within a wider drama concerned at least partly with a questioning of the justice of the gods.

Whereas in Hesiod transformation is a fairly standard example of a god's power, and divine lust is something that can be taken for granted, here there is a more obvious tension between myth and morality or theology. It is precisely the grotesque and primitive aspect of the transformation that seems the attraction here, since it poses in fairly extreme form questions and apparent contradictions about the gods and their purposes. The *Prometheus* takes an extreme view of the grotesque aspects; we have the contrast of the prophecies of Io as the 'famous wife'[23] of Zeus on the one hand and the brutal lust displayed by Zeus on the other. But a contrast seems also to exist in the *Supplices* between, for instance, the frustrated lust of

[21] For the *Tereus* of Philocles see *TGF* 24 F 1. For details of the other plays see Cat. 1*a* (Actaeon, Lycaon, Io).

[22] See especially Hes. fr. 124.

[23] *PV* 834.

290 ff. and the all-powerful Zeus of 85 ff.[24] In both plays the visually bizarre aspects of the cow is stressed, and it is treated as a monster:

> Men of those days, inhabitants of Egypt,
> Trembled at heart and were pale with terror
> At a sight so unheard-of and unnatural.
> They saw a creature at once human and brute,
> Part cow, part woman, and were speechless at the prodigy.[25]

In fact at various points the physical change is seen as a reflection of the internal disruption and madness of Io;[26] transformation is here a visible sign and grotesque intensification of the character's suffering.

We cannot say to what extent the lost plays adopted a similar approach to transformation. But it is obvious that the tragic poets were interested in the grotesque and the primitive as an expression of extremes of emotional or social disorder in a way that contrasts with Homer and the epinician odes of Pindar.[27] Apart from the popularity of the Io story (and the fragments of the *Inachus* suggest that Sophocles went still further in emphasizing the incongruous and bizarre aspects of the story) one may note also the cannibal feasts of Tereus or Thyestes, the popularity of themes of matricide, child-killing, or incest, and the resurfacing of folk-tale motifs in the magic bough of Meleager, the beast suitor of Deianeira, Heracles' struggle with death in the *Alcestis*, and the silent bride in Sophocles' version of Thetis' story.[28] When Pindar, by contrast, tells the story of Thetis he speaks of Peleus overcoming fire and lions to

[24] There is perhaps something deliberately paradoxical or ambiguous about l. 87 Διὸς ἵμερος οὐκ εὐθήρατος ἐτύχθη. ἵμερος is a strange word to use of the all-powerful will of Zeus since it normally suggests human desire and weakness (*Ag.* 1204 is an appropriate comparison).

[25] *Supplices* 564 ff. (tr. P. Vellacott, 1961). In both plays Io is a deformed human rather than a full cow.

[26] e.g. *PV* 673–4.

[27] But one has to be careful in generalizing about the lost works of Pindar. Fr. 91 tells of the rather undignified transformation of the gods to escape Typhon.

[28] For the bough in Greek tragedy see Paus. 10. 31. 4; for the monstrous forms of Achelous, Soph. *Trach.* 9 ff.; for Thetis' transformations and the silent bride, Soph. fr. 618.

marry her, without explicitly saying that these were transformations at all. He also corrects the stories of the cannibal feast of Tantalus and Apollo and the raven.[29]

It does seem that the rationalizations or religious censorship which we find in other fifth-century writers[30] leave little mark on the tragic presentation of fantastic myths;[31] in fact, the different climate of opinion makes more bizarre and incongruous, and hence more attractive, a divine transformation such as that in the story of Leda and the swan,[32] although in these divine changes we are dealing not so much with the expressive power of a primitive theme as with a self-conscious wit that is closer to some of the Alexandrian treatments of magic.

It is true that fantastic events tend to be reported rather than enacted and are often set in the remote past or in the future. There is a reluctance to present grotesque events on the actual stage, whether in the sense of indecorous or in the sense of fantastic and magical actions (and both these aspects are present in the stories of Io, Actaeon, and Callisto). But it is nevertheless true that such events play, in comparison with Homer, an important role in the plots of surviving plays, and a much greater role in some of the lost ones.[33] The breaking of deeply felt taboos and the confusion caused by the overstepping of natural boundaries is again and again the central theme or precondition of the story. The fact that Oedipus' incest and parricide take place before the beginning of the play does not diminish their importance to the tragedy. The cannibal feast of Thyestes and the final degeneration to an animal of Hecuba, though more remote from the action, are still seen to have an important

[29] Thetis: *Nem.* 4. 61 ff.; Tantalus: *Ol.* 1. 37 ff.; Apollo and Koronis: *Pyth.* 3. 8 ff.

[30] e.g. Herodotus 1. 1, on the story of Io. Outrage at the gods' behaviour in the poets is found before Pindar in Xenophanes (see frs. 11–12).

[31] There is the strange rejection of the poets' stories of the gods in Eur. *HF* 1341 ff., but this seems contradicted by the actual plot of the play.

[32] See Eur. *IA* 793 ff., *Helen* 16 ff., and especially the strange description at 255 ff. It has been argued that a doubt expressed by the speaker at *Helen* 16 ff. expresses an intellectual scepticism, but see T. C. W. Stinton, *Proceedings of the Cambridge Philological Society* 22 (1976), 60–89, who argues that this is a device to draw attention to the strangeness of what is being described rather than a rejection of its truth.

[33] Aeschylus' *Toxotides* and Euripides' *Melanippe* possibly even introduced a transformed character on to the stage.

causal link with it and thus differ from the colourful mythological reminiscences of the Homeric poems.

If the main interest of transformations to the tragic poets is as examples of grotesque disorder, they may also be seen, particularly when more loosely connected with the plot, as a compromise with some harsh reality. This is the way transformation is nearly always seen when it is referred to by way of comparison. The chorus in the *Agamemnon* compare Cassandra and the nightingale in their wailing,[34] but Cassandra continues by contrasting the transformation of the bird with the savage death that she herself will suffer. In the *Antigone* the mourning Niobe is cited by the heroine as a parallel for her ambiguous state as someone alive in Hades;[35] the chorus reply that Niobe is divine, implying that there is something more than human in her peculiar state.[36] The sisters of Phaethon exist in a sort of timeless state remote from the ordinary world and half-way to the gardens of the gods.[37] In the case of the nightingale and the trees of Phaethon mourning and suffering become a thing of beauty through transformation. In all these instances, therefore, transformation represents an escape from reality,[38] which brings us closer to the transformations of the Hellenistic poets than to the straight punishment of Hesiod's stories.

In so far as they imply a mitigation or compromise with death these comparisons are similar to the prophecies of an unusual or ambiguous afterlife which conclude a number of plays (and for which Euripides has a particular fondness). Peleus will finally return to Thetis and the nymphs; Cadmus will not only become a snake, but will ultimately retire to Elysium; Iphigeneia and Hippolytus will enjoy a cult (though in the latter case this is certainly not an escape from death); and Rhesus has an especially peculiar position:

> Hidden in the caves of the silver-veined earth
> He will lie a living man-god.[39]

[34] *Ag.* 1140 ff.
[35] *Ant.* 823 ff.
[36] Cf. *El.* 150: Νιόβα, σὲ δ' ἔγωγε νέμω θεόν.
[37] See Eur. *Hipp.* 738 ff.
[38] Cf. *Helen* 380 (of Callisto's transformation): ἐξαλλάξας' ἄχθεα λύπης.
[39] *Rhesus* 970–1. Cf. the mysterious fate of Oedipus in Sophocles.

One may note not only a compromise in their fate (which usually has the form of a balancing of their previous sufferings), but also the strong aetiological interest displayed in these cases; like many of the Hellenistic transformation stories Euripides' plays often end with a local cult *aition*.[40]

Do these conclusions suggest anything about the inventiveness of the tragedians? Clearly we can recognize typical themes and ideas; we have noted an interest in transformations both as escapes and as examples of grotesque disorder, but we have seen that this interest is combined with an enthusiasm for other bizarre themes of traditional myths which, though not popular in the epic sources, are not likely to be new.[41]

We do have at least one likely example of the reshaping of a story to suit its context as a comparison or *exemplum*, in Cadmus' unusual account of Actaeon's crime in the *Bacchae*.[42] Cadmus says that Actaeon was transformed for boasting that he was a better hunter than Artemis; since this story is told to Pentheus to illustrate the moral that one should not insult the gods, it is possible that this motive has been invented to suit the context. But one should make two qualifications here. First, it seems to be rare for a transformation story to be actually invented by a tragedian or for a metamorphosis to be added to a story that lacks one. Even when there is no hint of an earlier treatment in art or literature the story is sometimes so allusively referred to that we can only conclude that it was already familiar. Examples are the strange stories of Hecuba's and Cadmus' ends in Euripides' *Hecuba* and *Bacchae*. Secondly, the invention of details that does take place seems to follow what one can recognize as familiar mythical patterns (Actaeon's boasting, for instance, about his hunting is perhaps modelled on the similar boast

[40] See e.g. the local cults of Hippolytus or Iphigeneia, the tomb of Hecuba, a local landmark, or *Helen* 1673 where Helen gives her name to an island off Attica.

[41] On the newness of one primitive theme that first appears in tragedy one can note Pausanias' comments on the magic bough of Meleager (10. 31. 4): 'Phrynichus has not worked out the story in detail as an author would do with a creation of his own; he has only touched it as a story famous all over Greece.' But see J. Bremmer, in C. Calame (ed.), *Métamorphoses du mythe en Grèce antique* (Geneva, 1988), 37–56, who argues that the motif had been incorporated into the story of Meleager relatively late.

[42] 337 ff.

of his fellow-hunter Orion). In this respect, the innovations seem much less bold than Homer's invention in the story of Niobe.

With regard to the more fully told stories that appear in the main narrative or on stage it seems quite likely that all our later sources will depend on a definitive version of one of the tragedians (Sophocles' *Niobe*, for instance, or his *Tereus*), and the extent of their innovation is therefore hard to judge. However, it does not seem that these stories are in their basic points invented, though their themes and colouring may be distinctive. Thus Procne apparently obtains her name in Sophocles' version, but it seems that all three characters and hence the structure of the story existed well before him.[43]

THE LATER POETS

The transformations that appear after the classical period form by far the largest group. In the earlier period we have some thirty-five transformations; in Ovid there are about two hundred and fifty. Some of these may have been told in lost classical works, but most, one assumes, appear first in the Hellenistic poets. It is in this period in particular that we first find poetic collections of transformations. Boios wrote an *Ornithogonia* in two books; the scale of his enterprise can perhaps be imagined from his claim that every type of bird was once a man,[44] and in the few surviving reports we can see how fairly slight stories are crammed with *aitia* for different sorts of birds. His work was perhaps adapted or translated by Aemilius Macer,[45] a friend of Virgil's, and several of his stories appear in Ovid. But Ovid's most important source is Nicander, who wrote a *Heteroioumena* in four or five books which recounted transformations to various animals and objects. We also have reports of collections of metamorphoses by Theodorus, Parthenius, Didymarchus, and

[43] Tereus is mentioned in *Supplices* 60, while the swallow daughter of Pandion is mentioned by Hesiod and Sappho.

[44] Ath. 393 E.

[45] See E. Baehrens, *Fragmenta Poetarum Romanorum* (Leipzig, 1886), p. 344.

Antigonus, of which we know little.[46] Later on, the mythographers give us prose summaries and lists of metamorphoses.[47]

The most basic general difference of these metamorphoses from those of the earlier poets is that they are virtually all both aetiological and terminal; their function is to explain some present creature or landmark, and they bring the story to an end. There are earlier stories of this type, most notably the stories of Niobe or the nightingale, but now this becomes the standard form. Aetiology plays an important role in Hesiod, in Pindar, where institutions, cities, and families are set in a context of local stories,[48] and in endings of Euripides' plays, but it is only in the Hellenistic writers that it is applied on a large scale to the natural world; a close parallel to these transformation stories is the mythical explanations of stars in Eratosthenes.

Since these stories form the bulk of our material it is naturally important to decide whether they are pure invention, as is perhaps the case with many of the catasterisms, or whether they are a traditional type that was ignored by the epic tradition. We must consider the basis of their attraction for the Hellenistic poets and their relation to other Hellenistic genres, and if we decide they are not complete invention we must consider the sort of ways in which these poets may have reshaped or elaborated them.

Of these Hellenistic writers we have evidence for really only two, Boios and Nicander; this takes the form of a prose summary of a number of transformation stories by Antoninus Liberalis.[49] He is otherwise unknown, but his name and his language suggest a date of the second or third centuries AD. The work takes the form of a series of stories which the author makes no attempt to link to one another; nor is there any obvious principle of order. For each story sources are cited. These are nearly always Nicander or Boios, but occasion-

[46] For Theodorus see Probus on *G* 1. 399, Lafaye, 36; for Parthenius, Lafaye, 35; for Didymarchus and Antigonus, AL 23.

[47] See esp. Antoninus Liberalis, and the papyrus list of transformations in T. Renner, 'A Papyrus Dictionary of Metamorphoses', *HSCP* 82 (1978), 277–95.

[48] See Jannacone (op. cit. n. 1), 10–11.

[49] On Antoninus Liberalis see E. Oder, *De Antonino Liberali* (diss. Bonn, 1886); Papathomopoulos, pp. ix–xxiii.

ally other writers are cited in addition or instead.[50] Contrary to normal practice these citations appear not at the beginning or end of each story, but to one side. This might suggest that they do not stem from Antoninus himself; but the question of the authenticity of these citations is less important than that of their accuracy. One must decide whether Antoninus' summaries are reliable evidence for the actual form of the stories in these writers, or whether, as has been argued with the Homeric scholia, a particular character or story was merely mentioned in the work cited.

It seems relevant that most of the stories appear in Ovid too. Since Antoninus Liberalis is unlikely to have derived his stories from Ovid, it seems probable that they have a common source. However, one must be careful here since Ovid and Antoninus frequently differ in their details, and it may be that either one of them knew Nicander only through an intermediary. We should at least expect if Antoninus was using Nicander as a source that there would be less variation and originality in his bald and distinct summaries than in Ovid's poetic reworking.

In the case of several stories we have independent evidence for details of Nicander's version. Thus, the scholia of Apollonius and Theocritus tell us that Nicander differed from other poets in making Hylas' father Ceyx and having him seized by a number of nymphs.[51] This is the version of Antoninus Liberalis, and his accuracy in these details at least is confirmed. Athenaeus[52] preserves a fragment of Nicander which describes letters inscribed on an apple; this has plausibly been supposed to belong to the story of Ktesilla (see AL 2), which describes how a girl accidentally reads out an oath inscribed on an apple.

Another case is more complicated. Athenaeus too reports Boios' story of the pigmy woman, but here there seem to be differences. Since this is the only place where we can compare a whole story of Antoninus' with the account of someone else it seems worth looking at these passages in some detail. Antoninus tells how the

[50] See Papathomopoulos, pp. ix–xxiii, who lists various other treatments of the problem of the citations. Cf. Oder (op. cit. n. 49), ch. 3.

[51] Schol. AR 1. 1236 on the nymphs; schol. Theoc. 13. 7/9a on his parentage.

[52] 82 A.

beautiful but arrogant pigmy queen, Oinoe, failed to honour Hera and Artemis. On the birth of her son the pigmies brought her many gifts, but Hera turned her into a crane. She still longed to see her son, but the pigmies now drove her away, and ever since then there has been a war between cranes and the pigmies.[53]

Athenaeus reports that according to Boios a beautiful pigmy woman, Gerana ('Crane'), was worshipped as a god by the local people and treated Hera and Artemis without respect; Hera in anger turned her into an ugly bird and made her the hated enemy of the people who had honoured her. He adds as a strange postscript that she gave birth to a tortoise. A fuller but very similar version of the story (apart from the detail of the tortoise) is given in Aelian.[54]

First, therefore, we have a difference in the name of the heroine, and this in itself suggests that either Athenaeus and Aelian or Antoninus were using an intermediary source rather than Boios himself. Secondly, only Antoninus mentions her son and makes this the reason for her war with the pigmies. The other sources, however, give a fuller and more coherent account of the relation of the other details of the story; it is the honours she receives that drive her to mad pride (Aelian says that she wages war against the pigmies because they ruined her with their excessive honours), and her beauty, the subject of her blasphemous boasting, is contrasted with the ugliness of the bird. In Antoninus her beauty and the honours she receives have no explicit connection with her disregard of the gods (and we are not told that among these honours she was worshipped as a god). Finally the bizarre reference to the tortoise does not appear in Antoninus.

Although we cannot be sure, perhaps the most natural conclusion is that it is Aelian and Athenaeus who are using the intermediary. First, Athenaeus precedes his account by mentioning the transformation of Kyknos: 'Boios in his *Ornithogonia*, or Boio, as says Philochorus, said that Kyknos was turned into a bird by Ares.' This may imply that Philochorus was Athenaeus' source for Boios' story of Kyknos (although it may be simply the name Boio that

[53] AL 16.

[54] Ath. 393 E; Aelian *NA* 12. 59.

appeared in Philochorus).[55] Secondly, Ovid, in a brief refence to the story, refers to the heroine as a mother.[56] It seems likely, therefore, that he knew a version of the story close to Antoninus', and in this case Ovid is an important witness since he is by far our earliest source. Thirdly, what is missing in Aelian and Athenaeus is detail of the plot and the personal name, whereas Antoninus lacks the moral framework and the motivation. The latter is perhaps quite likely to be missed out through the abbreviation of the prose mythographer, whereas another proper literary treatment of the story would be unlikely to retain the redundant features of the plot that we find in Antoninus. I am not quite sure what to make of Athenaeus' reference to the tortoise; he makes no attempt to fit this into the rest of the story, and it would in any case seem to be out of place in an *ornithogonia*.

In this story, therefore, it seems that Antoninus was probably using the original source, or a fairly accurate report, but that the original relations of details and even the motivation of the story may have been left out in an abbreviated and possibly distorted account.

There are a number of more positive arguments in favour of the accuracy of the citations. One can note first the predominant role given to Nicander and Boios; of the forty-one citations thirty-one mention one of these two.[57] Secondly, there is the detail of the citation, which usually mentions a particular book of the work cited. But the main argument is the clear difference in character between the stories attributed to the two poets; this is so great that scholars have been able, with fairly general agreement, to assign most of the unattributed stories to either one of them. Perhaps, finally, the composition of the work suggests an acquaintance with the poet's original order. Consecutive Nicander stories in Antoninus frequently come from the same book of Nicander; of Boios' stories of which the book number is given, the first three in Antoninus come from Book 1 and the next and final five come from Book 2. Though the stories have been reorganized and mixed together, we

[55] As is argued by Jacoby on *FGH* 328 F 214.

[56] *Met.* 6. 90.

[57] Their names normally come first.

may have here (perhaps in an indirect form) the influence of the original structure.

It has been suggested that, even if we accept that Nicander's and Boios' accounts are the main sources of these stories, we should expect to find contamination, improvement, or the missing out of details by Antoninus Liberalis. Some of the stories have complicated introductions of little apparent relevance for the main transformation stories, or else digressions or comparisons with other stories. Thus the story of Byblis begins with an account of the birth of her father Miletus, and the adventures of his youth, though he plays no part in her story.[58] The prayer of Leucippus' mother that her daughter may change her sex includes an account of most of the other sex changes in Greek mythology. Sometimes we even have incoherence or redundancy within a story,[59] but before we assume that this must be the work of some late writer we must remember that digression was a feature of Hellenistic narrative,[60] and we do not know enough about Nicander's ability as a story-teller to conclude that he is any more likely than Antoninus to have avoided incoherence. It is interesting to note that Ovid's story of Byblis also begins with the story of her father Miletus, which does perhaps suggest that this structure at least is not Antoninus' work.

NICANDER

Though there is some dispute,[61] Nicander is usually thought to have lived in the second century BC; the lives tell us that he was a citizen of Colophon and a hereditary priest of Apollo of Claros, but that he

[58] See AL 30.

[59] e.g. in the story of Ktesilla: see AL 1. The Meleager story includes both the Bacchylides version (of the burning log) and the Homeric motif of the attempted persuasion by his mother; this does not seem to make sense, since if she is trying to persuade him to defend the city why does she then kill him by burning the log when he goes out to fight?

[60] We can note in particular that the story of Kragaleus, who judges between the gods, is a transparent frame for the stories the gods tell in their speeches; this shows that such a linking of stories was a feature of Nicander's method of composition, and therefore other digressions in the text may well go back to him.

[61] See A. S. F. Gow and A. F. Scholfield, *Nicander* (Cambridge, 1953), 4–8.

originally came from Aetolia, where he spent much of his life.[62] The list of works attributed to him appears to show a very varied interest. His surviving works are the *Theriaca* and the *Alexipharmaca*, which deal with venomous animals, mainly snakes, and cures for poisons. We also have substantial fragments of his *Georgica*, a work on husbandry, and reports of an *Aetolica*, an *Oetica*, and a *Colophonica*, presumably works of local geography and legend, a *Prognostica*, and three books about oracles. The *Suda* calls him a grammarian, poet, and doctor. It is possible that some of the lost works should be attributed to another poet of the same name.[63] But if, as the ancient lives suggest, the same writer combined a taste for versifying scientific treatises with an interest in the mythical and magical stories of the *Heteroioumena*, this would not be unusual for a Hellenistic poet. He would be following the precedent of, for example, Aratus. However, this strange combination of interests is a feature even within the scientific works; a detailed and careful account of animals and herbs will be followed by the most primitive superstitions and magic,[64] some very improbable facts of natural history,[65] and mythical *aitia*.[66] One can compare here the popularity of books of natural marvels. These absurd, though not strictly mythical, accounts find their way into the works of otherwise respectable geographers and natural historians.[67] One may note that Boios in the course of his bizarre stories reveals a detailed knowledge of an enormous number of bird species and habits; many of his descriptions come very close to those of Aristotle's *Natural History*.

What both the scientific and the mythical works have in common is that both are displays of learning and that the knowledge revealed

[62] For his life see schol. to *Theriaca* intr. (s.v. Νικάνδρου γένος) and *Suda* (s.v. Νίκανδρος. He himself says in *Ther.* 958 and *Alex.* 9 f. that Claros is his home.

[63] See J.-M. Jacques, *Ktema* 4 (1979), 133–49.

[64] e.g. *Ther.* 98 ff. which describes a magic protecting ointment that can be made by boiling snakes found copulating at a crossroads.

[65] e.g. that scorpions are born from dead crabs: *Ther.* 790 ff.

[66] e.g. that all venomous creatures were born from Titans' blood: *Ther.* 8 ff.

[67] e.g. the fantastic stories about the production of amber (Pliny, *NH* 37. 30 ff.). Pliny is sceptical, but it is interesting that he still gives such a long account of these mistaken beliefs, rather as a Hellenistic poet will recount alternative myths and then reject them (e.g. Callim. *Hymn* 1). Elsewhere he is less sceptical and claims to have seen a centaur (*NH* 7. 35): see Lafaye, 16 f.

(though it may be tempered to some extent by natural observation or judgement)[68] is primarily a knowledge of traditional belief.

This is important when we come to consider how much of their own invention we find in the myths these poets record. While learning can be displayed in narrating the most improbable legend and *aition*, and even in condemning it, even knowledge in this loose sense can hardly be displayed in pure inventions (one should remember Callimachus' claim that he sang of nothing that was unattested).[69] This applies to even the most characteristic Hellenistic stories; at the end of the romance of Acontius and Cydippe, the archetypal Alexandrian love story for the Roman elegists, Callimachus reveals that his source for the story was the fifth-century local historian Xenomedes.[70] The story of Hecale with its typically humble view of a heroic figure and legend seems to have been taken from the *Attic History* of Philochorus.[71]

The interest in local stories or in the details of the major ones meant that a taste for novelty could be satisfied without a recourse to pure invention, and local histories became an important source of material. Among the other sources cited for the Nicander stories of Antoninus and the stories of Parthenius are a number of local historians.[72] The use of myth in the *Theriaca* and the *Alexipharmaca* is comparatively rare, but it does often involve some unusual local variant of a myth,[73] and the story is often so briefly referred to that some further knowledge on the part of the poet,[74] if not the reader, seems implied.

In the *Heteroioumena* we can assume that most of the stories were rather more fully told, but we find some of the same tendencies. The first point is that they are not usually about the well-known epic heroes or if these do appear then the emphasis is given to some

[68] How far Nicander's works reveal firsthand medical knowledge is disputed. Contrast the views of Jacques (art. cit. n. 63) and O. Schneider, *Nicandrea* (Leipzig, 1856), 181–208.

[69] Fr. 612.

[70] *Aitia* fr. 75. 50 f.

[71] See Plut. *Thes.* 14 (*FGH* 328 F 109).

[72] e.g. Athanadas' *Ambrakika* (AL 4): see further Catalogue under Galinthias, Byblis, Alcmena, the Teumesian fox.

[73] *Theriaca* 685 ff.; the reference to the Phlegyan herb and the river Melas suggests an unusual location for a detail of the Heracles and Hydra story.

[74] e.g. *Ther.* 608 f.

lesser-known detail of their story (e.g. not the Calydonian boar hunt, but the fate of Meleager's sisters, or not Peleus' relations with Thetis, but his pursuit by a wolf). Like this story of the wolf many of these myths appear only in Nicander and in Ovid, who may be following him. They are also all stories with a strong local tie; all are set in a particular place and are related at the end to some local landmark or more often a religious rite or object for which they are the *aition*.[75]

It is curious perhaps that Nicander shows more interest in this *aition* than he does in the transformations themselves which are the theme of his work. We can contrast the Boios stories where, more naturally perhaps, the only *aitia* are for the birds the characters become. Nicander often does not describe his creatures, and sometimes there is no suggestion that their transformation is the *aition* for a species.[76] Where he does have a normal animal *aition* (for instance, for the mating habits of the weasel), this is usually combined with a religious *aition* as well.[77] In this case Galinthias, the weasel, is worshipped at the festival of Heracles at Thebes. Where the habits of the bird or the animal are described they follow much less obviously than in Boios from the nature or actions of the human being.

There is also no evidence that he gave much detail in his descriptions of the transformations; there is no hint in Antoninus, who is anyway always perfunctory, but the longest fragment we have, which describes the transformation of Hecuba, does not suggest much more:[78] 'She leapt into the sea and changed her aged form to that of a Hyrkanian hound.' Often indeed he will miss an opportunity of describing a transformation, so that we have a person simply disappearing and then an object appearing in their place.[79] Here transformation becomes a sort of cult miracle, the opposite of an epiphany, which leads to the real heart of the account, the concluding *aition*.

[75] Where the transformation is to a stone, tree, or spring, transformed object and local *aition* are the same thing. This is a particular favourite (see AL 4, 23, 30, 31, 32).

[76] The species of the Leros temple birds is not mentioned (AL 2). There is no description of the birds in AL 1, AL 9, or AL 12.

[77] AL 29.

[78] Fr. 62.

[79] Cf. Dryope, Byblis, Britomartis.

It is clear that some poets found the theme of metamorphosis and the bizarre ideas it could give rise to a stimulating one. Of the earlier poets we have seen how Aeschylus combines the physical and mental disorder of Io, and Euripides describes the grotesque incongruities of Zeus' relations with the bear Callisto. Among the Hellenistic poets and their Roman imitators we find equal ingenuity. Apollonius goes one better than Homer in his description of the mixed shape of the pigs of Circe or of the ambiguous trees of Phaethon.[80] Above all we have the strange conceits of Ovid.

However, what attracted Nicander about these stories seems not to have been the scope for the psychologically or physically grotesque description, but rather the air of simple-minded magic and superstition which so obviously suited the local cults and landmarks of his stories; indeed, it seems possible that such transformation stories did actually play a substantial role in local *aitia*.[81] This taste is not peculiar to Nicander; one of the features of Callimachus' *Aitia* and of his hymns is the pose of naïve belief (*Hymn* 6, for instance, which narrates the story of Erysichthon, is put into the mouths of a group of simple women devotees of Demeter). In its rustic form this pose can be seen in the pastoral poems of Theocritus.[82] In Nicander's *Theriaca* too one can perhaps detect a similar affectation, with its rustic superstitions and its declared purpose of allowing Hermesianax to sleep out in the fields in safety. We do not know who Hermesianax, a kinsman of Nicander, is, but Nicander himself was a man 'ab agro remotissimus'.[83]

In the *Heteroioumena* it seems significant that not only are his main characters often humble people,[84] but the gods who work the transformations are often not the major Olympians. Zeus does not appear once; one can contrast Boios, where almost every transformation is worked by Zeus or Apollo. Most of those in Nicander are worked by the nymphs; Artemis, a popular goddess of the

[80] AR 4. 672 ff. and 603 ff. See further Lafaye, 20–3.

[81] e.g. the function of Hecuba's transformation as a local *aition* at the end of Euripides' play.

[82] Especially when the poet himself enters this pastoral background in *Idyll* 7.

[83] See Cic. *De Or.* 1. 69.

[84] The stories in AL 31, 35, and 22 are about shepherds and cowmen. Leucippus' father is too poor to bring up his child unless it is a boy.

countryside who takes many local forms, is connected with four more. Sometimes no explanation is given of the transformation at all,[85] and we have to suppose the working of some unknown spirit.

Quite frequently rather than an actual transformation we get the miraculous disappearance of a body,[86] a characteristic pattern of local hero-*aitia*.[87] The gods are in general more primitive and mysterious figures than in Hesiod or tragedy. There are certain simple rules; if you make fun of gods to their faces[88] (as Askalabos mocks Demeter, or Kerambos the nymphs) they will punish you. But they often act unpredictably—unexpectedly dangerously, for instance, in the case of the nymphs and Hylas or of the oracle that demands a human sacrifice for no apparent reason,[89] or unexpectedly taking pity, like the nymphs who save Byblis from committing suicide.

The extent to which these aspects are an important element in Nicander's work emerges particularly clearly when we compare his stories in Antoninus with the versions in Ovid. Ovid uses all except three of Nicander's stories, and in nearly every case there are important differences. The most consistent change is that Ovid ignores the cult *aition* at the end. He tells the story of the sisters of Meleager, for instance, without reference to their life as temple birds on Leros, or of Galinthias without mention of her place in the festival of Heracles.[90] Similarly, instead of the miraculous disappearance or translation, he has a straight transformation in the stories of Dryope[91] and Byblis. In this last story Nicander differs not only from Ovid but from all the other versions of the story.

What Ovid tends to add in place of the cult *aition* is a more obvious explanation of animal features and an emphasis on the continuity of human traits. The Pierides for instance, all become

[85] See e.g. AL 8 (Lamia) or 38 (the wolf enemy of Peleus).

[86] e.g. Ktesilla or Aspalis; compare the list of disappearances of living people (above, n. 79).

[87] Cf. Kleomedes (Paus. 6. 9. 7) or Euthymos (Paus. 6. 6. 10).

[88] There do not seem to be any cases of a more general *hybris*. The gods have to be insulted in person.

[89] In the story of Metioche and Menippe, AL 25.

[90] Meleagrides: 8. 536 ff.; Galinthias: 9. 306 ff.

[91] 9. 331 ff.

magpies and thus preserve their 'raucous chatter'; in Nicander they become nine different birds which are not described.[92] In particular, there is very often a moral symbolism in Ovid's *aitia*. Thus the petrification of Battos is shown to be an appropriate punishment for his perjury by a detail that is not in Nicander: Battos promises 'that stone will speak before I do'.[93] In the story of the Lydian herdsmen who refuse to let Leto wash her children in a river and are punished by being turned into frogs, the main interest for Nicander is not the *aition* for the frogs, but a second *aition* for the name Lycia and the cult of Apollo; Ovid ignores this and develops Nicander's simple *aition* (Leto punishes the herdsmen by pushing them into the water where they will live from now on) by having them continue their anti-social behaviour: 'and even under the water they try to curse'.[94] Nicander's Messapians become trees that moan in the wind; Ovid has a tree whose wood retains the *acerbitas* of the sinner's human speech.[95] The suggestion of naïve and primitive awe about these mysterious trees in Nicander has changed to moral symbolism.

The pose as a naïve recorder of local miracles is one that might be expected to preserve rather than distort or reshape the pattern of these stories. It is possible, of course, that though transformation stories did form an important element in such traditions their number has been greatly increased by Nicander; but how does one distinguish the faked ones?

One might try to identify alien Hellenistic themes and tendencies. An obvious one perhaps is the tendency to introduce or emphasize erotic or sentimental themes in the heroic stories[96] and in certain cases to pick on bizarre sexual relationships.[97] But one feature of Nicander is his reticence in this respect; only three stories contain an important romantic element.[98] In the Meleager story he has apparently dropped the Euripidean innovation of the hero's love

[92] See Cat. 2 (Emathides).

[93] 2. 269. Cf. Askalabos who in Ovid (5. 460 f.) is covered with spots as a mark of his shame.

[94] 6. 376.

[95] See Cat. 3*a* (Messapian Shepherds).

[96] e.g. the love story of Medea in AR, Book 3.

[97] As we see in e.g. the erotic stories of Parthenius.

[98] Those of Hylas, Byblis, and Kyknos.

for Atalanta. In two cases, here and in the story of Leucippe, Ovid has introduced a love story that is not in Nicander; in the story of Leucippe being brought up as a boy it is not fear of her father's discovery of the deception that leads to problems, but the heroine's love for another girl. In the story of Byblis Nicander is much more restrained than Ovid and the other accounts; instead of revealing her incestuous love she goes away to kill herself. The opportunity for an incestuous intrigue and an emotional confrontation has been ignored. The story of Hylas is a romantic view of a heroic saga, but Nicander has inherited this; his innovation is in the cult *aition* at the end which is possibly a much older element.

Another new element might be particularly Hellenistic poetic conceits. Poetic imagination of any sort is something Nicander seems to be short of; the one passage that is quite striking in its unusual extravagance is the description of Mount Helicon rising in pleasure at the sound of the Muses' singing until Pegasus stops it by stamping with his hoof, possibly creating the Hippocrene spring.[99] Is this an exaggeration of Hellenistic conceits about the sympathy of nature, or the relic of a primitive animist view of the countryside?[100] It seems at any rate that the connection of spring and horse is not merely Alexandrian word play but a traditional feature of Greek myths.[101]

Thirdly, there is the question of composition; the overall form of a work may have an important effect in reshaping the individual stories. It is possible, for instance, that Ovid's story of Daidalion's transformation into a hawk has been invented to contrast with the peaceful and wife-loving halcyon of Ceyx, his brother. But there is no evidence that Nicander's poem took the form of a continuous narrative like that of Ovid. In so far as one can see any principle of composition it is perhaps the unpoetic criterion of loose categories of subject. All the stone stories in Antoninus, for instance, come from the first book of Nicander (and all the tree stories from the

[99] Antoninus does not actually state this, but see Papathomopoulos, 89 n. 15.

[100] H. J. Rose regards this as 'the kind of rubbish produced when an Alexandrian poet tries to improve on an original story' (*A Handbook of Greek Mythology*[6] (Oxford, 1958), 180 n. 34).

[101] See Ninck, 17.

first two), while all the birds and animals come in the third and fourth books.

Finally, one might expect in view of Nicander's particular purpose that the metamorphosis or *aition* of the story might be an invention and addition of his own even if the rest of the story conforms to traditional patterns. But it is no easier to distinguish a typically Hellenistic poetic *aition* from a genuine product of folklore than it is the rest of the story; mythical aetiology of all types clearly had a very old and wide role in Greek life and religion, and Pausanias, for instance, makes no attempt to distinguish early or late ones. There are no obvious criteria for such a distinction. We might suppose, for instance, in view of the grammatical interest of the Alexandrian poets, that etymological *aitia* would be an Alexandrian type, but we find many old ones.[102] One possible guide is relevance to the rest of the story; but the fact that an *aition* tends to come at the end of a story and appears to play no part in its structure can be deceptive. If we only knew Nicander's version of the story of Meleager, the metamorphosis at the end would be an obvious candidate for an example of Hellenistic innovation, as would the mourning trees of Phaethon, since Meleager's and Phaethon's sisters do not otherwise appear in the story. But in fact both these transformations go back to classical sources.

If the *aitia* and aetiological metamorphoses do operate according to a kind of logic that depends on traditional habits and belief, then we should expect Nicander to have as much familiarity with these and understanding of them as anyone (one can remember also the report that he was a hereditary priest of Apollo). Everything we have considered so far suggests that if Nicander is innovating he is at least doing it according to the rules and in a framework that does not belong just to his own times, and that therefore even his innovations would be a valuable source for the study of Greek myths.

[102] e.g. Aphrodite from ἀφρός, Hes. *Theog.* 195 ff., cf. fr. 234.

BOIOS

No actual fragments of the *Ornithogonia* survive and almost nothing is known of its author.[103] The name of the author cited in all our definite references to the work is Boios, but it is possible that Philochorus knew him or her as Boio.[104] Boio was the name of an ancient Delphic poetess,[105] or a soothsayer whom Clement classes with the mythical prophetesses Hippo and Manto.[106] It seems likely that the poet of the *Ornithogonia* attributed his work to one of these ancient figures, or at least that he was deliberately recalling her name. In the stories attributed by Antoninus to Boios particular attention is paid to the function of the birds in augury, and it is possible that the *Ornithogonia*[107] is a blending of the Hellenistic genre of the catalogue of metamorphoses with the older genre of the *ornithomanteia*. The date of the work is impossible to determine.[108] Its subject matter suggests that it is a Hellenistic work. Athenaeus implies that Philochorus (fourth–third century BC) knew the work and, if this is correct, it is the earliest of the collections of transformations that are known to us.

As has already been suggested, the stories of Boios in Antoninus are very different from those of Nicander, and some of the reasons for accepting Nicander as a reliable source make one feel doubts about Boios. Firstly, Boios has more obviously set himself a programme, claiming that all birds were once men; so one might expect a considerable amount of invention to get them all in. Each story ends with a general transformation of even irrelevant characters into different birds. Many stories are very simple and seem

[103] See Lafaye, ch. 2; Jacoby on *FGH* 28 F 214.

[104] See the citations in Antoninus, Ath. 393 E. Jacoby (loc. cit. n. 103) argues that Athenaeus mistook Philochorus' reference to the ancient poetess Boio for a reference to the author of the *Ornithogonia*. There seems no particular reason to believe this.

[105] Paus. 10. 5. 7.

[106] Clem. Al. *Strom.* 1. 132. 3.

[107] See Jacoby (loc. cit. n. 103), who imagines that the ancient Boio may have written such an *ornithomanteia*. As an example he cites the *ornithomanteia* included in some manuscripts of Hesiod's *Works and Days*.

[108] Jacoby (loc. cit. n. 103) supposes it is late Hellenistic, but the only evidence he produces is the absence of any earlier references to it.

little more than an excuse to fit in a number of birds. For instance, the family of Mounichos are attacked by robbers, and the gods in pity turn them into birds; most of the account in Antoninus is taken up with the description of the different kinds of birds.[109]

Secondly, whereas the stories of Nicander have a strong local element, and his characters are often derived from local cult or genealogy, in Boios the local element is almost completely lacking. His *aitia* are always for birds' habits rather than local landmarks or rites. Many of the characters have generic bird names and thus have no background in local legend and may be the invention of the poet; when the names are not generic bird names they are often obviously meaningful names which have presumably been invented for the story. Thus, the violent sons of the pious Kleinis are called Lykios ('Wolfy') and Harpasos ('Snatcher'); the sons of Autonoos, a farmer who can grow nothing but weeds, are called Akanthos and Schoineus, and his wife who is unable to prevent her son being eaten by horses is called Hippodameia.[110] The transforming gods are not the local nymphs and gods of the countryside, but in almost every case Zeus or Apollo; the divine powers have thus been standardized and have no local colouring. Most of the stories are given a location, but in several stories this is an exotic and fairy-tale place (such as the land of the pigmies or Babylon). Only two of the stories are set in mainland Greece.

Of course, generic and meaningful names and vagueness of location are a feature of the traditional animal fable, which we know did exist in ancient Greece, but though such fables may have been one of the influences on Boios' stories it would be a mistake to see the folk-tradition as his main source. The most important influence on him seems to be literary. In nearly every case one can see the starting-point of his stories in some more famous legend, or detail of a legend, recounted in the earlier poets. Thus Pindar told how the Hyperboreans sacrificed donkeys to Apollo; this becomes the starting-point of a story of Boios about the disastrous attempt of Kleinis who has just returned from the land of the Hyperboreans to introduce a donkey-sacrifice in his own home.[111] The report in

[109] AL 14. [110] Kleinis: AL 20; Autonoos: AL 17. [111] See Cat. 2 (Kleinis).

Homer of the war of the pigmies and the cranes gives rise to the story in Boios of how the crane was once a pigmy mother. The self-blinding of Oedipus after incest with his mother prompts the story that Aegypios' mother attempted to blind him after she had slept with him, and that even now as a bird she plucks out the eyes of dead animals.[112]

Boios' normal approach is to give these motifs from the heroic myths a bourgeois context. Thus, Aedon, normally the daughter and wife of kings, becomes the wife of the carpenter Polytechnos. The family of Merops, who in other sources is an ancient king of Cos, become farmers who refuse to attend the city festivals.[113] The story of Aegypios, though it seems to be modelled on that of Oedipus, makes incest not a tragic coincidence, but the conclusion of a story of petty intrigue, bribery, and adultery. No story that is definitely ascribed to Boios tells of kings or warriors; when his characters are distinguished it is for their wealth rather than royalty or power. I suggested that in some of Nicander's stories the heroes were humble people, but these tend to be shepherds, who have a recognized place in the heroic and primitive landscape, whereas the characters of Boios' stories seem to belong to a more developed society and would not be out of place in the Hellenistic world of their author.

All these considerations make one wary of regarding Boios as a source of ancient myths; in fact we find that only one story of his, that of Aedon, is mentioned in any earlier source. Nevertheless, I think that these stories should not be ignored. Even if they have been invented by Boios himself, and though they are given a bourgeois setting, it does seem first of all that they may preserve details of older beliefs and legends, and, secondly and more important, they still exemplify the patterns and themes that make up the main body of Greek mythology. An example of the first point is the story of the Cretan thieves, which is composed of a number of possibly ancient beliefs and legends. It includes references to the annual boiling of the afterbirth of Zeus, to the bees that fed him as a child, and to bronze-clad figures in the cave where he was born.[114]

[112] AL 5. [113] AL 15. [114] See Cat. 2 (Thieves).

That religious details should be preserved and form an important element in his stories is hardly surprising when we remember that Boios seems to have taken on the name of an ancient prophetess and that the function of the birds as omens is always given attention in his stories. Despite the many differences between Boios and Nicander, this pose of naïve belief is a common element in their works. The many examples of basic mythical themes and patterns in his stories will be looked at when we come to consider the individual myths in more detail. We may simply note here that these include transformation into a bird after incest, punishment by Aphrodite for choosing virginity, the conflict of Olympians and worshippers of the earth, and the ambiguous view of sacrifice as an act not only of religious worship but also of dangerous violence. In no case can we be sure that Boios is not repeating an older story, and we very often find that one of his stories, whether an invention or not, is a useful commentary on a better established myth.

Our other main source is, of course, Ovid, but to discuss the use of myth in the *Metamorphoses* would be far beyond the scope of this brief survey; his treatment of the stories is remarkable for its comprehensiveness and variety.[115] I noted above certain differences from Nicander in the treatment of the latter's stories; in fact, when he wishes, Ovid is himself perfectly capable of adopting the tone of simple piety and narrating the cult miracle (e.g. the story of Philemon and Baucis), or he can use Nicander's preferred type of the miraculous disappearance (e.g. the deaths of Kyknos or Kaineus), or he can abandon the moral symbolism of, for instance, the story of Battos and tell stories of amoral magic (e.g. the transformations of Mestra). He tells both the regular classical stories (Io, Callisto, and Actaeon) and the Alexandrian aetiological kind; he even includes all the different *aitia* for the same bird.[116]

[115] Ovid's treatment of metamorphosis has been much discussed: see the lists of works cited and discussed by H. Herter, in *Kulturwissenschaften: Festgabe für W. Perpeet* (Bonn, 1980), 185–228 (and also L. Barkan, *Gods Made Flesh* (New Haven, 1986), ch. 2). Herter sensibly concludes that Ovid did not take one single view of metamorphosis.

[116] There are three different swan transformations and two versions of the story of the halcyon: see 11. 410 ff., 7. 401 and 12. 243 ff., 2. 367 ff., 7. 371 ff.

Since his is the fullest account of most of our stories, and one of the few sources that give a moral and psychological colouring as opposed to the bare details of the plot in the mythographers, his view of these myths will naturally be a continual object of discussion. He does have special interests and particular ways in which he is likely to reshape the myths; for instance, there is a special emphasis on the relation between bodily transformation and speech which we do not find in the other sources (whether this takes the form of a nightmarish inability to communicate or whether change or continuity in the habits of speech becomes the *aition* of the story), and in such cases we may suspect Ovid's invention as opposed to use of a source, but these particular tastes will be discussed in context.

One interest, however, has some relevance to this survey; it was suggested that it was the existential ambiguity necessarily involved in transformation that was one reason for the rarity of human change in the *Iliad* and the *Odyssey*; such an ambiguity seems to have been a feature of Euripides' endings and the stories of the Hellenistic poets, but it is in Ovid that we see it most fully developed. Not only does he take pleasure in descriptions of the transition from man to animal, but more specifically transformation is again and again seen as a state between life and death inducing an uncertainty of response in the observer.[117]

[117] See e.g. 10. 485 ff., 10. 232 f., 13. 669 ff., or 1. 578 where the rivers are unsure whether to console or congratulate the father of Daphne.

2

Animals, I

The Ritual Theory

IT is the stories of transformation into large mammals that have most frequently prompted religious explanations, for several reasons. First, most of them appear early and have therefore been seen as belonging to the more primitive stage of Greek mythology. Secondly, most of them are not aetiological in form and therefore cannot be explained as animal just-so stories. Thirdly, in most of them the gods play a central role as characters and often have an intimate connection with the human heroes: Io, Callisto, and Taygete are all loved by Zeus, and Actaeon is Zeus' rival in love. Fourthly, the animals of the transformations have a close connection with the gods of the stories as their sacred animals: Io is a cow, the sacred animal of Hera; Callisto, Taygete, and Actaeon are bears and deer, the sacred animals of Artemis.

For an earlier generation of scholars the conclusion was obvious: we should seek the origins of these myths in historical animal cults. Cook wrote: 'I think we may venture on the general statement that within the bounds of Hellenic mythology animal metamorphosis commonly points to a preceding animal cult.'[1] Bubbe in his dissertation on metamorphoses used this principle to explain all the transformations into animals.

Although the influence of ritual on myths is now treated more cautiously by many scholars,[2] and the notion of an animal-god is no longer a fashionable one or a starting point for new research, it seems worth devoting some space to considering what appears in

[1] *JHS* 14 (1894), 160.

[2] See e.g. J. Fontenrose, *The Ritual Theory of Myth* (Berkeley, 1966); G. S. Kirk, *The Nature of Greek Myths* (Harmondsworth, 1974), ch. 10; W. Burkert, *Structure and History in Greek Mythology and Ritual* (Berkeley, 1979), 56–8.

many standard reference books as the explanation of metamorphosis stories.

There has recently been much more interest in explaining myths in terms of initiation rituals; in the second part of this chapter I shall consider whether these theories throw any light on the stories we are considering.

THE ANIMAL-CULT THEORY

In its traditional form this view supposed a general evolution from a naïve worship by primitive people of the animals around them to a belief in remoter anthropomorphic beings;[3] these new gods are, however, unable to shake off their animal associations completely and transfer their animal form to a human servant or enemy in a transformation story. This theory has been applied to all the stories,[4] but most frequently and with greatest enthusiasm to those of Io and Callisto, who are considered to be in origin the bear-goddess Artemis and the cow-goddess Hera. Since similar arguments arise in the case of every story I shall confine myself to considering these two.

Before we look at the individual stories, however, it is important to consider what the notion of an animal-god actually means, what form (if any) animal-gods took or had taken in ancient Greece, and how we may expect them to have influenced myths. Rather than assume some general a priori scheme of religious evolution, it seems more helpful to look for particular illustrations of what is meant by animal-cults among the Greeks' neighbours in the Near East.

As far as the Greeks were concerned the place most notorious for

[3] See e.g. S. Eitrem, *RE* s.v. *Tierdämonen*.

[4] See e.g. on Taygete, Rose, *Handbook*, 111–19; on Actaeon, Bubbe, 3, S. Reinach, *Cultes, mythes et religions* (Paris, 1908), iii. 24–53; on Hecuba, *RE* s.v. *Hekabe*, col. 2662; on Lycaon, the works cited in M. P. Nilsson, *Geschichte der griechischen Religion*[3], i (Munich, 1967), 398.

its animal-gods was Egypt. Here one can distinguish at least three forms of animal-worship:[5]

1. the worship of particular animals, for example, the bull Apis, who was kept in a special enclosure, regarded as having magic powers of fertility, fed and bathed by special attendants, and given an elaborate and ceremonial burial; according to Greek writers he had actual priests and was called a god;[6]
2. the worship in a more limited sense of a group or a whole species; these were surrounded with special taboos and again received sometimes a special embalming and burial;
3. the representation in physical images and hymns of the major gods in animal form; among the Egyptian remains are cult statues of gods in wholly animal form, and in particular in the characteristic animal-headed human form.

However, these simple categories raise important problems of interpretation. We may wonder first of all about the exact relation of Apis to the gods. His cult seems to have assumed a much greater importance in later times, but he is thought in the earlier stage of his worship not to have had his own priests. He lived not in his own temple but in that of the god Ptah, with whom his relation is a vague one; he is described as the herald of Ptah or the soul or manifestation of Ptah, never as Ptah himself. There was clearly felt to be some distinction between the manifestation of the god and the god himself.

The force of the animal representations of the major gods is also not clear; it has been suggested that the mixed type, for instance, are not portraits at all, but what Frankfort calls pictograms,[7] a symbolic representation of some sort. This raises the obvious question of

[5] In this discussion of Egyptian animal-gods I have drawn upon: W. Helck and W. Westendorf (ed.), *Lexikon der Ägyptologie* (Wiesbaden, 1972–), s.v. *Tierkult* and *Götter, Tier-*; T. Hopfner, *Der Tierkult der alten Ägypter* (Vienna, 1913); H. Frankfort, *Ancient Egyptian Religion* (New York, 1948), 8–14; E. Hornung, *Studium Generale* 20 (1967), 69–84, and *Conceptions of God in Ancient Egypt* (Eng. trs. London, 1983), ch. 4; *ANET*. The main Greek sources are Hdt. 2. 37 ff.; DS 1. 83 ff.; Strab. 17. 1. 38 ff.; Plut. *De Is. et Os.* 71 ff.

[6] See e.g. Hdt. 3. 27. 9.

[7] See Frankfort (op. cit. n. 5), 12; cf. E. Hornung, *Conceptions* (op. cit. n. 5), 109–25.

pictorial metaphors and convention. From the earliest times we find representations of the king as a bull. We can assume that nobody thought the king looked like this or ever became a bull; we may wonder, therefore, whether he is not so much becoming an animal-god in the strict sense as demonstrating the power and strength that the gods too can manifest in the form of a bull. In the same way the honorific title 'mighty bull' is applied to gods and kings. Also it is quite normal for a god to have various manifestations; Thoth is connected with the ibis, the moon, and the baboon. In such a case it seems necessary to suppose that Thoth exists apart from any of his manifestations.

If the link between god and animal is a complex one somewhere between metaphor or symbol and identification, it also seems that the evidence of historical Egyptian cults does not support a simple evolutionary pattern of change from primitive animal to human gods. We have noted that the Apis cult only assumed a special prominence later on, and the huge graves of embalmed sacred animals are also a late phenomenon; the mass of animal superstitions and taboos reported by the Greek writers belong to their own time and are not necessarily a picture of earlier beliefs. Frankfort argues against the view that the mixed figures are a transitional form between primitive animal representations and human ones; in fact some gods receive animal images throughout Egyptian history, and some totally human figures appear right at the start.

We find similar uncertainties in a stronger form with the gods of Mesopotamia.[8] We do not hear about individual animal-worship here. What we do find are frequent references in hymns and myths to the gods as bulls and representations of them in art wearing crowns of horns.[9]

Here the connection of the bull with fertility is particularly clear; for instance, the partners in the sacred marriage ceremonies are

[8] See *ANET*; S. N. Kramer, *Sumerian Mythology* (New York, 1944); L. Malten, *Jahrbuch des deutschen archäologischen Instituts* 43 (1928), 90–139; K. V. H. Ringgren, *Religions of the Ancient Near East* (London, 1973); J. R. Conrad, *The Horn and the Sword* (London, 1959); M. C. Astour, *Hellenosemitica* (Leiden, 1965), 85–91.

[9] We also find, at a lower level, a class of demons who have a mixed or monstrous form: see J. Black, *Bulletin of the Society of Mesopotamian Studies* 15 (1988), 19–25. There seems no reason to believe that these were the predecessors of the major anthropomorphic gods.

described as bulls and cows. This seems part of a wider system of natural metaphors for fertility,[10] though the bull can also be seen as a destructive force. What counts against the view that bull and god should be closely identified is that we very frequently find in the same hymn a whole series of other titles and metaphors (e.g. most commonly the lion),[11] and as in Egypt these are applied to human beings as well as gods.[12] Also the myths treat the gods as human beings even when they describe them as mighty bulls. Such myths do not offer support for the view that transformation stories arose as a means of explaining animal-gods; and in fact the earliest recorded transformation is of an anthropomorphic god to other human beings.[13]

How much of this do we find in Greek religion? As has often been pointed out, the worship of particular animals is almost non-existent, and although there seem to have been local taboos on certain animals, these take a very much more limited form than in Egyptian practice.[14] The main gods too are hardly ever worshipped in animal images or referred to as animals; the animal names in some of their epithets can usually be explained in some more obvious way.[15] Plutarch's comment on the Greek attitude to animals by contrast with the Egyptian seems to support this:

For the Greeks in these matters speak correctly and consider the dove to be an animal sacred to Aphrodite and the snake to Athene . . . but most of the Egyptians serve and treat these animals themselves as gods.[16]

[10] Compare the metaphors of ploughing and plant growth for the marriage of the goddess (*ANET* 637–45), and the connection of bulls and water.

[11] e.g. *ANET* 578: 'Ishkur lion of heaven, noble bull'.

[12] See e.g. the hymn of *Shulgi* (*ANET* 585) who calls himself a lion, a donkey, and a horse. The gods also tend to be closely linked with natural phenomena such as storms and water.

[13] In the story of the begetting of Nanna: see Kramer (op. cit. n. 8), 43; H. Behrens, *Enlil und Ninlil* (Rome, 1978), 220–7.

[14] See Nilsson, *GGR* 212–16; W. Burkert, *Greek Religion* (Eng. tr. Oxford, 1985), 64–6.

[15] Some explicitly make a distinction (e.g. ἐλαφηβόλος), some refer to a sacrificial victim (e.g. ταυροφάγος), some refer to a special sphere of activity presided over by a god (e.g. Athene ἱππία), and some are thought to suggest an apotropaic function (e.g. Apollo σμινθεύς).

[16] *De Is. et Os.* 71.

The obvious exceptions to this attitude are the worship of Dionysos and the river gods.[17] Dionysos is pictured in later art, though not in earlier representations, as horned, like one of the Near Eastern gods; he is also summoned in cult hymn as a bull.[18] However, two qualifications are necessary. First, Dionysos belongs to a class of magical shape-shifters;[19] in myths he goes through a whole series of different shapes and can also inspire delusions. This magical power is perhaps different from a permanent nature as a particular animal. Secondly, and in keeping with this, we find him being summoned by his devotees in a variety of animal forms simultaneously;[20] this again recalls the Eastern hymns and the distinctions between the god and his cult title and particular manifestation.

The rivers too are sometimes depicted in bull form or half bull form.[21] The important point in this case is perhaps that river-gods already have a basic natural embodiment in water. The bull here is necessarily a secondary development and of metaphorical origin. With both Dionysos and the river-gods bull form seems connected with metaphors of fertility, as it was with the Mesopotamian bulls.[22]

Rather than arguing, therefore, that these traces of bull-worship in the case of Dionysos and the rivers are a memory of a stage when Dionysos was simply a bull, we should see them as a belief, or a memory of a belief, in animal manifestations or the animal epiphany, something more than metaphor but less than the worship of actual animals. Just as the Eastern parallels suggest an ambiguous nature for the animal-god and certainly do not suggest a clear pattern of evolution from animal to human worship, it seems that in Greek religion the worship of the bull Dionysos became most

[17] It is sometimes thought that the role of the bull in Cretan religion is another exception. However, although the bull plays an intriguing role in the myths of the Cretan royal family there is no evidence of a historical cult: see Burkert, *GR* 40.

[18] For Dionysos as a bull see H. Grégoire, in *Mélanges C. Picard*, ii (Paris, 1949), 401–5. For artistic representations in bull form see Plut. *De Is. et Os.* 35; *LIMC* s.v. 'Dionysos', nos. 154–9.

[19] See below, ch. 8.

[20] See e.g. *Bacchae* 1017 ff.

[21] See *RE* s.v. *Flussgötter*, col. 2780.

[22] This is seen most clearly in the concept of Achelous' horn of plenty. For Dionysos and the fertility of the earth see *Bacchae* 705 ff.

popular in the later period, and that the evidence for Minoan-Mycenaean animal-gods is very limited.[23]

Having arrived at this more restricted view of what is meant by an animal-god we should perhaps consider whether general considerations or the comparative evidence suggest anything about the way such a conception might have influenced myths. First of all, we might expect the belief in animal epiphanies to be reflected in stories of the appearance of the god in animal form even when human beings are not present. We do in fact find this both in Greek and Near Eastern myths.[24] But whereas it is one thing for gods to manifest themselves in animal form in culture and myth it seems quite another for humans to do so. One may wonder why a belief in epiphanies of the gods should give rise to the stories of the transformations of human beings. In fact the transformations of human beings, though a dominant type in Greek myths, seem comparatively rare in Mesopotamian mythology. In the tale of Gilgamesh, Gilgamesh and Enkidu are frequently compared to bulls but they are never transformed. Dumuzi attempts to escape the demons in the form of a gazelle, and Gilgamesh recounts the transformations of the lovers of Ishtar into a wolf and a mole, but in both these cases the choice of animal is clearly dictated by the logic of the story and seems to have no special connection with the gods concerned (in particular there is no transformation into a bull among Ishtar's lovers).

We can conclude, therefore, first that there is little reason to assume a simple general change in Greek religion from the worship of animals to a conception of human gods; even in Egypt and Mesopotamia the picture seems to be more complicated than this. Secondly, the Near Eastern parallels do not suggest that belief in animal epiphanies is a likely origin for stories of the transformation of human beings.

Once we cease to assume a general religious evolution of the type

[23] See M. P. Nilsson, *The Minoan-Mycenaean Religion and its Survival in Greek Religion*[2] (Lund, 1950), 48–9 and 368–82.

[24] e.g. the transformation of Seth into a hippopotamus in his fight with Horus is perhaps connected with his worship in this form: J. G. Griffiths, *The Conflict of Horus and Seth* (Cardiff, 1960), 46–7.

proposed by the animal-cult proponents the particular evidence in relation to the stories of Callisto and Io looks much less convincing.

CALLISTO

Callisto is a virgin huntress and companion of Artemis who is seduced by Zeus and then expelled from Artemis' band and turned into a bear. She gives birth to Arcas, the ancestor of the Arcadians, and is then either shot or set in the stars.[25]

The animal-god theory runs that Callisto is in origin Artemis herself, a bear-goodess and ancestress of the Arcadians, but that when the comparatively recent conception of Artemis as a virgin made her motherhood an impossibility a companion was invented to whom her stories were transferred. With her role as a bride and mother Artemis also handed over to Callisto her bear form. In support of the identification of Artemis and Callisto it is pointed out that not only are they very similar figures, both virgin huntresses, but that, more specifically, a reputed tomb of Callisto lay beside a temple of Artemis Calliste near Cruni in Arcadia.[26] In support of the claim that Artemis was a bear-goddess there is cited the ritual *arkteia* ('bear-service') at Brauron, in which little girls consecrated to Artemis lived for a period as 'bears',[27] and the fact that the priestess of Artemis at Cyrene was known as 'bear'.[28] Supporters of this view, therefore, reconstruct an older myth in which Zeus and Artemis, the bear, bore the father of the Arcadians.[29]

[25] Fo a fuller account of the myth see Cat. 1*a* s.v.

[26] Paus. 8. 35. 8.

[27] See L. Deubner, *Attische Feste* (Berlin, 1932), 205–7; L. Kahil, *AK* 20 (1977), 86–120; E. Simon, *Festivals of Attica* (Wisconsin, 1983), 83–8; C. Sourvinou-Inwood, *Studies in Girls' Transitions* (Athens, 1988); and the works cited in n. 58, below.

[28] See *LSS* no. 115b. 16. Cf. Hsch. s.v. *arkos*.

[29] See K. O. Müller, *Prolegomena zu einer wissenschaftlichen Mythologie* (Göttingen, 1825), 73–6; L. R. Farnell, *The Cults of the Greek States* (Oxford, 1896–1909), ii. 435; G. Maggiuli, in *Mythos: Scripta in honorem M. Untersteiner* (Genoa, 1970), 179–85; P. Lévêque, *L'Information historique* 23 (1961), 94–8; Kahil (art. cit. n. 27); J. Fontenrose, *Orion: The Myth of the Hunter and the Huntress* (Berkeley, 1981), ch. 4. J. J. Bachofen, *Der Bär in den Religionen des Altertums* (Basle, 1863), sees a common ancestor for Artemis and Callisto in a mountain mother-goddess who took bear form.

This argument is open to objection at every stage. First, it seems entirely unnecessary to suppose that Callisto has replaced Artemis herself in the myth.[30] The conception of the virgin hunter/huntress is thought to have its origins in primitive hunting taboos,[31] and thus the virgin Artemis is not necessarily a new civilized creation as opposed to the ancient nature-goddess. Her companions too should be seen as an integral part of the conception of the goddess rather than as a group of substitutes; they seem to correspond to the groups of young girls associated with her in historical cults.[32] The evidence of the names is hardly conclusive; there are other cases of companions and priestesses of the gods receiving as names the epithets of the god, and this is different from saying that they have taken over the myth of the god; one could also argue that the goddess has taken over the name of one of her companions or local rivals.[33]

Secondly and more fundamentally, there is no real evidence that Artemis ever was a bear-goddess. In no myth does she take the form of a bear, nor do any of her epithets or any representations of her in art suggest that she had ever been imagined in bear form.[34] Indeed a bear epiphany would be very strange since the bear is invariably ascribed a repellent character in ancient sources:[35] 'bear' could hardly be a laudatory metaphor as 'bull', 'horse', or 'cow' could be. She is of course *potnia theron*, mistress of wild animals;[36] and bears,

[30] This identification has been questioned by W. Sale, *RhM* 108 (1965), 11–35; cf. L. Bodson, *ΙΕΡΑ ΖΩΙΑ* (Brussels, 1978), 136–44; P. Borgeaud, *Recherches sur le dieu Pan* (Rome, 1979), 51.

[31] See Burkert, *GR* 150.

[32] See Burkert, *GR* 151. The *arkteia* is an obvious example.

[33] In the first group are e.g. Hekaerge and Opis (see Paus. 5. 7. 8). We need not assume that their stories as well as their names were derived from Artemis. For the second group see e.g. Zeus Agamemnon or Dionysos Cadmus, or the relations of Apollo and Hyakinthos.

[34] Contrast her connections in myth and art with deers. She is ἐλαφοκτόνος and ἐλαφηβόλος. In one story she becomes a deer: Apollod. 1. 7. 4 (for further connections see Paus. 2. 30. 7; 7. 18. 12; 8. 10. 10). As for representations in art, Kahil (art. cit. n. 27) cites a vase illustrating the *arkteia* which shows the priestess wearing a bear mask (although Simon (op. cit. n. 27) considers that this is a depiction of the myth of Callisto). But since the picture also shows the goddess in completely human form it seems rather to distinguish priestess and god.

[35] It is seen as the type of irredeemable savagery, often in contrast with the 'noble' lion: see Ael. *NA* 3. 21; Artem. 4. 56; Oppian, *C* 3. 157).

[36] *Il.* 21. 470.

considered the wildest of animals, came under her care. In this sense bears are parallel to the consecrated girls at Brauron, or a priestess of the goddess, and this seems a sufficient explanation of why these human servants of the goddess should be called bears.

Thirdly, the animal-god explanation at best explains just one element in the story, that Callisto is a bear rather than any other animal. It does not explain the pattern of punishment and persecution or the change from human to animal that are the story's distinctive features. In reconstructing an original myth as a story that the bear Artemis and Zeus had a child we have lost most of the point of the story.

IO

Io is a priestess of Hera at Argos who is seduced by Zeus and then turned into a cow by, or in fear of, Hera.[37] As Callisto is considered to be a double of Artemis, so Io is considered to be in origin Hera herself; her union with Zeus and her transformation are, according to this view, a sacred marriage of the great gods in cow form similar to the marriage of Ningirsu and Baú celebrated in an annual ritual in Sumeria.[38] An obvious question is why Hera should be replaced in the myth by a mortal, even though, unlike Artemis, Hera did not develop a role as a virgin goddess but rather continued to be the regular partner in the Greek sacred marriage.[39] It is therefore argued that the direct source of the myth was a ritual in which the priestess impersonated the cow-goddess Hera in the sacred marriage, as a sacred slave represented the goddess in the Sumerian form of the rite.[40]

Hera clearly had a close connection with cows. In Homer she is

[37] For a fuller account of her myth see Cat. 1*a* s.v.

[38] For Ningirsu and Baú see Astour (op. cit. n. 8), 85.

[39] See Nilsson, *GGR* 429–33; Burkert, *GR* 132–5, and more generally, S. N. Kramer, *The Sacred Marriage Rite* (Bloomington, 1969); G. W. Elderkin, *AJA* 41 (1937), 424–35. For new Attic evidence see F. Salviat, *BCH* 88 (1964), 647–54, and R. Parker, in T. Linders and S. Nordquist (ed.), *Gifts to the Gods* (Uppsala, 1987), 142–3.

[40] See A. B. Cook, *Zeus: A Study in Ancient Religion* (Cambridge, 1914–40), i. 437–57. Cf. F. Wehrli, *AK* Suppl. 4 (1967), 196–200.

known as *boopis* ('cow-eyed') and her image at Samos appears to be decorated with horns. Her cult at Argos involved cows in a number of different ways: they were offered to her in sacrifice, her priestess was brought to the city on a cart drawn by oxen, her temple stood on a hill called Euboea ('rich in cows'), and a herd of cattle belonging to the goddess was kept nearby.[41]

It is also true that some accounts suggest a sacred marriage of the traditional Eastern type. Io is described as the 'famous wife' of Zeus,[42] and her cow form is sometimes seen as a symbol of fertility and motherhood, and linked with the general fertility of the land.[43] Most striking perhaps is the version of the story in which the earth brings forth flowers for the cow Io after her union with Zeus in a way that recalls not only Eastern hymns and myth but the union of Zeus and Hera in the *Iliad*.[44]

However, again the theory is very implausible. First of all, as with Callisto, the evidence falls short of suggesting that Hera was ever an animal-goddess. The Argive evidence points to her ownership of, and wealth in, cows rather than to identity with the cow and can perfectly well be understood in terms of the more limited concept of the holy animal.[45] It makes sense that Io, the human servant or property of a goddess whose holy animal is a cow, becomes that holy animal in a myth; we need not suppose that in doing so she becomes the goddess. The epithet *boopis* and the horned image do not take us very far either. In Homer *boopis* is used of other women and clearly refers to no more than their beauty; and the horns at Samos seem more likely to be a decorative feature borrowed from Eastern models than to reflect the original animal nature of the goddess:[46]

[41] For *boopis* see e.g. *Il.* 1. 551; see further U. Pestalozza, *Athenaeum* 17 (1939), 105–37. For the Samian image, Cook, *Zeus*, i. 444–5; C. Kardara, *AJA* 64 (1960), 343–58; Burkert, *SH* 129–32. For the Argive connections, W. Burkert, *Homo Necans: Interpretationen altgriechischer Opferriten und Mythen* (Berlin, 1972), 181–7.

[42] Aesch. *PV* 834.

[43] See e.g. Aesch. *Supp.* 41 f; cf. 300. Zeus as father of the cow's child becomes φυτουργός and φυσίζοος: Aesch. *Supp.* 592 and 584.

[44] See A. Westermann, *Mythographi* (Brunswick, 1843), 374, and *EM* s.v. Euboea.

[45] In fact the holy marriage myth connected with the image of Hera at her Argive temple was of her seduction by the cuckoo Zeus: Paus. 2. 17. 4.

[46] See G. Zuntz, *Persephone* (Oxford, 1971), 131–5; Kardara (art. cit. n. 41), 353.

no Minoan-Mycenaean evidence suggests the existence of a cow-headed goddess.[47]

As for the sacred marriage with a masked priestess, the sacred marriage was a feature of Greek religion; however, we simply do not know what role was played by the priestess of the god,[48] and we have no evidence at all that animal masks ever played a part in such rites, or indeed in any cult of Hera.[49]

The fact that the myth plays upon ideas associated with the traditional sacred marriage does not require us to imagine that Io is Hera herself. In fact, whereas Hera is above all the goddess of the order of marriage,[50] the story of Io celebrates (in so far as there is any celebration) the more basic themes of fertility and motherhood within the context of an illegitimate liaison. Hera is almost invariably seen, in cult and myth, as a wife, not a mother, whereas Io is above all a mother and an ancestress. The essence of the story of Io lies in the distinction between the goddess and her errant priestess: its distinctive feature, as with the story of Callisto, is her punishment, her transformation and frenzied flight, which an identification of goddess and mortal does not begin to explain. One may compare by contrast the Sumerian cult myth of Sin and Amat-Sin[51] which told simply of the seduction of a cow.

My conclusions therefore are basically negative. The explanation of transformation stories by reference to a theory of animal-gods is first, and most fundamentally, open to a charge of circularity: in each case the chief evidence for the existence of an animal-cult is the very metamorphosis story that such a cult is supposed to explain. But we have seen already that the comparative evidence does not suggest that animal-cults do give rise to such stories. Secondly, such

[47] See Nilsson, *GGR* 350 n. 4.

[48] See Burkert, *GR* 108–9.

[49] On masked priests the best evidence is perhaps the bull masks discovered in Cyprus (see V. Karageorghis, *HTR* 64 (1971), 261–70), but we do not know their function and how much they represent Eastern rather than typically Greek customs. The many masks found at the shrine of Artemis Orthia tend to be grotesque human rather than animal ones (see G. Dickins, *JHS*, suppl. 5 (1929), 163–86). Animal masks are most popular in the *komos* and old comedy, but the relation of this to rituals of the kind we are considering is uncertain. See further Burkert, *GR* 65 and 103–5.

[50] See Burkert, *GR* 132–5.

[51] See Astour (op. cit. n. 8), 85.

explanations are inadequate. At best they explain one feature of the story, why the heroine becomes a particular animal, without in any sense explaining the story as a whole. It is a general criticism of such explanations that they tend to treat a myth as a quite arbitrary collection of details from which some motif may be extracted and identified with some external cult practice or belief.[52] This leads on to a third charge, of redundancy. While over-determination may well be a feature of Greek myths, and an element may be explained in terms both of its part in the structure of the story and of its ritual and historical origin, it is much less plausible to look for an inevitably speculative ritual explanation of a myth when we can already explain its details in some other way. I hope to show in the following chapter that these myths do form coherent structures.

If the animal-god is not a helpful notion, none the less the connection of the god with his or her particular animals does play a part in the story, particularly in that of Io. It is clearly not coincidental that Io, a priestess of Hera, becomes a cow, and Callisto, a companion of Artemis, becomes a bear. But it should be stressed that such a connection only takes us so far. No more than the supposed animal-cult can it explain what is really distinctive about these stories, why a human being is transformed into an animal at all.

INITIATION

It has become increasingly common to explain Greek myths by reference to initiation rituals.[53] It is claimed that the myths reflect rituals similar to the elaborate rites of passage that in various primitive societies accompany the passing of a person from one

[52] The limitations of such an approach to Greek myths are discussed in Vernant, *Myth and Society*, 186–242.

[53] See e.g. J. Bremmer, *Studi storico-religiosi* 2 (1978), 5–38; P. H. J. Lloyd-Jones, *JHS* 103 (1983), 87–102; Burkert, *HN* 189–200; P. Vidal-Naquet, in R. L. Gordon (ed.), *Myth, Religion, and Society: Structuralist Essays by M. Detienne, L. Gernet, J. P. Vernant, and P. Vidal-Naquet* (Cambridge, 1981), 147–62; and for more wholesale approaches, A. Brelich, *Paides e Parthenoi* (Rome, 1969), H. Jeanmaire, *Couroi et Courètes: Essai sur l'éducation spartiate et sur les rites d'adolescence dans l'antiquité hellénique* (Lille, 1939), and C. Calame, *Les Chœurs de jeunes filles en Grèce archaïque* (Rome, 1977), *passim*.

social state to another. The major attraction of such theories is that they offer an explanation not just of one motif of the stories but of their whole structure. Such rites tend to have a common pattern of separation from family and society, a liminal period often associated with a reversal of status (and sometimes including a disguise or disfigurement) and a final reintegration into society.[54] These elements suitably translated into mythical terms bear an obvious relation to the patterns of many myths.

It might seem that initiation is a particularly appropriate explanation in the case of metamorphosis stories, since it is the ritual concerned with a process of change;[55] and it has indeed been claimed that the transformations of Callisto and of Lycaon, the Arcadian king who becomes a wolf, correspond to the liminal stage in a ritual initiation.[56]

This is not the place for a general discussion of the initiation theory, but I would like to begin with a number of preliminary reservations about this whole approach. First, it is necessary to emphasize the highly speculative nature of the theory. Evidence for age-group initiations in ancient Greece is extremely scarce,[57] and so most discussion has been concerned with the ritual consecrations of a small group such as the *arkteia* at Brauron;[58] it is argued that these are survivals of a more general rite.

Secondly and more fundamentally, it is not clear what explanatory force is being claimed for such hypothetical rites. It is claimed that the heroes of these stories are mythical prototypes of the initiands: but does this mean that a pre-existing story was adopted as a model for the experience of the initiands (in which case we learn little about the creation of Greek myths), or that the myth was created by a process of translating the various stages of the ritual into mythical episodes? The problem with the second account is

[54] See A. van Gennep, *The Rites of Passage* (Eng. tr. London, 1960); V. Turner, *The Ritual Process* (London, 1969) and *The Forest of Symbols* (Ithaca, 1967).

[55] See e.g. M. Eliade, *The Quest: History and Meaning in Religion* (Chicago, 1969), 112: 'The novice emerges from his ordeal a totally different being: he has become another.'

[56] On Callisto see Lloyd-Jones (art. cit. n. 53), 98; R. Arena, *Acme* 32 (1979), 6–26; cf. Borgeaud, 51–5. On Lycaon see works cited in n. 68, below.

[57] They appear to have existed in classical times only in Crete: see Burkert, *GR* 260–1.

[58] See e.g. Jeanmaire, *Couroi*, 257–64; Brelich, *Paides*, ch. 2; Lloyd-Jones (art. cit. n. 53).

that the initiatory pattern reduced to its most basic terms is essentially the pattern of most traditional stories: a boy or girl is removed from his or her home and undergoes a number of adventures before being restored to live happily ever after. With a certain amount of ingenuity almost any Greek myth can be made to reveal an initiatory structure (and any aberrant features can be explained away as imaginative extensions of the ritual motif). In short, the theory that such rituals gave rise to the transformation stories, or to any other group of myths, is almost impossible to prove or disprove.

In order to give the theory some useful explanatory role one would need to be able to look at a number of connected rites and myths and identify a common pattern of translation from ritual to myth. However, if we look at the stories told in connection with the historical ritual consecrations that we know of, it is very hard to produce such a scheme. In the most common pattern the consecration or service is an act of expiation for an earlier crime, usually an unlawful killing which has caused a plague or famine.[59] It makes little sense to talk here of translation from a ritual into a mythical structure. It is undoubtedly interesting that consecration is seen as an expiation for a death, but one should emphasize that such stories do not reflect the ritual structure of separation/marginalization/reintegration: myth is not here being used to give imaginative expression to the stages of the rite, but to establish an imaginative background against which the rite is set.

But this leads on to a third point, which applies as much to any ritual explanation as to the initiation theories. If the original appeal, and hence the origin, of these stories depends on their listeners' experience of certain rituals, why did the stories continue to appeal once the rituals had been forgotten? This is another form of the argument from redundancy. In so far as one can provide a coherent analysis of the stories in terms of their appeal to a classical listener, one may wonder why it is necessary to posit an entirely hypothetical ritual to explain their meaning for their original audience.

[59] See e.g. the *aitia* for the *arkteia* in honour of Artemis Brauronia and Mounichia (in Brelich, *Paides*, 248–9), or for the consecration of seven boys and girls in the shrine of Hera Akraia at Corinth (schol. on Eur. *Med.* 273) cf. the *aitia* in Paus. 7. 19. 1 (the shrine of Triklarian Artemis), and Paus. 3. 16. 9 (the shrine of Artemis Orthia).

Turning now to the particular stories that this theory has been applied to, I shall deal first, and fairly briefly, with Callisto. No source connects her with any ritual consecration or indeed with any rite at all. But it is claimed that she is a mythical parallel to the young girls at Brauron, who during their consecration were known as 'bears'.[60] As I pointed out above, one cannot prove that her story is not a mythical projection of such a ritual, and it is quite likely that some of the same attitudes to the wilds and to the goddess Artemis underlie the story of the transformation and the metaphorical description of young girls as bears; on the other hand Callisto's experiences are so far removed from such a ritual consecration that any direct influence of ritual on myth seems very implausible.

Callisto's transformation and exile is not a preparation for re-integration into society and a model marriage but a prelude to death (or catasterism); it follows rape by a married god and is closely linked with illegitimate childbirth. It is not connected with a period of devotion to the goddess, but rather with her expulsion from Artemis' band. There is a much more obvious episode in the story that does correspond to the initiatory exclusion, and that is when she joins the band of Artemis in the first place.

The theory is sufficiently flexible to get round all these points of difficulty. Callisto's death, it is said, is a symbolic one,[61] or her experiences are a warning of what can go wrong and illustrate the dangers of transition.[62] But since, as I shall argue in the next chapter, the story can be understood in terms of a purely mythical logic, there seems little incentive to try to force the myth into such a scheme. One may note finally that there is already a cult story attached to the Brauron *arkteia*; this belongs to the pattern noted above, in which the consecration becomes an expiation for a past death, and bears no resemblance at all to the story of Callisto.[63]

The story of Lycaon requires more detailed consideration. He is

[60] See the works cited in n. 56 above.

[61] See Brelich, *Paides*, 263, and more generally in *Myths and Symbols: Studies in Honour of M. Eliade* (London, 1969), 195–207. Cf. R. Arena (art. cit. n. 56). For the idea that rebirth inevitably involves death of the old self compare M. Eliade, *Birth and Rebirth* (Eng. tr. London, 1961), 13–14.

[62] Cf. Calame, 270–2, on the 'plant' heroines.

[63] See above, n. 59.

an early king of Arcadia who entertained Zeus as a guest and served him up a human child (normally his grandson Arcas). Zeus turned him into a wolf. Unlike any of the stories we have considered so far, this myth is linked by an ancient source to a rite. 'They say', says Pausanias, 'that since the time of Lycaon a man always turns into a wolf at the sacrifice to Zeus Lycaeus, but not for life, for if he abstains from human flesh, in the ninth year he changes back again.'[64] Earlier he has told us of Damarchus, an athlete who is supposed to have done this before becoming an Olympic victor.[65] He refuses to speak of the sacrifice itself, which he says is a secret, but Plato[66] tells us a *mythos* about the shrine of Zeus Lycaeus on Mount Lycaeon which has been thought to refer to it. Human flesh is mixed with the meat of other animals which is then shared out; whoever eats the human flesh becomes a wolf. There is also a report in Pliny and Augustine about an Arcadian werewolf custom:[67] a man from a certain family is chosen by lot and led to a pond; he hangs his clothes on an oak tree, swims across, and becomes a wolf. If he avoids human flesh for eight years he can swim back and become a man again. Some think that the same rite is being referred to, perhaps in a more developed form.

It has been suggested that the cannibal feast is the first step in an eight-year initiation ordeal for an Arcadian secret society.[68] The obvious models for this interpretation are African secret societies (e.g. the leopard men), but it is argued that a Greek parallel exists in the Spartan *krypteia*, the institution by which young Spartans spent a certain period in the wilds living virtually as outlaws. They would hide during the day, and at night would come out and murder passing helots. This was a preparation, it is argued, for joining an élite group of Spartan soldiers.

With regard to the legends of mount Lycaeon, it is thought to be significant first that Damarchus, the Olympic victor mentioned by Pausanias, spent eight years as a wolf before his victory; his period as

[64] 8. 2. 6. [65] 6. 8. 2. [66] *Resp.* 565 D.

[67] Pliny, *NH* 8. 81; Aug. *De Civ. D.* 18. 17.

[68] See Jeanmaire, *Couroi*, 540–69; Burkert, *HN* 98–108; cf. R. J. A. Buxton, in J. Bremmer (ed.), *Interpretations of Greek Mythology* (London, 1987), ch. 4; Lloyd-Jones (art. cit. n. 53), 98.

a wolf is therefore a preparation for a successful reintegration into society as a highly honoured citizen. Secondly, it is argued that the werewolf story in Pliny and Augustine shows familiar rite of passage motifs (removing clothes, immersion in water, crossing a river), while the communal cannibal feast in Plato's story is a feature in ancient and modern secret societies.[69] (Note, however, that whereas in these the communal guilt from the shared cannibal feast seems to be an important binding factor, here we have a single cannibal isolated from his companions). The myth of Lycaon is therefore a mythical projection of this rite, and Lycaon is the mythical prototype of each of the wolf men.

There are two problems here, the first as to the historical existence of the initiation rite, the second as to Lycaon's connection with it.

There is no external archaeological evidence that people ate each other on Mount Lycaeon. All the reports of this feast in ancient writers appear to derive from the playful allusion in Plato (even the account of the Arcadian Polybius cites Plato).[70] In fact it seems likely that Pausanias did not regard it as a local story at all: he speaks of the werewolf tradition with contempt and contrasts it with the ancient Arcadian story of the transformation of Lycaon.[71]

One might well be sceptical therefore about the tradition of the cannibal feast, but to combine this with the story of Pliny and Augustine seems even more questionable. This latter story has no link with Mount Lycaeon or with any rite, and in particular it misses out the human sacrifice that is a vital part of the other story. Furthermore, the story shows the familiar motifs of later werewolf stories (most obviously in the removal and careful preservation of the werewolf's clothes).[72] This story perhaps only shows that there were in fact Arcadian werewolf stories which did originate in the sacrifice on Mount Lycaeon.

[69] See H. Webster, *Primitive Secret Societies*[2] (New York, 1932), 35.

[70] Polyb. 7. 13. 7.

[71] Further, in his report of the werewolf athlete Damarchus he infers that the story of his transformation is not a tradition that the Arcadians held themselves since otherwise it would have been recorded on the inscription at Olympia. Whatever we may think of the grounds for this inference this at least shows that the story was not in Pausanias' time recognized as a local Arcadian one.

[72] Cf. Petronius 62 and Aesop 301 (ed. A. Hausrath[2], vol. ii, Leipzig, 1959).

In short, werewolf stories are a common feature in the European folk-tale; they are found frequently in late antiquity and probably existed in Arcadia. It may well be that one of these later became attached to the sacrifice on Mount Lycaeon, the secrecy of which may have encouraged dark rumours.[73] Perhaps the myth of Lycaon itself prompted such a development.

One may note further that there is no independent evidence for this secret society. The Spartan *krypteia* is perhaps not such a helpful parallel. Rather than a survival of primitive initiations it seems to have been an institution especially created or adapted for the Spartans' peculiar and relatively new problem of suppressing the helots.[74]

We clearly do not know enough to say that there could not have been such a rite or secret society. But their existence is at least highly questionable, and this means that rather more hangs on the second issue of the inherent suitability of Lycaon as an initiatory model. In fact it is extremely difficult to see how he could have been invented for such a purpose.

First of all, he is the wrong age. Those figures normally considered to be initiatory models are heroic or divine equivalents of the initiands, young men or women like Theseus, Apollo, Artemis, or the daughters of Cecrops.[75] But Lycaon is invariably an old or middle-aged man.[76]

Secondly, Lycaon's transformation is not a temporary prelude to reintegration or even to death. He is a permanent wolf, and his story belongs rather with the aetiological stories which explain animal characters in terms of past human crimes; we can compare the close parallel of the transformation of the savage Lyncus into a lynx. Lycaon is a real wolf, not a werewolf. It could of course be that the myth illustrates the dangers of what could go wrong at the rite, but this leads on to a third and most crucial point: Lycaon's crime is murder and abusing the rules of hospitality, never cannibalism; we

[73] See Nilsson, *GGR* 397–401; cf. Halliday on Plut. *GQ* 39.

[74] See P. Vidal-Naquet, in Gordon, 180–5.

[75] Or Pelops, Melikertes, Archemoros, the children of Medea, Iphigeneia, Kaineus, or Achilles.

[76] Ovid speaks of his 'canities' persisting in the wolf, *Met.* 1. 238.

find the same pattern in the story of Tantalus, where the only cannibal is the goddess Demeter. It is difficult to see how Lycaon could be an imaginary archetype for the banqueters at Plato's cannibal feast, where it is eating rather than killing that is at issue.

The myth and cults of Mount Lycaeon do not, therefore, provide a clear example of how a mythical structure can be explained by that of a rite. Again one is forced to rely on the myth itself as evidence for the existence of the rite that is supposed to explain it, and again, on closer examination, the myth is not very helpful material for such a purpose.

3

Animals, 2

Myths as Stories

It was suggested in Chapter 2 that although the overall structure of these stories and the theme of transformation itself do not have their origin in the practices and conceptions of historical Greek cult, the cult relations of an animal may go some way to explain why it is this animal rather than any other that appears in a particular story.

One need not stop at cult relations, of course. These animals point to various other things outside their story. Etymologizing is common. Sometimes it is explicit; sometimes it is not. Various sources explain that the name of Callisto's son Arcas is derived from the bear form of his mother. Since in fact Arcas obviously derives his name from the people of which he is the ancestor and eponym, the Arcadians, one can reverse this and argue that the story of the transformation of the mother might be prompted by the name of the son. The fact that Lycaon's name is so similar to the Greek word for a wolf makes it inconceivable that he could be turned into any other animal. It is clear that here too the name is not specially invented to suit the story since Lycaon has an essential connection with, and clearly derives his name from, Mount Lycaeon or Zeus Lycaeus.

The geographical background of these heroes and their stories, as well as the meaning of their names is probably important. It is presumably no coincidence that a princess who lives in the fertile plain of Argos should become a cow while Lycaon and Callisto who live in the wild mountains of Arcadia become a wolf and a bear. This may be a direct influence, or perhaps an indirect one in that the geography of the area will affect the nature of the god, which in turn may be the direct influence on the story.

Often the external influence may be some mythological relative of the character. Hippo, for instance, becomes a horse at least partly because she is a daughter of Cheiron. We have an explicit *aition* in the case of Philyra, who because of her transformation into a horse bears the centaur Cheiron (as Demeter and Erinys are turned into horses to bear the horse Arion).

These external factors may help not only to explain the origin of the story, but to give it part of its meaning, in the sense of its appeal. It is possible that even when the story is not explicitly aetiological, as in the case of the story of Lycaon, some satisfaction is derived from the recognition of the appropriateness of the change.

However, we need to go beyond these external factors. In so far as these *aitia* are developed into stories they acquire an interest quite distinct from their explanatory function. *Aitia* are not an entirely distinct category of stories which have to be studied apart from other Greek myths;[1] they use the themes and episodes of the general body of Greek myths. When we come to consider the aetiological metamorphoses we shall see that they make use not only of the same themes as non-aetiological stories, but also of similar structures; the aetiological transformation is itself a narrative element which may be replaced, for instance, by suicide or madness.[2] With regard to the mammals, I shall try to show that the aetiological transformation of Leto (to bear Apollo Lykegenes) has a similar structure and themes to the non-aetiological changes of Io or Callisto.

I have already suggested in the previous chapter that pointing to external historical or religious reasons why a particular animal, a bear for instance rather than a lion, appears in a story will not explain the structure of the story as a whole. But having accepted that the structure of a story must be explained in terms of an internal logic, one must assume that this internal logic, these narrative factors that make a story a satisfying whole, will at least partly govern the choice of any particular episode or feature within it. Therefore, if a feature or object has to be explained or given a story, a story will have to be chosen that is appropriate according to these narrative or mythical criteria. Had, for instance, *Lykegenes*

[1] As seems implied in M. P. Nilsson, *A History of Greek Religion* (Oxford, 1925), 48.

[2] Cf. e.g. the Pherecydes story of the nightingale (*FGH* 3 F 124) with the story of Themisto (Hyg. *Fab.* 4).

suggested a birth from a lion rather than a wolf it seems unlikely that we should have our present story of the transformation, exile, and hiding of Leto. A lion is traditionally too powerful and aggressive an animal to behave in this furtive way. Perhaps in this case we would have had a story more like the birth of Dionysos from Persephone, in which Zeus masters and rapes the goddess after she has turned into a formidable snake. For understanding these stories, therefore, their aetiological starting point is only a starting point.

In this chapter I shall be particularly concerned with the nature of the imaginative appeal of these myths as stories. I shall argue that these stories play upon traditional ideas and metaphors about the relation between men and animals to present an imaginative and mythical expression of familiar human concerns. We can assume, I think, that most ancient Greeks were not seriously worried that they would suddenly become animals; we should perhaps assume, therefore, that metamorphosis stories will normally depend for their appeal on involving their audience, probably not fully consciously, in some metaphorical or symbolic perception of the story. In this sense, therefore, to say that Leto's transformation into a wolf is an *aition* for Apollo Lykegenes only goes some way towards explaining what that story would mean and why it would be satisfying to its audience.

This imaginative or mythical projection of a human concern can have various levels of contact with reality. In the case of the group of young women who all at some time take to the wilds we are dealing with a wholly imaginative or metaphorical construction. Athenian women, for instance, would probably have no contact with the wilds at all except for the few who served as maenads or the élite who entered a symbolic wilderness as young bears. In particular, the female hunter, one of the basic figures of Greek mythology, seems entirely a fantasy.

The case of the male hunter, Actaeon, seems more complicated. At one level hunting is a direct reflection of experience. Among certain classes of people hunting was still popular in classical Greece. However, this was a restricted group. More generally hunting is a realm of imagined experience in which one can set fantasies about dangerous and destructive activities and mysterious journeys into the wilds. More specifically hunting may be a mythical projection of other more familiar dangerous and destructive activities such as being a soldier. However, at a third level I shall argue that hunting becomes the mythical model of not just a dangerous, but a specifically masculine activity. At this level, the myth is concerned with the relations of men and women, and the wild goddess is a projection of the ordinary woman hidden in her house.

One must be careful here. Mythical projections are not the same as metaphors or symbols, though a study of traditional metaphors may help to explain them. One is not saying that colourful mythical actions can be reduced to everyday behaviour, but rather that some point of contact with the emotional experience of the hearer is necessary. In the story of Actaeon the mythical hero is rather more than the contemporary soldier or voyeur. On the one hand the myth magnifies and heightens the experiences by giving them to heroes and gods, but also the different levels of the story are not alternatives, but operate together and the myth brings together different levels of experience. The story of Actaeon derives its excitement from arousing curiosity about hidden and forbidden women and at the same time evoking and blending with this the imagined excitement of hunting, killing, and the wilds.

There is a danger that any attempt to analyse the imaginative appeal of a myth will seem subjective and arbitrary. Even if one can show that certain ideas or metaphors are pervasive in classical literature and culture it is difficult to show that they underlie our stories. Many of our older sources are lost, and we thus have only reports of their plots. What these reports indicate about the choice of details in the original sources can be revealing, but this is not a full substitute for their own words. We can to some extent make up for this by seeing how the various motifs of our stories are used in different myths. We find the same motifs occurring again and again in Greek mythology, and we can fix more precisely the meaning and associations a particular motif brings to any one context by looking at its use in others. To anticipate a later discussion, it is a very common pattern for seers to acquire their power of prophecy through an encounter with snakes. Thus, although Teiresias' encounter with snakes is in no source the direct cause of his gift of prophecy, we may assume that this earlier incident is closely linked with his later career. The significance of a motif is also clarified by establishing which other motifs may be used as regular alternatives for it. (It was pointed out earlier that suicide or madness often replaces transformation.) Much of my argument, therefore, will be concerned with setting the motifs of our stories in their wider mythological context.

However, any attempt to consider the imaginative appeal of these stories will inevitably rely on the fuller later sources, particularly Ovid. It will naturally be objected that these later writers are misleading: they belong to a different world from the earlier tellers of these stories and they have their interests and purposes in telling them. We clearly need to be cautious, but we do at least have some idea of what we are dealing with: nearly all Ovid's stories can be compared with other versions, in some cases with full earlier versions, so that we can build up a good picture of what his special interests are and what themes or elements in these stories he is likely to distort or omit. On the other hand, the imagination Ovid shows in his treatment of the stories can often be a help in interpreting them. He will point to or bring to the surface underlying themes which must have been a part of the appeal of the earlier versions of the story even if they were never made explicit. In a sense the best commentary on the interest of these myths as stories will be an imaginative retelling of them. Provided, therefore, that we do have some kind of check Ovid can be very useful. In fact, we do not find in Ovid the kind of bold distortions of character and incident that we take for granted in, say, Shakespeare's *Troilus and Cressida*, and which obviously turn a myth into a completely different story.

We can now turn to the stories. There is little point in treating them together. The stories of Lycaon, Actaeon, and the young women clearly have different themes and play upon different ideas about the relations between men and animals. There is, however, perhaps one basic element in common in all these cases. In each story the transformation into an animal is a part of a wider disruption of order. It is very often associated with madness or pollution and, of course, a taking to the wilds (even when the transformation is into a domestic beast as in the case of Io). Io, Atalanta, Callisto, and Hecuba all become, in some sources at least, not merely animals, but mad animals. In the story of Actaeon the madness and pollution are not his own, but that of his dogs; it is a combination of madness and transformation that leads to the catastrophic disorder as the dogs eat their master. The story of Lycaon is, of course, concerned with the original *miasma* of the table and concludes not merely with his own transformation but with the destruction of his house. The cause and nature of the disorder is different in each case: sexual pollution in the stories of the young women, the abuse of the table in the story of Lycaon, and the confusion of normal relations in the story of Actaeon, but it is important to see right at the start that we are dealing with rather more than simply a change from particular human being to particular animal. The stories play upon the antithesis of man and animal in a much wider sense.

I should finally add that I do not intend in this chapter to consider the very enigmatic transformation of Hecuba into a dog. This story raises special questions, and it makes more sense to discuss it in the catalogue. It does share some of the more general characteristics of the stories of transformation into animals in that Hecuba's transformation follows a more general disruption of order in which she has been deprived of home, city, and family; but more specifically it belongs to a pattern like that of Cadmus' transformation into a snake, and Niobe's into a stone, in which transformation comes as the final and ambiguous episode in a series of misfortunes.

THE YOUNG WOMEN

The stories of the young women form a group distinguished to some extent by common themes and a common pattern. These are the stories of Io, Callisto, Atalanta, Taygete, and Hippo, of the Proitides who suffer the delusion that they are cows (and in one source actually become cows), and of Leto who becomes a wolf to bear Apollo, and Philyra who becomes a horse to bear Cheiron. All these heroines have as the central action of their stories some illicit sexual experience, usually the illicit loss of virginity. This is usually followed by a taking to the wilds, transformation (these two are closely linked), birth of a child, and either a final marriage or an end to all relations with men or animals (i.e. in death or catasterism). Transformation, like exile to the wilds, usually comes after seduction and before the birth of the child,[3] but in some versions of these stories it is closely associated with the initial seduction, and sometimes it follows the birth of the child. In the case of the companions of Artemis, who have already taken to the wilds, the exile has two stages: first they voluntarily leave their father's home, and secondly they are expelled or withdraw from the band of Artemis.

As I have already indicated, I consider that the most useful way of exploring the function of transformation in these myths is by considering the animal metaphors used of women in Greek literature and life and seeing if they shed any light on the act of becoming an animal in myths. Women are most commonly compared to animals in respect of their sexuality: sometimes the comparison suggests their physical fertility, sometimes their sexual appetite, and most commonly, in a largely external sense, it suggests that they are attractive or interesting to men.[4]

The effect of these metaphors is not only to celebrate the physical functions which women share with animals, but to suggest a certain wildness about sex and the sexual nature of women. This may take the positive form of an exciting and enticing wildness or else suggest an outrageous or disorderly sexual behaviour. In either case we have an implicit or explicit opposition to the order of the house. There is much evidence in ancient texts for the wilds as a

[3] This is the pattern of the story of Io, the Hesiodic and Callimachean versions of Callisto's story, the story of Leto, the Hesiodic version of the story of the Proitides, and one version of the story of Hippo. The Euripidean version of Taygete's story makes no mention of a child, but here too transformation and expulsion appear to follow seduction; cf. the story of Atalanta. Euripides' version of Callisto's story appears to associate seduction with transformation; Ovid has Callisto transformed after giving birth. The major exception to this scheme is the confused account of the story of Taygete in the Pindar scholia, where she appears to evade seduction altogether.

[4] For animals in an inviting sense see the comparisons in the marriage hymns of Alcman, fr. 1. 45 ff., and Theoc. 18. 30, or Anacreon, fr. 417; ἀταύρωτος/η means 'virgin' in Aesch. *Ag.* 246 and Ar. *Lys.* 217. For human mothers as animals see Eur. *Andr.* 711 or Pind. *Pyth.* 4. 142. For sexual appetite suggested by animal names or comparisons see Arist. *HA* 572ᵃ; Antig. *Mir.* 115; Photius s.v. πεζὰς μόσχους. Cf. also Ar. *Lys.* 1308 ff.; Pind. fr. 112; Hor. *Carm.* 2. 5 and 3. 11.

place without sexual order: animals commit incest,[5] they show no respect for shrines,[6] and, as we have seen, particularly shameless women may be described as animals. The story of Polyphonte who takes to the wilds, is maddened by Aphrodite, and mates with a bear is an extreme expression of this attitude.[7] The more positive attitude is equally important: the wilds may be contrasted with the parents' home as an exciting and inviting place.[8] Very often too we find a paradoxical association of the wilds with female virginity.[9] Young women are seen as animals to be hunted and tamed by their lovers,[10] while in mythology Artemis and her band of huntresses roam through the woods resisting or succumbing to various male advances. Although these women are chaste wild creatures they are essentially objects of male pursuit, and it is their wildness that makes them enticing and appropriate objects of such pursuit. We find in fact that the dominant metaphors for Greek marriage or even sex outside marriage are those of subduing, taming, or yoking.[11] The woman is seen as an element of the wilds that a man must take in hand. We may compare those metaphors in which the woman is opposed to the man as the land to the farmer.[12] Even the aggressively chaste huntresses are not asexual beings, but their wildness expresses a sexual potential that is tamed and brought under a male order by the husband or lover.

Women may, therefore, be thought of as animals in respect of their sexual nature, sometimes in a complimentary, sometimes in a negative sense. Since in our stories transformation follows or has a close relation with a sexual experience it seems reasonable to look for the influence of such ideas here. This is not to deny that there

[5] See Ov. *Met.* 7. 386 f. or 10. 324 ff.

[6] Hdt. 2. 64.

[7] See AL 21; compare Pentheus' speculation in the *Bacchae* (215 ff.) on the likely behaviour of women in the wilds.

[8] e.g. Anac. fr. 346.

[9] Detienne (*Dionysos Slain*, 25–6) discusses the wilds as a place of unorthodox sexuality, either of promiscuity and bestiality or of unnatural chastity.

[10] See Hor. *Carm.* 3. 11; Anac. fr. 408. Cf. Anac. fr. 417; Hor. *Carm.* 2. 5. On this theme see C. Sourvinou-Inwood, *JHS* 107 (1987), 131–53; Calame, i. 414.

[11] A basic word is δαμάζω. Cf. Anac. fr. 417. See Sourvinou-Inwood (art. cit. n. 10); Calame, i. 411–20.

[12] See J. P. Gould, *JHS* 100 (1980), 53.

are not other important elements in these stories (for instance, the relation between man and god). But the one feature that is present in all of them is the connection between women, sex, and the wilds.

Let us now turn to the myths themselves. There seems to be a direct reflection of the positive animal metaphors in some of our stories. Taygete as a deer and Io as a cow may be seen as inviting objects. Zeus' pursuit of Taygete in deer form seems to be a literal version of the metaphors of the hunt, while the god is imagined approaching in bull form 'the fine-horned cow' of Io.[13] Io is not only an attractive cow, but a fertile and maternal one. The chorus in the *Supplices* refer to their cow-ancestress in a way that recalls, for instance, Pindar's metaphorical reference to the mother of Kretheus and Salmoneus as a cow.[14] In the *Prometheus* Io vividly describes how dreams would come to her in her *parthenon* ('maidens' apartment') calling her to the deep meadow outside where her father's cattle grazed and Zeus awaited her; this comes very close to the description in a fragment of Anacreon of a timid girl sitting at home frightened of the meadow outside where the horses of Aphrodite graze.[15] Here the movement from inside the house to the outside, and even the change to a cow, are not Hera's punishment, but necessary for Io's union with Zeus. In the most direct sense, therefore, transformation and the movement to the outside reflect a readiness for Zeus' approaches (though a physical rather than a psychological one; Io's own wishes are never in question).

However, this is not normal. On the whole, transformation stories do not reflect the positive metaphors of invitation, but the negative side of the link between animals, women, and sex. Transformation normally comes as a punishment after seduction, and the transformed woman is usually an unattractive object and not at all inviting (the desirable wildness of the women comes more often in their earlier human state as huntresses); it is a punishment for a sexual transgression, and it expresses the degeneration from humans to animals that follows from this sexual activity. This is more explicit in the case of Atalanta. Though she becomes a sexless animal

[13] Aesch. *Supp.* 300; cf. Bacchylides, *Dith.* 19. 24.

[14] *Supp.* 41 f. and Pind. *Pyth.* 1. 42.

[15] *PV* 652–3 and Anacr. fr. 346.

it is the desecration of a shrine through sex that has brought this about, and such behaviour is a traditional characteristic of animals as opposed to human beings.[16] In the story of the Proitides a taking to the wilds is sometimes a part of the disorderly sexual behaviour, sometimes a consequence of it.[17]

The form of the stories makes the point particularly clear here, but I think similar ideas underlie the other changes. The cases of Atalanta and Callisto show that the animal need not in itself be an erotic one; here, in fact, it is anti-erotic. Though the sexual experience of these women has made them animals we have a reversal, and these animals are repellent ones. Atalanta's and Callisto's forms are extreme cases of reversal; they tend to be described in terms of an opposition to the sexual act that produced them. Lions are traditionally not fertile, but according to the *aition* of our story they are sexless creatures that never mate with each other.[18] Bears were regarded as sexually active animals, but the point taken up by our sources is their off-putting appearance for men: 'and when Hera saw', Ovid says, 'the hideous face of the savage beast on Jupiter's mistress, "let him enter its embrace", she said.'[19] There may be a deliberate irony in the name of the heroine Callisto ('most beautiful') and the reversal implied by it.

Both lions and bears are savage and formidable animals that cannot be approached by men, but we find similar treatment given to Io's potentially inviting and fertile cow form. Io takes to the wilds and becomes a wild and unmanageable creature like Callisto and Atalanta (similarly the Proitides take to the wilds in spite of the fact that they think they are domestic beasts; they are said to have 'a savage heart').[20] As was noted earlier, all these transformed heroines

[16] Hdt. 2. 64.

[17] In Hesiod it seems to be a consequence (see frs. 132 and 133). Aelian tells how they were made μάχλοι by Aphrodite and ran round the Peloponnese: *VH* 3. 42.

[18] See Serv. *A* 113.

[19] *Fasti* 2. 179–80. Cf. the incongruous picture in *Helen* 375 ff. of the bear climbing into Zeus' bed. For their general appearance see Opp. *C* 3. 141. See further O. Keller, who sees a humorous incongruity in pictures showing Cupids playing with bears (*Die antike Tierwelt* (Berlin, 1909–13), 276). The story that Cephalus mated with a bear (*EM* s.v. Ἀρκείσιος; Eust. *Il.* 2. 631) is not evidence for the attractiveness of bears but rather plays upon the incongruity of such a union.

[20] In Callim. 3. 236; their father Proitos sets up a shrine to Artemis.

become not merely animals, but animals in whose lives there has been a complete breakdown of order: they are diseased, polluted, or maddened animals. Callisto is not only expelled as a bear from the band of Artemis, but becomes a constellation that is not allowed to set in the sea because of her crime and impurity.[21] Artemis' immediate reaction to her pregnancy is 'Begone . . . and pollute not our sacred spring'.[22] There are repeated suggestions of the disease and pollution of Io in the *Supplices* and the *Prometheus*, and she is seen as a monster rather than as a real cow.[23] Perhaps this idea is most explicit in the case of the Proitides, who are afflicted with a disfiguring disease as an alternative, or in addition to, the belief that they are cows. Closely linked with disease and pollution is the madness that appears in nearly all these stories as an addition to or substitute for physical change. In the case of the Proitides it replaces transformation, but Io is normally driven mad as well as being transformed; her distraught wandering in the *Prometheus* recalls that of the polluted Orestes in the *Oresteia* (and later versions have her too pursued by a fury).[24] Atalanta also in one version becomes the maddened lion of Cybele; here the madness might be argued to come from the *aition* rather than the logic of the story, but in another version she is maddened by Artemis.[25]

In conclusion, therefore, I would suggest that, just as the sexuality of women may be expressed in terms of a metaphor of animals or the wilds, transformation reflects the traumatic effect of an unorthodox or illegitimate change from young girls to sexual objects. Sometimes this may be partly a positive expression of their sexuality and fertility as in some descriptions of Io, but more often it suggests a frightening and repellent outbreak of wildness opposed both to the childhood home and to marriage.

Before I consider the individual stories in more detail there is perhaps one final objection I should consider. It may be suggested

21 In Ov. 2. 530 Juno asks Tethys 'ne puro tingatur in aequore paelex'; cf. Hes. fr. 354.

22 Ov. 2. 464; cf. *Fasti* 2. 174.

23 See *Supp.* 566 f.; *PV* 690 f. In *PV* 606 and *Supp.* 586 there is explicit mention of disease.

24 e.g. Ovid or Valerius Flaccus: see Cat. 1*a* (Io); cf. the ghost of Argos in Aesch. *PV* 568.

25 Nonn. 12. 89. Callisto is not mentioned as mad by any of our literary sources, but Lyssa appears on a vase representation of her story (see Cat. 1*a* (Callisto)).

that to argue for a close link of transformation and sexual behaviour is to distort these stories, since in each case it is male, not female, lust that is the motivating force. Women are merely the passive victims of male gods; yet it is they, and not the men, who become animals. This objection would have some force if one were to argue that animal form is an expression of lust; but lust is not really in question. In most stories of the loves of gods and heroes it is impossible to distinguish between rape and seduction; the woman's feelings are not usually mentioned. In myth women are continually punished for being raped;[26] it seems that Athenian law made no distinction between adulterous wives who had been willing partners and those who had been the victims of rape.[27] (Even in the transformation story where transformation is most directly and clearly a punishment for sexual intercourse, that of Atalanta, mention is made not of Atalanta's lust, but of Hippomenes'). There is clearly sympathy for the heroines of these stories, and there is no suggestion that they get what they deserve. The myths are not a direct illustration of Greek moral thinking: these stories are nightmarish fantasies which nevertheless have a sort of logic and are a distorted imitation of the patterns of real life.

IO AND THE PROITIDES

I have discussed in the previous chapter and in the catalogue those elements of the story of Io that point directly to external institutions and relations. All these elements have become part of a mythical narrative and have a meaning within this new structure. The fact that Io begins her story as a priestess not only points to a causal connection with the historical institution of the cult of Hera, but sets her apart from men at the start of the story and magnifies her crime.[28] In the alternative version of the *Prometheus* that pictures her

[26] e.g. Leucothoe, Psamathe, Alope, Arne, Danae; Aura, Pelopeia, and Taygete commit suicide.

[27] See A. R. W. Harrison, *The Law of Athens*, i (Oxford, 1968), 32–6.

[28] For the significance of being a priestess compare the story, apparently treated by Sophocles (frs. 77–100), that Auge was made a priestess by her father so that she would not bear a child.

as a girl in her father's home we still find a strong contrast between the enclosed area of her *parthenon* into which only dreams can penetrate and the invitation of the meadows and the outside. Both versions emphasize her virginal status and the order of the background.

Her misfortunes begin when she becomes the object of Zeus' interest. In most versions she is seduced by Zeus, and then either Zeus or Hera turns her into a cow. Zeus is trying to hide her from Hera, and Hera to punish her and keep her away from Zeus. The difference is perhaps not important; what matters is that transformation immediately follows illicit seduction and that it is worked by, or in fear of, Hera, both a goddess with a personal interest in this liaison and the goddess of the order of marriage and the home.

At the simplest level transformation expresses the disruption of order that Io's seduction has caused: 'at once my mind and shape were distorted', she says;[29] the fact that she was a priestess makes this disruption even greater. However, by contrast with the next stage of her story, her mad wandering, the change may be seen in a positive way, and as a cow Io may still be an object of desire; in Aeschylus' imaginative treatments of the story it is almost as if she must become a cow in order to satisfy the desire of Zeus.[30]

The next stage in the story in which Hera's herdsman, Argos, is killed and Io, from being a healthy cow living in a fertile meadow,[31] is driven mad into the wilds, is in one sense a repetition or reinforcement of the change from order to disorder of the original transformation (even the relation of the human Io and the cow to the goddess is similar: they are both her servants or property). But this time there is little ambiguity about the animal, which is sick, frightening, and polluted rather than desirable.

Finally, after wandering all over the world, she reaches Egypt and

[29] *PV* 673 f. Cf. Sophocles' *Inachus*, where we seem to have an incongruous description of transformation within a house, and Io is, or is compared to, a γυνὴ λέαινα: fr. 269a. 36 ff.

[30] In *Supp.* 300 Zeus takes on bull form for their union; cf. *PV* 652 ff., where she must leave her *parthenon* and go to her father's pastures in order to satisfy the desire of Zeus.

[31] The cow grazes on flowers in *Supp.* 41 and 539. Some sources have the earth bringing forth flowers or grass to feed Io.

Zeus, and bears her child. The way that her final marriage is described in the *Supplices*[32] supports the idea that her wild wandering is to be seen in terms of an opposition to marriage, the home, and sex. The site of the marriage is an 'all-nourishing grove' by contrast with the barren deserts she has been wandering through, but her surroundings are only a reflection of her own change from barrenness to fruitfulness, and her husband, Zeus, is described as a grower or gardener. The union with Zeus is a touching or holding that contrasts with Io's previous unapproachability. Thus Zeus is *ephaptor* ('toucher') whereas earlier men had shuddered on seeing the animal that was so 'hard to take in hand'.[33] Such references give literal form to the metaphors of taming that are characteristic of Greek descriptions of marriage. By contrast with her earlier and catastrophic union which provoked the disorder this is a successful taming or domestication.

It is important that the cow is not naturally a wild animal and that therefore its wild wandering is an incongruous phase that can only be explained by madness and the gadfly. In fact, the final restoration of order may be seen either as a transformation back to human shape or simply as the finding of a home for the cow (there is no explicit mention of her being transformed back in the *Supplices*). The choice of domestic beast rather than a permanent inhabitant of the wilds is therefore in keeping with the major general difference of this story from those of the huntresses, that it is a story of the successful setting up of a new home and family; it begins and ends in the order of the house, and the wilds are only a temporary interlude.

The different versions of the story of the Proitides[34] give a less consistent pattern, but we can detect a parallel structure to the story of Io. The story begins with the daughters of Proitos ready to be married and sought by suitors from all over Greece; the theme of

[32] 530 ff.

[33] The 'touch' of Zeus is depicted on a number of vase representations of the story: see E. Simon, *AA* 1985, 265–80.

[34] For the story of the Proitides see Hes. frs. 37 and 130–3; Apollod. 2. 2, citing Acusilaus (*FGH* 2 F 28); Bacchylides 11; Pherecydes, *FGH* 3 F 114; Ael. *VH* 3. 42; Callim. 3. 233 ff. For modern discussions see below, n. 35, and R. A. S. Seaford, *JHS* 108 (1988), 118–37.

marriage is thus introduced right from the start. The girls offend Hera and are punished with madness (and, in Hesiod, a disfiguring disease); they take to the wilds imagining they are cows. In Hesiod, where they are punished for their 'hateful lust',[35] we have a particularly clear case of disorder and disease following a sexual offence: 'transformation' is in effect an expression of sexual pollution. Later accounts speak of them scorning Hera in her shrine. Here too, though the pattern is less obviously spelt out, scorning the goddess especially concerned with the order of marriage leads to an outbreak of wild disorder. 'Transformation' into an animal follows an offence connected with the sexual sphere of women's lives.

As in the case of Io, this period in the wilds is a prelude to their successful restoration and marriage. After bargaining with their father, Melampus cures the women[36] and wins them as brides for himself and his brother. They successfully found a dynasty of kings and seers. Again, therefore, women 'become cows' as a temporary preparation for a successful marriage and motherhood. This pattern contrasts with that of the wild huntresses, Callisto and Atalanta, who are permanently isolated after their change to wild animals.

CALLISTO AND ATALANTA

Just as the stories of Io and the Proitides complement and help to explain one another, so do the stories of the huntresses Callisto and Atalanta. Callisto's story begins when she rejects marriage and her father's home and joins the band of Artemis. Up to a point this move corresponds to Io's service as a temple priestess. In each case the heroine is set apart from men,[37] and the sexual lapse that follows is exaggerated since it is also a betrayal of the goddess. But this is a superficial resemblance: joining the band of Artemis and becoming a huntress is an extreme and aggressive rejection of men and the family quite different from the passive isolation of the priestess or

[35] Fr. 132. But this may not be their original crime: see F. Vian, *REA* 67 (1965), 25–35. Cf. the text in A. Henrichs, *ZPE* 15 (1974), 297–8.

[36] Thus performing an identical role to that of Zeus in the story of Io.

[37] See Burkert, *SH* 7, who sees a parallel in the seclusions of Io, Callisto, and Danae.

the girl in her *parthenon*. There is an arrogance in her attitude that can only invite trouble.[38] Callisto belongs to a wider group of women who choose to become wild huntresses, and it is interesting to note that almost none of them settle down to an orderly marriage and home.[39] Deianeira, a warrior and huntress, finally kills her husband. Dictynna leaps into the sea to escape pursuit, while Daphne kills her lover and becomes a tree. Antiope, the Amazon, is killed by her lover, Theseus, or her former companions (and her son Hippolytus suffers an equally tragic fate). Aura eats her children. Procris is accidentally killed by her husband. Polyphonte mates with a bear and brings forth cannibal sons. Nicaea kills her lover. In fact, hunting and killing animals is closely connected with killing men, and Callisto is naturally presented as a soldier as well as a huntress.[40]

In taking to the wilds, therefore, Callisto has more or less determined her fate. However, though the huntress has a potential for savagery, she is quite different from the animal Callisto becomes through transformation. Callisto as a huntress is still desirable and inviting. As I suggested earlier, the chief role of the wild huntresses is to be pursued by men. In one sense, therefore, this period is parallel to the period that Io spends as a cow under Argos' protection; at this stage Io is wild only in a limited sense and in an inviting form, and this is contrasted with the later mad wandering.

Callisto is then raped by Zeus, discovered, and expelled from the band of Artemis. In some versions she is transformed by Artemis herself, in some by the jealous Hera. Again I do not regard the difference of the gods as important; both are goddesses who have a special interest in sexual lapses. As with Io, what matters is that as a result of illicit sexual activity she becomes an animal. It was argued earlier that this animal is not merely wild, but anti-erotic. There is little doubt either about Callisto's sexual pollution.[41] If there is less emphasis on disease and madness this is because, unlike the cow, the bear is not a domestic animal which may be seen as attractive and

[38] She says 'Salve numen, me iudice . . . audiat ipse licet, maius Iove': *Met.* 2. 428 f.

[39] The one possible exception that I can think of is the lion-fighting Cyrene of whom we hear nothing after her marriage to Apollo.

[40] 'Miles erat Phoebes': *Met.* 2. 415.

[41] See p. 68.

fertile, but is itself a symbol of savagery and completely unapproachable. For the bear a savage life in the wilds is not a temporary incongruity but its natural state.

In her bear form, Callisto has a child. We should not, however, suppose that the bear is here a symbol of motherhood.[42] I noted in the last chapter that the bear is not seen as an ideal mother, but more importantly, in every version of Callisto's story the child is immediately removed, so that the transformation isolates her from her child as much as from Artemis and her family. In the Hesiodic version the boy is brought up by shepherds, and the climax of the story comes as her son pursues her in ignorance. This version ends with her perpetual isolation as a star; not only is she removed from men, but even now she is not allowed to touch and pollute the water of the sea. The other main version has her shot by Artemis, whether in ignorance of intentionally. Here again, we have an immediate separation from her child, which is given to Maia to nurse. Both versions also end with her being hunted; cows may be caught and tamed, but bears may only be hunted and killed. (Various stories tell of apparently tame bears whose natural savagery breaks out in the end.)[43] Although, therefore, there may be external factors that help to explain the bear form we can see that there is a structural explanation not only for Callisto's change from human to animal, but for the choice of a bear. The irredeemably savage animal is in human form a wild and potentially savage huntress, while the temporarily wild cow is a priestess or a timid girl in her *parthenon*. The bear is the animal to be hunted and killed; the cow becomes a wife and mother.

In the story of Atalanta we find the themes of the story of Callisto greatly exaggerated. Like Callisto, Atalanta is a member of the band of Artemis, but the opposition to men and the home, the desire for freedom, and the potential for savagery are all more extreme. She is exposed at birth and suckled by a bear, and her wildness, therefore, goes back much further than that of Callisto.[44] We

[42] See Borgeaud, 53.

[43] See the Brauron *aitia* (schol. Ar. *Lys.* 646) or Ael. *NA* 4. 45.

[44] For the earlier adventures of Atalanta see Apollod. 3. 9. 2, Ael. *VH* 13. 1. It is suggested in a couple of ancient scholia (on Theoc. 3. 40 and Eur. *Phoen.* 150) and by some modern

have stories of how she fights off and competes with various men, but her most famous story gives this antagonism and rivalry a formal character. She sets up a race for her suitors and lays down that everyone she defeats must die.[45] This means that her eventual marriage becomes literally a defeat or conquest, when, with the help of Aphrodite and her apples, Melanion or Hippomenes tricks her into losing.

On her way to their new home the newly married pair are overcome by lust and desecrate a shrine of the mother of the gods or of Zeus; in punishment they are turned into lions. Although, therefore, Atalanta is not seduced but actually married, this desecration makes their intercourse still a crime.[46] Sex is the crucial motivating theme in her end as it is, through her rejection of it, in her life.[47]

Much of what I have said about the bear applies to the lion. They are interchangeable symbols of savagery and unapproachability, especially in the female form;[48] Atalanta, who becomes a lion, was suckled by a bear. Just as several stories tell of tame bears going wild, the lion fable of the *Agamemnon* tells how a lion introduced into a human home reveals its true nature and destroys it. This lion clearly stands for a woman (Helen or Clytaemnestra). More specifically, as I noted earlier, the lion is an animal opposed not only to the home, but to sex altogether.

One tradition has Atalanta and her husband transformed not

writers (e.g. C. Robert, *Die griechische Heldensage* (Berlin, 1920–6), 83–4 and 93–5) that there are two different Atalantas: an Arcadian huntress who eventually yields to Melanion, and the Boeotian runner who is conquered by Hippomenes. This seems an unreal distinction: see Fontenrose, *Orion*, 175–6; Detienne, *Dionysos Slain*, 30–1.

45 Apollodorus has her pursuing her suitors in full armour: 3. 9. 2. Here again we have an ambiguity of soldier and hunter.

46 Nonnus (12. 89) alludes to a version of a story in which she was transformed by Artemis after her marriage. Here too the lapse is primarily sexual; it would appear that it is dangerous for a huntress to abandon virginity even in the context of a legitimate marriage. Sourvinou-Inwood (art. cit. n. 10), 152–3, points out that Atalanta's marriage is a wild one which has not succeeded in taming her animality, since unlike the normal wife she continues to hunt in the wilds.

47 See further, on the themes of sex and wildness in this story, Detienne, *Dionysos Slain*, ch. 2.

48 Euripides possibly calls Callisto a lioness in *Helen* 379: see A. M. Dale, *CR* 10 (1960), 194–5. But see also R. Kannicht's commentary (1969) on this line. He brackets the phrase as a gloss.

into ordinary animals, but into the mythical beasts that are yoked to the chariot of the mother of the gods. First of all, this perhaps reinforces the sexlessness of the animals; Cybele's other mythical servant, Attis, and her historical servants, the Galloi, are also sexless (maddened lion and maddened Attis are brought together by Catullus in Poem 63). Secondly, the idea that she is now yoked or made subservient[49] gives a final twist to the antitheses of freedom and servitude, marriage and the wilds, which are particularly emphasized in this story. Until Atalanta was physically conquered by Hippomenes her flight to the wilds had enabled her to avoid the yoke of marriage. She is now permanently wild, and yet paradoxically not free but yoked or tamed as if she were married.[50]

LETO

The story used to explain the epithet of Apollo Lykegenes is that Leto came to Delos in the form of a wolf (*lykos*) to escape Hera,[51] but an *aition* for Lycia also connects her with wolves. In this story, which perhaps makes more explicit certain aspects of the other, she wishes, still in exile, to wash her new-born babies, but is turned away from the water by some cowherds; she is received by wolves and guided to the streams of Xanthus.[52]

These stories are explicit *aitia*, and up to a point it would be true to say Leto becomes a wolf because she is mother of Apollo Lykegenes. However, in so far as we have not merely an explanation but also a story, the myth requires a different approach. In fact, it shares some of the themes of the stories we have been considering. Leto is different from the other heroines in that her transformation is a self-willed temporary disguise, but it is still connected with a journey into the wilds and with pregnancy. The wolf is clearly not a sexually inviting animal. Leto is closer to Callisto than to Io in this

[49] See e.g. Ov. *Met.* 10. 704.

[50] One thinks of Aura (Nonn. 48. 260 ff.), who dreams that she, as an unconquerable lioness, is captured and yoked by Eros.

[51] See Aelian, *NA* 10. 26; Antig. *Mir.* 56; Arist. *HA* 580ª.

[52] AL 35.

respect, and also in the way that she bears her children in homeless exile. The theme of pollution emerges most strongly in the Lycia *aition*, where being received by wolves is connected with her unclean state after giving birth and where, like Callisto, she is not allowed to share the communal water; but her impurity is perhaps also behind the refusal, in the story, of any land except the floating island of Delos to allow her to bring forth her child.[53]

In the ancient world the wolf was not merely, like the lion or bear, a symbol of animal savagery, but more particularly a symbol of the outcast, fugitive, or outsider.[54] In early Hittite laws we find: 'Thou art become a wolf' (as a penalty for muder).[55] In Greece we have the Arcadian wolf-men who are exiled after a cannibal feast; here too the wolf has an almost metaphorical sense. Very close to the Leto story is that of Athamas who, banished after killing his sons, is told to found a new city in a place where he is entertained by wolves.[56] Danaos is identified with a wolf, as an outsider, in an omen to the people of Argos.[57] (This is an *aition* for the worship of Apollo Lykeios, but it shows that such an *aition* might be expected to play upon the general character of the wolf.) In our story the connection of the wolf with the social outcast fits in with the theme of the exile and isolation of Leto, with Apollo's links with Delos, a barren and remote island, and with the curiously ambiguous mythological conception of Apollo himself: on the one hand he is Zeus' right-hand man, the guardian of Olympic order, while on the other he goes through a series of punishments and exiles. Here, therefore, the wolf has a function that goes beyond simply explaining Apollo's epithet.

[53] Cf. the later regulation, after the purification of Delos, that nobody should die or give birth there (Thuc. 3. 104).

[54] See L. Gernet, in *Mélanges F. Cumont* (Paris, 1936), 189–208; R. G. A. Buxton, in Bremmer, 63–4.

[55] See M. Gerstein, in G. J. Larson (ed.), *Myth in Indo-European Antiquity* (Berkeley, 1974), 134.

[56] Apollod. 1. 9. 2.

[57] Paus. 2. 19. 3.

HIPPO

One story of Hippo tells how she is transformed by the gods for revealing the secrets of the gods (and she possibly remains a prophet in horse form). The other tells how after being seduced by Aeolus she flees into the forest to hide from her father and is turned into a mare (or else that she was transformed when she ceased hunting, and worshipping Artemis). Thus the familiar pattern of seduction, shame, and transformation of the wild huntress is the alternative version of the story of a seer. This latter story belongs to another familiar type in which seers and doctors are repressed by the gods;[58] but this form of punishment, change to an animal, sets the prophetess in the context of a contrast between civilization and savagery, and gives her some of the same ambiguities as her father, Cheiron.[59] On the one hand he has a horse body, lives in a cave, and belongs to the race of wild centaurs; on the other he acts as an educator and civilizer of men. In the case of the daughter too we have a tension between her savage roots and habitat and her civilizing role (Ovid describes her in human form, but with hints of the change to come in her unbound hair hanging to her shoulders like a mane).[60] Since she embodies simultaneously the two extremes, the potential for reversal from one to the other is always present. In a sense her position is a reflection of the peculiar role of female prophets in general. They live in a state that is both opposed to marriage and yet free from the restraints of the parental home and normal female modesty.[61] In Ovid's description of Hippo's unbound hair we have not only a hint of the horse but the unorthodox appearance and freedom of the prophetess.[62]

[58] The most common form of repression is blindness: see R. G. A. Buxton, *JHS* 100 (1980), 22–37.

[59] For the ambiguity of Cheiron and the centaurs see Kirk, *Myth*, 152–62.

[60] *Met.* 2. 635.

[61] See M. Beard, *JRS* 70 (1980), 12–27, on the status of the Vestal Virgins. Cicero, *De Div.* 1. 31, quotes from a tragic writer a reproach to Cassandra: 'ubi illa paulo ante sapiens modestia?'.

[62] Bömer, on *Met.* 2. 635, notes that untied hair is characteristic of prophetesses and maenads. It is also characteristic of huntresses: see e.g. of Daphne, *Met.* 1. 497.

On the one hand, therefore, her transformation is prompted by the fact that she is Cheiron's daughter; it is not really conceivable that she could become any other animal. On the other hand her horse form does not merely express the fact that she is the child of a centaur, but forms part of the same framework of ideas that characterizes her father's nature.

However, this peculiar position of the female prophetess and civilizer is actually a sort of parallel to that of the huntress who is seduced in the other story. Like the prophetess the huntress is an anomalous figure, a woman who has removed herself from the home and family and lives the shameless and yet chaste life of a man. Like the huntress this prophetess and civilizer has an ambiguous relation to the wilds; she lives there, and wildness is an essential part of her nature (since civilization is seen in these myths as something that must come from the outside, and since on a more personal level it is only in the wilds that she can be free of the normal restraints of the Greek home), and yet both prophetess and huntress are in continual danger of a reversion to the wild beasts around them. We can, therefore, see how one story could very easily suggest and be replaced by the other.

I can perhaps now summarize my conclusion about this group of heroines. Their change and taking to the wilds is not a reflection of any actual practice or activity of Greek women, though it has certain parallels to some ritual practices, and it is, therefore, to be seen entirely as an imaginative and metaphorical pattern. In each case the central theme of the story and the controlling metaphor is the idea that becoming an object of sexual interest and indulging in sexual activity makes one into an animal, in a way that is sometimes positive, more often demeaning and frightening. The latter idea is particularly strong in these stories where the sexual activity is always illicit. Transformation becomes part of a larger breakdown of order in the lives of these women and is usually associated with pollution and madness.

ACTAEON

The story of Actaeon, the hunter who is turned into a deer by the goddess Artemis and torn apart by his own dogs, is one of the most familiar of all transformation stories. The reason for the goddess's anger varies; in some versions Actaeon makes the mistake of pursuing Semele as a rival to Zeus, in others he comes across the goddess bathing, and in one account he boasts he is a better hunter than Artemis.[63]

The first point is that one cannot attempt to explain the transformation in isolation. In every account it is immediately followed by Actaeon's death; it is in a sense only a device to bring about the real disaster, his being torn apart by his dogs. It is this reversal of the normal order of things that is the heart of the story, and the death of Actaeon is in a sense a family crime like the tearing apart of Pentheus by his mother and his aunts, or the cannibalism of Tereus.[64] The horror of the disorder is emphasised by the way that not only is Actaeon transformed but his dogs are maddened. The disorder does not stop with Actaeon's death. Our sources speak of the restlessness of his ghost,[65] the breakup of his home,[66] and the exile of his polluted dogs.[67]

How one analyses the nature of the reversal and disorder of Actaeon's death must depend on what one considers its cause. Since Actaeon's crime varies in our sources one might argue that the cause of his fate is unimportant and that the essence of the story is a hunting nightmare in which the hunter identifies with his victim. A number of stories speak of a hunter being mistaken for his animal prey: for instance, Orion and Callisto are in various stories shot under the impression that they are wild animals. The identification

[63] See further Cat. *1a* s.v.

[64] A crucial point is that he is torn apart by creatures *ἃς ἐθρέψατο*: *Bacchae* 337.

[65] See the ghost story of Pausanias 9. 38. 5 or Nonnus 5. 287 ff. These are late sources, but it seems likely that the search for Actaeon's body and the issue of his burial may be early (see p. 198).

[66] His father leaves home after Actaeon's death, just as Cadmus and Harmonia leave Thebes after the death of Pentheus: DS 4. 82.

[67] See p. 199.

and sympathy of the hunter with his prey, and the sense of guilt he feels in killing, have been recognized as an important element in many old hunting rituals and superstitions.[68] A similar feeling may underlie this story.

However, although Actaeon's crime takes different forms it is always an important part of the story, and the different forms do have certain things in common. It is always Artemis who punishes him, and his crime has something to do with women.

That the connection with women is significant is confirmed by looking at the stories of the other mythical hunters.[69] Orion, Cephalus, Hippolytus, Adonis, Attis, and Heracles are all great hunters who suffer a catastrophe arising from their relations with women. Among non-Greek stories the myth of the Canaanite Aquat tells of a hunter who is eaten by eagles after refusing to give his bow to the goddess Anath; this story has been felt to be very close to, and even an ancestor of, that of Actaeon.[70] The various versions of the myth of Actaeon thus conform to a wider pattern of the story of the hunter, and it is this wider pattern that must be the starting point of any attempt to explain his particular story.

It has been suggested that the story of the hunter has its origins in primitive hunting belief, in particular the belief that sex before the hunt invariably leads to failure and death. Burkert argues that traces of this belief can be seen in the story of Enkidu, who is shunned by the animals after he has been seduced by a woman, and Kessi, a hunter whose excessive devotion to his wife and neglect of hunting leads to failure and possibly death when he returns to the wilds.[71] Among Greek hunters he argues that the pattern is clearest in the story of Adonis, but that it also lies behind the conception of the chaste hunters Artemis and Hippolytus.

[68] See K. Meuli, *Gesammelte Schriften*, ii (Basle, 1975), 948–80; Burkert, *HN* 20–31. Cf. K. Sälzle, *Tier und Mensch* (Munich, 1965), 158–70.

[69] For a general discussion of these stories see Fontenrose, *Orion*. For Adonis and hunting see Detienne, *Dionysos Slain*, ch. 2.

[70] See *ANET* 149–55. For an attempt to derive Actaeon's story from Aquat's see M. C. Astour, *Hellenosemitica* (1965), 163–8.

[71] See *SH* 118–22 and *HN* 72–3. He discusses the myth of Actaeon in *HN* 127–33 and argues, somewhat speculatively, that it reflects an ancient hunting ritual in which men dressed as dogs pursued and killed a man disguised as a deer.

There may be traces of such a taboo in the Near Eastern stories, and possibly even in the conception of Artemis, but I do not believe that such a taboo really helps to explain very much in the stories of the hunter as they have developed in Greek mythology. The Greek mythical hunter is hardly a throw-back to an age when men lived by hunting. He does not hunt to live or to feed his family, but exclusively for his own glory.[72] There is no equivalent to stories of game shunning a polluted hunter (no Greek hunter fails to find his prey, although he may be killed by it), and the attitude of the game is never in question.[73]

The Greek stories are not really concerned with hunting, which had for a very long time played a fairly marginal role in Greek life. Hunting has, for the purpose of these stories, a primarily imaginative and metaphorical significance.[74] It is the supreme and purest masculine heroic activity[75] and (following on from and perhaps explaining this) the activity that more than any other takes the hero into the wilds away from the home and ordinary civilized society. It is the dangers arising from this function of hunting, illustrated above all in the hero's relations with women, that are the theme of these stories.

One can break down this theme a little further. There are three closely related aspects of the wilds in these stories. First of all, the wilds are opposed as a masculine habitat to the home as the place of the family and of women. Secondly, the hunter often takes on the savage character of the animals he kills and lives among; thirdly, the

[72] See Fontenrose, *Orion*, 252.

[73] Hippolytus is a chaste hunter, but his fall is caused not by a sexual lapse but by his very ascetism and misogyny. The most plausible illustration of the taboo is in the link of hunting and virginity among women, but one suspects that in the case of women hunting is simply an expression of the free unattached life as opposed to the yoking and taming of marriage; i.e. the female hunters are entirely an imaginative construction rather than historical relics.

[74] It has been argued that such stories are not so much a throw-back to prehistoric hunters, but reflect more recent initiation rites in which young men were forced to leave their families and hunt in the wilds (see e.g. P. Vidal-Naquet, in Gordon, 147–62). It is not necessary to argue against such views here: it does not seem that outside Crete any form of initiatory hunting existed in classical times. For those who told or listened to these stories, in classical times and later, hunting had a purely imaginative significance.

[75] By contrast the soldiers' achievements are often tied to social responsibilities and obligations.

wilds may be seen as a place of danger and mystery, and the hunter as a trespasser or intruder. These themes are all central to the stories of the misfortunes of the hunter and, as we shall see shortly, to the story of Actaeon himself.

Let us begin with the masculine character of the wilds and of hunting. Whereas the life of the normal woman in Greek mythology and life is completely defined in terms of her place in the home and the family, the man moves between the world of the home and the outside.[76] The most extreme form of the outside is the wilds and the life of the hunter. This is a sphere the woman will never enter unless she denies her nature as a woman, adopts the life of man, and becomes a virgin huntress.

However, the hunter's movement between the home and the wilds causes tensions in many myths. Thus a number of stories have their starting point in suspicions of women about what hunters do while they are away from home, or in their resentment about the time and energy devoted to hunting.[77] This applies not only to hunting but to war, which again removes men from the home and in which women can take no part: one thinks of the trouble caused by the jealousy of the wives of Agamemnon, Diomedes, or Heracles. The man's movement outside the home is repeatedly seen as a threat by women inside. Among the men a counterpart of the women's resentment can be the misogyny of the male hunter who demonstrates his masculinity by abandoning the home and the world of women altogether: 'such was young Melanion, who fled marriage for the wilds . . . so great was his loathing for women'.[78] Hunting is the pure masculine activity, and hunters therefore have a tendency to hold women in scorn.

Secondly, the wilds are the sphere not only of men but of wild animals, and the hunter's profession consists in killing them. Men living in the wilds among animals and hunting them inevitably take on a certain animal savagery; sometimes this is carried over into the

[76] See Burkert, *HN* 25–8. The two spheres of the man's life are linked, he says, with two forms of social organization, the family and the *Männerbund*.

[77] e.g. those of Leucone and Procris who are accidentally killed when they go in jealous pursuit of their husbands: *Met.* 7. 694 ff. and Parth. 10. One version of Aedon's story has her killing her son after suspecting his father of having an affair with a dryad: Phot. *Bibl.* 5. 31.

[78] Ar. *Lys.* 785 ff. Cf. Hippolytus in Euripides.

home where it causes destruction. The greatest of all hunters, Heracles, takes on many of the qualities of the animals he kills and tames and in whose skins he dresses; in various incidents we find his aggression wreaking havoc, above all in the killing of his wife and children. Orion is another example: he clears Chios of wild beasts, but then rapes the daughter of the king.[79] Their savagery in sexual affairs is one of the basic characteristics of these hunters. The career of Orion, the archetypal hunter, is a history of rapes. Even as a constellation he is endlessly pursuing the Pleiades. Often savagery is incorporated not so much in the hunter himself as in his helpers, the 'tame' dogs and horses: their tameness is a state of tension that can quite easily be disrupted and lead to aggression against their master and his family (e.g. the dogs of her husband which tear Leucone apart,[80] or the horses of Hippolytus). This brings us very close to Actaeon.

The third theme is the role of the wilds as a place of danger and mystery in which the hunter is the intruder. In this respect he is similar not so much to the soldier as to the shepherd and the woodcutter who also move in the wilds. Here, as well as facing wild beasts, he also meets the gods, who tend not to appear in crowded cities. There are many stories of the meeting and sexual relations of hunters, shepherds, and woodcutters with nymphs and dryads, but even the major gods prefer to appear in such surroundings. The lovers of goddesses in particular tend to be always shepherds or hunters, and their meetings are in remote places.[81]

One aspect of this mystery of the wilds takes us back to the connection of the wilds with virginity; this is the idea that certain areas of the wilds are of special privacy and inaccessible to men, for instance the holy grove or the holy spring, each of which may have the status of a female preserve. This is almost a reversal of the way that according to the first pattern women are associated with the home and men with the outside, but we do have many stories of male intrusion upon, and violence to, some secret female area in the wilds. The spring, with its bathing nymphs and goddesses, is the

[79] Parth. 20.

[80] See above, n. 77.

[81] See e.g. *Hymn. Hom. Ven.* 76.

most common example: Teiresias, Leucippus, Hermaphroditus, Hylas, and Actaeon himself all come to grief through such intrusions at a spring. But trees too are inhabited by female spirits and threatened by male woodcutters, and there are stories of violations of holy groves by Erysichthon and Triopas. Even the animals are sometimes seen to be under the protection of Artemis in her function as Mistress of the Animals. Sometimes she will punish killers of her animals; sometimes the prey of the hunter is revealed to be the goddess herself.

The *Hippolytus* has a famous description of the pure untouched meadow,[82] and springs are often described in a similar way.[83] It seems that the most obvious point of comparison or metaphor for the inaccessibility of the mysterious natural place is that of female ownership in general and female chastity in particular, and the reverse of this is also common in poetry, so that a chaste young girl can be compared to a flower in a hidden garden.[84] The most extreme form of this conception is of course Artemis' band of virgins, who live in the woods and endow it with some of their character. Many hunting stories concern the abuse of her or one of her companions by a hunter.

In a curious way, therefore, the sanctity of the inaccessible female preserve of the interior of the house is here attached to its apparent opposite, the wilds. (Orion's attempt to rape Artemis in the wilds is parallel and alternative to his rape of his bride before her marriage in the *parthenon* of her father's house.) The hunter who wanders into the woods is in special danger since he offers in his violence and his masculinity a double threat. It is not surprising, therefore, that Orion's and Actaeon's crimes are either assaults on the goddess or boasts about the killing of animals (Orion boasts that he will kill all the animals in the world).[85]

To recapitulate, therefore, we have noted three dominant themes in the hunting stories. First, there is the way that hunting in

[82] 76 ff.

[83] See Serv. on *A* 7. 84: 'nullus enim fons non est sacer'. The words καθαρός and *purus* are frequently used of springs and streams.

[84] See Catullus 62. 39 ff. Cf. Sappho fr. 105c.

[85] See Hes. fr. 148; Ov. *Fasti* 5. 540.

the wilds is seen as a purely masculine activity and contrasted with the life of the home; this may lead to male arrogance and scorn of women. Secondly, there is the danger of the savagery of the hunter getting out of control. Thirdly, there is sometimes an association between venturing into the wilds and intrusion into a forbidden or female sanctuary.

All three themes are relevant to the story of Actaeon. The supposed Alexandrian version, in particular, which has Actaeon blundering in on Artemis or attempting to rape her, is a particularly clear illustration of our third theme. The hunter is here the trespasser. His crime can be seen as the violation of the spring (it is called Parthenius in one version:[86] its waters are often described as pure or holy)[87] or as the violation of the tree he climbs to see the goddess.[88] Diodorus sets the attempted rape in the goddess's temple,[89] an interesting alternative to the secret spring. In Euripides his crime takes place in a piece of land sacred to the gods.[90] There are hints that his enthusiastic hunting is itself a desecration of the mountains and the woods (Ovid describes the mountain as stained with the blood of the beasts he has killed).[91] In Callimachus the very similar story of the blinding of Teiresias after blundering in on the goddess Athene bathing is seen as Helicon's revenge for his hunting. There is a possible variation of Actaeon's story in which he shot Artemis' holy deer.[92] All these passages suggest a wider intrusion of the hunter.

In the story of Hesiod and Stesichorus, though the disastrous climax happens in the wilds, the cause is not Actaeon's offence against Artemis, but his pursuit of his aunt Semele as a rival to Zeus. Our evidence is too fragmentary to reveal what moral colouring the story had, but on the face of it Actaeon would appear to be a similar figure to Orion, a wild hunter who in this story disrupts his own

[86] Hyg. *Fab.* 181.
[87] See Stat. *Theb.* 3. 210 f.; Nonn. 5. 484.
[88] Nonn. 5. 476.
[89] 4. 81.
[90] *Bacchae* 340: see Dodds's note on this line; E. Norden, *Aus altrömischen Priesterbüchern* (Lund, 1939), 22–31; and the inscription about the ὀργὰς ἵερα at Elcusis (*LSCG* 32).
[91] *Met.* 3. 143. The idea that a mountain is the mother of wild beasts is a common one. Cf. *Hymn. Hom. Ven.* 68. Note also the way that a mountain, like springs or rivers, may be called Parthenius.
[92] See p. 201.

family by his incestuous lusts and offends Zeus by his presumption. Here we perhaps have the second theme, savage behaviour carried over to sexual relations.[93]

It is interesting to note that Aeschylus, the rest of whose story is obscure, appears to make Actaeon a puritanical misogynist like Hippolytus.[94] One assumes that eventually he succumbs and offends against Semele or Artemis. Here our second theme, that of the wild aggressive hunter, seems in a sense to be only an exaggeration of the first, the conflict of the masculine world of the hunt with women and the home. It is in this light perhaps that we should see Euripides' version in which Actaeon boasts that he is a better hunter than Artemis: perhaps like Aquat he disparages the goddess's hunting because she is a woman.

One problem in discussing the story of Actaeon is that we have no full early account of the story. It is illuminating, therefore, to compare the story of his cousin Pentheus as it is treated in the *Bacchae* (and with whom Actaeon is compared in that play). In a sense they are opposites: Pentheus is not a hunter but a king who attempts to defend the order of the home and prevent the exodus of women to the wilds, whereas Actaeon is someone who spends his whole time in the wilds. But both adopt a pose of masculine superiority and scorn women. In both cases over-emphasis leads to a reversal and the breakdown of the masculine-dominated order, in which Actaeon is killed by his dogs—a part, if a humble part, of his own house (and they are inspired by a woman)—and Pentheus by his women.[95] In both cases we have a change from hunter and master to victim; Pentheus becomes in a sense both a woman and an animal (and in both cases this reversal leads not only to their own deaths but to the destruction of their whole house).[96]

[93] Nonnus speaks of his *ἄγριον θράσος*: 5. 311.

[94] Fr. 243.

[95] Compare the way that dogs and women are the two alternatives in the story of the tearing apart of Euripides himself (e.g. *Suda* s.v. Euripides). The connections of Actaeon's dogs with the maenads (who are addressed as 'hounds' in the *Bacchae*) seems implied in the prophecy that Dionysos will use the dogs afterwards (*POxy* 2509). We may compare also the Corinthian version of the story in which Actaeon is torn apart by his family.

[96] Actaeon's father, Aristaeus, leaves home: DS 4. 82; the dogs are left miserably searching for their master: Apollod. 3. 4. 4.

In Actaeon's case the initial threat to order is implicit in his role as a hunter; in Pentheus' case it is in a sense external, coming with the arrival of Dionysos, but from that point their stories advance in a remarkably similar way. It is not perhaps coincidental that hunting metaphors pervade the *Bacchae* and our other sources for Pentheus' story. It shares what I have noted as the three hunting themes, masculine pride, savagery misdirected at one's own family, and intrusion into a wild female area, and it allows us to see how these themes fit together and follow from the opposition of men and women.

In summary, therefore, the mythical hunter is the model of specifically masculine achievement. He is also someone who moves in mysterious places in the wilds and whose life is devoted to killing and destruction. All these aspects of the hunter are related and expose him to particular dangers: the great hunter tends to be someone who over-emphasizes his masculine virtues and brings an assertive and wild quality to his relations with other people, especially women. He tends to transgress normal boundaries both in the wilds and when he returns home.

Having attempted to set the general structure of Actaeon's story in a wider mythical context I turn finally to consider the specific motif of his transformation. As I have already suggested, the transformation is less important in itself than as a prelude to his outrageous death: the deer is above all the animal for hunting and killing and has a metaphorical meaning in literature, myth, and ritual as 'victim'.[97] The central incident of the story, as in that of Pentheus, is a nightmarish outbreak of disorder in which the male master of the house becomes a helpless victim of its normally subordinate members. The transformation of Actaeon from hunter to prey is one aspect of this larger reversal; it is parallel to the maddening and 'cannibalism' of the dogs.

There is perhaps a special relevance in the choice of prey. It is interesting that, while the female hunters, Callisto and Atalanta, become fierce wild beasts, Actaeon becomes a deer. If the hunter was the supreme example of masculinity and daring the deer is the

[97] See Plut. *GQ* 39. Cf. the description of a man being disguised as a deer before being torn apart in Dionysius' *Bassarica*: Page, *GLP* 536–40.

traditional symbol of cowardice and weakness;[98] it is with this psychological change that Ovid completes his description of the transformation: 'and last of all she planted fear within his heart'.[99]

This last reversal brings Actaeon closely into line with some of the literal and metaphorical emasculated hunters and soldiers. The comparison with Pentheus is perhaps particularly obvious; Pentheus is a soldier who dresses up as a woman before he is torn apart. Attis is literally castrated. Siproites becomes a woman after, like Actaeon, seeing Artemis naked.[100] Orion is blinded, which may be a symbolic castration.[101] Heracles is forced to become the slave of a woman and dress up in women's clothes. Cephalus is made to exchange roles with his wife.[102] Aquat loses his bow, the symbol of his strength and virility.[103] In each of these stories a masculine assertiveness closely identified with and resting on excellence in hunting leads to some outrage or intrusion (appropriately, but not always directed against women), which is punished by the removal of that dominant masculine status and by a reversal.

In conclusion, therefore, I think that while it is possible that at the literal level the sympathy and sense of identity which the primitive hunter is supposed to feel with his prey may play a part, the dominant aspect of the transformation and death of Actaeon, by contrast with the fate of the huntresses who turn into savage and polluted wild animals, is the reversal of a clearly defined order in which masculine superiority is opposed to women, animals, and the wilds. Actaeon is an extreme example of masculine achievement, bringing in record numbers of dead animals, devastating the countryside, and uncovering forbidden female preserves. Artemis is simultaneously a creature of the wilds, a woman, and a goddess; the combination of these three characters in one mythical figure is the

[98] See e.g. *Il.* 1. 225 and 4. 243.

[99] *Met.* 3. 198.

[100] See AL 17. 5.

[101] This is argued by S. Eitrem, *Symb. Osl.* 7 (1928), 53–82. For blinding as a symbol of castration see G. Devereux, *JHS* 93 (1973), 36–49; for a castrated Adonis, Burkert, *SH* 108.

[102] See AL 41. 6.

[103] For the sexual symbolism in this story see D. R. Hilliers, in H. A. Hoffner (ed.), *Orient and Occident* (Kevelaer, 1973), 71–80. But see also H. Dressler, *Ugarit Forschungen* 7 (1975), 217–20.

source both of the prurient excitement of the story and of the triple resentment that brings Actaeon down.

LYCAON[104]

The myth of Lycaon has a key position for our understanding of the animal stories. It deals directly with the theme that underlies the other stories, the opposition of the house and the wilds. In the other stories this theme was the background or context given to a conflict of men and women; here it assumes a central and explicit role in the story of the original king and founder. He sets up the order that is undermined in the other stories.

That his function as a founder is central to his mythical character is suggested by his name, which connects him with Mount Lycaeon and its holy grove, the ancient cult of Zeus Lycaeus, the Lycaean games, and the city of Lycosura.[105] These were all supposed to be of great antiquity and were treated with veneration by the Arcadians. They claimed that Lycosura was the oldest city in the world and the model for all other cities.[106] Pausanias in his history of Arcadia explicitly makes Lycaon the founder of these institutions, and further characterizes him as the son of Pelasgus, the first man, in whose time men fed on acorns, and as the father of Arcas who introduced cereal growing.[107]

It is in the light of his role as founder and creator of the present order of human culture that we should interpret his story. I shall argue that the details of his crime and punishment are dictated by, and help to define, the nature of the order with whose birth he is connected. It seems important that Lycaon's crime is connected by the myth both to the gods, as his victims, and to animals, and it seems reasonable to suppose that the relations of gods and men, and men and animals, are an important aspect of this new order.

[104] The myth is very fully discussed in G. Piccaluga, *Lykaon: un tema mitico* (Rome, 1968); cf. R. Merkelbach, *Gnomon* 42 (1970), 182–5.

[105] He is also the founder of the cult of Hermes of Cyllene, and his sons are founders of the other cities of Arcadia: see Cat. 1*a* s.v.

[106] Paus. 8. 38. 1.

[107] Paus. 8. 2. 1.

Let us begin with the role of the gods, the abused guests of Lycaon. Lycaon's relation with the gods both in our tradition as a whole and within individual stories is an ambiguous one. Sometimes he is the pious and just king who receives the gods as friends and guests, and the crime is committed by his evil sons; sometimes he is the impious monster and enemy of the gods.[108] We may note that Lycaon and his sons have associations with the giants[109] and that the Arcadians as a whole, as the oldest men, are associated with primitive violence.[110]

However, this ambiguity is central to the historical perspective of the story. Lycaon's crime belongs to a familiar pattern of the original separation of men and gods.[111] That men and gods once shared the same table is a commonly expressed belief,[112] and various stories are concerned with the cause of this separation. Some speak of an abuse of the gods' hospitality by men. There is Ixion, who takes advantage of Zeus' hospitality and attempts to rape his wife, and Tantalus who in one story steals the food of the gods;[113] in another story, he is closer to Lycaon and serves the gods a cannibal feast. Some versions of Lycaon's story have his crime followed by the flood, and this serves to emphasize the break and new beginning in human history.[114] These versions and perhaps the whole tradition of the flood are late, but even so their invention takes its starting point from, and draws attention to, the perhaps older idea that the crime of Lycaon marks a new beginning for mankind.

It is in this context of the mixed attitude to the new age that we

[108] See Cat. 1*a* s.v. Tantalus has some of the same abiguities: see Piccaluga, 186–9.

[109] See p. 217.

[110] See Lyc. 481 ff. and scholia, Borgeaud, 21–3. For primitive Arcadia as a land of cannibals see Paus. 8. 42. 6.

[111] This is one of the main themes of Piccaluga.

[112] e.g. Hes. fr. 1. 6.

[113] Pind. *Ol.* 1. 60 ff. See Piccaluga, 156–90.

[114] There is a similar tradition about Tantalus' feast: see schol. Pind. *Ol.* 9. 78, and Piccaluga, 156–90. Piccaluga makes the flood a central element in her analysis of the story, and sees Lycaon's role as the bringer of the fertilizing rain which makes Arcadia capable of growing crops. This seems to give the wrong emphasis to the myth. Even in Pausanias' account Lycaon is not an agricultural innovator like Pelasgus and Arcas, but a founder in a social and religious sense. The wolf he becomes is not a destroyer of crops but a predator on sheep. (For the view of the sacrifice as a rain rite cf. W. Sale, *RhM* 108 (1965), 11–35).

should see the ambiguities of Lycaon. The first men may be imagined as belonging to a golden age and to have deserved the favour of mixing with the gods;[115] the birth of the present age may then be seen as a decline. But secondly, there is also a tendency to see the past as a time of wildness and primitive barbarism, or at least of hardship. Men may have been closer to the gods, but often this took the form of rivalry, and the most characteristic figures of this period are the giants. Just as Prometheus and his innovations are seen in a very ambiguous light, so is Lycaon. On the one hand we have positive foundations and achievements, on the other the criminal act and its unintentional consequences. His crime may be seen as the aberration of a golden-age friend of the gods or as the reversion of a primitive giant to his true nature. (Thus Pausanias makes Lycaon a well-meaning but misguided religious innovator, the son of pious Pelasgus. In Ovid he is a criminal born from the blood of the giants, and all his race has to be destroyed.)

The relation to the gods is one defining feature of this new age, and this explains one aspect of Lycaon's crime. The shared table is at least partly a symbol of closeness to the gods, to which Zeus' action in turning this table over signals an end. But this explains only one aspect of the story and Lycaon's crime. Of more basic importance is the wolf: the story concerns man's relations not only to the gods but also to the animal world.

It is of course appropriate that a savage man should be transformed into a savage and greedy animal, the wolf. In particular the notorious hunger of the wolf (which can even extend to cannibalism)[116] seems particularly appropriate for the holder of cannibal feasts. In a similar way Tantalus endures perpetual hunger in Hades, while the cannibal Tereus becomes a bird of greed, the hawk or hoopoe.

But the wolf is not merely a savage and greedy animal; it has a more specific role in Greek and Near Eastern mythology as an outsider,[117] its defining characteristic being its opposition to human society. What we have here is the reversal of Lycaon's role, from being the king, a protector and ruler of society, to becoming its

[115] See Hes. *Op.* 109 ff. and fr. 1; cf. Pind. *Ol.* 1. 54; Catull. 64.

[116] Ael. *NA* 7. 20.

[117] See above, n. 54.

enemy; the closest parallel is the story of Tamuz in the epic of Gilgamesh who changes from shepherd to the wolf, killer of the flocks.

One can take this further. The desecration of the table and Lycaon's greed can be seen in a wider and symbolic sense. Detienne and Vidal-Naquet[118] have shown that a distinction in terms of eating is one of the main ways of characterizing the social order of the community on the one hand and the world of primitive man and animals on the other: the latter are seen either in a positive way as vegetarians or a negative one as cannibals. Hesiod's attitude in the *Works and Days* is typical in the importance it attaches to eating:[119]

> The son of Kronos laid down this law for men
> that fish and animals and winged beasts
> should eat each other, since there is no justice amongst them;
> but to men he gave justice.

According to this scheme Lycaon is a traditional figure who upsets the delicate balance of meat eating and the blood sacrifice as opposed to cannibalism, and when Zeus overturns the table at the end of the meal, in a gesture which has a symbolic and ritual significance,[120] he acknowledges not merely the end of the fellowship between men and gods, but the end of the human order of Lycaon's house.

It is in this context of the wider historical contrast of civilization and the wilds that the wolf should be seen, and not just as an expression of individual cruelty. If the myth in one sense marks a separation of men and gods, through the transformation it also marks the separation of men and animals. If the human order is defined or expressed on the one hand in its differences from the gods, so also, as we saw in the Hesiod passage quoted above, it may be defined in terms of differences from animals. From the historical perspective we find that early man is often thought of as living in an animal way

[118] See Detienne, *Dionysos Slain*, ch. 3; P. Vidal-Naquet, in Gordon, 163–85.

[119] 276 ff.

[120] It is a feature in the Stepterion at Delphi (see Burkert, *HN* 144–7). For the metaphorical significance of the overturned table as sign of animal disorder see Lyc. 137 f. A similar gesture follows the cannibal feasts of Thyestes (see Aesch. *Ag.* 1601–2) and Tereus.

or with close links with the animals just as he has close links with the gods.[121] Lycaon's building of the city sets men apart, and his flight as a wolf establishes a precedent for what is human and what is animal behaviour. Unlike the other transformation stories we have been considering this is an aetiological one, that is to say, it sets up distinctions between men and animals that still exist, and does not deal just with a temporary or isolated change. In this sense, therefore, Lycaon is both the first civilized man and also the first animal, and the wolf here is a symbol of one side of the animal world, its enmity and opposition to man and his institutions.

Compared with the myth of Tantalus, therefore, there is a difference of emphasis in Lycaon's story. Though both tell of a separation of gods and men and imply the birth of a new age Lycaon is much more closely associated with the foundation of human order and its opposite. Unlike Tantalus he is a founder and a civilizer, and although Tantalus' cannibal feast may suggest a metaphorical animal savagery it is only in the case of Lycaon that we have an actual change to a wolf. The motif of the animal balances and corresponds to Lycaon's role as a civilizer and must be seen and understood in this context.

That there is a close link and contrast between wild animals and social institutions in this story, rather than just a reflection of Lycaon's personal moral character and emotions, is suggested also by the other two stories of this type, those of Lyncus and the Cerastae,[122] which both also concern the abuse of hospitality. Lyncus was a king of Scythia who received Triptolemus as he was travelling all over the world offering the gifts of Demeter to men. During the night he attempted to kill him and take the gifts for himself, but Demeter transformed him into a lynx. Triptolemus is here opposed to the barbarian king as one of the great civilizers of men.[123] Ovid's account has much of the same sybolism as in the

[121] The animal life of early man is a basic feature in the historians of human progress (e.g. Archelaus T 4 (D.-K.); Moschion, *TGF* 97 F 6; DS 1. 8), but in a positive way and in a quite different context this is also the prehistory of Aesop's fables: see Babrius, *Fabulae Aesopeae*, Preamb. 1–13, which speaks of an original comradeship of men and animals and men and gods; cf. Cratinus, fr. 171. 13 *PCG*; Callim. fr. 192. 1 ff.

[122] Both under Cat. 1*b*.

[123] *Met.* 5. 656–7: he brings 'alimentaque mitia . . . Barbarus invidet . . .'

story of Lycaon's transformation; but the story of Lyncus does not have the full reversal that follows from Lycaon's role as a culture hero (Ovid's story of Lycaon too is simplified and he becomes simply an outrageous villain). The threat is not seen here to come from within the very institutions that the hero has set up, but has been externalized in the form of a savage outsider. The threat from inside is particularly clear in the sacrifice version of Lycaon's story, and we can compare it with various other stories, including several bird metamorphoses, that illustrate the dangers inherent in the violence of the sacrifice.[124]

This danger is also seen in the story of the Cerastae, horned and giant inhabitants of Cyprus, who sacrifice strangers to Zeus Xenios until Aphrodite turns them into bulls. A historical framework is given to this story first by their name (Cerastia was the ancient name of Cyprus),[125] and second by the persistent mythological and historical tradition connecting human sacrifices with ancient Cyprus.[126] Again, we have a pattern of bad old days in which wild men, whose animal-like nature is reinforced by their horns, abused human institutions until this was brought to an end in a new order indicated by a change in the name of the island, in which they become literal wild animals.

[124] See p. 110.

[125] See schol. Lyc. 447.

[126] e.g. the sacrifices of Teucer, or Aglauros and Diomedes. A seer from Cyprus was supposed to have advised Busiris on his human sacrifice.

4

Birds

IN many ways the stories of mammals form a group of their own. The great mass of transformation stories describe the change of men into birds, plants, and stones; they tend to be first of all terminal, in the sense that transformation ends the story in which it occurs and the transformed person remains permanently in his new state, and secondly, and more basically, aetiological, in that they explain the creation not merely of one animal but of a whole species. Unlike, for instance, Io, the heroes of the bird stories live on in the birds around us. The transformation of Lycaon was, of course, of this type, but most animal changes are not.

It may seem that there is very little to say about aetiological stories, since their function is quite explicit. Their starting point is the object to be explained, and their form and nature will depend on that object. However, I think one needs to go further. One wants to know first of all why certain creatures and particular traits of those creatures receive aetiological stories. Why, for instance, are there nearly fifty aetiological stories of birds and hardly any of animals, when animals have much more intrinsic importance and interest for human beings? Or why are there six different explanations of the owl when the hen does not seem to receive a single one? We find that birds tend to receive stories explaining their natural characteristics, while trees receive stories explaining their relation to the gods. It seems plausible to suggest that one of the reasons for the existence of a story about a bird or a trait of a bird is that these objects suggest a satisfying story. In the next few chapters I shall attempt to draw some general conclusions about which traits of birds and plants and stones generate stories, and why they do.

One must clearly be cautious here. I am not suggesting that narrative considerations are all-important. Boios, for instance, had a programme to explain every single bird by a story. One must assume, therefore, that many birds are included simply for the sake of completeness rather than because they suggest a good story. Nicander had a special interest in these stories. He was concerned not merely with the origin of birds and plants, but with the origins of local cults. Clearly, therefore, his criteria for choosiong a story are complicated. We must nevertheless suppose that telling stories of transformation had sufficient intrinsic appeal for Boios to undertake his programme and Nicander to choose this type of cult *aition*.

Secondly, the aetiological conclusion does not necessarily explain the rest of the story. Often the explanatory function is not the origin, or the main point of interest in the story. There are certain simple stories where it is: the spider, for instance, is a spinning creature; in its previous life, therefore, it was quite naturally a human weaver who competed with the goddess of the craft, Athene. The *monedula* is a bird that loved money; it was, therefore, a woman who betrayed her city out of greed. The eagle is a bird loved by Zeus; it was, therefore, naturally a human lover of Zeus.[1] It seems likely that there were many fables of this kind which never achieved the status of myths[2] (in the sense that they never became attached to a particular heroic family or location). But these stories are not typical. Aetiological change is normally a final reflection or comment on an independent pattern of human suffering. It has a place in a larger imaginative structure, and it is the human tragedy rather than the bird habit that is the chief interest of the story.

At the opposite extreme from the simple *aition* are, for instance, a number of stories in which the transformation is attached to an already existing story, prompted perhaps partly by a coincidence of names.[3] Sometimes we find that the *aition* of a bird transformation will change in different versions; but we can still speak of the same

[1] *Monedula*: Cat. 2 (Arne); eagle: Cat. 2 (eagles: Aetos).

[2] For instance Aristotle, *HA* 619[a], reports a story that the eagle, which in old age starves to death because of its curved beak, was once a man who refused hospitality to a stranger. Compare the report in Dionys. *Av.* 2. 5 that seagulls were once fishermen, or the fable that the ant was once a thieving farmer: see M. Davies and J. Kathiramby, *Greek Insects* (London, 1986), 4.

[3] e.g. Kyknos, son of Poseidon, and Kyknos, son of Ares.

story.[4] Often we find that the *aition* is a very general characteristic of trees or birds, such as the mournful sound of birds' songs, and that a more specific link of bird and man is merely an individual story-teller's elaboration. Even in Boios, who goes into considerable detail in describing bird habits and deriving these from episodes in his stories, it is very rarely that we can point to a specific bird habit as the starting point of the story as a whole. It is true that the specific name of the bird may limit the choice of a story or even suggest one. For instance, we find that a bird or tree with a feminine name will nearly always be explained as a woman, and one with a masculine name as a man (it is no accident that all the Kyknoi are male and Peleia is invariably a woman), but such considerations only take us a certain way; one still wants to know why, for instance, female birds are usually criminals while female trees are innocent lovers of the gods.

Rather, therefore, than assuming in each case that the explicit aetiological conclusion is the original and main interest of the story it makes more sense to look at the story as a whole and see in what way the transformation into a bird forms an appropriate conclusion; very often the answer is a complicated one. We find that there are certain characteristic patterns among these stories which appeal, often not explicitly, to the character of birds, trees, and stones in general and to their role in ancient metaphor, beliefs, and religion. At one level there are simple narrative motifs that can be found in all our categories of stories. We find the motif of the transformed mourner, for instance, used in the story of the cypress, of Aedon, and of Niobe. Within this, however, one can make distinctions. The story of Aedon belongs to a common type in which transformation into a bird follows a crime of pollution and family murder, the story of the cypress also exemplifies the pattern in which a tree is the dying lover of a god, and the mourning of Niobe is a permanent anomaly in which even a lifeless stone expresses human grief. I shall therefore look separately at each of the main categories of birds, trees, and stones and try to identify some of the common patterns and themes, starting in this chapter with birds.

[4] e.g. Hesiod apparently made the story of the nightingale an *aition* for its sleeplessness (fr. 312). This is found nowhere else.

It was once customary to explain stories of transformation into a bird in terms of beliefs in bird-gods and bird-souls.[5] I do not propose to devote much space to considering these theories. The conceptions of bird-gods and souls are as problematical as those of animal-gods; also they do not seem to offer a plausible explanation of bird metamorphosis in general, since in most of the bird stories (compared for instance with those of trees or stones) the gods or the afterlife do not play a central role. A number of stories do play upon a looser connection of birds and gods, and more importantly birds and the dead, and I shall consider these later on, but in the main part of this chapter I shall concentrate on the more characteristic patterns of these stories. Perhaps the best way to begin is by considering in detail the oldest, most popular, and best-documented of the bird stories, that of the nightingale.

THE STORY OF THE NIGHTINGALE

The main story of the nightingale, which received definitive form in Sophocles' *Tereus*, is well known: it tells how Tereus, the king of Thrace, marries the Athenian princess Procne and then rapes her sister Philomela and cuts out her tongue. Unable to speak Philomela sends a message to her sister woven in a piece of cloth, and the sisters take a horrible revenge by serving Tereus up his son in a cannibal banquet. When the enraged father attempts to pursue the women all three are turned into birds,[6] Procne into a nightingale, Philomela into a swallow, and Tereus into a hawk or hoopoe.

The story is a striking and complex one. It has been suggested that it has its origin in a simple folk belief that the nightingale is mourning for its lost bird young.[7] This may be true as far as it goes—it is certainly true that the mourning of the nightingale is a motif that has an existence quite apart from any particular transformation

[5] For the bird-god theory see e.g. J. E. Harrison, *Themis*[2] (Cambridge, 1927), 115–17. For the soul-bird theory see below, n. 60 and text.

[6] For a fuller account of the various versions of the story see Cat. 2 (nightingale).

[7] See e.g. *RML* article on Aedon; cf. W. R. Halliday, *Indo-European Folktales and Greek Legend* (Cambridge, 1933), 85–112.

story[8]—but it does not explain very much about the developed version of our story: the main interest of this story is not ornithological lore but the relations of human beings.

The most immediately obvious pattern in the story is the opposition between the husband and his home (and heir) on the one hand, and the wife and her family on the other. At the risk of appearing to move off at a tangent I shall begin not with Sophocles (of whose version we have only fragments), but with the highly idiosyncratic version of Boios, where this theme emerges in its most exaggerated form.[9]

Boios tells how a blissfully married couple, Polytechnos, a carpenter, and Aedon ('nightingale'), a weaver, incur the displeasure of the gods by boasting that their marriage is happier than that of Zeus and Hera. The gods inspire a rivalry between husband and wife in which the wife achieves a temporary victory: the husband then rapes her sister Chelidon ('swallow') and presents her to his wife as a slave (i.e. Aedon is now identified with her father's family, and hostility towards them is a way of getting back to her). The two sisters respond by killing Aedon's child, thus destroying the husband's home and heir, and then return to their father's home. The idea that the son is an extension of the husband and that a mother may be torn between loyalty to her father's family and to her husband and son is not unusual: we can compare the story of Meleager and Althaea (whereas we have many stories of wives killing their child to hurt their husband, we do not find cases of husbands killing their child to hurt their wife).

Polytechnos is then captured by the wife's father Pandareos and thrown out of the house into the stables: Polytechynos' rape was a crime against the father-in-law himself. The wife, however, falls in love with the husband again and goes to the stable to try to rescue him. The father and the brother angrily set on her to try and kill her (clearly she has changed sides and now identifies herself again with the house of Polytechnos). Zeus intervenes to save the house of Pandareos from family murder, and they are all turned into birds;

[8] See Page, *GLP* no. 95. Parthenius (11) has the nightingales mourning for Adonis; cf. Moschus 3. 36 ff.

[9] AL 11.

but the distinction of the two houses is preserved in the bird world, the sea-birds of Pandareos and his wife and son[10] being contrasted with the land-birds Polytechnos, Aedon, and Chelidon.

Boios' interpretation is perhaps not in itself very important, but if we now look at the few surviving fragments of Sophocles we can recognize, in spite of the obvious differences of style and genre, many of the same oppositions. The first point is the heroine's isolation from home in Thrace, which is apparently an important feature of the play: thus our longest fragment is a complaint about marriage in which she contrasts the blissful life girls lead in their father's house with the problems of adapting to a new home and master: 'we are pushed out and sold away from our parents and our family gods', she says.[11] It seems that this aspect remains central to the story, since in later sources Tereus is sent to fetch Philomela because of Procne's loneliness.

This grim view of marriage and the lot of women is reminiscent of another contemporary speech, that of Medea in Euripides: she too is a foreigner among strange people and describes how marriage involves learning new customs and laws; in particular she bitterly regrets the loss of her family.[12] In fact in her story we have a similar opposition between her father's family and her husband or lover. Medea betrays her father and kills her brother to save her lover, but her story ends in the same way as that of Procne: she too kills her own children to spite her husband.

Procne's position is from the start an insecure and potentially ambiguous one. The effect of Tereus' crime is to disrupt the fragile family order and confuse its relations, and this will lead to the ultimate disruption, the eating of the son by his father. 'You have thrown everything into confusion', Philomela cries to Tereus in Ovid's account:[13] roles and relations have been turned upside down to such an extent that in Procne's eyes *pietas* towards her husband becomes a crime against her father.[14]

However, this disruption of the house leads us on to a second

[10] His son becomes a hoopoe, not apparently a sea-bird, but our source says that it keeps company with the sea-birds.

[11] Fr. 583. 3 ff.

[12] See Eur. *Med.* 238 f., 253 f., and 257 f.

[13] *Met.* 6. 537.

[14] *Met.* 6. 635.

opposition even more fundamental than that of husband and wife as representatives of two houses; this is the opposition between the family order of the house and the wilds. This is seen most clearly in the experience of Philomela, who is in a sense a double of her sister Procne. Procne moves from one house to the other with all the proper formalities of marriage. Tereus and Philomela too leave Philomela's home with her father's blessing, but end up in the wilds where she is raped. In many of our sources this rape is treated as a savage parody or contrast with her sister's marriage.[15] It takes place not in a house, but in an animal stable or beside the road (in a 'way-side bedchamber').[16] Her mutilation is linked with the loss of her virginity,[17] but it also has the effect of reducing her to a dumb animal.[18] The motif of weaving is also important in this respect, since traditionally it symbolizes the wifely and homely virtues (weaving was the special accomplishment of Aedon herself in Boios' version of the story; in the story of the Minyades the women prefer to stay at home weaving than to join in the wild rites of Dionysos). Here weaving becomes the pathetic last resource of a woman who has lost all social and even human status. A final pathetic touch comes in the way that while the nightingale and the hoopoe fly off to the open country the swallow still clings to the roofs of human houses.[19]

Philomela is the passive sufferer in a process of degeneration; Tereus, the main cause of this, merely reveals his true character as a savage barbarian,[20] someone who never did belong in the house. He is continually described in Ovid as *saevus* and *barbarus*.[21] From the surviving fragments of Sophocles' play it appears that the opposition between Greek and Thracian barbarian was important,[22] as in the parallel story of Medea. Tereus' mistake, not dissimilar to that of Dr

[15] See e.g. *AP* 9. 451; Nonn. 4. 320 ff.

[16] Nonn. 4. 325.

[17] See Nonn. 4. 320 ff., where the blood from her rape and her mutilation mixes together, or Ach. Tat. 5. 3–5, where cutting out her tongue becomes her wedding present.

[18] Or, more particularly, a non-Greek: see e.g. *AP* 9. 451.

[19] See e.g. AL 11.

[20] In most sources Tereus is a barbarian. Pausanias comments mildly that his rape of Philomela was contrary to Greek *nomos* (1. 5. 4).

[21] Cf. 6. 460 'flagrat vitio gentisque suoque'.

[22] See e.g. fr. 587; cf. frs. 584 and 582.

Jekyll, is to imagine that two opposite roles, that of civilized father and husband and that of savage rapist, can be kept apart and played out with different sisters.

Finally, Procne herself literally and metaphorically enters the sphere of the wilds when she goes in search of Philomela. In many sources this happens in the course of a Bacchic rite, the one ritual which introduces an element of wildness into the civilized Greek home. By then bringing her sister into her house she inevitably wrecks it, since the one home cannot have two brides.[23] Her behaviour after this is, in one sense, no longer that of a woman, but an animal: she is 'lion-hearted'.[24] The story ends with both Tereus and Procne taking to the wilds and deserting their home altogether. Tereus in particular becomes a bird that is opposed to all human civilization: the hoopoe lives as far away from men as it possibly can and covers its nest with excrement to keep away human beings.[25]

Perhaps we can take this a little further by considering the central act and climax of the story, the cannibal banquet of Tereus. As we have already seen in the case of Lycaon, cannibalism, like the eating of raw flesh, is a defining act of the animal as opposed to the human world. Even if here it is not intentional it still puts Tereus outside the world of men. But in fact it is also parallel to the intentional act of incest, which is also a defining animal act. This parallel of incest and cannibalism seems worth pursuing further, since here eating and the table are more than a symbol of civilization in general as opposed to the world of animals (which was their function in the story of the culture hero Lycaon). Here they have a more particular relevance to the family.

There is in Greek myth generally a metaphorical relation between eating and sex, and more particularly between eating one's own family and incest.[26] This takes two forms, both of which are relevant to our story. First, the table can be seen as a symbol of family solidarity, and since a crucial foundation of the family order

[23] In the Boios version Polytechnos attempts to introduce the sister into the house as a slave.

[24] Nonn. 44. 267.

[25] Ael. *NA* 3. 26. Soph. fr. 581 has the birds live among deserted rocks and thickets.

[26] Cf. R. Parker, *Miasma* (Oxford, 1983), 98.

is the sexual bond sexual offences may be seen as offences against the table. Thus, for instance, Paris' crime against Menelaus can be described in terms of the table: Lycophron describes him as a fugitive from justice, 'having kicked over the table and having spat out Themis'.[27] The feast of Tereus was, we are told by Pausanias, the first *miasma* of the table, and it is followed by Tereus' symbolic knocking over of the table; but since sexual crimes inevitably cause and can be represented by an outrage to the family table this can be seen as a fitting, almost an inevitable consequence of Tereus' incestuous rape.

However, there is a parallel in the motivation as well as the results of crimes of the table and sexual crimes; the action of eating is itself more closely parallel to sexual and incestuous relations since both are clearly forms of taking possession or greed.[28] For example, the seduction and swallowing of Metis by Zeus are seen as parallel conquests.[29] More relevant perhaps is the way Thyestes' unholy feast on his sons is explicitly paralleled by the rape of his daughter (the oracle tells him that in order to obtain vengeance for his misfortune he must bear a son by his daughter).[30] The feast was itself an act of revenge for Thyestes' incestuous seduction of his brother's wife; this is a situation very close to that of Tereus and Procne. One might note also that in this case, as in that of Zeus and Metis, the episode comes in the context of a more general power struggle. This perhaps supports the idea that it is the theme of greed in the sense of desire for power and possession that underlies these parallels of sex and eating.

Still more relevant to our myth is the story of Harpalyke and her father;[31] here as in the nightingale story we have the conflict between father, daughter, and husband. In one version of this story she is a wild Amazon who refuses marriage and is devoted to the

[27] Lyc. 137–8. Compare the anger of Oedipus after being served on the table of Cadmus (*Thebais* fr. 2); the point may be that his sexual crime pollutes this.

[28] Greed and lust are often metaphorically interchangeable; see e.g. the description of Paris and Theseus (as seducers of Helen) in Lyc. 147. For incest as a form of greed compare C. Lévi-Strauss, *The Elementary Structures of Kinship* (Eng. tr. Oxford, 1968), 58.

[29] See below, ch. 8 n. 63.

[30] Apollod. *Epit.* 2. 14.

[31] Cat. 2 (owls s.v.).

support of her father. In another this close relation of father and daughter takes on a grimmer aspect: Klymenos, her father, rapes her and then after her marriage takes her away from her husband; she then serves up their child to him. Here again we have a man who commits a crime of greed on two levels. Of course, greed is not the conscious motivation of the human eaters since no man deliberately eats his own children,[32] but I think it is fair to say that in these stories the reason why this meal is such a fitting punishment for, or balance to, a crime of incest is that it is a symbolic re-enactment of the crime. This metaphorical equivalence of eating and sex finds perhaps its most striking expression in a passage of the *Suppliants* where Danaus compares a forced marriage of his daughters to the sons of Aegyptus to the impure eating of one bird by another.[33] The sons of Aegyptus are in this passage described as hawks: that is, they are metaphorically what Tereus becomes literally (in earlier versions of the story he appears to have been transformed into a hawk).[34]

These comparisons provide a context for Tereus' eating; it is because he too, this time as a husband, attempts to take more than his fair share, by demanding both sisters that he finishes by eating his own child. He ends up as a bird of prey forever eating swallows and nightingales (i.e. perpetuating his double greed). The hawk is, of course, the traditional bird of greed, but it is interesting to note that the greed of the hoopoe takes a particular form; Pliny says it is a bird that eats filth.[35] Tereus' disgusting appetite is thus perpetuated in a striking way. Other greedy heroes who become birds of prey will be discussed in the second part of this chapter.

I hope we can see, therefore, that the details of a story of transformation from humans into birds have been used to illustrate and give metaphorical expression to several important human themes and contrasts: there is first the ambiguous position of Procne, the wife and mother, as the link between two houses, secondly the

[32] Although it is among the gods. Kronos deliberately eats his children to retain power.

[33] *Supp.* 226.

[34] Ovid anticipates the final transformation by comparing Tereus' rape of Philomela to a hawk's attack on a dove.

[35] *NH* 10. 86. In Boios the metaphor of eating is given a further twist: Tereus' double greed is balanced by Pandareos' 'gift' of never being full. This reinforces the theme of the opposition of the two houses and the competing demands of father and husband.

danger of incestuous greed in the husband and father Tereus, and thirdly, underlying these themes, the contrast of the fragile order of the house and family with the world of savage animals. Clearly we are dealing with something more complicated than a simple folk belief or an observation about the mournful sound of the nightingale.

It remains perhaps to make a couple of further points about the actual transformation. We may begin by summarizing the points already made. First, the change plays its part in the opposition between the house and the wilds. The house is wrecked (according to Ovid its inner room drips with gore),[36] and wife and husband both abandon it, while the unmarried Philomela pathetically clings to it. But in an obvious sense they are all in exile, cut off from human life and society; in this sense their separation may also be seen as a marking-off of the human and animal worlds that follows the committing of the original crime (we may compare Lycaon again).

However, this leads on to a second point: that their crime is a *miasma* which they can only remove or escape by transformation. The escape prayers of Greek tragedy perhaps provide a context for such a view of transformation. Usually the object of these prayers, which often use the traditional formula of asking to be buried under the earth or to fly into the sky, is to escape some immediate danger. But sometimes the formula is used after a polluting crime: for instance Heracles, after murdering his family, asks where, in the sky or under the earth, he can find release from his troubles.[37] Most striking perhaps from our point of view is Artemis' taunt to Theseus in the *Hippolytus* after he has killed his son: 'Why don't you hide under the ground in shame or change your life for that of a bird to escape this misery?'[38]

It is significant, therefore, that in Pherecydes' version of the nightingale story, where there is no cannibal feast, the husband does not become a bird.[39] That he does become a bird in the normal story

[36] *Met.* 6. 646.

[37] Eur. *HF* 1157 f.

[38] Eur. *Hipp.* 1290 ff. In *Med.* 1327–8 and 1296–7 both an immediate escape from danger and a general escape from pollution are expressed in this formula, and Medea's final flight in a magic carriage is in a sense a fulfilment of such an escape prayer and half-way towards a transformation into a bird.

[39] *FGH* 3 F 124.

makes it clear that the transformation is not simply a means of escape from immediate danger for the sisters: a crucial factor is that in this story he has undergone a polluting action himself. This function of transformation, though most important in the bird stories, can also be seen in other transformation stories where incest or family murder plays a part. Myrrha, after sleeping with her father, prays that in order not to violate the living or the dead she be driven from both realms:[40] she is then turned into a tree.

PATTERNS OF DISORDER IN OTHER BIRD STORIES

The story of the nightingale is the fullest of our bird stories, and in none of the others do we find quite the same richness of detail or such elaborately developed themes; nevertheless, our conclusions about that story do seem relevant to a large number of others, in particular those of the birds of the night and birds of prey. There is in fact a greater number of these stories than is necessary for strictly aetiological purposes: we have eight different stories of owls, six stories of hawks, and two stories of vultures (and of course the nightingale too is a bird of the night). Clearly such birds offered scope for certain particularly popular types of story.

There were two closely related themes that seemed particularly important in the transformation of the nightingale: pollution, and the opposition between the house and the wilds. Both were illustrated in terms of eating; and indeed we shall see that the symbolic function of eating is a pervasive feature of the bird stories. I shall begin with pollution.

Transformation into a bird often follows a family crime. First of all, there is a group of stories of incest. Harpalyke and Nyctimene became owls after incest with their father. Harpalyke also kills her own child. They are now shunned by their fellow-birds and hide in the darkness. Aigypios and Neophron become vultures: Aigypios has seduced the mother of Neophron, and in revenge Neophron has seduced Aigypios' mother and then tricked Aigypios into sleeping with her himself. Again the climax of the story is incest. Having

[40] Ov. *Met.* 10. 484 f.; cf. AL 34.

discovered what has happened Aigypios looks up to the sky and prays that they could all be removed from the face of the earth. Aigypios' mother also becomes a scavenger bird, and none of these birds appear together. Iktinos attempts to rape his daughter, but is transformed into a kite. Here transformation prevents a crime of pollution, but the criminal still becomes a rapacious predator in a similar pattern to the story of Tereus.[41]

There are also several stories of family murder. Harpalyke's child-killing has already been mentioned. The Minyades are seized by a Dionysiac frenzy and kill the child of one of them. All the sources conclude with an account of how they flee the light of day and become birds of the night, though there is divergence on the species of bird; one source says that they were rejected even by their fellow maenads before their transformation. Scylla becomes a sea-bird, the *ciris*. Her pollution comes from her crime of parricide; Minos tells her, 'I will not allow so vile a monster to set foot on Crete, the cradle of Zeus';[42] as a result she is as isolated as the birds of the night and leads a savage life among the lonely rocks.[43] Further, like the swallow and the nightingale she is forever pursued, since her father becomes a sea-eagle. We may compare the story of Arne, who also betrays her city and is then transformed, though we know none of the details. The story of Botres concerns a family killing, but here it is the victim rather than the agent that is transformed. Botres is killed in a fit of rage by his father after he has eaten the raw brain of the sacrificial animal; he becomes a bee-eater before the eyes of his remorseful father. Similarly, the daughter of Sciron is thrown into the sea by her father in punishment for her promiscuity and becomes a halcyon. Finally, there is the story of Combe, which appears to involve a family killing of some sort, or at least a threat of it.[44]

Moving away from the strictly family crimes, we should note the story of Polyphonte.[45] She has been polluted by sex with a bear, for

[41] See Cat. 2 (owls, Aigypios, Iktinos). For the shunning of Harpalyke and Nyctimene by the other birds see Euph. *SH* no. 413, and Ov. *Met.* 2. 594 f.

[42] Ov. *Met.* 8. 99 f.; he also says 'tellus tibi pontusque negetur': 8. 98.

[43] See *Ciris* 518: incultum solis in rupibus exigit aevum.

[44] See Cat. 2 (owls, the Ciris, Botres, halcyons, Combe).

[45] See Cat. 2 (owls s.v.).

which she is expelled from the band of Artemis and shunned by the animals; her sons grow up as monsters which kill and eat strangers. She becomes a *styx*, an ill-omened harbinger of war and conflict, and interestingly (in view of the metaphorical equivalence of eating and sex noted earlier) a bird that does not eat, though her sons become vultures which retain their polluting taste for human flesh.

But these polluting crimes can be generally described as outbreaks of wildness, and it is the more general opposition between the wilds and human order that is the basic structure of these stories.

I have already tried to show how this theme provides a basic structure for the story of the nightingale: the cannibal meal introduced the animal world into the house (following on from the savage marriage of Philomela in the stable). Almost identical with the structure of this story is that of the story of Polyphonte: after mating with a bear in the wilds she returns to her father's house. Introducing this wildness into the house inevitably wrecks it; she bears giant sons who abuse the table and eat the flesh of strangers. (Lycophron's description of Paris' symbolic kicking over of the table cited earlier is revealing here; such savage ways, Lycophron suggests, must have been learnt from his bear nurse.)[46] They finally all leave the house in the form of birds. Again desecration of the table and transformation follow an outrageous sexual act in the wilds.

The Minyades stay at home weaving, having rejected the night wandering of their companions (their motivation opposes the family to the wilds; Aelian says that they wanted husbands). However Dionysos enters their house and transforms it into an image of the outside as vines and ivy grow all over it. He drives them to kill their son and go off into the mountains where they eventually become night birds, permanent creatures of darkness and the wilds. Here too their food is important: their diet on the mountains is not grain but ivy and laurel, the special wild food of the Dionysiac votaries.[47]

We can develop the antithesis in various directions. Staying for a moment with eating we can note that an important theme in some

[46] Lyc. 137 f.

[47] See Plut. *RQ* 112 for chewing ivy as part of the Dionysiac festival.

stories is the danger represented by the killing and eating within the order of the family sacrifice. Thus Botres is prompted to eat the raw brain of his victim (for the savage significance of this we can compare the story of Tydeus who deprives himself of immortality by eating the brain of his enemy); he has become an animal and introduces into the rite an infectious savagery that ends with his father's murderous attack on him. In the story of Kleinis the introduction of wild asses instead of goats in the sacrifice leads to an outbreak of animal savagery as the asses eat up the whole family including the pious father, Kleinis himself.[48]

Some stories make explicit the antithesis of the home and the wilds only in the *aition* at the end; in these cases the wildness within the story is sometimes a metaphorical one in the form of particularly inhuman or savage behaviour or the breakdown of the social order and the destruction of the house. This is well illustrated by the story of Scylla. She kills her father and is responsible for the destruction of her city and her home (even Minos is shocked by her inhuman behaviour and calls her a monster).[49] Her life as a bird is a wild and homeless one among the deserted rocks.[50] Earlier I cited this transformation as an example of isolation following a polluting crime; we can now see how this wild new life is more specifically the inevitable consequence of her destruction of her home.

Having been raped by her father, Nyctimene takes to the woods where she hides until she is transformed into an owl. Daidalion runs mad into the wilds before he throws himself off a deserted cliff, but his transformation is already anticipated in the description of his inhuman emotional state (he was no more to be comforted, says Ovid, than a rock or the sea).[51] In the story of Harpalyke we have only the metaphorical wildness of open incest and cannibalism, but it is interesting to note that in her other story she is a wild Amazon and robber (as suits her name 'snatcher'), who is finally caught like an animal in the hunters' nets.[52]

[48] Cat. 2 s.v., and more generally on wildness in the sacrifice J. L. Durand; in *La Cité des images* (Lausanne, 1984), 49–54.

[49] In Ov. *Met.* 8. 100. Aeschylus calls her κυνόφρων: *Cho.* 621.

[50] See above, n. 43.

[51] *Met.* 11. 330 ff. See more generally Cat. 2 (hawks s.v.).

[52] See Virg. *A* 1. 316 f. and Servius on these lines.

A third aspect of this opposition of the wilds and the house is shown in a group of stories which are concerned with farming. Just as the order of Kleinis' home is savagely destroyed when his family are attacked by wild asses, so Anthos and his family are eaten by the horses he has tried to keep away from his meadow. Here farming and wild horses are opposed; we can compare this with the story of the companions of Diomedes, Dorians and farmers who are killed by their wild Illyrian neighbours, jealous of the efficiency of their farming.[53] Here the order of the house has taken on a wider aspect as the order and controlled environment of the farm.

It is important to stress that for the Greeks there was a close connection between the social order and the order of the land[54] (Demeter is the goddess both of the crops and of civilized life).[55] We therefore find that a number of heroes of bird stories start as favourites of Demeter or the earth, and their initial prosperity, the initial order of their house, is expressed in terms of the productivity of their land. But this sometimes leads to an over-reliance and a neglect of the other gods which must bring about a reversal. Hierax is a rich farmer who gives food to starving Trojans in defiance of Poseidon: he becomes a rapacious and anti-social bird hated by its fellow creatures. Meropis and her family, who are worshippers of the earth, refuse to leave their home to attend the public festivals of the other gods.[56] The aggrieved gods appear at night and transform them into birds. Strikingly, in this story the Olympians appear as subverters of the order of the house, in a role more commonly played by Dionysos.[57]

To summarize briefly, therefore—the basic framework of a large number of the bird stories, and in particular those of the birds of the night, and birds of prey and their victims, depends on the opposition between the family order and the outside or animal world; transformation into a bird often follows the breakdown of this order and is itself characterized as a movement from the house to the wilds.

[53] See Cat. 2 (Birds of Diomedes).

[54] See e.g. Aesch. *Sept.* 16 ff.

[55] See e.g. Isocr. *Paneg.* 28; Serv. on *A* 4. 58.

[56] Hierax: Cat. 2 (hawks s.v.); Meropis and her family: Cat. 2 (owls s.v.).

[57] The Furies make this accusation against Apollo in the *Eumenides*: see e.g. 198 ff.

Perhaps finally I should make one more general qualification. The emphasis on punishment, pollution, and greed might seem to conflict with what I have said elsewhere, that bird transformation tends to be at least an ambiguous change. It is important to stress, therefore, that being transformed into a bird is quite different from being transformed into an animal. In the latter case, one becomes a monster and the change has no redeeming features. Although the heroes of the bird stories do not fully escape their guilt and pollution they are at least no longer felt to be a threat to human beings (as Io is, for instance, or Callisto). Their new state has a certain detachment or remoteness about it. Perhaps the important point is that the birds' main punishment comes during their human lifetime and their bird state is not actually a period of suffering. In the case of Aedon, for instance, or the singing birds, transformation turns suffering into a thing of beauty; Aedon actually becomes the 'messenger of Zeus' in spite of her crime.[58] Even Tereus, who is transformed from an evil man into an evil bird, has already been sufficiently punished by the sisters in his human form, and his ruthless bird behaviour is treated with some sympathy. This perhaps takes us back to the most basic narrative difference between these stories and those of animals: not only are birds remoter creatures from human beings than animals, but bird stories tend to be aetiological stories explaining species that still exist. Since they are describing everyday facts of nature and since the present birds are no longer really the original transformed people these birds will tend to be less alarming or extraordinary than the unique freaks created by transformation into an animal; also the position of these transformations at the end of their story, and the fact that they will last for ever, removes any sense of urgency about the heroes' behaviour or state of mind as birds, and produces a perhaps artificial sense of serenity about their new state. They are now free from any further human tragedy, in comparison with which neither the suffering of birds nor any further evil that they do among each other needs to be taken too seriously. This remoteness of birds leads on appropriately to the final part of the discussion.

[58] Soph. *El.* 147 ff.; cf. Cassandra's comparison between the sweet life of the nightingale and the grim fate awaiting her: *Ag.* 1147–9.

BIRDS AND THE OTHER WORLD

It is important to stress first of all that although the gods do usually appear at some point in the stories of transformation into birds it is often only to work the final transformation, and they are a major point of interest in very few of them. Many stories do tell how a human being becomes the sacred bird of a god,[59] but in the more substantial bird stories the religious *aition* at the end has little to do with the rest of the story. (The pattern of the *aition* for the holy object is more important in the tree stories, and I shall consider it in more detail in the next chapter).

Death is a more important issue in some of these stories. Since aetiological transformations are terminal and end the career of the hero they correspond, formally at least, to the death of the hero in other stories. More particularly death is often explicitly referred to in these stories. Sometimes transformation actually follows the death of the hero; sometimes the hero dies and his mourners are transformed; in other stories, though nobody dies, transformation is said to be a substitute for death. In such cases the birds retain some otherworldly characteristic or some close connections with the world of the dead.

It is the relation of transformation and death that I shall be mainly concerned with in this section. Those few stories in which a link with a god is important tend to be also those in which the death and afterlife of the hero is an issue (in particular the stories of eagles and doves). In these stories the oppositions between men and gods and between mortality and immortality are very closely connected. I shall try to show how various Greek beliefs about the connections of birds with the world beyond may underlie some of these stories of transformation into birds.

I shall begin by dealing very shortly with the theory of the soul-bird. It has been argued that all stories of transformation into a bird have their origin in a general Greek belief that the souls of the dead took the form of birds.[60] But there is no reason to believe that the

[59] e.g. the stories of the eagle, two stories of the dove, two stories of the owl, and the story of the crow.

[60] See Weicker, *Seelenvogel*, *passim*, and *RML* article 'Seirenen'.

Greeks ever did hold such a belief. The Siren, the human-headed bird, has a wide role in Greek art as an otherworldly symbol, but it cannot be specifically characterized as the spirit of a dead man in the way that its Egyptian equivalent, the Ba bird, can.[61] The Homeric poems speak of the spirits of the dead flying to Hades and compare them to birds[62] (and in later art tiny winged figures apparently indicate the spirits of the dead).[63] But the point of comparison is a limited one; it is the flight of the soul at the moment of death and the dead spirits' insubstantiality (they are also compared to shadow, smoke, and dreams).[64] By contrast we do have depictions of the soul as a butterfly, and we know that it was sometimes imagined as taking the form of a snake.[65]

The soul-bird does not in any case seem a plausible explanation of the stories of transformation into a bird. In these it is the body, not just the spirit that changes its form, and a view that Hades was inhabited by strange bird-like creatures does not seem relevant to most of our stories, which are aetiological and seek to explain the ordinary birds around us.

However, we do have evidence of various looser connections of birds with the other world. Though it does not make much sense to talk of a general belief in bird-souls we do find, later on at least, that birds perform an important role as a sign in the public miracle of apotheosis. In Roman times seeing an eagle or a star at the funeral of an emperor became the regular way of recognizing his apotheosis, and we find the belief expressed that the souls of men are carried to heaven on an eagle, or become eagles to get to heaven.[66]

[61] See E. Kunze, *MDAI(A)* 57 (1932), 124–41; E. Buschor, *Die Musen des Jenseits*, Munich, 1944; J. Pollard, *Birds in Greek Life and Myth* (London, 1977), ch. 22; Nilsson, *GGR* 197–9. For the Ba bird see L. V. Zabkar, *A Study in the Ba Concept in Ancient Egyptian Texts* (Chicago, 1968).

[62] See e.g. *Od.* 11. 605 f. and 24. 5 ff.; *Il.* 22. 362 and 16. 586.

[63] See E. Vermeule, *Aspects of Death in Early Greek Art and Poetry* (Berkeley, 1979), 8–11.

[64] Contrast the fully visualized bird-like dead in the underworld of the epic of Gilgamesh: *ANET* 87.

[65] For the soul as a butterfly see Davies and Kathiramby, 99–109; for the soul in snake form, Burkert, *GR* 195. Cf. J. Bremmer, *The Early Greek Concept of the Soul* (Princeton, 1983), 80 and 82.

[66] See Herodian 4. 2. 11; Dio Cass. 56. 42; *AP* 7. 62; Artem. 2. 20; Lucian, *Peregr.* 39;

It is important to stress that this transformation applies only to the moment and means of escape; there is no suggestion that the divine emperors continued to live as eagles. The bird epiphany is really only the public sign of a more mysterious and invisible change of status. The pattern perhaps owes less to any specific connection of birds and souls than to the belief that birds act as a link between gods and men;[67] birds share the home of the gods in the sky,[68] and the science of augury depends on the belief that birds are sent by the gods as signs to men. We may compare the way that gods sometimes reveal themselves in Homer by flying away as birds. In the context, therefore, of the funeral of a great man this special character of the bird makes it an obvious sign of apotheosis.[69]

One should be wary of ascribing too much influence to a pattern that reaches its fullest development only in Roman times. Also, as I pointed out earlier, most of our bird stories are aetiological and explain birds that remain around us rather than tell of birds disappearing into the sky. However, there does seem to be a small and quite distinct group of stories which owe something to the role of birds as a sign of apotheosis. Ktesilla is a girl from Ceos who dies in childbirth after being separated from her lover. When she is carried out for burial her body vanishes and a dove flies away; as a result a cult is set up to Aphrodite Ktesilla.[70] This story does not explain the origin of a type of bird: it is *a* dove, not the first of all doves, that appears. Also rather than a transformation we have a death followed by the disappearance of the body and the appearance of a bird; such a miraculous disappearance is very frequently the starting point of a cult in local temple stories (sometimes it is followed by the appearance of a tree, stone, or cult statue).

Another case is the final transformation of Kaineus. Ovid tells how the invulnerable hero disappears under a heap of branches and a bird with golden wings appears, which is greeted by the seer

F. Cumont, *Afterlife in Roman Paganism* (New Haven, 1922), 102, 113, and 157–9; S. Price, in D. Cannadine and S. Price (ed.), *Rituals of Royalty* (Cambridge, 1987), 94–5.

[67] See Bodson, 94–101. Euripides calls birds 'heralds of the gods'; fr. 989a; cf. Soph. *El.* 148.

[68] Aesch. *Ag.* 57 calls them μέτοικοι of the gods.

[69] And the eagle is the appropriate bird since it is the bird of kings.

[70] See AL 1.

Mopsus as the reborn hero.[71] It seems likely that this bird is the phoenix and that we have here the rebirth that is the central element in the myth of the phoenix. Mopsus' speech performs the role of the recognition speech that is an essential feature in the pattern of apotheosis.[72] Kyknos too is an invulnerable warrior, but is finally throttled by Achilles. He then disappears and Achilles finds only his empty armour, but a swan flies away (it is *a* swan in Ovid's account, not *the* swan).[73] Kyknos and Kaineus do not receive cults like Ktesilla, but both were super-human figures in their human lives, and Kaineus at least becomes a divine bird.

The transformations of Kyknos and Kaineus appear only in Ovid, where they are explicitly compared, and it does seem that Ovid is particularly fond of the bird epiphany.[74] However, Nicander's cult legend of Ktesilla shows that the idea is not a peculiar fantasy of Ovid's. If Ovid has invented, it is probably in accordance with a traditional pattern.[75]

However, this type comprises a very small group of stories, and these are not the most characteristic or most popular of the bird stories. This is perhaps not surprising since transformation has here a very limited expressive role. It is a public sign which tells us nothing about the state of mind of the transformed hero: its importance is rather its effect on the observers.

A more complicated use of connections between birds and the dead is found in a second group of stories that tell how the companions or mourners of a dead hero are transformed into birds which continue to look after his tomb or temple. These are the 'hero

[71] *Met.* 12. 525 ff.

[72] Or epiphany; cf. Nestor's recognition of Athene's epiphany at Pylos: Hom. *Od.* 3. 375 ff.

[73] *Met.* 12. 143 ff. The story of *the* swan is recounted at 2. 367 ff.

[74] Elsewhere he goes even further and has the soul of a city arising from the burnt Ardea: *Met.* 14. 567 ff.

[75] The closest parallels among Greek stories are the appearance of trees or stones after the miraculous disappearance of a hero in local cult *aitia* (see e.g. AL 23, 13, 40, 33, 30). The flying away of a bird appears to be an alternative amplification of such cult legends, and perhaps has its origins in Eastern stories: we may compare the story which made the flying away of a dove the sign of the apotheosis of Semiramis (DS 2. 20). For the view that the pattern of the royal apotheosis had its origins in the East see Cumont (op. cit. n. 66), 157–9, and *Études Syriennes* (Paris, 1917), 108; cf. A. Roes, *Mélanges C. Picard*, ii (Paris, 1948), 881–91.

birds'.[76] Best known perhaps, and apparently told by Sophocles, is the story of the Meleagrides, the sisters of Meleager, who were transformed into guinea-fowl as they mourned beside their brother's tomb. According to some accounts they live far in the East and weep magical tears of amber; other accounts report that they are now the sacred birds of Artemis on the island of Leros and once a year perform a ritual mourning for their brother.[77]

The other stories have a similar pattern. After Memnon's death his companions were transformed, and every year they return from the East, the home of the hero, and fight mock battles or sprinkle water over his tomb or cenotaph. The birds of Diomedes live on the uninhabited island of Diomedeia in the Adriatic, where they look after the temple or tomb of Diomedes. They were companions of the hero who were transformed after he or they were treacherously killed. On their island they remember their Greek origin and fight off any barbarians who land. The birds of Achilles also belong in this group, although in no source are they transformed men. These birds are the hero's attendants in his mysterious afterlife on the island of Leuke. Along with various wives and other heroes these birds keep the hero company and look after his temple.[78]

In a sense the hero birds belong to a much wider group of transformed mourners that includes other birds, the cypress tree, the mourning stone of Niobe, and above all the mourning trees of Phaethon, which in their tears of amber come very close to the birds of Meleager. Perhaps the starting point of stories of this type is the pathetic fallacy: exceptional respect or sorrow for a dead man is shown by having a normally unfeeling nature weep for a human tragedy. Some stories tell of the mourning of natural objects or animals even without a transformation story,[79] or the weeping of a transformed person may be mentioned without referring to their transformation. Secondly, the remoteness of these transformed

[76] See R. Holland, *Heroenvögel in der gr. Mythologie* (Leipzig, 1895).

[77] See Cat. 2 s.v.

[78] Birds of Memnon, birds of Diomedes: see Cat. 2 s.vv.; birds of Achilles: see Eur. *IT* 435 ff., Pind. *Nem.* 4. 49 f., Philostr. *Her.* 211 f.

[79] See e.g. the many stories which tell how the earth sends up a plant in memory of a dead hero, or the swallows that weep for Adonis (Parth. 11), or the general mourning of nature in Bion's lament for Adonis.

people is relevant to their grief; in a sense their transformation is part of a more general removal, in both place and time, from the normal human world, that allows a complete and eternal submersion in their role as mourners. The sisters of Phaethon are removed to the mysterious West, for instance, and Niobe mourns, not in Thebes where she was queen, but 'in the lonely mountains'.[80] More important perhaps is the fact that time no longer exists for them. To understand the significance of their eternity of mourning we should perhaps turn to the speeches of Ajax and Oedipus in Sophocles.[81] It is a characteristic of the world ruled by time that human attachments and feelings do not last. It is only through transformation into another realm of existence, even though the change is merely from one natural object to another, that one can achieve a release from the normal laws of nature.

Finally perhaps, and almost conflicting with this last idea, is the suggestion that the detachment which comes with transformation leads to a certain, if not mitigation, at least transformation or elevation of grief into a thing of beauty. This is particularly clear in some of Euripides' descriptions, for instance that of the Phaethontiades, or the nightingale which in spite of her grief and her terrible crime produces a beautiful song.[82]

These considerations, however, take us only a certain way with the hero birds. This group has differences from the other mourners. Their actions are much less an expression of internal private grief than an external and public honour. Their dead comrade is not merely a dead man but a hero and sometimes even a god, and their service helps to establish his status. We find in fact that there is a tendency to regard these birds as extensions of the dead hero: Ovid for instance has the birds of Memnon born from the hero's ashes.[83]

Since these stories have the form of an animal *aition* and purport to explain the curious actions of still existing birds one might offer a very simple explanation of their story: birds which perform acts appropriate to human beings are quite naturally given stories of

[80] *Il.* 24. 614.

[81] OC 616 ff.; *Ajax* 646 ff.

[82] See e.g. *HF* 1021 ff.

[83] In Hesychius they are called ἀντίψυχοι (s.v. ἀντίψυχοι).

how they were once human beings. But the question is more complicated than that. Although the descriptions of these birds have acquired an air of scientific reality by being taken up in works of natural history, and though there was a tendency in later writers to link them with particular places and identify them with familiar real birds, these reports seem to be complete fantasy.[84] One has therefore not merely to explain why these birds acquire a story of transformation, but to offer an account of an imaginative construction in which birds are connected with a tomb and with the dead.

As in the case of the stories of apotheosis, I think that the role of these birds as pointers to the other world is central. They provide a link between our world and the departed hero. An obvious comparison with the hero birds is the real sacred birds which were kept at temples in Greece and the Near East.[85] In one version of their story the Meleagrides were actually identified with the temple birds on Leros. Such temple birds seem to have been regarded with some reverence.[86] To an even greater degree than ordinary birds which were the objects of the art of augury they were felt to have special access to the god whose home they shared, and stories and fantasies tended to grow up around them; some accounts even describe them as the servants or attendants of the god.[87] We often find the idea that the birds accompany the gods to places where men cannot go. The arrival and departure of the temple birds at Eryx was supposed to be a sign of the arrival and departure of Aphrodite herself.[88] We may compare the swans that were supposed to draw Apollo's chariot from the inaccessible land of the Hyperboreans.[89] Swans were also supposed to join in the rites of the Hyperboreans, purifying Apollo's temple with water[90] (just as the birds of Achilles, Diomedes, or Memnon purify the tomb or temple of the hero).

The belief that special birds may have privileged access to a place which belongs to the gods or a hero is an important element in our stories. The birds of Achilles and Diomedes live not merely by a

[84] See under the individual stories in Cat. 2.

[85] See Arist. *HA* 614[a] for the general custom, and Bodson, 99.

[86] See Ael. *NA* 4. 42.

[87] See Ael. *NA* 17. 46.

[88] See Ael. *NA* 4. 2.

[89] Alcaeus, fr. 307.

[90] Ael. *NA* 11. 1.

temple or a tomb but on mysterious and deserted islands. One is tempted to see in these islands a form of the Isles of the Blest. This is quite clear in the case of Leuke,[91] which Achilles shared with a large number of translated heroes and ghosts. It is interesting that alternative versions of the stories of Achilles and Diomedes have them living on in the Isles of the Blest.[92] We do not know whether the Meleagrides lived on an island in Sophocles' play, but later versions locate them either on the mysterious island of the Electrides by the mouth of the Eridanus or as temple birds on the island of Leros.

That birds should be inhabitants of, or fly to, the Isles of the Blest is perhaps not surprising. They are the only animals which regularly form part of the heroes' environment there, and as sirens they frequently accompany banquets of the dead in art.[93] Their power of flight enables them to reach places normally denied to men. The chorus in the *Hippolytus* pray to become birds in order to fly to the Eridanus and then to the gardens of the gods.[94]

The case of Memnon is somewhat different in that his tomb is on the Hellespont, not on one of these mysterious islands. But the birds actually live in the home of Dawn in the East to which the hero has been removed or where he has been made immortal, and only return to the ordinary world to pay honour to his tomb or cenotaph. Just as the birds on the sacred island of Achilles or Diomedes are the only link with the invisible dead or translated hero, so the flight of the Memnon birds provides a point of contact between our world and the next. They are, in a sense, like the migrating doves of Eryx which announce to men the arrival and disappearance of Aphrodite.

In keeping with this role as intermediaries the birds are not direct continuations of the dead hero, but transformed human beings who are not completely translated like their master. These stories belong to a pattern that we often find in stories of heroization or translation, in which the removal of the hero is balanced by the change

[91] E. Rohde, *Psyche*[4] (Tübingen, 1907), ii. 371, thought that the island of Leuke was a mythical fantasy inspired by Homer's reference to the white rock at the entrance to the underworld (*Od.* 24. 11).

[92] In a skolion to Harmodius, *PMG* 894 (cf. Pind. *Ol.* 2. 79 f.).

[93] See Weicker, *Seelenvogel*, 14–15. We may compare among literary sources e.g. Lucian *Ver. Hist.* 2. 14, where a chorus of birds sing to the dead heroes.

[94] Eur. *Hipp.* 734 ff.

into a bird, plant, or stone of a human companion, or enemy, or witness.[95] We may compare in particular the stories of the translation of Ino and the disappearance of Persephone: the companions of Persephone become sirens to continue their search for their vanished mistress over the sea, while those of Ino continue to hover as *aithuiai* over the sea where she disappeared.[96] Once again, while the hero is fully translated, the companions go only part of the way and are left behind as memorials or pointers.

However, while these heroes have received some sort of elevation they are also all men who have died. Their stories tell of violence and suffering, and the reports of the fighting of the birds have darker, otherworldly associations. They are reminiscent of the reports of ghostly battles endlessly refought on the site of the battle of Marathon or on Achilles' island of Leuke.[97] The mock battles of the Memnon birds (and those of the birds of Meleager) should be understood not only as a service to the hero but also as a ghostly re-enactment of his own life and death: we have grim descriptions of how these birds, ever mindful of their warrior past, carry on fighting until they are all dead.[98] It is not so much perhaps that the hero lives on in the birds as that their fighting is an echo or *eidolon* of his own death.

There are thus a number of themes in these stories. The birds may be seen as symbols of eternal grief, like the other transformed mourners. But as well as expressing grief their actions have a public function: like the flight of the birds in the apotheosis stories they are an honour and a proof of the status of the dead hero. In this respect, whether they are the only earthly inhabitants of some distant and mysterious land or island, or whether they fly from there to us, the birds may be seen as intermediaries or pointers to the other world. Their actions are a continual miracle that corresponds to bird omens or the epiphanies of the gods in bird form.

One theme is perhaps peculiar to these stories. The service of

[95] Cf. e.g. AL 23, where two women who see and report the translation of Dryope are turned into trees.

[96] Persephone: Ov. *Met.* 5. 552 ff.; Ino: see Cat. 2 (Ismenides).

[97] Marathon: Paus. 1. 32. 4; Leuke: Philostr. *Her.* 214.

[98] See especially Ov. *Met.* 13. 613 ff.; QS 2. 653 ff.

these birds, whether it is caring for the hero's tomb or fighting commemorative battles, is a human cultural pattern, but the grief and violence expressed by these actions are appropriate to animals (and so perhaps is service to a god): what we have here is the incongruous transferring of a human cultural pattern into the non-human world. Indeed Aelian explicitly compares the actions of the Memnon birds with the human funeral games for Pelias or Achilles.[99] They offer a compromise between the natural world, with its inherent lack of respect for human order, and the familiar cultural patterns of human society. There are two oppositions here, between the living and the dead, and between human culture and nature, and a bridge between the first two is created by a compromise between the second two.[100] The cultural behaviour of these birds does not extend merely to caring for a tomb; perhaps its most extreme form is in Lycophron's description of how the birds of Diomedes actually produce a Greek city on their island, building rows of streets in imitation of Amphion and Zethus, the builders of Thebes.[101]

There are two further patterns of bird stories in which the other world or death is a central theme, but which apparently owe nothing to the local cult *aition* or to stories of heroization and translation. These are the *aitia* for eagles and heavenly birds, and the stories of the drowned heroes who become sea-birds.

Eagles occupy a special place in the Greek bird world. Although they are savage birds of prey they do not tend to be given the evil character that the Greeks attributed to the closely related hawks and vultures, and their transformation stories are quite different from those of the other birds of prey. They have become the birds of Zeus, and as such they are removed both from men and from the normal natural world and become birds of heaven.[102]

[99] *NA* 5. 1.

[100] It is possible, particularly in the case of the birds of Memnon, that there is something paradoxical about the respect for a human corpse shown by traditionally greedy birds of prey. Aelian says that though they are hawks they do not eat meat, and show self-control in their eating habits: *NA* 5. 1.

[101] Lyc. 601 f.

[102] In two cases, Aetos and Merops, transformation into an eagle is followed by catasterism. To some extent doves may also be seen as birds of heaven. They bring ambrosia for the gods in the *Odyssey*, and in the form of the Pleiades are set permanently in the sky. All the

Periphas was an early earth-born king of Athens who was worshipped by his people as Zeus himself. Zeus in anger turned him into an eagle but set him beside himself in heaven, made him king of the birds, and let him guard his sceptre. Similarly, Merops was an early king who once entertained Rhea at his home. Later his wife was killed by Artemis for daring to compare herself with the goddess, and Merops mourned her inconsolably until Rhea, in return for his hospitality, turned him into the bird that sits beside Zeus.[103]

Although these are especially privileged birds, they represent not so much an apotheosis or a simple elevation as a compromise between man and god. These transformations are not public signs suggesting a more mysterious unseen process, but a permanent change of nature, in which the heroes have won a place in heaven only at the expense of their human status. Merops was transformed to stop him feeling grief for his dead wife; we are explicitly told that as a bird he has lost human consciousness. Since Periphas' transformation is a punishment we must suppose that he too has lost something important. These myths reflect the limitations of human ambitions. These men may be kings, hosts of the gods, or even worshipped, and they suffer no ordinary human death, but they cannot quite cross the gulf which separates gods and men.

One can see a similar theme in Boios' story of the thieves.[104] These are four men who break into the sacred birthplace of Zeus to steal honey from the holy bees. This honey is clearly the food of the gods, and their action puts them alongside such celebrated sinners as Tantalus, who stole the food of the gods for his mortal companions. For this sacrilege they are turned into birds, but as in the case of Periphas this is a compromise rather than a simple punishment; we are told that because they saw the blood of Zeus the birds are very good omens. Rather, therefore, than simply being reduced to subhuman status, in one important sense they stand between men and gods.

The final pattern I want to consider is that of the drowned heroes

transformation stories of doves concern their relation to the gods or their heavenly associations: see Cat. 2 (doves).

[103] Periphas and Merops: Cat. 2 (eagles s.vv.).

[104] See Cat. 2 (thieves).

who become sea-birds. Ceyx is drowned in a shipwreck, and his wife throws herself into the sea in grief; she becomes a halcyon, and in some versions he too is transformed. Aisakos, Kyknos, the daughters of Alkyoneus, the daughters of Kinyras, and Hyperippe also attempt to drown themselves by a suicidal leap into the sea or lake. The Ismenides, companions of the drowned Ino, become sea-birds as they attempt to follow their mistress into the sea. The daughter of Sciron is pushed into the sea by her father, and Scylla is drowned by Minos in punishment for betraying her city. Sometimes transformation saves these heroes from actual drowning, sometimes it follows their death.

Underlying these stories is, I think, the idea that those who die at sea are in a peculiar and anomalous position: there is an essential connection between the manner of death and the peculiar afterlife in transformed form. We find in fact that often, even when a drowned or drowning hero does not become a bird, he is transformed into something else (a rock or an island, for instance),[105] or else he undergoes a different sort of metamorphosis altogether and becomes a god.[106] This pattern seems to owe less to belief in the magical transforming power of water[107] than to the desolate nature of the death that faces the heroes of these stories.

The Greeks and Romans recognized various categories of abnormal and restless dead, including those committing suicide and those suffering violent premature deaths.[108] But what is more relevant to drowning is that from Homer onwards[109] the unburied dead form a special class that cannot enter Hades. Those drowned at sea form an obvious category of the unburied, and the two are often linked. Perhaps the clearest statement of a special fate for the drowned is a passage of Achilles Tatius:[110] 'They say that the spirits

[105] e.g. Lichas, Perimele, Asteria, Hylas, Syrinx, Derketo.

[106] e.g. Dictynna, Ino, Palaemon, Glaucus, Derketo, Aegeus. For modern discussions of this pattern see R. Ginouvès, *Balaneutike* (Paris, 1962), 417–20; S. Eitrem, *Laographia* 7 (1923), 127–36; Jeanmaire, *Couroi*, 324–37; C. Gallini, *SMSR* 34 (1963), 61–90.

[107] For this view see Ninck, 138–80; S. Viarre, *L'Image et la pensée dans les Métamorphoses* (Paris, 1964), 61–90.

[108] See e.g. Lucian, *Philops.* 29.

[109] See the appeal of Patroclus' ghost in *Il.* 23. 71 ff.

[110] Ach. Tat. 5. 16.

of the drowned do not descend to Hades, but remain here wandering over the sea.' The Greek epigrams emphasize the homelessness of shipwrecked sailors and frequently link them with gulls.[111]

Whether the Greeks shared the common folk belief that the wandering spirits of drowned sailors took the form of gulls is uncertain.[112] However, we do not need to appeal to this general belief to argue that the special desolate fate of the drowned hero has influenced the stories of the transformations of particular heroes into sea-birds (in the *Ciris*, for instance, Scylla anticipates her desolate unburied death in language that recalls the shipwrecked sailors of the epigrams).[113] These transformed beings are not ghosts, but as in ghost stories the assumption is that a desolate unburied death which isolates the hero from other men and from the normal cultural pattern of burial leads to an anomalous and homeless afterlife. Thus we are told of the new life of the transformed Scylla:[114] 'Unhappy girl, saved from death in vain, she draws out a savage (*incultum*) life among the desolate rocks.' One might add that the lonely death of the heroes of these stories is not only technically unorthodox but also an expression of their emotional desolation and isolation even before their deaths: most of them are suicides, and the others are involved in family murders.

Finally, although the birds of these stories are not spirits it does seem that sea-birds were often thought of as uncanny mysterious creatures. A number of semi-mythical sea-birds, including the halcyon, the *kerylos*, and the *ciris*, were associated with strange superstitions and even given magical powers;[115] it is these birds of course that tend to collect transformation stories (the halcyon has four).

I have tried in this section to identify four patterns in which transformation to a bird and death are closely related. In all these

[111] e.g. *AP* 7. 374 or 285.

[112] Dionys. *Av*. 2. 5 says that gulls were once human fishermen, but does not mention their death. According to Charon of Lampsacus (*FGH* 262 F 3) white doves first appeared in Greece when the Persian fleet was wrecked off Athos.

[113] 441–2.

[114] *Ciris* 517 ff.

[115] See under these birds in W. D. Thompson, *A Glossary of Greek Birds*[2] (Oxford, 1958). The *aithuia* too is a mysterious bird, which was closely associated with Athene.

stories the change from man to bird is an ambiguous process that provides a link between this world and the next; and they all play upon the feeling that an object of intense grief or extreme violence cannot disappear without leaving something behind. But in each pattern the compromise suggested by transformation is of a different sort. In the first the stories describe how a bird appears as a sign of a mysterious translation. There is here no permanent identity of bird and hero, and the story serves rather to evoke the temporary wonder of the observer of a cult miracle than to express a fantasy about the survival of individual human consciousness. In the second pattern we again have the translation or death of a great hero, but in this case his mourning companions are transformed into mythical birds that continue to pay him honour. Unlike the birds of the first type, which appear only at the moment of translation, these appear regularly and are in some ways parallel to the birds that are kept in temples. At the imaginative level of these stories, however, they act as a compensation or balance for the hero's death[116] and serve as a permanent link between him and ourselves. The transference of human cult practice into the natural sphere is a mitigation of death, though only a mitigation; these birds are not the vehicles of the soul of the dead hero, neither do they suggest the immortality of his companions. These are nameless and unimportant in themselves, and it is the eternity of their grief and service rather than personal immortality that is the theme of the story.

Our third pattern describes how men come close to bridging the gap between men and gods but in the end are transformed into birds. Although the hero has won a place in heaven, or even immortality, he has lost his human status. Here transformation is not a symbol of some mysterious unseen process, but a literal and permanent change. In our final group the heroes who drown themselves in despair and now live a homeless and marginal existence on the sea-shore also win immortality of a sort; but this is akin to the homeless wandering of ghosts, and for them transformation ensures not so much a continuation of their personality as perpetual suffering and isolation. For these heroes Hades is not so much

[116] The birds of Memnon are called ἀντίψυχοι: see above, n. 83.

something to be conquered, but the normal community of the dead that is permanently closed to them.

I do not wish to imply that these stories form a group completely distinct from those considered in the earlier sections of the chapter. Many stories that play upon the link of birds with the dead also exemplify the pattern in which the home is opposed to the wilds. What one can say about all these stories is that the birds always point to a world beyond or opposed to our own. In most of the stories, but particularly those of the birds of prey and their victims, and those of the birds of the night, that other world is the world of animal disorder; in the stories of the heavenly or miraculous birds and the birds of the sea it may be instead, or as well, a supernatual beyond.

5

Plants

THERE are certain features common to all or most of the stories of transformations into plants. Heroes of these stories are often early or primitive men.[1] Natural forces and natural symbolism tend to play a much more important part than in the stories of birds or animals. The heroines are often daughters of rivers or the earth; the sun, winds, or water are often important characters in these stories;[2] and the transformation is most usually worked by the earth. But in spite of these common elements the stories fall into certain obvious groups.

The oldest stories, those of Smyrna and the Phaethontiades, belong to the pattern, discussed in the previous chapter, of the transformed mourner. In some ways they are closer to contemporary stories of mourning birds or stones than to the other tree stories. The story of the Phaethontiades, for instance, is similar to the stories of the hero birds and in particular to that of the Meleagrides, which first appears soon after it and may be influenced by it. The story of the myrrh tree also belongs to a pattern of transformation as an escape after an outrageous crime and is thus similar to that of Procne.[3] In later examples of the mourning tree (e.g. Platanos, Elate, or Philyra) the motif is often incorporated into the more common pattern of the story of the lover of a god (as in the story of the cypress).

[1] One source makes Daphne the oldest woman: Eust. on Dionys. *Per.* 416. Elate and Platanos are the sisters of giants. Some stories are set among primitive tribes such as the Messapians and Dryopes, and primitive wild figures such as Pan often occur.

[2] The winds are lovers of Hyakinthos or Pitys and enemies of the flower that Adonis becomes. Boreas also plants the first cypress in memory of his daughter. River-nymphs transform Syrinx. Klytie and Leucothoe are lovers of the sun, and the Phaethontiades are his daughters.

[3] The story of the myrrh tree is a little more complicated in that the transformation is a prelude to a miraculous birth from a tree. For the sort of ideas that may underlie this see Cat. 3*a* (Philyra; Platanos and Elate).

A second group of stories, mostly stemming from Nicander, characteristically take the form of local cult *aitia*. Here we have *aitia* not for types of trees but for particular ones, and the stories tend to be concerned not with the major gods but with the nymphs.[4]

But the third and by far the largest group comprises the normal *aitia* for types of plant. Here the stories take the form of *aitia* for the holy plant of a god and tell how a human favourite or lover of a god becomes the god's favoured plant.[5] They show few individual features, but tend to use just two plots, those of the stories of Daphne (transformation to preserve virginity) and of Hyakinthos (the dying lover). None of these stories appear before the Hellenistic period, and many of them are perhaps imitations of a familiar type by later poets and scholars rather than the product of separate local traditions. As the characteristic type of tree story it is with these that, after some preliminary observations, this chapter will be concerned.

It is immediately obvious that religion plays a larger role in each of these groups than in the bird stories. In the case of the mourning trees the historical practice of planting trees or flowers at a grave has undoubtably been an influence.[6] Such grave trees were often regarded as having a special link with a dead hero, and this was sometimes thought to give them ambiguous status. Thus the trees that grew beside Alcmaeon's tomb were called *parthenoi* (maidens)[7] and in this way assimilated to the groups of female mourners who were a traditional part of a hero's funeral. It is an easy step from this to the sisters of Phaethon, who are transformed as they mourn beside their brother's tomb and as trees still 'cradle him in their arms'.[8] In fact, in one story, that of Phyllis, our sources show a legend of mourning beside the tomb developing into a story of transformation.[9]

[4] e.g. the stories of Dryope, the Messapian shepherds, or Lotis: see Cat. 3*a*.

[5] e.g. Daphne, Syrinx, Pitys, Kyparissos, Ampelos, Myrsine, Melus, Mekon, Leuke, Leukothoe, Klytie, Elaia.

[6] For the general custom of planting grave trees see Serv. *A* 5. 760. For trees at the graves of particular heroes, *Il.* 6. 419; Hdt. 4. 34; AR 4. 1476 or 2. 843 f.; Paus. 2. 28. 7, 8. 24. 7, 9. 25. 1; Pliny *NH* 15. 119.

[7] Paus. 8. 24. 7; it was forbidden to cut down these trees. Cf. the trees round the grave of Hyrnetho: Paus. 2. 28. 7.

[8] Eur. fr. 782.

[9] See Cat. 3*a* s.v.

The local *aitia* (our second group) tell not of ordinary trees but of trees that have some special connection with the nymphs. Nymphs were regarded as having a close association with trees: in Homer they merely live in groves, but later sources and inscriptions reveal a much closer relationship of nymphs with particular trees.[10] Nymphs plant them, own and take pride in them, and sometimes live in them; in the *Homeric Hymn to Aphrodite* they die with their trees.[11] Ovid goes still further and gives us trees with human spirits.[12] Clearly such beliefs have influenced stories such as that of Dryope, in which Nicander tells how when Dryope mysteriously disappeared and became a nymph a tree and a spring appeared, and two women who witnessed her disappearance were turned into trees.[13] The third group, the *aitia* for sacred plants, feature the gods not only in their aetiological conclusion, but as the main characters in their stories.

What all this shows is that the myths can make diverse use of the various religious connections of plants; it certainly does not mean that one can offer a wholesale explanation of transformation in terms of some concept such as the tree-god, the tree-spirit, or the tree-soul.[14] There is little evidence that the Greeks ever believed in tree-souls or tree-spirits in so far as this implies an identity of plant and human being. The reflection of a dead man in his grave tree is a limited and external one: that Alcmaeon's trees were known as *parthenoi* suggests, if anything, an ambiguity between trees and mourners rather than between the trees and the dead hero himself. While trees do have close connections with the nymphs, in Greek sources at any rate this falls short of imagining a tree with a human spirit.[15] It is only in Ovid that we find anything approaching this, in

[10] Homer: *Il.* 20. 8–9. For the later closer associations see A. Henrichs, *Bull. Soc. Am. Pap.* 16 (1979), 85–108.

[11] 256 ff. This becomes a regular explanation in the scholia of the word 'hamadryad': see e.g. on AR 2. 476.

[12] e.g. *Met.* 8. 771.

[13] AL 32.

[14] For the tree-god explanation see Boetticher; L. Malten, *Hermes* 74 (1939), 176–206, and 75 (1940), 168–76. For the idea that the stories have their origin in the notion of the hamadryad, see W. Mannhardt, *Wald- und Feld-Kulte*², ii (Berlin, 1905), 4–20.

[15] More common are stories of a nymph's mourning or anger when her favourite tree is cut down: e.g. Callim. *Dem.* 85; AR 2. 471 ff. When ancient sources explain the function of grave trees, tree-souls are never mentioned; typical is the comment of our source on the

the bleeding tree of Lotis or the one that Erisychthon cuts down,[16] and it is more plausible to consider this an Italian belief, or a literary conceit following on from and going one step further than Virgil's description of the bleeding bush of Polydorus,[17] than a traditional Greek belief.

Besides, as noted earlier, both the stories of mourning trees and the local *aitia* have more in common with other categories of transformation stories than with the typical tree stories, and belief in the tree-soul is therefore unlikely to be the origin of the type as a whole. The largest group of tree stories, on the other hand, the generic *aitia* of gods' holy plants, do form a characteristic type quite unlike the patterns of the stories of birds and animals; but although they do feature gods and sacred plants there is no reason to believe that they have their origin in the worship of tree-gods. We know that tree cults existed in classical Greece,[18] but these stories do not end with the worship of a tree; nor could they, since they are generic *aitia* explaining a whole species, not particular holy trees.[19] It is perhaps significant that Artemis, the goddess who is more than any other associated with trees and tree worship,[20] does not play an important role in a single story of transformation into a tree. To understand this type one needs to take a wider view of the imaginative associations of trees and plants.

So much for preliminary observations. We turn now to the generic *aitia* for plants. They usually take the form of explaining the relation of a god to his holy plant by telling how his human favourite

cypresses that spring up when the daughters of Eteocles fall down a well: they are a τέρψις ἀνθρώποις καὶ μνήμη ἐπ' αὐταῖς (*Geop.* 11. 4).

[16] Lotis: *Met.* 9. 344 ff.; Erisychthon: 8. 739 ff. (Ovid is the only source who sees the death of a tree-spirit in the cutting down of this tree).

[17] *A* 3. 24 ff., where there is, however, a clear distinction between the hero beneath the ground and the bush.

[18] For tree cults see Boetticher; O. Kern, *RE* s.v. *Baumkultus*; Malten (the two articles cited in n. 14); Nilsson, *GGR* 209–12; Henrichs (art. cit. n. 10).

[19] The only exceptions are Ovid's story of Philemon and Baucis, and a Syrian version of the story of Daphne (see Philostr. *VH* 1. 16). These are both set in Asia Minor, where we know that tree cults were particularly popular: see Malten, *Hermes* 74 (1939), 197–202; V. Müller, *Röm. Mitt.* 44 (1929), 59–86.

[20] See Nilsson, *GGR* 486–92; she has a number of epithets including καρυᾶτις, δενδρεᾶτις, δάφνια, κυπαρίσσια.

or, more often, lover either dies or is transformed to preserve her virginity. There are two obvious questions about this type. First, why should the cult relations of plants be taken up, whereas birds tend to be explained in terms of their natural features? Secondly, why do these plant stories take the form they do? Among bird stories even those which do tell of the special relation of birds to a god do not necessarily take this form. (The story of Meropis, for instance, the owl of Athene, is the story of a human enemy.) Stories of stones may tell of the sexual relations of men and gods, but the characteristic heroes of these stories are punished rapists.

One could make various guesses in answer to the first question. Perhaps the relation of sacred plant and god was considered a closer and more intimate one than that of a god and his favourite bird. Trees do not have the differences in behaviour, song, and social groupings that characterize birds. The study of bird behaviour for purposes of augury became a specialized skill, and pseudo-scientific works full of their supposed hatreds and friendships offer material for many of Boios' transformation stories. But perhaps the answer to our first question is closely connected with the answer to the second one. It was because trees provided an opportunity for a sentimental love story that these stories became the *aitia* for the favoured plants of the gods. (We find the story of the dying lover who is transformed into a plant even when this plant is not connected with a god.)[21] What is it about plants that inspires such stories?

Certain aspects of the story will follow from the name of the plant. It is generally true that the sex of the hero will depend on the gender of the plant that he turns into. Trees, which in Greek are feminine, are therefore usually women, and flowers, which tend to be masculine, are usually men, or rather boys.[22] However, these connections do not in themselves take us very far. The principle that the gender of a name will dictate the sex of the hero is one that applies in all types of aetiological stories (though in the case of the bird stories women are often not favourites or lovers but enemies of the gods). We may take it that the stories are illustrations of some

[21] e.g. Narcissus, Smilax, Smyrna.

[22] There are exceptions. ἡ κυπάρισσος is a transformed boy. Presumably the masculine ending of the name was considered more important than actual gender.

expression such as 'Apollo loves the laurel'. The question is why this formula has prompted such a story in the case of trees and not, for instance, in the case of Apollo's love for the swan or for the lyre.

Since these stories tend to be late and in many cases probably have a literary origin it seems useful to look at the metaphorical use of plants by ancient poets. First, we find that the garland of a god or victor may be said to have a partiuclarly intimate relation with its wearer, sometimes even a sexual one: for instance, Pindar describes how the people of Sicily are joined[23] with the golden leaves of their Olympic victories. This imaginative view of the role of the sacred plant takes us some way towards the spirit of our stories. We are told that Apollo's love for Daphne did not cease and that he is now a lover (*erastes*) of its leaves,[24] while Ovid pictures him embracing and kissing the tree itself.[25] More generally the relation of a god with a heroine who does not become a tree may be described as if she were a plant: Zeus is a 'gardener' and a 'grower' as a lover of Io,[26] while marriage or seduction is often described in terms of plucking fruit or leaves.[27] It would be possible to see transformation stories as a literal reflection of such metaphors. We may compare here the sexual metaphors that colour Apollo's relations with his prophetess, the sibyl[28] (who at Delphi at least is closely associated with, and in some ways even corresponds to, his holy plant).[29]

Flowers have much more obvious erotic associations. They are regularly seen as symbols of, enticements to, and products of love.[30] It would perhaps be surprising, therefore, if a flower story was not

[23] μιχθέντα: see *Nem.* 1. 17 ff. (the sexual sense of μιχθέντα is reinforced by the reference to μναστῆρα in l. 18). Cf. fr. 20, *Nem.* 2. 22; 4. 21.

[24] Lib. *Narr.* 11.

[25] *Met.* 1. 555.

[26] Aesch. *Supp.* 584 and 592.

[27] See e.g. Pind. *Pyth.* 9. 109 f. or 37.

[28] For the prophetess as bride of the god see e.g. Paus. 10. 12. 2; K. Latte, *HTR* 33 (1940), 9–18. For, more specifically, the sibyl's ecstasy as sexual possession see E. Norden, *Aeneis VI*[4] (Darmstadt, 1957) on 6. 77. In Longinus 13. 2 the Pythia is 'pregnant with the god's spirit'.

[29] At Delphi she was known as Daphne or Daphnis: see Paus. 10. 5. 5 and DS 4. 66. The Pythian priestess was supposed to shake the laurel as she spoke, and the laurel became a symbol of the god's prophetic power (see e.g. *Geop.* 11. 2). In one version Daphne herself became an oracle: Plut. *Ages.* 9; cf. Nonn. 42. 389.

[30] Flowers spring up when Zeus and Hera make love (*Il.* 14. 347 ff.) or from Aphrodite's tears (see Bion, *Lament for Adonis* 65–6). A narcissus entices and traps Persephone (*Hymn. Hom. Cer.* 5 ff.).

an erotic one. Among our stories of flowers and shrubs there are some that stress the erotic associations in the *aition*. In nearly all of them these associations also help to determine the plot: thus Krokos becomes the *anthos eroton*, 'the flower of love', and Karpos is described as a 'flower of love' while still a boy.[31]

Secondly, we may note that trees (and also flowers) are frequently comparisons for human growth and beauty; the most famous early example is the comparison of Nausicaa to the palm at Delos.[32] Certain descriptions like *habrokomes* ('of soft hair' or 'of soft leaves') can be applied both to women and boys and to trees.[33] Not surprisingly the heroes of the transformation stories tend to be beautiful young girls and boys. In particular, the daughters of Eteocles who fall down a well become lovely trees resembling the young girls they once were;[34] Ovid says of Daphne's change that only her beauty survived her transformation.[35] In the case of flowers the link with youth and beauty is still more obvious.[36] By contrast we are never told that birds are beautiful: at best they have a beautiful song, and even then it is a mournful beauty.

Such comparisons may take on morbid associations, since the flower of youth is very frequently contrasted with old age or with death. We find a *topos* of this form in Greek and Latin epitaphs, which compare the death of a young girl or young boy to the withering of a flower.[37] Not surprisingly, therefore, all the stories of flowers are morbid ones: they tell of boys who die prematurely (Ovid, for instance, in a simile that is distinct from the actual transformation, compares the dying Hyakinthos to a broken flower).[38] This is true of a number of the tree stories too, since although the tree lives on, the death of its leaves is again a traditional comparison for human mortality[39] (and it is often the leaves of the tree, the garland of the god, that are important to the *aition* of our stories).

[31] Krokos: Nonn. 12. 86; Karpos: Nonn. 11. 397.

[32] Hom. *Od.* 6. 163.

[33] See *AP* 12. 256, which plays upon both meanings and compares a group of boys to a grove of plants. Cf. Nonn. 13. 91.

[34] *Geop.* 11. 4.

[35] *Met.* 1. 552.

[36] See, for instance, expressions of the form 'the flower of youth' (e.g. Aesch. *Supp.* 663).

[37] See R. Lattimore, *Themes in Greek and Latin Epitaphs* (Urbana, 1942), 195.

[38] *Met.* 10. 190 ff.

[39] Most famously in *Il.* 6. 146 ff.

Not only do plant heroes die prematurely, but two of the stories concern lovers of Hades. With these we may compare those epitaphs which compare or contrast the death of a young girl with a marriage; these too sometimes use plant metaphors, for instance 'no husband, but grim Hades plucked her bloom'.[40] Part of the point of these stories is the way that the plants suggest both the beauty of the hero and his fragility and premature end: 'but short-lived is his flower; for the winds from which it takes its name shake off the flower so delicately clinging and doomed too easily to fall.'[41] The plant is often blood-coloured or bears the marks of grief.

This leads on to a further important point: in spite of the suggestions of growth and fruitfulness which plants carry, all these stories are to some extent tragedies in which the love of god and mortal is unfulfilled. In the cases just mentioned it is a premature death that is responsible for this (in the case of the lovers of Hades it was impossible for the relation to be a fruitful one in human terms and for the lover to bear a child).[42] In a number of stories, however, it is the heroine's extreme love of virginity that frustrates the god, and the tree perpetuates her virgin state.

Plants are often used in Greek and Latin poetry as symbols or metaphors for virginity. One thinks, for instance, of the garland from the uncut meadow in Euripides' *Hippolytus*; in Catullus' wedding hymn virginity is praised as a flower in a hidden garden unpolluted by human touch, and in what is probably the model for this comparison Sappho describes the hyacinth which shepherds have not trampled on.[43] Such associations colour ancient descriptions of Daphne's tree. It is a symbol of chastity[44] (in fact Callimachus' description of the holy laurel, 'I am holy and no men trample on me',[45] recalls the passage of Sappho). One account explains its evergreen bloom as due to Daphne's remaining untouched by Apollo.[46] Syrinx, who escaped Pan's love, became a

[40] See Lattimore (op. cit. n. 37), 193.

[41] Ov. *Met.* 10. 737 ff. Cf. Adonis' anemone.

[42] On the infertility of Hades see R. Garland, *The Greek Way of Death* (London, 1985), 72–3.

[43] Catull. 62. 39 ff.; Sappho, fr. 105c.

[44] See e.g. Ov. *Met.* 10. 92 'innuba laurus'; cf. Nonn. 48. 261.

[45] Fr. 194. 39.

[46] Schol. Lyc. 6.

test of virginity in a shrine of Artemis.[47] More specifically the *topos* of the untouched plant suggests not just virginity but a removal from normal human contact, whether in a hidden garden, as in Catullus, or (more commonly) in the wilds, as in the *Hippolytus*. This perhaps helps to explain why the virgin heroines, Daphne, Lotis, Pitys, and Syrinx, are all hunters in the wilds; they are located there not only because that is where their tree must originate,[48] but because their virgin life in the wilds is a literal form of the metaphors of the untouched plant.

There is clearly a conflict between the role of the plant as a symbol of virginity and the suggestions it carries of growth and fertility. In fact the relation between the god and his sacred plant implied by our stories is an ambiguous one. The transformation into a tree is a form of miraculous compromise or mediation. It enables the heroine in plant form to be both a lover of the god and yet to retain her virginity and purity. A plant can suggest all the metaphors of love and of luxurious growth and fruitfulness, and yet since plants do not reproduce by sexual intercourse it can avoid the suggestions of pollution and sickness that invariably accompany the transformation of a lover of a god into an animal. This ambiguous state is one that is also seen in the case of Apollo's prophetesses, who are both virgins and lovers of the gods.

A second ambiguity is that these stories tell both of a death and of life and growth. I have suggested that certain plants, and the flowers in particular, may be seen as symbols of mortality and fragility in themselves; in all cases, however, the plant has an important role as a balance or compromise with death worked by the god's love. There is on the one hand a tendency to regard transformation into a plant as a form of death even where there is no explicit mention of the hero dying first.[49] On the other hand the plant is often seen as a symbol of growth and life that contrasts with and qualifies the

[47] Ach. Tat. 8. 6.

[48] In cult and myth the laurel is seen as a wild plant. It is brought from the 'steep mountains' in Callim. fr. 194. 34 f. It also covers the Cyclops' cave in the *Odyssey*.

[49] The transformation of Pitys is a μόρος αὐτόχθων (Nonn. 42. 261). Pliny says that the *smilax* is 'lugubris' and pollutes the holy rites because it is a transformed woman: *NH* 16. 154 f.

hero's death: 'in the only way you can be', Orpheus tells the dead Hyakinthos, 'you are immortal.'[50]

This tension between growing and dying follows from the unusual nature of this type of transformation. Descriptions of transformations into trees have a characteristic form which tells of the hero being swallowed up by the earth and in exchange a plant miraculously arising out of the earth;[51] we do not merely have a change from one form of life to another. The plant in this sense mediates between what is under the earth, from where it appeared and where it still has its roots, and the living. This mediation becomes particularly striking in the case of plants that originate not merely beneath the surface of the earth but in the underworld. Leuke, for instance, was a lover of Hades who was brought to the surface by Heracles in tree form. Minthe was another lover of Hades who was trampled into the earth by Demeter and reappeared as a plant.[52] In a sense the miracle of transformation becomes an illustration of a much more basic belief which sees the appearance of even ordinary plants as a miraculous act of giving birth by the earth. There are many stories of the mysterious appearance of trees from the earth even without a transformation. We often find the same language used of the birth of human beings and of plants;[53] Daphne is said to have earth as her mother. Such a metaphor already implies an ambiguity of man and nature which takes us halfway to the stories of transformation.

In conclusion, therefore, it is not difficult to see why *aitia* for the gods' holy plants take the form of stories of their dying lovers. Trees are used in these stories to express a series of tensions, between love and virginity, between living and dying (and in particular between the earth as a source of life and as the resting place of the dead), and

[50] Ov. *Met.* 10. 164 ff.

[51] See Cat. 3*a* under Daphne, Syrinx, Pitys, Leucothoe. Disappearance into the earth can take various forms: Daphne begs to be swallowed up, Leucothoe is buried alive as a punishment, Minthe is trampled into the earth, the daughters of Eteocles fall down a well.

[52] See Cat. 3*a* (Leuke; Minthe).

[53] The word *φύω* is used frequently both of men and of the earth's production of plants. *τίκτω* is sometimes used of the earth as well as human beings, e.g. Aesch. fr. 44; cf. Eur. fr. 839. Bion's *Lament for Adonis* says that the bloody ground *τίκτει ῥόδον* (66). In Servius this becomes a transformation: *A* 10. 18.

between the gods and men. If the stories are tragedies, they at least end with a birth and new life. By contrast, the stories of petrification, which will be considered in the next chapter, work a rather bleaker mediation between the world of the living and the world below.

6

Stones

THERE are a number of obvious common features in the stories of petrification. First, their character is dominated by the lifelessness of stones. Trees are animate only in a limited sense and, like stones, tend to be memorials rather than continuations of the human being, but whereas trees are living and positive memorials stones tend to be more often grim reminders or warnings.[1] Secondly, petrification permanently fixes an object in a place; these stories, unlike most of the others we have been considering, concern particular landmarks and objects, and being petrified is sometimes described in terms of being rooted to the ground.[2] Thirdly, as in the tree stories, the gods, or otherworldly figures of some sort, play a crucial part; but whereas transformation into a tree is normally worked by the love or pity of a god petrificiation is normally a punishment for their enemies. Any discussion of these stories must take account of these features.

It has been suggested that the explanation of these stories is very simple: they are prompted by the need to account for certain stones that appear to have human or animal form.[3] This answer, however, only takes us a certain way. Although they all have an aetiological form it seems likely that only a few of these stories explain and are thus prompted by real stones of this sort.[4] So it must be that the

[1] See Ovid on Battos' stone (2. 706 f.): 'qui nunc quoque dicitur index, | inque nihil merito vetus est infamia saxo.'

[2] e.g. *Od.* 13. 163, of the Phaeacian ship; cf. AL 39. 6, of Arsinoe.

[3] See Bubbe, 23.

[4] See the discussion of the individual stories in Part 4 of the Catalogue. In most cases there are reasons for supposing that the stone has been invented (typically e.g. AL 38 tells us that the stone form of the wolf that attacked Peleus' flocks remained there for a long time, i.e. that it no longer exists). Sometimes we can see a story of a human-shaped rock developing from a story of a rock known as 'the stone of X' (see Cat. 4*a* under Lichas or Kerkopes). Sometimes the stories explain cult statues. The only well-documented human-shaped rock is that of Niobe on Mount Sipylus. But even here the story is earlier than reports of the rock.

characteristic pattern of the stone stories had some appeal in itself, and it is the imaginative interest of this pattern that I shall be looking at here.

There are two possible approaches to these stories. The first takes its starting point in the peculiar relation of these stones to the gods and to death. The second looks at stones as metaphors for human behaviour and considers why petrification is an appropriate punishment for particular heroes.

I shall begin with their relation to the gods and to death. It was noted earlier that a transformation into a bird sometimes had an important public function as a sign or epiphany. This function was also noted in a few of the tree stories: not in the generic *aitia* for species of trees but in the stories of the miraculous appearance of particular trees. However, it is in the stories of stones that this aspect of transformation is most important. Since stones are particular, fixed, and permanent they make ideal markers or memorials. Moreover, petrification is a peculiar sort of transformation: it is not a change of shape but rather a continuing anomaly in which an inanimate substance assumes a human or animal form. Whereas the bird or tree stories explain the ordinary objects around us petrifications explain stones that are exceptional or unusual. These stones are therefore not only memorials of a past miracle but continuing wonders. Quintus Smyrnaeus calls the petrified Hecuba 'a great wonder even for men to come'.[5]

Two of our earliest transformations, that of the snake at Aulis and that of the Phaeacian ship, are explicitly described as divine signs. The ship was petrified as a warning from Poseidon, and the petrification of the snake made it clear that this animal was a divine portent.[6] In fact there are a number of petrifications of animals and objects in later myths.[7] In most cases the fate of the animal or object is not an issue, and the petrification is not a reflection of its character or behaviour; what matters is how these changes demonstrate the attitude of the gods to human characters in the story.

[5] QS 14. 351.

[6] See ch. 1 n. 3.

[7] e.g. those of the wolf enemy of Peleus, the snake enemy of Orpheus, the golden altar of Midas, the ship of Pompilos: see Cat. 4*b*.

A second group of stories in which petrification functions as a sign is, like the bird epiphanies, concerned with apotheosis. Aspalis hangs herself, her body disappears, and a cult statue appears in the temple of Artemis. The disappearance of Dictynna and Alcmena is followed by the appearance of a cult statue and a holy stone.[8] One may compare the more orthodox transformation of Iodama.[9] She was a priestess of Athene who was petrified after entering the goddess's temple at night. She still stands there and receives the ritual chant 'Iodama lives and asks for fire'. Like the bird epiphany of Ktesilla the appearance of these stones is a sign: they are the *aition* for a cult. These petrifications differ from those of the animals in that their function is not an entirely external one: these translated women are the heroes of their stories, and their fate is of interest in itself (Iodama, we are told, still lives). In their continuing relation to a translated human being, therefore, these stones have a mysterious or otherworldly character. They are in a sense doubles or substitutes that provide a point of contact with an unseen world. Vernant has discussed this function of stone images:[10] he draws attention to the way that binding a statue of Actaeon to a rock helps to control the ravages of the hero's ghost.[11] Particularly relevant to the stone of Alcmena, which is found in her empty coffin, are the stone doubles found in an empty tomb at Midea.[12] In these cases at least petrification is a sign of some mysterious invisible process, and the stone figure is a compromise not only between natural material and human form, but between men and the other world.

In many other transformation stories, however, the stones are not signs, and the petrification is important chiefly to the person being transformed. There are two observations one might make about the role of the gods and death in these stories:

1. Many of them make petrification a consequence of direct contact with or, more particularly, intrusion upon some god or otherworldly spirit. At the simplest level, in a pattern that has many

[8] See Cat. 4*a* (Aspalis, Britomartis, Alcmena).

[9] See Cat. 4*a* s.v.

[10] J. P. Vernant, *Mythe et pensée chez les grecs* (1965), 251–64. Cf. E. Benveniste, *Rev. Phil.* 6 (1932), 118–35; P. Guillon, *Rev. Phil.* 10 (1936), 209–35; G. Roux, *REA* 62 (1960), 5–40.

[11] Paus. 9. 38. 5.

[12] See C. Picard, *Rev. Phil.* 7 (1933), 343–54; Nilsson, *GGR* 379.

folk-tale parallels, heroes are petrified with horror and fear on seeing the Gorgon (or in another story Cerberus). This simple amoral pattern becomes in other stories a pattern of punishment for intruding or spying upon a higher god. We find occasional instances of this pattern in the other categories of transformation stories, but among stone stories it is the dominant type.[13] It is possible that part of the reason for this is that the continuing anomaly of the human-figured stone has helped to prompt a story of some unusually direct contact with the god.

2. Most heroes of petrification stories die rather than being translated like Iodama or Aspalis (Perseus is described as bearing a 'stony death').[14] Nevertheless their death is a peculiar one in that instead of descending to Hades they remain among us for all to see. In our descriptions of Niobe, for instance, there is an ambiguity first between woman and stone and secondly between the living and the dead: her mourning is such an intense identification with the dead that it isolates her from the living and makes her stand permanently between the two worlds. The first ambiguity is seen already in the Homeric description: 'even as a stone she broods over her woes'.[15] The references in tragedy show that this ambiguity may be reduced to the second. In Aeschylus she sits on the tomb of her children and will not leave it.[16] In Sophocles' *Antigone* she is seen as a parallel to Antigone, who is going alive to Hades (i.e. being buried alive); in the *Electra* we are told how she weeps in her rocky tomb.[17] It is interesting that the petrifications of Cadmus and Harmonia, Lichas and Hecuba all take their starting points in reports of tombs of these heroes.[18]

We come now to the second approach proposed at the start of this

[13] Thus e.g. Orphe and Lyko spy on Dionysos, Battos and an old Cyprian woman reveal the hiding-places of Hermes and Aphrodite, Pandareos trespasses into the cave of Zeus and steals his holy dog, Aglauros imposes herself between Hermes and her sister, Iunx interferes with the marriage of Zeus and Hera, Kalydon sees Artemis naked, Kelmis and Pyrrhos both attempt to assault Rhea.

[14] Pind. *Pyth.* 10. 48.

[15] *Il.* 24. 617.

[16] Fr. 154a.

[17] *Ant.* 823 ff. (cf. 811); *El.* 150 ff.

[18] In the case of those petrified on seeing the Gorgon or Cerberus it is perhaps appropriate that those who see a creature of the underworld become themselves a form of the underworld in the world of the living: cf. J. P. Vernant, *La Mort dans les yeux* (Paris, 1985), 79–82.

chapter. These stones are not only points of contact with the gods and the dead; most of the stories have a logic according to which petrification reflects human qualities and behaviour. I have suggested that animal and plant metaphors tell us something about the meaning of transformation into an animal or plant; here too it seems reasonable to ask what it would mean for a man to be described as a stone.

In the case of birds and animals transformation is often closely linked with some particularly savage or inhuman behaviour. We might expect something similar here. Stone metaphors often suggest an inhuman or cruel quality in an attitude or character.[19] There are a few reflections of such comparisons in our stories: Arsinoe who lets her lover commit suicide is an obvious example of cold-hearted cruelty.[20] In Ovid's descriptions we sometimes find a direct moral symbolism, so that petrification becomes only an intensification of an already existing stone-like state.[21] But one may suspect that in these cases the colouring of the story is Ovid's own invention; we find nothing like it in our other sources, and even those stories which appear only in Ovid are sometimes open to a different interpretation.[22]

In fact we very rarely find that petrified heroes are symbols of stone-like qualities; most are not hard-hearted or cruel but prying or lacking in judgement. Their characteristic crime is not savage behaviour but betrayal of a god. What we normally find is that the peculiar qualities of stone are actually a reversal and sometimes a pathetic contrast with the nature of the human being.

There is first of all a group of stories in which petrification is a punishment for lust, particularly male lust. In this class belong Pyrrhos, Kelmis, and Daphnis; the first two assault Rhea, and Daphnis is unfaithful to his nymph lover.[23] We may also include the

[19] Usually in a passive sense, in such expressions as 'your heart is harder than stone' (e.g. *Od.* 23. 103), but also in a more active sense: see schol. *Il.* 13. 136.

[20] See Cat. 4*a* (Arkeophon and Arsinoe).

[21] e.g. *Met.* 10. 241 f. and 2. 822 ff.

[22] It has been argued in ch. 1 that one of the main differences between Ovid and his sources is the moral symbolism of his versions. Ovid is particularly fond of stone metaphors: see D. F. Bauer, *TAPA* 93 (1962), 1–21.

[23] Daphnis' alternative punishment is blinding, another regular punishment for sexual crimes; see above, ch. 3 n. 101 and text.

chief victims of the Gorgon's head, Polydectes and Phineus.[24] It has been pointed out[25] that both are aggressors against Perseus' women, his mother and his bride, and it is to protect these that they are transformed. I noted earlier that on the most basic level they belong to the folk-tale pattern in which those who see a magical figure are transformed; we can now see that they also exemplify this further pattern of crime and punishment. In all these cases transformation is the negation of human feeling and sensation, and is therefore a reversal of excessive desire or lust. We may compare Propertius' prayer that his rival should turn to stone in the middle of making love, or Callicles' description in the *Gorgias* of a life without pleasure as 'the life of a stone'.[26]

Most commonly this is a male pattern, but there are at least two stories of sexual crimes of women. The Propoitides are transformed after a period of promiscuity, and Iunx becomes either a stone or a magic bird after either seducing Zeus herself or making him fall in love with Io.[27] It has been suggested[28] that the bird and the stone represent opposite extremes of continual movement or none at all. Since the continual movement of the bird induces a sexual fascination and is thus a continuation of Iunx's power it is possible that the petrified state, the other extreme, is a reversal of this power.

In some cases we have not so much a punishment for lust as a pathetic contrast of stones and human love. Thus the loving couple Olenos and Lethaia become stones on Ida ('once two hearts joined in close embrace', as Ovid puts it, 'but now stones');[29] the unusually loving Haemon and Rhodope are now neighbouring mountains.[30] In both these stories it is arrogance that is the crime, but it is perhaps the heroes' love that dictates their punishment. One may compare passages such as the description of the eyeless statues in the *Aga-*

[24] See Cat. 4*a* (victims of the Gorgon's head).

[25] See T. P. Howe, *AJA* 58 (1954), 209–21.

[26] Prop. 2. 9. 47 f.; *Gorgias* 494 A, and see note in commentary of E. R. Dodds (Oxford, 1959).

[27] See Cat. 4*a* s.vv.

[28] M. Detienne, *The Gardens of Adonis* (Eng. tr. Hassocks, 1977), 84–5.

[29] *Met.* 10. 69 f.

[30] See Cat. 4*a* (Haemon and Rhodope). Ps.-Plutarch makes them an incestuous pair. Lucian refers to Rhodope as one of the μαχλόταται heroines.

memnon, which are now hateful to the deserted husband 'since Aphrodite is absent from their empty eyes'.[31] Ovid's story of Pygmalion describes the opposite process in which a lifeless statue becomes a human lover.[32]

Secondly, stones are not only incapable of feeling or desire; they are also proverbially silent.[33] Again in most stories the stone is not so much a memorial of the unusually silent man as a reversal. Petrification is an appropriate punishment for a crime of speech, since being turned into stone ensures that the criminal will never speak again. Battos witnesses Hermes' theft of Apollo's cattle, and then promises his silence: 'that stone will speak of your theft before I do', he claims.[34] Needless to say he immediately breaks his promise, and Hermes turns him into stone (his very name 'Battos' appears to characterize him as a talker).[35] In a similar story a gossiping old woman reveals the hiding place of Aphrodite and is also turned into stone.[36]

The Kerkopes are petrified for lying.[37] An alternative story has them being turned into apes, but here too there is a link between speech and punishment: 'But first he took from them the power of speech, the use of tongues born for vile perjuries, leaving them only the power to complain in raucous tones.'[38] No speech at all and meaningless chatter are complementary punishments for unscrupulous talkers.

Niobe's immediate punishment is not her petrification but the killing of her children. But it is interesting that she too belongs to this pattern in that her crime is 'boldness of speech'.[39] Several accounts contrast her previous love of chattering with her present silence.[40]

Thirdly, stones cannot move. As was noted earlier, permanence

31 Aesch. *Ag.* 416 f. Cf. Eur. *Alcestis* 348 f. on a statue of Alcestis.

32 *Met.* 10. 243 ff.

33 See e.g. Theognis 567; *AP* 7. 380; Pl. *Symp.* 198.

34 *Met.* 2. 696.

35 See Cat. 4*a* s.v.

36 See Cat. 4*a* (Cyprian old woman).

37 See Cat. 4*a* s.v.

38 Ov. *Met.* 14. 98 ff.

39 See e.g. *AP* 16. 131; cf. Aesch. fr. 154. 17 or Ov. *Met.* 6. 213.

40 See e.g. *AP* 16. 134. We may compare Kragaleus, the judge who gives a verdict against Apollo, Pandareos, in one version a perjurer, or Haemon and Rhodope, who call themselves Hera and Zeus.

and a fixed position are important features both of those transformed animals which act as a sign or warning from the gods and of those stones which are seen as a memorial of, or link with, vanished heroes. Sometimes, however, there is a more particular relevance. Perhaps the most obvious case is the story of the Phaeacian ship petrified for taking Odysseus home and as a sign that free passage across the seas is no longer allowed. Homer describes how it is rooted to the sea-bed, and has the Phaeacians ask each other who had bound the swift ship in the sea.[41] We may compare the story of the Teumessian fox and the dog of Cephalus. Since the one can never be caught and the other can never miss its prey Zeus resolves the dilemma by turning them both into unmoving stone.[42]

It is questionable whether the blindness of stones is relevant to our stories in so direct a way, although the motif of looking is important. In the basic folk-tale pattern of those who are transformed after seeing a witch or magician it is more natural to describe the petrification as an instinctive reaction of shock and helplessness than as an appropriate punishment which ensures that the criminal does not see again. In so far as these stories do exemplify a pattern of crime and punishment the crime may be defined in a more general way and the punishment may be seen as a wider insensitivity. As was noted earlier, the victims of the Gorgon's head are all victims of lust. Calydon's seeing of Artemis is a sexual intrusion that perhaps puts him in the same class as the rapists Pyrrhos or Kelmis. What one can say is that the eyes and seeing have an important expressive function in Greek myths and poetry. It was in the emptiness of the eyes of Helen's statues that the absence of Aphrodite was most apparent, and in Greek mythology blinding is a common punishment for a sexual offence. The blindness of statues therefore sometimes has a metaphorical if not a literal relevance in these stories.

The story of Niobe needs further consideration, since it is slightly different from the others and rather more complicated. First, we have seen that her story belongs to the pattern of crime and punishment in which talkers become silent stones. But this pattern is less important here since Niobe is primarily a symbol of grief.

[41] *Od.* 13. 168. [42] See Cat. 4*b*.

Secondly, we saw in the first part of our discussion that Niobe as a mourner stands between the living and the dead. The special qualities of stone, its silence and its stillness, are clearly relevant to the isolation of the mourner;[43] in this respect petrification is an expression of her human state rather than a reversal of it. But what has complicated her story is that petrification is the second stage of her story, her reaction to her initial punishment rather than the punishment itself; while therefore petrification is a continuation or intensification of her final state it is still a reversal of her position at the start of the story. The happy mother among her children, a picture of vitality and fertility, has now become the isolated and lifeless mourner. One can compare here another stone, the 'unsmiling stone'[44] on which Demeter sat fasting in silent mourning for her child. She is again in self-imposed exile from her community, that of the gods. Again a stone has become a symbol of human mourning.

But the antithesis of stone and human qualities also has a special and quite different role here. Though she is dead in every other respect Niobe's grief defies the defining qualities of stone and she continues to weep even after her petrification.[45] We have seen examples of the pathetic fallacy, according to which nature feels human grief, in the stories of the mourning birds and trees, but it assumes its most striking form in the weeping stone. In a similar way the exceptional power of Orpheus' music is shown in the way that he can charm not only men and animals but even stones. In Ovid and the Hellenistic poets the pathetic fallacy has become extremely popular, but it is plausible to imagine that such incongruous stones have their origin in the folk-tale (one may compare, for instance, the singing stones of Megara).[46] While therefore there is nothing incongruous in a stone expressing the isolation, barrenness, and silence of the mourner, Niobe's stone is different from the others we have been considering in that the opposition of stone and human

[43] See e.g. Cic. *Tusc.* 3. 63: 'Niobe fingitur lapidea propter aeternum, credo, in luctu silentium.' Cf. Philemon, fr. 101.

[44] See Hsch. s.v. *ἀγέλαστος πέτρα*.

[45] First in Homer: *Il.* 24. 617; cf. *AP* 7. 599.

[46] Paus. 1. 42. 2.

feeling is transcended by her exceptional grief. In her case we can say that the mysterious human-figured stone is a compromise not only between this world and the next but between unfeeling nature and human grief.

In this chapter we have been able to point to certain broad differences between petrification and the other types of transformation. Petrification tends to be a direct consequence of a crime, and it makes sense to consider these stories as patterns of punishment in which the petrification is an appropriate reversal of criminal qualities rather than a mitigation or ambiguous reflection of human suffering. But petrification also permanently fixes a figure of the past before our eyes; not only does the stone give monumental form to and act as a memorial for a human being or an animal, but it is a permanent anomaly in which human form and sometimes even human expressions are given a substance that is cold and lifeless. Such stones will naturally be seen as signs from the gods, or as pointers to translated beings, or at least as mysterious reminders of someone who has had direct contact with the gods or powers of the other world. The pattern of crime and punishment will therefore very often involve some kind of interference with the gods.

7

Sex Changes

THERE are only a few stories of sex change, but these are generally agreed to be some of the most striking and imaginative of all Greek myths. The two most popular stories tell how Kaineus changed from a woman to an invulnerable man and how Teiresias changed his sex twice before becoming a seer. There is also a cult *aition* at Phaistos describing how a girl was brought up disguised as a boy, Leucippus, and then transformed as she was about to be discovered.[1]

Any attempt to interpret these myths must go beyond the stories themselves and explore their background. Literal and metaphorical sex change seems to have been a subject of considerable imaginative interest in the ancient world and had some importance in ancient religion. Attempts have been made to link these stories with a number of phenomena and beliefs. Writers of natural history and historians report some real sex changes: these almost invariably tell of the appearance of male genitals on what was apparently a woman. Such cases, like the births of bisexual babies, were treated as striking portents: Pliny says that hermaphrodites were regarded as prodigies, and Diodorus tells how at Rome and Athens such people were burnt alive.[2] The superstitious fears surrounding bisexuality are vividly expressed in a story recounted in Phlegon.[3] The citizens of an Aetolian city, faced with a bisexual child, prepared to take it out of the city and burn it. The dead father of the child then

[1] There is also an obscure allusion in Ov. *Met.* 4. 280 to the sex changes of Sithon; and Nicander (see AL 17. 5) refers briefly to the otherwise unknown story that Siproites was turned into a woman on seeing Artemis bathing. I shall not be considering Mestra here since she is a magical figure who transformed herself into all sorts of animals as well as a man.

[2] Pliny, *NH* 7. 34 (in 36 he describes how a girl who changed into a boy was sent to a desert island); DS 32. 10. Cf. the cases in Phlegon 6, 7, 8, 9, 10. One case led to the setting up of a cult of Zeus Alexikakos, and another to the consultation of the Sibylline books.

[3] Phlegon 2, citing Hieron of Alexandria or Ephesus.

appeared and ate it, leaving only the head, which spoke and prophesied the destruction of the whole people. Here bisexuality is linked with the further miracle of a return from the dead and the magical power of prophecy; it is a portent of terrible disaster and an anomaly that must be destroyed.

We do not find natural changes from men to women, but emasculation played an important part in the religious life of some of the Greeks' neighbours, most notably in the castrated priests of Cybele. There are also references in several writers to androgynous seers among the Scythians. One may compare the reports of shamans in Siberia who adopt the life of women, marry, and are sometimes supposed literally to become women.[4]

One must also consider the metaphorical change of transvestism. Myths of a number of heroes or gods tell how at one time or another they dressed up as women: best known perhaps are stories of the transvestism of Achilles, Heracles, and Dionysos. We also have historical reports of tranvestite rituals; transvestism is most common in the worship of Dionysos and in the *komos*, but it is reported also of marriage rites in several places.[5] It is often suggested that mythical sex changes are imaginative extensions of such ritual changes of dress. The stories of Kaineus and Leucippus who change from young girls to adult men are said to be mythical projections of the liminal stage in age-group initiation rituals; parallels may be found in various parts of the world for the custom of boys spending a period as women before becoming men.[6]

Sex change is thus capable of a variety of symbolic and imaginative meanings. It is not merely a curious fact of natural history but at the least a strange sign or portent; it may also be a way of describing the isolation of a priest or seer, or possibly the change from normal boys to normal adult men. We should not expect, therefore, that these myths are literally concerned with the psychological and practical problems of those who suffer from physical sexual

[4] For Siberian shamans see H. Baumann, *Das doppelte Geschlecht* (Berlin, 1955). For Scythian androgynous seers, see Hdt. 4. 67 (cf. 1. 105); Hippoc. *Aer.* 17–22; W. R. Halliday, *BSA* 17 (1910–11), 95–102.

[5] At Argos women wore beards, and on Cos men wore a woman's robe: see Plut. *Mor.* 245; *GQ* 58. Cf. brides at Sparta: Plut. *Lyc.* 15.

[6] See W. R. Halliday, *BSA* 16 (1909–10), 212–19. Cf. Jeanmaire, *Couroi*, 321–3.

ambiguity or from unorthodox sexual preferences. The distinction of the sexes is the most basic of human divisions and pervades every level of thought, religion, and society. Movement between the sexes is perhaps the most obvious and striking example of a confusion or transcendence of categories and therefore a symbol of very varied potential.[7]

Sex change is a common theme in later folk-tales of other cultures.[8] These have certain similarities with the details of some of our stories, and the story of Leucippus in particular has close parallels in later folk-tales, but most folk-tales of sex change are very different from the stories of Teiresias and Kaineus. These folk-tales have various patterns, but where they differ from the Greek myths is that they are not concerned with the careers of exceptional beings and supermen. Their heroes are ordinary people, and the miraculous element in their stories tends to be entirely externalized in the form of a magic spring, or plant, or pill. Most commonly sex change is a device that enables a marriage to be consummated or thwarted. One Indian story tells how a wife cannot be wooed until the hero disguises himself by being turned into a woman. An Arabian story tells how an eager suitor is bewitched before his wedding day and must be transformed back before he can be married.

The closest parallels to such stories in Greek mythology are not the stories of human sex change but the transformations of the gods. Zeus, for instance, takes the form of a woman to seduce Callisto. In such cases sex change is merely an alternative to disguise as a man or as an animal. In fact, whereas animal changes may be felt to appeal to the conception of the god as an animal the sex changes belong in the class of superficial disguises and seem to have no deeper significance at all.

Perhaps we should now turn to the myths themselves. The obvious story to begin with is the Cretan cult *aition*, the story of Leucippus, since it is the simplest and has an explicit link with ritual.

[7] For the variety of imaginative responses produced in different cultures to the physical reality of hermaphrodites see C. Geertz, *Local Knowledge* (New York, 1983), 80–5.

[8] Sex change as a folk-tale theme is discussed by N. M. Penzer, *Ocean of Story* (London, 1927), vii. 223–33; H. Gaidoz, *RHR* 57 (1908), 317–22.

It is the normal starting-point for those who believe that all the myths should be explained in terms of initiation.

LEUCIPPUS

Lampros, a poor shepherd living at Phaistos, tells his wife that they cannot afford to bring up their child if it is a girl. When a girl is born the mother, encouraged by dreams and prophecies, dresses her up as a boy and calls her Leucippus. The child grows up, and her mother, realizing that she can no longer conceal the deception, flees with her into a temple of Leto and begs the goddess to change her sex. Leto does so, and this change of sex becomes a triple *aition*: first, the people of Phaistos sacrifice to Leto Phytia ('grower'), who made male genitals grow on a girl; secondly, they gave the name Ekdysia ('taking off') to this festival because the girl took off her *peplos* (robe); thirdly, it is a custom that before marriage girls lie beside the statue of Leucippus.[9]

Ovid[10] tells what looks like the same story but with different names. His child is called Iphis, and the parents Ligdus and Telethusa; also it is not Leto who performs the transformation but Isis. But the main change is to have the crisis prompted by the marriage of Iphis. This may be Ovid's invention, but the marriage does provide a reason for the crisis, which is unexplained in Antoninus' version, and would account for the aetiological link with marriage. Also this detail would bring the story into line with a familiar folk-tale pattern. We may compare, for instance, an Indian story which tells how two kings agree that their children should marry, but both have only girls. One king therefore brings up his girl disguised as a boy until the time comes when they are to be married. The girl bridegroom flees to the temple of Devi and prays for help. She comes out from the temple a man, and the husband and wife live out a happily married life.[11] Interestingly this story too is an *aition*: the king builds a series of temples in gratitude for the miracle.

[9] AL 17, citing Nicander.
[10] *Met.* 9. 668 ff.
[11] See Penzer (op. cit. n. 8), 229–30.

The *aitia* and the Cretan setting perhaps suggest that the story of Leucippus should be explained in terms of initiation rituals. The Cretan cities appear to have preserved a series of collective age-group rituals long after most of the rest of Greece, and we have full reports of some of these. In particular there is epigraphic evidence to suggest that the Ekdysia was connected with the change of dress that marked the transition from boyhood to manhood.[12] It has been argued that the story is an *aition* for a collective ceremony in which boys assumed female dress and then removed it.[13]

But this theory of a transvestite rite is not at all convincing. Although we have full reports of Cretan initiations there is no mention of transvestism in any of these.[14] Elsewhere, as was pointed out earlier, we do have reports of transvestite marriage rites, and later on of transvestism in Dionysiac festivals, but not in the context of age-group initiations. Again, exponents of this theory, like exponents of other ritual theories, turn to myths as evidence of the earlier existence of such rites. In particular they refer to the stories of Heracles and Achilles dressing up in women's clothes; but in each of these cases the transvestism can be explained in terms of the context of their stories.[15] The one ritual which seems at all relevant

[12] In the Dreros oath: see R. F. Willetts, *Aristocratic Society in Ancient Crete* (London, 1955), 119–21.

[13] M. Delcourt, *Hermaphrodite: Myths and Rites of the Bisexual Figure in Classical Antiquity* (Eng. tr. London, 1961), ch. 1; cf. P. Vidal-Naquet, in Gordon, 147–62; Jeanmaire, *Couroi*, 354–8. Delcourt compares the story of the Elean Leucippus, who dresses up as a girl in pursuit of Daphne and is discovered and killed when Daphne's companions remove their clothes to bathe: see Cat. 3*a* (Daphne).

[14] See the account of Ephorus, *FGH* 70 F 149.

[15] For Heracles in women's clothes as a slave of Omphale see E. G. Suhr, *AJA* 57 (1953), 251–63; for his disguise as a woman after temporary defeat in his war against the Meropes, Plut. *GQ* 58. Female dress is closely linked with servitude and humiliation in both stories, and thus forms an integral part of the hero's mythical career in which his fantastic achievements are constantly balanced by a humbling. Achilles is hidden as a girl on Scyros (Apollod. 3. 13. 8; Stat. *Achil.* 1. 259 ff.). This is just one of a series of futile maternal attempts to thwart his fate and death (see also the interruption by Peleus of Thetis' immortalizing rite, the inadequate dipping in the Styx, the fatal killing of Tennes, and of course Achilles' attempt to retire from the war in the *Iliad*). The inevitability of his fate is constantly being re-established by setting up an apparent alternative; here the fact that the alternative is an absurd opposite reinforces the inevitability of his true role. The way in which a female element helps to highlight or define masculine heroism is discussed further with the story of Kaineus.

is the Oschophoria at Athens in which two young men processed in female dress and which is linked with the supposed initiatory hero Theseus.[16] But one should be wary of attaching too much weight to this one rite, which anyway does not immediately suggest an initiatory pattern (the change of dress applies only to two boys, there is no hint of withdrawal or consecration, and there is no emphasis on the removal of these clothes).

It has been more plausibly suggested that the change of dress at the Ekdysia is the change from the clothes of a boy to those of a man.[17] If the child's clothes were seen as sexually ambiguous by contrast with the man's this might help to explain how a story arose that Leucippus was once a woman. However, I can find no evidence that a boy's clothes were thought of in this way.[18] We certainly need not assume this, since there is already an obvious way in which the ritual reflects the rite: the change from girl to a man is an exaggeration of the change from boy to man celebrated by the rite. Thus if Leto Phytia is responsible for the growth of the city's young men her power is demonstrated even more emphatically in this miracle, and the statue of Leucippus in her temple remains the proof of it. Sex change therefore becomes a metaphor for the growth of boys into men. We may compare how in many soures the relation of man to woman is regarded as equivalent to that of the adult to the child.[19] If the statue is a figure of unusual fertility then the change is even more exaggerated: Leucipus changes from someone less than a man to someone greater than one.

It should be stressed that to recognize this parallel of myth and ritual is not to accept that ritual is the explanation of the mythical fantasy of sex change. Here myth has given an imaginative level to a rite. While it may be that such ambiguities were inherent in the rite

[16] See Plut. *Thes.* 23; Deubner, 142–7.

[17] See Willetts (op. cit. n. 12), 120–1; id., *Cretan Cults and Festivals* (London, 1962), 175–8; P. Faure, *Fonctions des cavernes crétoises* (Paris, 1964), 159.

[18] It would appear at least that the characteristic adolescent garment in Crete as in Athens and Sparta was a short cloak (see R. F. Willetts, *Ancient Crete* (London, 1965), ch. 9). The evidence of vases is that the undifferentiated dress of children is closer to male than to female dress: see C. Sourvinou-Inwood, *Studies in Girls' Transitions* (Athens, 1988), 119.

[19] e.g. the story of Kaineus is rationalized in terms of a change from a boy to a great man (Heraclit. *Incred.* 3). In Artemidorus (1. 50) for a woman to dream she has become a man is a sign of marriage, the mature state of the woman.

itself and in other rites, we have no evidence of this. What we do know is that the pattern of explaining or highlighting extreme masculinity by giving it a girlish aspect is a well-established mythical one, seen most obviously in the stories of Heracles and Achilles. This pattern receives its most remarkable development in the story of Kaineus' sex change, a more complex and a much more popular story than that of Leucippus.

KAINEUS

Kaineus is mentioned by Nestor in the *Iliad* as one of the Lapith heroes of his youth who fought in the war against the Centaurs.[20] There is no mention of anything unusual about his sex or death. According to Phlegon the story of his sex change was told by Hesiod,[21] but our earliest account is that of Acusilaus.[22] Kaine (in later sources Kainis), daughter of Elatus, after being seduced by Poseidon is transformed into an invincible warrior Kaineus, who becomes king of the Lapiths and wars against the Centaurs. But then, overreaching himself, Kaineus sets up his spear in the marketplace and orders his subjects to worship it, thus offending Zeus who sends the Centaurs against him. Since he is invulnerable they drive him into the earth, a rock is put on his head, and he dies. The story seems to have been a popular one: the strange death of Kaineus was a favourite subject in early art;[23] Pindar describes how he was driven unbending into the ground;[24] *Kaineus* was the name of a tragedy by Ion of Chios and of comedies by Antiphanes and Araros of which we know little (the latter play at least may have been concerned with his sex change rather than his heroic death);[25] Theophrastus

[20] *Il.* 1. 264.

[21] Phlegon, 5; Hes. fr. 87; cf. fr. 88. See J. Schwartz, *Pseudo-Hesiodeia* (Leiden, 1960), 476–83.

[22] *FGH* 2 F 22 (*POxy* 1611).

[23] The earliest depiction dates from the seventh century; see K. Schefold, *Myth and Legend in Early Greek Art* (Eng. tr. London, 1966), pl. 27c. For vases see F. Brommer, *Vasenlisten zur griechischen Heldensage* (Marburg, 1973), 499–501.

[24] Fr. 167; cf. AR 1. 63. Apollonius says that poets sang of his death; this was clearly a popular theme in poetry as well as art.

[25] Ion: *TGF* 19 frs. 36–41; Antiphanes: frs. 4–7; Araros: fr. 112.

mentions that the spear of Kaineus was a proverbial symbol of rule by violence,[26] while the invulnerability of Kaineus was also proverbial.[27]

The transformation seems to have become a more popular aspect of the story in the Hellenistic period. Gellius speaks of 'that familiar old song of the ancient poets about Caenis and Caeneus'.[28] It was mentioned by Nicander, Virgil, and Ovid, as well as in most of the mythographers and scholia.[29] In Ovid Kaineus is finally transformed into a phoenix. In Virgil he appears in the underworld transformed back into a woman. The motive for the sex change varies. In Acusilaus it is mysterious: 'it was not holy for her to bear children'. Ovid makes it her indignant reaction to her rape. The scholiast to Lucian has her outwitting Poseidon and receiving the gift without losing her virginity at all.[30] As to Kaineus' end, the scholiast to Apollonius says he strove with Apollo and was defeated; whether this is just another motivation for the Centaurs' attack or a different ending of the story is uncertain.

The story is full of striking themes, although the relation between them is not immediately clear. For Rohde and a previous generation of scholars Kaineus' strange death is the central theme of the story: he is in origin an underground hero like Trophonius or Amphiaraus and the story has developed as an *aition*.[31] In an extension of this argument it is argued that the sex change is a sign of belonging to, or having some contact with, the underworld.[32] For other scholars it is the sex change that comes first and explains the rest of the story. Devereux and Delcourt point out the ambiguity of his career as a warrior:[33] the word used to describe his invulner-

[26] See *POxy* 1611.

[27] See Apost. 4. 19.

[28] 9. 4.

[29] Virg. *A* 6. 448 and Servius; Ov. *Met.* 12. 169–209 and 459–532; Nicander in AL 17. 4; Agatharch. 7; Apollod. *Epit.* 1. 22; Hyg. *Fab.* 14; Plut. *Mor.* 75 E; schol. *Il.* 1. 264; *Myth. Vat.* 1. 154, 3. 6. 25; Heraclit. *Incred.* 3.

[30] Schol. Lucian *Gall.* 19.

[31] Rohde, *Psyche*, i. 115. Cf. O. Berthold, *Die Unverwundbarkeit in Sage und Aberglauben der Griechen* (Giessen, 1911). Against this see J. T. Kakridis, *CR* 61 (1947), 77–80.

[32] See H. Kenner, *Das Phänomen der verkehrten Welt in der griechisch-römischen Antike* (Klagenfurt, 1970), 151.

[33] G. Devereux, *Int. J. Psycho-analysis* 38 (1957), 398–401; M. Delcourt, *RHR* 144 (1953), 129–50, and *Hermaphrodite*, ch. 3. Cf. Kirk, *Myth*, 201, who seems to go along with Delcourt's position.

ability could also suggest that he is inviolate in the sexual sense,[34] the spear which he worships is a phallic symbol, and his strange death driven erect into the ground continues the sexual metaphor. For Devereux the story is a fantasy reaction to rape in which the woman is awarded a phallus: for Delcourt sexual and metaphorical potency are the consequences of initiation; she sees the story of Kaineus, like that of Leucippus, as a reflection of a rite in which men gain manhood and heroic powers by briefly adopting women's dress. The name Kaineus, which on one interpretation means 'new', itself suggests initiation.

It is implausible, I think, to explain the story as an *aition* for a Chthonic god. None of our sources gives any hint of worship of Kaineus or any reference to his continued existence under the ground. In particular this explanation does not provide a convincing reason for the sex change; no other Chthonic heroes are given this sort of story.

Neither, although the sexual metaphors within the story are important, is the hypothesis of an initiatory rite helpful. I have already pointed out that there is almost no evidence for transvestite age-group rituals in ancient Greece, and the story of Leucippus itself is neither evidence for a transvestite rite nor for the imaginative equivalence of transvestism and transformation.

It is perhaps safest, therefore, to approach the story as an entirely imaginative construction. It falls into two apparently distinct parts, the story of the sex change and the story of the hero's strange death. But these two parts are not equally independent of each other. Whereas the arrogance and the strange death of the invulnerable hero can exist as a story in its own right, and perhaps did exist before the other part of the story, the story of the sex change is only found as a prelude to the story of Kaineus' death: it is not a story in itself. Even the hero's invulnerability, though it is gained with the sex change, can be understood quite independently of the earlier events of the story. Kaineus belongs in a group of supermen for whom invulnerability acts as a narrative foil to some spectacular death. In each case the man's invulnerability merely reinforces the point that men cannot escape death.[35]

[34] He is ἄτρωτος: for 'wounding' used in a sexual sense see e.g. Aesch. fr. 44.

[*See p. 158 for n. 35*]

If, therefore, sex change was invented as a prelude or introduction to this other more famous story we must assume that its structure is determined by the latter, and approach it by considering why a story that he was once a girl was considered an appropriate start to the career of an invulnerable hero.

In the first place it seems possible that one miraculous aspect of Kaineus was felt to prompt another. This man who had apparently crossed one natural boundary (of gods and men) could perhaps plausibly be imagined to have crossed another basic one. We may compare Teiresias, who not only changed his sex but lived for seven generations and retained his consciousness in Hades. In later writers bisexuality in men and animals is associated with various supernatural powers.[36] It is interesting that in Ovid's account a third miracle has been added to Kaineus' career: he rises from death to become the immortal bird, the phoenix.

But this is a very general point. We should expect a more specific significance in the sex change story. It seems likely that there was a deliberate contrast or opposition between Kainis the girl and Kaineus the invulnerable man, giving us a balance between the invulnerable warrior who is something greater than a man and the girl who is something less than a man. The story emphasizes his greatness by diminishing his origins—a point that is presumably at the root of the rationalizations of the story which claim that the sex change was only a way of describing how he changed from a boy to a great man.[37] We may compare the dramatic contrast in the change from Achilles disguised as a girl to Achilles the invulnerable warrior or in the conception of the girlish warrior Parthenopaeus.[38] This formal scheme in which the particular quality of a hero is given emphasis by introducing its opposite somewhere else in his career is one of the basic structures in Greek mythology: we read of a whole series of kings and founders who begin as outcasts.

[35] See Berthold (op. cit. n. 31). He points out that invulnerability is a characteristic of mortals, not of gods, who can be wounded.

[36] See L. Brisson, *Le Mythe de Tirésias* (Leiden, 1976), 74–7.

[37] See Heraclit. *Incred.* 3.

[38] In Aesch. *Sept.* 533 ff. there is a contrast of name and appearance on the one hand, *βλάστημα καλλίπρῳρον, ἀνδρόπαις ἀνήρ*, and his nature on the other, *ὁ δ᾽ ὠμόν, οὔτι παρθένων ἐπώνυμον φρόνημα*.

But although this formal contrast of more-than-a-man and less-than-a-man may be a starting-point of the story of the sex change I believe that the developed story involves more than this and is concerned with the relation of men and women. It is important to consider its psychological motivation as well as its formal structure. Perhaps we should begin by considering why the woman Kainis decides to become a man.

Ovid's account, our fullest, is the only one which is explicit about Kainis' motivation: he has her pray to become a man so that she can never suffer such an injury again. This is not a peculiarly Ovidian view of divine rape. Far from being a particularly happy experience rape by a god is nearly always seen as something shameful and humiliating (unless it is in the context of marriage). This is true not only of mortal women who are at the mercy of their parents, but of goddesses too. When Demeter is raped by Poseidon, for instance, she retires in anger to a cave and the earth becomes barren.[39] Such a view of seduction underlies also the variant which has Kaineus outwitting Poseidon by becoming a man before he can enjoy her. Male/female rivalry rather than love is the main element in this story too. The only other motive that is offered in our sources is that of Acusilaus, that it was not 'holy' for her to bear children. The reasons for this are not clear. What is important perhaps is that in this version sex change is not a gratuitous honour but a form of compensation for being deprived of her natural fulfilment as a woman.

The circumstances of her sex change seem relevant to the fact that what Kaineus becomes it not an ordinary man, or even a superman, but an unusually aggressive man and a killer. Other Lapith heroes have a more colourful character in which they are wild rapists as well as warriors. Kaineus, however, is single-minded. His name was derived from *kaino* ('kill');[40] the spear for which he demanded worship was a poverbial symbol of violence. It seems possible that this aggression was felt to be explained by the sexual rivalry of the earlier part of the story and in particular by the injury she suffered as a woman. At the very least one can explain Kaineus'

[39] Paus. 8. 42. 2.

[40] See Eust. *Il.* 1. 264. He had a Hellenistic double, a murderer called Kaineus who could not be executed (Val. Max. 9. 10).

aggression as a form of over-compensation and over-reliance on masculinity of a woman who has unnaturally acquired it.[41] Again female origins are important in Kaineus' motivation and not just as a formal element characterizing his superhuman powers. It is interesting that Virgil at least seems to have regarded Kaineus as a woman all along since he makes her revert to female form in Hades.

This interpretation of the story may be supported and clarified by two mythical parallels. Kaineus is frequently compared with the male transvestite heroes, but it is more illuminating to compare him with those women who adopt a male life and dress and become competitors with men, the huntresses. (It is interesting that Atalanta, in Plato at least, undergoes an actual sex change in choosing to become a male athlete in her next life.)[42] As was noted earlier, what these women actually become is not so much men as characters of an extreme nature with a potential for violence and savagery. In particular their savagery is directed towards the men who attempt to marry or rape them, and it is normally in an attempt to avoid this that they become hunters in the first place. All begin their stories with a rejection of marriage. It is interesting to note that Kainis too begins her story, in Ovid, by rejecting all her countless suitors, exactly like Daphne or Atalanta. These myths do suggest, I think, how women who become men might be expected to behave and that Ovid's interpretation of the desire to become a man as a desire to avoid sexual humiliation is in harmony with a wider mythical tradition.

The only other figure in Greek mythology who worships his spear is Parthenopaeus.[43] There are female associations in his name and appearance that appear to contrast with his warlike nature, but which may be an essential part of it. Vernant,[44] for instance, argues that the virgin girl becomes a symbol of the dedicated warrior because she can become totally identified with her role whereas the male hero will probably also be a father and a husband. Yet it is not only Parthenopaeus' appearance but the motivation of his career that is female. He is the abandoned child of Atalanta, the virgin

[41] Devereux (art. cit. n. 33) sees the story as a fantasy pattern in which a woman is awarded a penis in compensation for rape.

[42] *Resp.* 10. 620 B.

[43] Aesch. *Sept.* 529 f.

[44] *Myth and Society*, 24.

huntress who refuses to give up her life and accept the loss of her virginity. In an obvious sense Parthenopaeus is an extension and result of her anomalous career (compare Hippolytus, another one-sided figure and a misogynist who is the son of an Amazon).

The female huntresses together with their sons represent one strand of sexual hostility or rivalry in Greek myths. Another is the resentment felt by female gods against Zeus and the Olympian order; Kaineus, we may remember, is not only a killer but a scorner and rival of the gods. The general structure given to the conflict between Olympian gods and their rivals and predecessors is first of all sky as opposed to earth, but secondly male as opposed to female. Various stories explain uprisings of giants or monsters in terms of the resentment of a female god;[45] most commonly the offended goddess is Earth, who sends up a succession of children against Zeus, but it may be Hera herself.[46] Kaineus is not a god, but in his magical invulnerability and his relation to Poseidon he closely resembles some of the famous giant enemies of the gods.[47]

A closer parallel, though, is the story of Thetis. As I shall discuss more fully in the next chapter on shape-shifters, she too is a figure who represents through her son a threat to the Olympian order. As the story is told by Pindar the gods conspire to make sure that her son will die by marrying her to a mortal. She herself is humiliated; the marriage was, she says in the *Iliad*, endured much against her will.[48] Achilles' life is a succession of episodes in which he nearly gains immortality before he is finally put down by Apollo. The motivating force in these episodes is his mother's love and ambition. The myths of the goddesses and those of the huntresses suggest that sexual rivalry or resentment may be an important element in the motivation of the story of Kaineus.

Finally, there is a certain appropriateness in his death through a strange alliance of the Centaurs and Zeus and Apollo (the Olympians and the Centaurs are normally enemies). In a sense this ending

[45] See e.g. Apollod. 1. 6. 1.

[46] *Hymn. Hom. Ap.* 305. It is also Hera who persecutes Zeus' representative on earth, Heracles.

[47] Most obviously the Aloades.

[48] Pind. *Isthm.* 8. 36 f.; *Il.* 18. 433.

to the story is already fixed quite independently of the story of the sex change. Kaineus is a Lapith and thus a traditional enemy of the Centaurs. His death at their hands may have been a popular story before the story of the sex change was invented. But if we are looking for reasons why a sex change may be thought a suitable opening to this story it may be relevant that the only thing Zeus and Apollo and the Centaurs have in common is their aggressive maleness. The Centaurs are symbols of unbridled male lust and power, and normally appear as rapists (they are descended from Ixion who attempted to rape Hera). Kainis is an outrage to their masculinity: 'we are conquered by a half-man', they complain.[49] Zeus and Apollo are guardians of a male order which is continually opposed to Chthonic and female powers. The ex-woman Kaineus is an appropriate figure to threaten both these masculine groups.

To sum up, therefore, the story of Kaineus makes a complex use of the theme of sex change and the antithesis of male and female. The basic opposition of male and female is transcended by a miraculous hero; and there is a further dramatic contrast in that Kaineus passes from something less to something more than a man. But if one goes deeper it appears that the motivation of the unbalanced and murderous superman has its origins in female resentment and rivalry. In this sense perhaps Kaineus never was a man but a woman who was suddenly given superhuman powers.

TEIRESIAS

Teiresias is first mentioned in the *Odyssey*. He is a blind seer in Hades who alone of all the dead has been allowed to retain his mind.[50] There is no account of his life on earth, or reference to any sexual ambiguity. He seems also to have featured in the pseudo-Hesiodic *Melampodia*.[51] We find ascribed to this work a story that Zeus and Hera once argued about which partner derives greater pleasure from sexual intercourse, and they decided to consult

[49] Ov. *Met.* 12. 499 ff.

[50] *Od.* 10. 492 ff.

[51] Frs. 275 and 276; see I. Löffler, *Die Melampodie* (Meisenheim, 1963), 43–5.

Teiresias, who had been both a man and a woman. He had once come across two copulating snakes and on striking one of them had become a woman; coming across a similar or the same pair eight years later he struck the other and became a man again. He now answered that the woman derived far more pleasure than the man. Hera punished him with blindness, but Zeus granted him prophetic power and a life of seven generations.

We have no further references to this story or to Teiresias' female form in any pre-Hellenistic source, although the blind Teiresias appears as the seer of Thebes in several tragedies. But a different story of his blindness and gift of prophecy was ascribed to Pherecydes[52] and later made popular by a hymn of Callimachus.[53] This told how he came across Athene bathing, was blinded, and then granted prophecy, a staff, a long life, and consciousness in Hades. (The Callimachus story at least is clearly influenced by the Homeric account. The specific details mentioned in Homer, his blindness, his staff, and his consciousness in Hades are all explained in this story.)

According to Phlegon,[54] Dicaearchus, Clearchus, and Callimachus told the story of the sex change. The reference to Callimachus at least may be a confusion with the other story. It is in Lycophron[55] that we first have a definite reference to Teiresias' transformation and arbitration, and it is in Ovid that we first find an account of the story.[56] Our later sources do not vary very much.[57] The scholia to Lycophron combine the two stories and say that Teiresias was turned into a woman after coming across Athene bathing. Apollodorus mentions a third story, that Teiresias was blinded for revealing the secrets of the gods[58] (this is a standard motif in stories of seers). Finally, we find an extraordinary

[52] *FGH* 3 F 92. U. v. Wilamowitz, *Hellenistische Dichtung* (Berlin, 1924), ii. 23, suggested that Pherecydes might have taken this story from that of Actaeon.

[53] Callim. *Hymn.* 5. 75 ff. Cf. Prop. 4. 9. 57 f.; Nonn. 5. 337 ff.

[54] Phlegon, 4.

[55] 683. The story was apparently told in a digression by Nicander: see AL 17.

[56] *Met.* 3. 316 ff.

[57] See further Apollod. 3. 6. 7; Hyg. *Fab.* 75; Ov. *Ibis* 262; Ael. *NA* 1. 25; schol. *Od.* 10. 494; schol. Lyc. 683; schol. Stat. *Theb.* 11. 95; Fulg. 2. 5; *Myth. Vat.* 1. 16 and 2. 84. The sources are set out in full by Brisson, 135–42.

[58] 3. 6. 7.

elaboration of the story, which told how he went through seven changes and was eventually transformed into a mouse.[59] This is probably an invention of Ptolemaeus, who wrote pastiches of famous myths,[60] and one assumes that the starting point of this strange fantasy was the epic tradition that Teiresias' life was prolonged to seven generations.

That there is no hint of the story of the sex change between Hesiod and the Hellenistic writers need not lead to the conclusion that the *Melampodia* merely told of Teiresias' arbitration and that the sex change is a Hellenistic invention.[61] It is not only the sex change itself but the story of the arbitration that is neglected by the classical authors, and we know that that at least is Hesiodic. It is hardly strange that the story does not appear in the tragic poets; we have already seen in the case of Io that the Hesiodic burlesque treatment of the quarrel of Zeus and Hera is quite different from that of our tragic sources (it is useful to remember that had it not been for the discovery of a papyrus-text of Acusilaus we would have no evidence for the sex change of Kaineus between Pseudo-Hesiod and Nicander). The story of the snakes is in any case a striking and unusual one, quite unlike the standard elaborations of later mythographers. There is further important evidence that the tradition of a sexually ambiguous Teiresias is an old one in the form of a fifth-century Etruscan mirror which shows Odysseus conversing with a youthful effeminate Teiresias.[62]

What is one to make of Teiresias' story? The form of the story of the sex change is perhaps not a surprising one. Coupling snakes are a common magical sign of varied significance in other cultures and in the ancient world.[63] The pattern of the story, the repeated en-

[59] See Eust. on *Od.* 10. 494; cf. Ptolemaeus in Photius *Bibl.* 146^{b}39.

[60] See Brisson, 78–83. However, K. H. Tomberg, *Die Kaine Historia des Ptolemaios Chennos* (Diss. Bonn, 1967), 172–3, considers that Ptolemaeus' attribution of the story to one Sostratos is genuine.

[61] This is argued by Schwartz (op. cit. n. 21), 211–20.

[62] See O. Touchefeu-Meynier, *Thèmes odysséens dans l'art antique* (Paris, 1968), no. 235; Brisson, 123–4; *EAA* s.v. Tiresias. Zeus and Hephaistos are sometimes portrayed on Etruscan mirrors as young men (see M. T. de Grummond, *A Guide to Etruscan Mirrors* (Tallahassee, 1962), 90 and 96). But these are heroic youthful figures whereas Teiresias is an effeminate one.

[63] See Frazer's note on Apollod. 3. 6. 6. Admetus' bedroom is filled with coupling snakes

counter, is a regular one in folk-tales of sex change. We may compare those stories which tell how a character comes across a magic spring or well and is transformed; years later he comes across the same spring and is returned to his previous sex.[64] However, the sex change is clearly, like that of Kaineus, not a story in itself but the prelude to what comes later, in this case the arbitration between the gods and the granting to Teiresias of the gift of prophecy. We need to know why it was thought a suitable opening for such a story.

There is of course the obvious narrative point that without the sex change Teiresias could not answer Zeus' and Hera's question. But there may be more to it than this: the snakes are not just a magical device of general significance; an encounter with snakes is the standard way of acquiring prophetic powers in Greek myths,[65] and it is difficult not to see an anticipation of the final gift of prophecy in this incident.[66] If this is accepted it becomes more likely that the sex change too has a further significance.

One approach is to compare the behaviour of shamans in various parts of the world who dressed and lived as women.[67] The story of Teiresias could be evidence of an earlier practice of this sort among the Greeks or of the influence of their neighbours' practices.[68] Perhaps the obvious objection to this appoach is that Teiresias is not, as a seer, bisexual or effeminate; by the time he is granted the power of prophecy he has been transformed back into a man. There is little evidence, either, of any Greek equivalents of the androgynous Scythian seers or the effeminate ecstatic priests of Anatolia. Teiresias himself is not an exotic inhabitant of the far North or the

by the offended Artemis (Apollod. 1. 9. 15). A pair of snakes are a sign of death for the father of the Gracchi: see Cic. *Div.* 1. 36; Plut. *Tib. Gracch.* 1; Val. Max. 4. 6. 1; Pliny *NH* 7. 122. Snakes copulating at a crossroads are an important ingredient for a magical potion: see Nicander, *Ther.* 98 ff. This seems to have influenced Nicander's telling of Teiresias' story, since he is the only source who has the snakes encountered at a crossroads: AL 17. 5.

[64] See Gaidoz (art. cit. n. 8).

[65] Cassandra and Helenus (schol. *Il.* 7. 44) and Melampus had their ears cleaned out by snakes; cf. Porph. *Abst.* 3. 4. Iamos (Pind. *Ol.* 6. 45 ff.) is fed by snakes. Apollonius of Tyana eats snakes (Philostr. *VA* 1. 20). Apollo kills a snake to win Delphi.

[66] A. H. Krappe, *AJP* (1928), 267–75, argues that the original form of the story told how Teiresias acquired his power of prophecy from the snakes.

[67] See above, n. 4.

[68] This is the approach of Delcourt, *Hermaphrodite*, ch. 3; cf. Burkert, *SH* 30.

East but is firmly fixed in Boeotia. Even so, we need not rule out the possibility of such an influence; the myth of Teiresias is a unique one, and this makes it more plausible that some unusual or external influence may be at work. However, there have also been structural approaches to the story which take us rather further.

A connection can be made between the sex change and the blinding. The blinding of seers is a common pattern in Greek mythology[69] and has been plausibly interpreted as an act of repression against someone who has overstepped the boundaries between gods and men.[70] Changing from a man into a woman may be seen as a similar lowering in status. In fact sex change is an alternative punishment for blinding in one version of the story of Teiresias' intrusion upon Athene; it is also the punishment imposed upon Siproites for a similar offence.[71] Of course in this story blindness and sex change are not structural parallels: again one needs to point out that Teiresias, though a blind seer, is not an effeminate one. However, it may be that the motif of the blind or repressed seer had prompted or was felt to be in harmony with defects or deviation in the sexual field: persistently in Greek myths a physical maiming or defect is connected with sexual unorthodoxy and ambiguity.[72]

Brisson[73] takes us further and shows how Teiresias' consecutive bisexuality fits in with the other incidents of his career in that it helps to characterize him as a mediator. Teiresias stands between men and the gods (since although he is not immortal he lives for seven generations of men), between the living and the dead (since he retains consciousness in Hades), and also between men and women.

However, I want to pursue further another way in which Teiresias' consecutive sex changes may be more closely associated with prophecy. There is perhaps a third way in which the story of

[69] Other blind seers include Phineus, Ophioneus, Euenios, and Phormion.

[70] See R. G. A. Buxton, *JHS* 100 (1980), 22–37; Brisson, 31–3.

[71] Teiresias' intrusion punished by sex change: schol. Lyc. 683; Siproites: AL 17. 5.

[72] Pleisthenes, according to one report, was 'hermaphrodite or lame and wore women's clothing': see M. Papathomopoulos, *Nouveaux fragments d'auteurs anciens* (Paris, 1980), 11–26; J. P. Vernant, *Arethusa* 15 (1982), 19–38. The house of Oedipus and the house of Cypselus (which claimed descent from Kaineus) are pervaded by deviancy in both spheres. G. Devereux, *JHS* 93 (1973), 36–49, has argued that blindness is very often a symbolic castration.

[73] Brisson, *passim*.

his sex changes can be seen as an appropriate introduction to his later prophetic career. I have noted above that the Pherecydes story in which Teiresias comes across the bathing Athene and the Hesiodic story of the arbitration share a common structure. In both cases Teiresias offends a god, is punished by blindness, and is then compensated by the gift of prophecy. But we see a still closer similarity if we consider why Hera punishes Teiresias. Of course Hera is angry that Zeus has won their argument, but the incident belongs perhaps to a wider pattern in which men are punished for witnessing and revealing the secret of some god. Here Teiresias offends against Hera not merely as a god but as a woman; his period as a woman may be seen as a form of involuntary spying or at least as the acquiring of information he should not have revealed. It is therefore an intrusion. Described in this way the episode has a resemblance to the Pherecydes story; there too we have not merely an offence against a god, but an intrusion, and an intrusion upon a woman. It would seem that the myth in both its forms suggests a close connection between intrusion upon women and prophecy. Further, it seems that the sex change of Teiresias is not merely an emasculation, an entirely negative experience, but more positively an unnatural way of acquiring knowledge.

The Pherecydes story of the encounter with Athene belongs to the pattern of a mysterious encounter of the hunter in the wilds; as was noted in the discussion of Actaeon, the hunter is often seen as an intruder on both women and the wilds. In the Hesiodic version this element is provided by the story of the snakes, the prelude to the arbitration and the cause of Teiresias' sex change. His wounding or killing of the snakes can be seen as an intrusion and an act of aggression comparable to his blundering on Athene (several stories tell of an intrusion upon snakes and its fatal consequences),[74] a mysterious encounter in the wilds that adds to his experience of another world. This episode gives to the Hesiodic story an element it otherwise lacks. The outside or other world experienced by Teiresias is represented not only by women but by the wilds. Seen as a whole, therefore, the myth not only sets the prophet in an

[74] See e.g. Ael. *NA* 11. 17; 11. 16; Plut. *Alex.* 3.

ambiguous relation with the gods but associates prophetic knowledge with an intrusion upon women and the non-human wilds. In the Hesiodic story these two intrusions form an extended pattern of aggression, punishment, and recompense; in the Pherecydes story the pattern is compressed into a single episode.

We can support and clarify this interpretation if we turn to some of the other myths of seers. Although none of them is as striking or as complex as the story of Teiresias, who is the greatest of the mythical seers, what they do suggest is that prophetic knowledge is something that must come from the outside. Of course in the first place it must come from the gods; nearly all seer myths make some reference to Apollo. But alongside this view of the prophet as sharer of the Olympians' wisdom there is the notion that he owes his knowledge to some non-human (if we count the Olympian gods as human) or non-masculine otherworld. The idea that the wilds or the animal world is a source of wisdom is a regular one; one thinks of Cheiron, the teacher of men who is half a horse and lives in a cave in the wilds. More particularly, the knowledge of the prophet is associated with the animal world. Cheiron's daughter Hippo, who becomes a horse, taught men prophecy. Proteus, the old man of the sea, is identified with a different element and with its evil-smelling inhabitants, the seals.

In the case of a mortal seer a single account may make his prophecy both a gift of Apollo and something acquired from the animal world. Thus Apollodorus[75] tells how Melampus was granted prophecy by Apollo, but also how snakes cleaned out his ears so that he could understand the language of the birds and thus become a seer. This sort of double motivation makes it more likely that Teiresias' meeting with the snakes is as important in his gaining of prophecy as his service to Zeus.

Very often the acquiring of knowledge from the otherworld involves an act of aggression against it. This is most obvious in the model and ideal form of all seers, Apollo. His myths, and in particular the myth of his conquest of Delphi, have a structure in which sky, male, and human are opposed to earth, female, and

[75] 1. 9. 11.

animal. He is opposed in various sources to Earth and her representative Python, Themis, the Sibyl, the Thriai, and of course, though we now move away from prophetic myths, to the Erinyes in the *Eumenides*. Teiresias is, like the other seers, a protégé of Apollo, and it is on the god's instructions that he attacks the snakes the second time he sees them. Sometimes the seers suffer aggression from this otherworld.[76] Mopsus, for instance, is killed by a snake[77] (as is Apollo himself in some versions of his story). Most striking perhaps are the monstrous female creatures that plague Phineus and leave behind them a terrible stench. In some cases at least, therefore, the otherworld can be seen as female rather than, or as well as, animal, though this is not so common. In the case of Chthonic creatures the ambiguity of animal and female is always present, since the earth is female, especially in opposition to Apollo.

Teiresias' encounter with the snakes and his sex change both look forward to his final gift of prophecy with which they have a causal connection. His sex change is not merely a reflection of the marginal position of seers, but like his encounter with snakes it is an intrusion upon an outside world that is distinct from the world of the Olympian gods. In other seer stories this may be seen metaphorically as the world of animals or the earth or sea, or of women. Here we have both forms of intrusion, and one is seen as the consequence of the other.

It is interesting to note that both in the story of Teiresias and in that of Kaineus the sex change belongs to a pattern of aggression between the sexes. This is perhaps one of the most obvious differences from the folk-tales and myths of other cultures, in which the change is normally motivated by hostility between two men or else some completely arbitrary magical occurrence. There is a striking contrast here between the story of Teiresias and an Indian story which uses the same theme of the difference in the enjoyment of sex of men and women.[78] A king with many sons is transformed into a woman after bathing in a lake, and he then bears more sons as

[76] In a story treated by Sophocles (frs. 390–400) the seer Polyidos learns the secret of immortality by killing a snake.

[77] AR 4. 1502 ff.

[78] See Gaidoz (art. cit. n. 8); Krappe (art. cit. n. 66).

a woman. When all his sons are killed a god in pity offers to restore one set of sons to life and asks him which he would prefer to have back. The king asks for the sons he bore as a woman, because a woman loves more than a man. The god then offers to restore his sex, but the king refuses because he says a woman enjoys sex more than a man. Here the spirit of the story is one of sympathy between the sexes rather than aggression.

To sum up, the sex change stories of Kaineus and Teiresias both deal with different types of exceptional men, and that of Leucippus quite possibly with a third type. The story of Leucippus probably concerns the origins of a statue of exceptional fertility, the story of Kaineus describes the career of a superhuman killer, and that of Teiresias tells of the gaining of prophetic powers and a qualified immortality. In each case we may say that crossing the basic natural boundary and belonging to two formally opposed worlds have much to do with the special powers of the hero. But we can also see a special relevance of the sex change to each particular hero. In the simplest case, that of Leucippus, where it is male potency that is at issue, the hero's change from a less than normal capacity to a more than normal one is an amplification of the normal process of growing up; in Kaineus' story the motivation of the woman that he once was explains the single-minded character of the hero he becomes; and Teiresias' sex change may be seen as a form of involuntary spying that has a causal relevance to his special knowledge.

8

The Shape-Shifters

THE stories of the shape-shifters, Proteus, Nereus, Metis, Nemesis, Thetis, Periclymenus, Dionysos, and Mestra are quite different from any of the transformation stories we have considered so far.[1] The defining feature of this class of heroes is that they undergo a whole series of transformations rather than a single one. Further, unlike the changes of most human beings these are self-willed and temporary; unlike those of the gods they have strong suggestions of magic.

In fact the language used to describe these transformations shows that they differ in nature from those of the gods. Whereas our early sources normally use words meaning 'seem' or 'appear as' of the transformations of the gods the word used in the case of the shape-shifters is *gignomai* ('become').[2] This difference in language reveals a difference in conception. Whereas the transformation of the Olympians is only a form of disguise under which the god continues to exist and behave as a god, the shape-shifter completely submerges his personality in the thing he becomes. Whereas too the gods generally become only living creatures and advanced forms of life the shape-shifter may turn himself into the lifeless elements fire or water.

There are many folk-tale parallels to these stories. Multiple change is a standard magical device that may be ascribed to demons, magicians, dead spirits, or bewitched persons.[3] Even in the ancient

[1] For general discussions of these stories see Ninck; M. Detienne, and J. P. Vernant, *Cunning Intelligence in Greek Culture and Society* (Eng. tr. Hassocks, 1978), especially 20–1 and chs. 3 and 4; Burkert, *SH* 95–7.

[2] See the description of Proteus in the *Odyssey* (4. 351 ff.), Nemesis in the *Cypria* (fr. 9), Periclymenus in Hesiod (fr. 33), Dionysos in the Homeric hymn (*Hymn. Hom. Bacch.* 44). See further F. Dirlmeier, *Die Vogelgestalt homerischer Götter* (Heidelberg, 1967), 1–2.

[3] See E. S. Hartland, *Science of Fairy Tales* (London, 1891), 242; J. A. MacCulloch, *Childhood of Fiction* (London, 1905), 45; R. Kühnau, *Schlesische Sagen*, ii (Breslau, 1911), ch. 4; A. Lesky, *Thalassa* (Vienna, 1947), 120–7.

world the closest parallels to these figures are the sub-mythological demons and wizards of which we receive only hints in the literary sources.[4] These stories take us back to the folk-tale roots of Greek mythology. However one should not stop here; one needs to look further at how and why these particular stories were incorporated as episodes into the larger patterns of the familiar Greek heroic stories. Have the Greek magical shape-shifters developed any characteristic features? And does the difference in spirit of these stories and characters from the more familiar types of Greek mythology serve any functional purpose in these new structures?

The stories exemplify a number of different patterns. It also seems that their origin may vary; in some cases at least it is possible that the starting point of a story of a series of transformations was the change to one particular significant animal. However, I am assuming as an esssential characteristic of the developed form of these stories that it is the bewildering number of changes rather than a particular form that is important; in most of these stories, in fact, we have a standard list of animals and elements. I shall not, therefore, be very much concerned with two figures who stand at the edge of this class and are normally treated as shape-shifters, Achelous and Mestra. Achelous is basically not a shape-shifter but a bull-shaped river-god.[5] In no early source does he go through a

[4] Compare the transformations of the demon Empusa in Ar. *Ran.* 289 f.; cf. schol. AR 3. 861; Lucian, *Salt.* 19. Shape-changing is a standard power of wizards or magicians: see Plato, *Resp.* 380 D and 383 A; Ov. *Fasti* 6. 131 ff.; Lucian, *Asin.* 12, *Philops.* 13 f. See further W. Burkert, *RhM* 105 (1962), 41. Plato asks whether the gods are wizards who can change their shape and cites the stories of Proteus and Thetis (*Resp.* 381 D; cf. *Euthyd.* 288 B). In later writers Proteus is the prime mythical example of a magician: see Eust. *Od.* 4. 401; Proteus appears to the mother of Apollonius and says he will be born in her son (Philostr. *VH* 1. 4).

[5] Early accounts and representations of his fight with Achelous have Heracles fighting a bull or a bull-man (Archil. fr. 287, Soph. *Trach.* 507 ff., Pind. fr. 249a; cf. Apollod. 2. 7. 5, DS 4. 35. For art see H. P. Isler, *Acheloos* (Berne, 1970) and *LIMC* s.v. Acheloos; S. B. Luce, *AJA* 27 (1923), 425–37). The most important element in this fight, and the reason for his bull form, is the capturing of the horn of plenty by Heracles. On one early gem there is a hint at a further transformation into a snake (*LIMC* no. 221. In the *Trachiniae* he appears in snake form as a suitor, though not in the fight). In Ovid he transforms himself into a bull and a snake in the fight (8. 879 ff; he has here a 'finita potestas novandi'). Finally in late authors he becomes capable of unlimited transformations (Hyg. *Fab.* 31. 7, Sen. *Herc. Oet.* 495 ff., *Myth. Vat.* 1. 58). He is frequently depicted as a man-bull, or a horned mask quite apart from

series of changes. Mestra[6] does become a large number of animals, none of which have any special importance, but these changes happen on separate occasions and do not form a baffling series, nor are they the response to an attack or an attempted binding like the changes in all the other stories.

Perhaps the most obvious common feature of the shape-shifters is their connection with water or rather with the sea. Nereus and Proteus are old men of the sea, Thetis is a Nereid, Nemesis and Metis are Oceanids, and even Periclymenus obtains his powers from Poseidon. Dionysos too has a connection with the sea or water, though a less important one. Already in antiquity this common feature was noted and seen as an explanation of their power. Thus Euphorion described Periclymenus as '*thalassios* (of the sea) like Proteus'.[7] In other folk-tales the power of transformation tends to be a power of spirits in general and not restricted to water spirits. Any study of the Greek stories will have to consider why a connection with the sea has become a distinguishing feature.

It has been suggested that these stories have their origin in simple natural symbolism:[8] as sea spirits the shape-shifters possess the natural fluidity of water, which is always shifting, assuming new shapes when put into different containers, and reflecting different images. It may be so; but this is not a view of water that is often expressed in ancient writers. Although the unpredictability and danger of the sea, and the continual flow of a river, are common themes the capacity of water to assume forms or reflect images is not, nor are shape-shifting stories ever explained in this way. We do not even find the later fantasies which see horses in waves.[9] The common epithets for the sea suggest rather its shapelessness, in the

depictions in this story. Snakes too have a special relevance to rivers (see Strab. 9. 13. 16 or 10. 2. 19, *RE* s.v. *Flussgötter*, col. 2782).

[6] See Hes. fr. 43; Palaeph. 23; Lyc. 1393; AL 17. 5; Ov. *Met.* 8. 846 ff.; T. Zielinski, *Philol.* 50 (1891), 137–62; K. J. Mackay, *Erysichthon* (Leiden, 1962); D. Fehling, *RhM* 115 (1972), 173–96; Ninck, 144–5.

[7] See fr. 64. Artemidorus grants the power of transformation to sea gods in general: 2. 38.

[8] Ninck, ch. 4. This is part of a wider argument which sees the origin of the fantasy of shape-shifting in dream images.

[9] The bull form of river-gods is explained in terms of rivers' noise, and their snake form in terms of their rivers' overall shape and bends: see Strab. 10. 2. 19.

sense of its vast pathless expanse or its hidden depths.[10] Such fantasies about shape-shifting as we find concern clouds, not water.[11]

What also points to a more complex origin of this pattern is that not all sea creatures are shape-shifters. Most obviously the greatest of the sea spirits, Poseidon himself, is not; although he changes his shape on occasions to seduce women and goddesses, as does Zeus or Apollo, he does not go through the magical series of changes. Nor do the various sea monsters; though the god or monster Triton sometimes takes the place of the old man of the sea on vases depicting the fight of Heracles with a sea monster, these vases never indicate transformations. This is quite in keeping with the literary sources. Of sea creatures it is only the old men or the women who have this power.

The aquatic nature of shape-shifters must therefore be part of a more complex mythical scheme.

THE OLD MAN OF THE SEA

The earliest attested stories of shape-shifting are those of Proteus and Nereus, the old men of the sea. In Book 4 of the *Odysssey* Menelaus tells how he and his men were stranded on the island of Pharos until a goddess, Eidothea, came to his help and told him he should capture and consult her father, Proteus, the old man of the sea.[12] Every day Proteus came ashore with his flocks of seals and slept for the afternoon. Menelaus should seize him as soon as he fell asleep and hold on to him through a series of transformations until he resumed his original shape. He would then tell Menelaus what he wanted to know. The goddess hides Menelaus and his companions

[10] We may note such Homeric epithets as ἀπείριτος, ἀπείρων, ἀθέσφατος, πολυβενθής.

[11] See Ar. *Nub.* 346 ff.; DS 3. 50. 4; Cic. *Div.* 2. 21. 49; Lucr. 4. 136 ff.

[12] *Od.* 4. 351 ff. Cf. Virg. *G* 4. 387 ff.; Ov. *Met.* 8. 730 ff., *Ars Am.* 1. 761 f.; Hyg. *Fab.* 118; DS 1. 62; Ath. 345 A; Nonn. 1. 13 ff., 43. 230 ff.; Lesky (op. cit. n. 3), 120–7; F. Fischer, *Nereiden und Okeaniden in Hesiods Theogonie* (diss. Halle, 1934), 115–19; K. O'Nolan, *Hermes* 88 (1960), 129–38; R. Goossens, *Mélanges F. Cumont* ii (Paris, 1936), 715–22; M. Detienne, *Les Maîtres de la vérité dans la Grèce archaïque* (Paris, 1967), 30–50.

under seal skins, and they capture the old man as she advises. Proteus tells them of the sacrifices Menelaus must perform in order to leave the island, of the fates of the other Greek heroes, and of Menelaus' eventual translation to Elysium. Later accounts do not add much; there is a certain amount of variation in the choice of transformations, and in later sources he is bound rather than being merely held down. Virgil transfers the episode to the story of Aristaeus and his bees but preserves the basic features of the Homeric account.[13]

Pherecydes is the first writer cited for the story of how Heracles fights with Nereus to get him to reveal the way to the Hesperides.[14] But the depiction of Heracles' fight with a fish-tailed man in art seems to be much earlier.[15] On a seventh-century relief the figure is called *halios geron* ('the old man of the sea') and transformations are indicated, while fragments of an early sixth-century vase actually name this figure as Nereus. On a series of later sixth-century vases the monster is called 'Triton', no transformations are indicated, and Nereus is sometimes shown as an onlooker. Finally at the end of the sixth century and in the fifth vases show a human-figured Nereus and again indicate transformations.

I think it is unnecessary to decide which of these figures is earlier. I shall consider them both as examples of the same figure, the 'old man of the sea' (a name which appears both in art and literature before Proteus and Nereus).[16] Their stories show more or less the same pattern: among the common features are a mysterious and remote location, the hero lost on his mission, the helping daughter, the old man coming ashore and sleeping, the transformations, and the winning of knowledge.

There are two important contrasts in this story. First, there is the contrast and confrontation of man and god. In each case a mortal

[13] A later, probably rationalizing, tradition makes Proteus a human king of Egypt: see Hdt. 2. 112 ff., DS 1. 62, and Eur. *Helen*.

[14] *FGH* 3 F 16A. Cf. Apollod. 2. 5. 11.

[15] See R. Glynn, *AJA* 85 (1981), 121–32; E. Buschor, *Meermänner, Sitz. München* 2. 1 (1941). Cf. S. B. Luce, *AJA* 26 (1922), 174–92; K. Shephard, *The Fish-Tailed Monster* (New York, 1940).

[16] In the *Iliad* the father of the Nereids is known as ἅλιος γέρων, not Nereus. In cults too Γέρων is primary: see e.g. Paus. 3. 21. 9; Dion. Byz. 49. See West on *Theog.* 233.

hero remarkably overcomes a god (as Menelaus points out, 'it is hard for a mortal man to subdue a god'[17]). Second, and perhaps more important for our understanding of the transformations,[18] there is a contrast between the old man of the sea on the one hand and the Olympian and heroic world on the other (in fact Eidothea never actually refers to Proteus as a god, nor does the narrative). Proteus belongs to a class of marginal figures who play a part in a number of heroic journeys, usually standing some way between humans and gods, and whom the hero has to consult. We may compare Teiresias in the story of Odysseus, Phineus in the story of the Argonauts, the Graiai in the story of Perseus, and perhaps Atlas in the story of Heracles, or Prometheus in the story of Io in the *Prometheus*. There is something ambiguous about the status of all these characters,[19] and all, as well as having mysterious knowledge, are contrasted with, and have become enemies of, the Olympian gods.

Proteus is not in Homer an actual enemy of the gods,[20] but the essence of his character lies in his contrast both with the hero and the hero's divine adviser. His basic attribute is his knowledge, but even in this he is distinguished from his daughter Eidothea. Whereas she, like the Olympians, helps men of her own accord, he is grudging in his information and has to have it forced out of him. Whereas she has apparently the wisdom of the gods,[21] he is characterized as the possessor of 'baneful knowledge'.[22] We may

[17] *Od.* 4. 397.

[18] Since, when he is seen as an unambiguous and positive divine figure in the *Theogony* 232 ff., he is not given the power of shape-shifting.

[19] They are all marginal figures. They live apart from men on the edge of the world, and in each case some striking physical disability balances their mysterious powers: blindness in the case of Phineus and Teiresias, only one tooth and eye in the case of the Graiai, being bound in the case of Atlas and Prometheus. The first three are also afflicted by old age (the Graiai are grey-haired from birth), while Atlas and Prometheus belong to the older generation of the gods.

[20] Although a different tradition, which locates Proteus in Pallene, makes his sons villains who are killed by Heracles: see Lyc. 115 f. and scholia; Conon, 32; Westermann, *Myth.* 383.

[21] Or else the appearance of the gods, depending on how one interprets the meaning of her name *Eidothea*. In either case she is a more conventional godlike figure.

[22] ὀλοφώια εἰδώς. The meaning of this is uncertain, but the phrase is used of Circe, a strange immoral magician, who, like Proteus, is overcome with the help of a higher god;

note further that the Olympian gods do not generally have a knowledge of the future; for this they have to rely on some older figure.[23]

This brings us to the second defining characteristic of the old man of the sea, his age.[24] Olympian gods do not become old however long they live; their immortality means perpetual youth, health, and beauty.[25] Although the myth is not referred to in literary sources a number of vases reveal a story in which Heracles threatens Old Age in the form of a repellent old man; the scene is similar to depictions of Heracles' pursuit of Nereus.[26] Not only is Proteus old, but he lives among the repellent-smelling seals; this smell is only overcome by the ambrosia which Eidothea gives to the heroes. The contrast between ambrosia and the smell of the deep is of the same nature as that between the meaning of the name Eidothea and the description of Proteus as the possessor of baneful knowledge.

Thirdly, there is the nature of his power. Like Circe's, it is characterized as a 'crafty skill';[27] this contrasts with the power of the gods and their favourites, which tends to be natural *arete* ('heroic excellence or valour').[28] His means of fighting is not the heroic battle, the method of the Olympian god who is modelled on the heroic warrior, but a succession of magical tricks. Although, unlike Circe, he makes no use of magical drugs the scholia, which (like Plato) assume that Proteus must be a magician, saw various magical elements in his story.[29] It is important that Proteus, in spite of his

Atlas, Aietes, and Minos are described as ὀλοόφρων. See W. B. Stanford on *Od.* 1. 52 (London, 1958).

[23] e.g. Themis, Prometheus, or the earth. Even Apollo, the god of prophecy, has to seize Delphi from the earth and in myth at least shows no special knowledge of the future.

[24] His old age or rather antiquity is reinforced by his name, presumably derived from πρῶτος.

[25] Their freedom from old age is a distinguishing mark of the gods as is illustrated by the story of Tithonus.

[26] See C. Smith, *JHS* 4 (1883), 96–110; F. Brommer, *Arch. Anz.* 67 (1952), 59–73. Sometimes even youthful enemies of the gods are differentiated as old men on vases: e.g. Alkyoneus or Antaeus (see *LIMC* s.v. Alkyoneus no. 17) or even Actaeon (see B. E. Richardson, *Old Age among the Greeks* (Baltimore, 1933), 98–100).

[27] δολίη τέχνη: *Od.* 4. 455.

[28] In Pind. *Nem.* 4. 57 f. Peleus overcomes the δόλιαι τέχναι of Hippolyte. The heroic craftsmen of Rhodes have a σόφια ἄδολος: Pind. *Ol.* 7. 53.

[29] For Plato see above, n. 4. Servius (*G* 4. 400) comments on his appearance at midday 'fere enim numina tunc videntur'; on midday demons in general see R. Caillois, *RHR* 115

magical arts, is finally mastered, as the Olympians, with one or two notable exceptions, are not. His story thus belongs to a type in which the magical power of the antagonist proves to be futile against the *arete* of an Olympian god or of a hero advised or supported by an Olympian. Like invulnerability it is a foil, a device introduced only to be overcome.

Fourthly, as well as by his knowledge and his age Proteus is distinguished from the Olympians by his home. The smell to which Menelaus objects is the smell of the deep,[30] and it is to this that Proteus belongs. Whereas Poseidon moves perfectly easily between Olympus and the sea (and on the land among human beings) it is impossible to imagine Proteus on Olympus or moving about among men. We can pursue this point further. The sea may be seen as a place of secret knowledge and skills and also as an alternative, older, and sometimes subversive world that is contrasted with the world of Olympians and of men in the same way as the world under the earth is.[31] Proteus may be compared with the Telchines and the Kabeiroi,[32] mysterious and magical craftsmen of the sea, who were supposed to be very old,[33] and who had an ambiguous relation with the gods (several stories tell how the gods finally destroy the Telchines[34]). The Telchines are called wizards and magicians[35] and, like Proteus, are jealous of their knowledge. The Kabeiroi are supposed to be Proteus' grandchildren by his wife Anchinoia.[36] The

(1937), 142–73; 116 (1937), 54–83 and 143–86. On his seals' usefulness for magical purposes see Eustathius on *Od.* 4. 402, and Detienne–Vernant, 261–9. The holding down of Proteus, a metaphorical binding which in later sources becomes a literal one, may be seen as an act of magical significance. Spells in Greek are bindings (*κατάδεσμοι*): e.g. the binding song in the *Eumenides*. See M. Delcourt, *Héphaistos ou la légende du magicien* (Paris, 1957), ch. 1.

[30] See *Od.* 4. 406.

[31] See Fontenrose, *Python*, ch. 6, which considers the links between the monsters of the deep and the underworld, and Ninck, ch. 1. Fischer (op. cit. n. 12), *passim*, argues that nearly all sea deities are in origin chthonic creatures.

[32] On the Telchines see Suetonius in Eust. *Il.* 9. 529; Strab. 14. 2. 7; DS 5. 55; Detienne–Vernant, ch. 9. On the Kabeiroi, B. Hemberg, *Die Kabiren* (Uppsala, 1950); Burkert, *GR* 420–6.

[33] The ancient name of Rhodes was 'Telchinia'; ancient images of the gods were known as Telchinian. The Kabeiroi at Pergamum were the oldest of the gods (Aristid. *Or.* 53. 3).

[34] See Suet., DS (both cited in n. 32); Callim. *Ait.* fr. 75. 64; Ov. 7. 365 ff.

[35] See Suet. (loc. cit. n. 32).

[36] Pherecydes, *FGH* 3 F 48.

depths of the sea are hidden and unknowable for men. Knowledge of them is an obvious model and image of knowledge of the future or any other hidden subject. Thus Proteus, whose primary characteristic is that he knows the depths of the sea, is also able to prophesy the future to Menelaus.[37] Among the exiles and subversive figures who hide in the sea are Hephaistos, Dionysos, Typhon, and Ophion and Eurynome, the previous rulers of heaven.[38] Like the earth the sea is the home or origin of countless monsters, and Poseidon, though an Olympian himself, is the father of most of the monstrous and violent enemies of the gods.[39]

This suggests, I think, a different way of seeing Proteus' connection with the sea and its relation to his powers of transformation. The sea does not so much directly explain his fluidity of form as help, like his age, his knowledge of the future, and his magic, to characterize him as someone standing outside the orthodox Olympian and heroic world. The power of transformation is appropriate to such a figure and is a further element in his differentiation. In the case of the old man of the sea, however, it is perhaps his physical and social as much as his geographical marginality that is relevant to his shape-shifting. At the purely narrative level an old man is no threat or worthy opponent to a young hero; the power of shape-shifting, the means of making him into a formidable opponent, has an essential connection with his old age and weakness (the other transforming sea deities are also weak figures, women).

[37] What Eidothea says is that her father will tell Menelaus the *ὅδον καὶ μέτρα κελεύθου | νόστον θ'* i.e. implying geographical instructions. What he actually tells him is how he has offended the gods, the fates of his companions, and his own future. For knowledge of the sea meaning one knows everything West, p. 233, compares orac. ap. Hdt. 1. 47.

[38] Hephaistos is thrown from Olympus into the sea (*Il.* 18. 394 ff.), Dionysos hides there from Lycurgus (*Il.* 6. 132 ff.). For the story of how Pan lured Typhon to the sea-shore see Oppian *H* 3. 15 ff. and scholia. He was the mate of Keto. See Fontenrose, *Python*, 142–4. For Ophion and Eurynome see AR 1. 503 ff.

[39] These include Antaeus, the Aloades, Polyphemus, Briareos, Sciron, Pegasus, the Laestrygonians, the Harpies, and Lamia. Cf. Hesiod's list of the children of Phorkys in *Theog.* 270 ff.

PERICLYMENUS

Before I turn to the female shape-shifters I shall briefly consider the story of Periclymenus. He is a magical and mortal hero of Pylos, who is killed in battle by Heracles aided by Athene, after going through a series of transformations and finally assuming the form of a bee. He was given the power of transformation by his grandfather, Poseidon.[40]

At first sight he only partly conforms to the scheme I have been suggesting; although he is an aquatic figure[41] whose trickery is vanquished by simple heroic virtue aided by the advice of a higher god, he is in other respects not a marginal figure but a regular hero and the son of a king, and his transformations take place in a heroic sphere on the battlefield. It is possible that his connection with the sea has, by a secondary process, led to the power of transformation being given to a regular hero, but it may be that he was once a more marginal figure subsequently given a more conventional heroic form by the epic tradition. In particular it has been suggested that Periclymenus is in origin Hades himself[42] and that the battle of Heracles with Periclymenus is in origin a battle with death. As a god of the dead he may have been imagined as an old man. This theory is based on his name (which is one of the names of the god of the underworld) and the names of his family, and on a tradition that Hades fought at Pylos.[43] This is speculation but not completely

[40] See Hes. frs. 33 and 35; Apollod. 1. 9. 8 and 2. 7. 3; AR 1. 156 ff. and scholia; Euphorion, fr. 64; schol. *Od.* 11. 281 and 285, and *Il.* 2. 333; Ov. *Met.* 12. 556 ff.; Hyg. *Fab.* 10; Nonn. 43. 247 ff. Ovid says he was finally shot in the form of an eagle, Hyginus that he escaped in the form of an eagle. That Poseidon had an ancient connection with Pylos is shown by the sacrifice of Nestor in *Od.* 3. 5 ff. and by the Linear B tablets found at Pylos (see Burkert, *GR* 43–4).

[41] See Euphorion, fr. 64, and for his connection with the sea-god Poseidon see above, n. 40.

[42] See most fully Fontenrose, *Python*, 327–30. Cf. Burkert, *SH* 86.

[43] Periclymenus and Clymenus are names of the god of the underworld (see Hes. fr. 136 and Hsch. s.v. *Περικλύμενος*). His father is Neleus and his brothers include *Ἀλάστωρ* and *Πυλάων* (Hades is elsewhere *Πυλάρτης*: *Il.* 8. 367). For the battle of Hades at Pylos see *Il.* 5. 397; Pind. *Ol.* 9. 29 ff.; Apollod. 2. 7. 3. We are left with the fact that Periclymenus has close links with Poseidon, the sea-god, and Poseidon is the traditional god of Pylos. But

implausible. The theory would help to explain the very unusual character of the warrior and the fact that he is the only mortal among the figures we are considering.

THETIS

Our first account of the story of the capture of Thetis by Peleus is in Pindar. He tells how the hero overcame fire, lions, and snakes to win her, and all the gods attended her wedding.[44] Here marriage with a god is simply a reward for Peleus' piety; elsewhere Pindar explains the background more fully: Zeus and Poseidon both pursue Thetis, but when they learn from Themis that she will bear a son greater than his father they marry her off to a mortal.[45]

It is uncertain what form the story took in earlier poets. Homer does not mention the transformation, but he does make Thetis say that Zeus forced her into a humiliating marriage.[46] In the *Cypria*, apparently, Thetis refused Zeus, and the god in anger swore that she should marry a mortal.[47] We do not know whether the *Cypria* mentioned the transformation, nor whether it combined the story of Thetis' rejection of Zeus with the normal story of the prophecy about her son, as Apollonius does.[48]

The later sources do not add much to Pindar's account.[49] Sometimes the prophecy is given not by Themis but by Prometheus.[50] Some accounts, such as those of Alcaeus or Catullus, emphasize the blessedness of the marriage of the god and mortal and therefore play down the violent capture of Thetis;[51] others emphasize the violent capture at the expense of the more decorous wedding. Thus

Fontenrose, *Python*, 327–30, argues that Poseidon can be a death-god. (According to Paus. 3. 25. 4 there was thought to be an entrance to the underworld in his temple at Cape Taenarum.)

[44] *Nem.* 4. 62 f. [45] *Isthm.* 8. 27 ff. [46] *Il.* 18. 433–4.

[47] *Cypria* fr. 2. Cf. Hes. fr. 210. [48] AR 4. 790 ff.

[49] Other sources for the transformation story: Apollod. 3. 13. 5; schol. Pind. *Nem.* 3. 60, which quotes two plays of Sophocles; schol. Lyc. 175 and 178, which cites Euripides; Ov. 11. 218 ff.; schol. AR 1. 582; QS 3. 618 ff.; schol. *Il.* 18. 433, citing the *νεώτεροι*; Paus. 5. 18. 5. The story is a very popular one in ancient art: see Brommer, *Vasenlisten*, 321–9.

[50] See Apollod. 3. 13. 5; Aesch. *PV* 908 ff.

[51] Alcaeus, fr. 42, and Catullus 64.

Sophocles spoke of the 'silent marriage' of Thetis,[52] while Euripides apparently had Peleus raping Thetis in a cave at Cape Sepia.[53] The scholia also attribute to Euripides a story of a bestial union after she assumed the form of a cuttle-fish (for which the Greek word is *sepia*[54]); it seems more likely that this particular transformation was a secondary development rather than the starting-point of the story of her multiple transformations. The normal sequel to the wedding is that Thetis quarrels with and leaves Peleus shortly after the birth of Achilles and returns to the sea.[55]

It is often pointed out that the story of Thetis is very similar to a common folk-tale pattern in which a man wins some otherworldly bride, either from the sea or in the woods.[56] After a period they quarrel or some accident happens and she returns to her own world. Sophocles' 'silent marriage' is particularly suggestive of such a pattern.[57] But it would be a mistake to infer from this, as some have, that we have two distinct traditions in the story of Thetis, on the one hand the myth of the plan of Zeus and the wedding feast attended by the gods and on the other a folk-tale that tells of Peleus' violent capture of a transforming sea spirit on his own initiative. It seems that Homer already knew of Thetis' discontent with her marriage, and Pindar combines the marriage feast of the gods with the story of the transformation, and the prophecy of Themis with the cave of Cheiron. The introduction of the plan of the gods into the story is not incompatible with the transformation but quite in harmony with it, since in all versions their intention is to humiliate Thetis. The sources which definitely exclude all reluctance on

[52] Fr. 618.

[53] See schol. Lyc. 178 (cf. *Andr.* 1265).

[54] See schol. Lyc. 175; schol. *Andr.* 1266.

[55] For modern discussions of the story see J. Kaiser, *Peleus und Thetis* (diss. Munich, 1912); K. Tümpel, *Bemerkungen zu einigen Fragen der griechischen Religionsgeschichte* (Neustettin, 1887), 11–17; F. Jouan, *Euripide et les légendes des chants cypriens* (Paris, 1966), ch. 2; A. Lesky, *Stud. Ital.* 27/8 (1956), 216–26 and *RE* article 'Peleus'; Detienne–Vernant, ch. 5; R. Stoneman, *Philol.* 125 (1981), 58–63.

[56] See Frazer, *Apollodorus*, App. 10; G. Benwell, *Sea Enchantress* (London, 1961); W. Mannhardt, *Wald- und Feldkulte*, ii² (Berlin, 1905), 60–70; J. C. Lawson, *Modern Greek Folklore* (Cambridge, 1910), 134–9.

[57] It is not clear whether 'silent marriage' refers simply to a rape, or to some story like the modern Cretan folk-tale of the silent bride: see Frazer (loc. cit. n. 56).

Thetis' part are very rare, and are normally making some special moral point.[58] While, therefore, the marriage of hero and god may sometimes be treated as a separate motif the story as a whole is nearly always a more ambiguous one, and the role of the gods is central to this ambiguity.

Thetis is a more complicated figure than the old man of the sea, and transformation is here connected with winning a bride rather than acquiring knowledge, but her story does reveal similar oppositions to that of the old man. She too may be seen, like Proteus, simply as a god, particularly in those accounts that stress the blessedness of the wedding, but in her case also what is most relevant to the shape-shifting is the opposition and contrast between the sea spirit and the Olympian gods. She shares the old man's sea character in the widest sense. Thus she too has magical powers quite apart from her shape-shifting. Most mysterious perhaps are her attempts to burn out the mortal parts of her children, but there are perhaps also hints of magical powers in the prophecy that she will bear a son greater than his father (the other person of whom this is said is the magical Metis). She also has prophetic powers: she knows and tells her son of his fate and warns him not to kill Tennes (in one tradition she is merged with Hippo the prophetic daughter of Cheiron).[59]

But her magical and prophetic powers are of course futile attempts to frustrate the purpose of the Olympians who have decided that her son must die. They are therefore closely parallel in function to her shape-shifting, since her marriage to a mortal is an essential first step in this plan. The overall framework of the story makes her a threat to the Olympians; she is in this sense quite explicitly a figure of subversion, and Peleus by winning her is explicitly fulfilling the plan of the Olympians. She is of course a passively subversive figure in that she is never explicitly given the motive of wanting to overthrow the Olympians. But in this respect

[58] Alcaeus wishes to contrast the disreputable affair of Paris with the blessed marriage of Peleus, while Catullus is presenting a romantic picture of a golden age in which gods and men mixed and even married.

[59] Burning her children: Hes. fr. 300 (cf. the stories of the 'witch' Medea, or Demeter at Eleusis). Metis: see the next section of this chapter. As Hippo: see *RML* article 'Thetis' (col. 785).

her initial motives do not really matter. Her threat is a real one, and it can be assumed that she will owe her first loyalty to her son, in the familiar pattern of the divine succession myth. To a large extent our picture of Thetis is coloured by the treatment of the *Iliad*, where she is an honorary Olympian and a close ally of Zeus: a more mysterious and darker figure emerges from our other sources.[60] It is interesting that even in the *Iliad* there are hints of her role as a representative of an alien or alternative world. She is described as looking after Hephaistos when he is exiled from Olympus, and she releases the monstrous Briareos, presumably from under the sea, who terrifies the gods into submission.[61] He too like Thetis' own son is, we are told, greater than his father. In her appearance she retains something of the darkness of the deep: she emerges from the sea wearing a dark veil 'than which no garment is blacker'.[62]

The contrasts that we find in the case of Thetis are thus familiar ones in the context of shape-shifting: magic is set against the plans of the higher gods and their hero; a marginal and apparently weak figure, this time a woman, is set against a male hero and two male gods; and again the heroic and Olympian world is set against that of the deep.

METIS

The story of Metis ('Cunning') first appears in the *Theogony* and in a Hesiodic fragment. She is, like Thetis, a goddess whose son will be greater than his father. This time Zeus, who has seduced or married her, swallows her whole and then gives birth himself, not to a son, but to the goddess Athene; in addition he now possesses 'cunning' inside himself. Metis' transformations, which are only mentioned in later accounts, are an attempt to escape Zeus, either in his initial wooing or when he attempts to swallow her.[63]

[60] See above, n. 59.

[61] See *Il.* 1. 397 ff.

[62] *Il.* 24. 94–5. See Detienne–Vernant, 158; they compare the ritual address κυάνεα (Philostr. *Her.* 208).

[63] See Hes. *Theog.* 886 ff. and fr. 343. For the transformation story see Apollod. 1. 3. 6, schol. *Theog.* 886, schol. *Il.* 8. 39. The two Hesiodic accounts are discussed by S. Kauer, *Die Geburt der Athena im altgr. Epos* (Würzburg, 1959), and West's note on *Theog.* 886 ff. See also

No historical cults of Metis are mentioned, and she is apparently an entirely mythical personification. It has been pointed out that her story is an amalgamation of three different elements.[64] There is first a common story of how Zeus puts an end to the pattern of divine succession in which a more powerful son overthrows his father; secondly, the explanation of the birth of Athene, the goddess of *metis*, from the head of Zeus; and finally, the *aition* for the *metis* of Zeus (he is given the epithet 'cunning' nineteen times in the *Iliad*).

Such an explanation of the story in terms of its parts can only take us a certain way. In bringing these elements together the story-teller has created a new structure which is more than the sum of its parts and which we should be able to explain in terms of the familiar patterns and themes of Greek myths. In fact this story of Metis does conform to the pattern of the shape-shifter: we have the same contrast of Olympian god and subversive outsider, of male and female, of the new order and the older generation of the gods, of magician and god, and of sea and sky.

The subversive character of Metis is explicit. We have the same motif as in the Thetis story in that she represents a threat to the established order through her son; here, however, she is crushed by Zeus himself (the further theme of the Peleus and Thetis and the Proteus stories, the confrontation of man and god, is completely absent). She is a daughter of Ocean and is thus characterized not only as belonging to a different element but to an ancient generation of the gods[65] (all Zeus' early brides are of this type). Later Orphic cosmologies expand on this and make Metis the previous ruler of the universe who is absorbed by Zeus.[66] As with the other sea figures her magic and knowledge is not restricted to her power of transformation (as is indicated explicitly by her name); it is Metis who prepares a special potion to make Kronos vomit up his

Cook, *Zeus*, iii. 739–47; H. Jeanmaire, *Rev. Arch.* 48 (1956), 12–19; N. O. Brown, *TAPA* 83 (1952), 130–43; M. W. M. Pope, *AJP* 81 (1960), 113–35; Detienne–Vernant, chs. 4 and 5.

[64] See West on *Theog.* 886–900.

[65] In the *Theogony* Ocean is made one of the Titans. In most sources he has a unique antiquity (see e.g. *Il.* 14. 201).

[66] See O. Kern, *Hermes* 74 (1939), 207–8; R. Merkelbach, *ZPE* 1 (1967), 21–32. Metis is thought of as a primordial power in Alcman's cosmology (see M. L. West, *CQ* 13 (1963), 154–6, and 17 (1967), 1–15).

children.[67] Not only does this episode draw attention to her magical skills; it also emphasizes the devious methods and subversive nature of this sea creature. In a previous reign too she was a threat to, and in this case actually conspired against, the established order. In fact, in this respect she closely resembles Prometheus, another god renowed for his cunning who helps to undermine the power of Kronos, and also tries to undermine that of Zeus. It is interesting that he too gets drawn into the story of Zeus' successor, since in the *Prometheus* he alone knows and will not reveal the name of the woman who will bear him.

Each of the consequences of Zeus' swallowing of Metis, his acquiring of *metis* and the birth of Athene, provides a compromise in the oppositions of the story. On the one hand we have an enlarged Zeus. Zeus is primarily a god of masculine strength and power who rules by the thunderbolt, the familiar sky-god of Near Eastern and Indian mythology; and yet in this story he uses and acquires the *metis* that is the characteristic compensation of the weak.[68] Athene, whose birth is the second consequence, is an anomaly: on the one hand she is a woman, and thus potentially an outsider and a rebel in Zeus' order,[69] and she is endowed with her mother's *metis*,[70] but on the other hand she is someone who totally identifies herself with her father and with men, and denies her nature as a woman.[71] She dresses as a man and fights as a heroic warrior, not as a shape-shifter like her mother. It is in fact Athene who helps Heracles destroy the shape-shifter Periclymenus.

Finally it is interesting that in the second Hesiodic account of the story and in that of Apollodorus the whole story is set in a context of sexual rivalry. Hera has given birth to Hephaistos without a man, and Zeus' seduction of Metis and giving birth to Athene is Zeus'

[67] Apollod. 1. 2. 1.

[68] See e.g. Melissus, the small athlete of Pind. *Isthm.* 4 who makes up for his lack of size with the *metis* of a fox. Cf. Antilochus in *Il.* 23. 306 ff. The great hero of *metis* is Odysseus who continually finds himself in unheroic and undignified positions. For the meaning of μῆτις see Jeanmaire (art. cit. n. 63), 18 f.; Detienne–Vernant, *passim*.

[69] Cf. Hera's continual opposition to Zeus' plans.

[70] See *Od.* 13. 296 ff.

[71] Most obviously in her judgement at the end of the *Eumenides*: τὸ δ' ἄρσεν αἰνῶ πάντα (737).

answer to this. Both the prelude and the consequence of the story of Metis, the birth of Athene, show that the antithesis and conflict of men and women is important in this story and not merely an incidental consequence of the fact that *metis* is a feminine noun.

NEMESIS

Nemesis is, like Metis, a personification; her name means 'retribution' or 'anger'. But unlike Metis she was actually worshipped as a goddess. Her most famous cult was at Rhamnus in Attica,[72] where she was worshipped as a daughter of Ocean. Her story first appears in the *Cypria*.[73] Pursued by Zeus through the whole world she changed from one form to another, until finally when she took the form of a goose Zeus adopted a similar form and raped her. The result was the egg from which Helen, the cause of the Trojan war, was born. (The story was later reconciled with the tradition that the mother of Helen was Leda by having Leda discover the egg, hatch it, and bring up the child.)[74]

In contrast to the stories of the other shape-shifters, there is here one transformation, the final change to a goose, that is significantly more important than the others. It may be, therefore, that the starting-point for her shape-shifting is the need to explain the egg of Helen[75] (as, for instance, the name of the hero Phocus is explained by a story that his mother was transformed into a seal). The spectacular series of changes perhaps owes something not just

[72] See Paus. 1. 33. Cratinus had her ending her flight at Rhamnus: see *PCG* iv. 179.

[73] Frs. 9 and 10; cf. Apollod. 3. 10. 7.

[74] See Apollod. 3. 10. 7; schol. Lyc. 88; Eratosth. *Cat.* 25; Paus. 1. 33. 7; Hyg. *PA* 2. 8. The story that Leda gave birth to the egg herself after being seduced in human form by a swan is found first in Eur. *Helen* 16 f.; cf. Paus. 3. 16. 1. Later the motif of seduction by a swan was transferred from Leda to Nemesis herself: see Isocr. *Or.* 10. 59; cf. Hyg. *PA* 2. 8. For modern discussions of the story see Jouan (op. cit. n. 55), 145–52; K. Kerenyi, *Mnemosyne* 7 (1939), 161–79; Cook, *Zeus*, i. 272–85; and the very full *RE* article by H. Herter.

[75] Helen's birth from an egg may be in origin an independent motif, not related to any particular mother: Neocles said that the egg fell from the moon (see Ath. 2. 57). Other poets had it fall from the sky (see Plut. *Mor.* 637 B). Sappho (fr. 166) refers to Leda finding it, but does not mention the mother. The birth of a remarkable hero from an egg is a common folk-tale motif (cf. e.g. Ibycus fr. 285).

to her watery connections, but to epithets, which suggest her unyielding nature[76] and her association with necessity. In this story even the unyielding and unconquerable goddess is conquered by Zeus, just as Metis the goddess of cunning is outwitted by him (there may be a deliberate paradox in the *Cypria*'s account of how Nemesis is overcome 'by harsh necessity'). Since Zeus' conquest is an impossible victory it perhaps invites an unusually spectacular flight and resistance.

But apart from these particular influences Nemesis' story has most of the characteristics of the pattern of the shape-shifters. We cannot show that she has other magical powers, since this is the only early story in which she appears; what we can see, however, is that her story and her character in the *Cypria* are similar to those of Thetis and Metis. It seems in fact that there is a special link between her story and that of Thetis in the *Cypria*: the marriage of Peleus and Thetis and the birth of Helen are parallel elements in Zeus' plan to start the Trojan War. Each story opposes a goddess's pride to the Olympian purpose, which is imposed only through her humiliation: we are told that Nemesis was racked by shame and anger.[77]

But she is also a god of a different type from Zeus. Some sources make her the daughter of Ocean; like Metis, therefore, she is a goddess connected with the sea and an older figure. She is also linked with a number of darker spirits. In Hesiod she is daughter of Night,[78] 'a source of misery to mortal men'; her brothers and sisters are Death, Sleep, Strife, the Fates, and Old Age (which is particularly relevant in the context of the shape-shifters). She is probably in origin a similar figure to the Erinyes.[79] As with them, anger is an essential characteristic, and it is often the anger of the dead.[80] Her story is actually very similar to that of the Erinys of Tilphusa,[81] whose anger is explained by a story that she was raped by Poseidon after turning into a horse to escape him. Perhaps we have an *aition*

[76] She is ἀπειθής: see *IG* 4. 444. That her association with necessity is early is seen from Eur. fr. 1022.

[77] *Cypria* fr. 9.

[78] *Theog.* 223.

[79] See Burkert, *GR* 185.

[80] See e.g. Soph. *El.* 792. Elsewhere she seems to have taken over from Hermes as guide of the dead: see F. J. M. De Waele, *The Magic Staff or Rod in Graeco-Roman Antiquity* (Ghent, 1927), 98. For Nemesis and death see *RE* s.v. Nemesis, col. 2365.

[81] See Paus. 8. 25. 4; cf. Paus. 8. 42. 1–4.

for Nemesis herself as much as an explanation of Helen; we are explicitly told that she feels *nemesis* herself.

Her relationship with the Olympians has some of the same ambiguity as that of the Erinyes; the Erinyes are their servants, but the relationship is sometimes strained and as gods who are older, female, and belonging to the earth and darkness they are strongly contrasted with them.

Finally, and most important, it seems that her femininity and specifically female anger are a crucial element in the story. The product of her humiliation is the most famous woman of all, a woman who will destroy countless men.[82] The destructive and sinister aspect of Helen is constantly emphasized; indeed, in the *Agamemnon* she becomes an instrument of the Erinyes.[83] The fact that a woman is humiliated is not an incidental feature of Nemesis' story but of central importance. Female anger is being manipulated by Zeus just as female *metis* was in the story of Metis. It is interesting that just as *metis* is seen as a characteristic of marginal creatures, so are anger and resentment; the gods of anger are apparently all female, and they are all given stories attributing their anger to a rape.

This story too, therefore, has a structure in which a marginal creature is contrasted with an Olympian. Nemesis is a dangerous sinister figure who is old, belongs to night or the ocean, and is a symbol of intense female pride and resentment; she becomes a tame servant of Zeus but only through violence. (Her resentment is unleashed on mankind instead.) She resists with the magical powers appropriate to such figures. She shares a necessary condition of the shape-shifters in being an Oceanid, and in her case the changes become an expression not so much of a special cunning but of the unyielding or unconquerable nature of a member of the physically weaker sex. But in the familiar pattern her magical transformations and her reputation as unconquerable prove futile and act only as a foil to the virtuosity of the hero.

I suggested in the discussion of Proteus that an important underlying psychological appeal of his story is the fear of old age and of

[82] In the *Cypria* Zeus' purpose in producing Helen is to reduce the number of mortals in the world. See also Aesch. *Ag.* 688.

[83] *Ag.* 749.

old people. Much the same applies to the women. The assertion of male dominance over a superhuman woman, especially a dangerous woman who threatens to upset the established male order, is a fantasy that is at the heart of these stories. (We may compare the stories of the conquest of the unconquerable huntresses: none of them escapes a man in the end.) The difference from the case of Proteus or Nereus is that, whereas the struggle with an old man is pure fantasy, the struggle with and taming of a woman reflects a social reality. Some of the commonest Greek metaphors for marriage and sex are those of taming and mastering[84] and even binding[85] (just as some marriage rituals appear to treat marriage itself as a rape). The language used of the struggle is often ambiguous: for instance, Sophocles uses *symplakeis*, which can describe both combat and sex, of the struggle of Peleus and Thetis. Ovid and Euripides have the struggle ending in a rape. In the story of Metis the seduction and the swallowing by Zeus (which is in effect a complete and permanent binding) are two different episodes, but they are parallel acts of mastering or outwitting and we find resistance to both attempts in the form of transformations. In the story of Nemesis there is no literal binding, but sex nevertheless is seen as a conquest and a violent act; she submits only 'under harsh necessity'. It seems likely, therefore, that the metaphors of sex and marriage are one starting-point for, or at least a close parallel to, these stories of a subduing of a bride. It is interesting to note that Thetis in the *Iliad* describes her humiliating marriage in a metaphor of this kind.[86] This could either be a hint of an already known transformation story or the starting-point for a later one.

Perhaps I should summarize these points more generally. These stories depend on an ambivalent attitude or feeling about the old and women. On the one hand they are a necessary part of the established order. Old age is something that comes to everybody except the gods and has to be accepted; more particularly the old may be seen as a source of knowledge and wisdom. Women are vital for the

[84] See C. Sourvinou-Inwood, *JHS* 107 (1987), 131–53.

[85] See e.g. the explanation of the bonds on the statue of Aphrodite Morpho: Paus. 3. 15. 11.

[86] *Il.* 18. 432; cf. *Theog.* 1006.

continuation of the family, the foundation of the social order. On the other hand the old and women are marginal figures within this order, since the central figure in the heroic world is the male warrior, and they are often suspected of subversion and of resentment or envy. This applies particularly in those spheres where they make their contribution; the old may be suspected of being unwilling to reveal or share their knowledge, or else using it to defy or undermine the authority of the ruler (as, for instance, Teiresias so often is). Women very often represent a threat through their children, either in being over-protective of their children at the expense of the father or else in getting back at the husband by killing their child. In the first class is Thetis[87] or Rhea, in the second Procne or Medea. When women or the old are attacked, their natural method of resistance will not be an orthodox trial of strength but devious and non-heroic means, particularly magic and transformations. The shape-shifters' power to change their form has its origin in the marginal character of these figures, and their connection with the sea is an imaginative expression of that character.

DIONYSOS

We come finally to Dionysos. At first sight he is quite unlike the other shape-shifters both in his nature and his stories, since he is a major god and a young man, and his transformations are not futile attempts to escape but always the means to an overwhelming victory. However, I think it can be shown that, though he is a complex figure who fits various categories, in certain important respects he belongs in this same class.

There are several stories which show his nature as a shape-shifter, though no one story combines all the familiar elements of the other shape-shifters' stories. In the *Homeric Hymn to Dionysos* he is captured by pirates and bound, like a typical shape-shifter. There follow magical transformations, as a lion and a bear appear and

[87] Thetis belongs in both classes. On the one hand she cares for Achilles but abandons his father; on the other we are told she threw her sons into the fire ὡς ἀνάξια πάσχουσα ἑαυτῆς (schol. Lyc. 178).

terrify the sailors, who then turn into dolphins. Only the lion is actually a transformation of the god; the bear is merely an apparition. In the Dionysiac stories transformation and apparition are closely related and are perhaps in origin the same thing.[88] Other versions have other animals, in Ovid tigers and a lynx, in Apollodorus snakes.[89]

In another story Antoninus Liberalis, citing Nicander, tells how Dionysos appears in the house of the Minyades and maddens them. He appears first as a woman and then goes through a series of other forms, including a bull, a lion, and a leopard[90] (we may compare the variety of forms in which he is invoked in the *Bacchae*).[91] Here, though we have a proper series of transformations, there is no binding. But the idea of Dionysos being bound or imprisoned is a basic one and occurs, apart from the story of the pirates, in the stories of Lycurgus and Pentheus; the latter is especially interesting, since some have seen in the miracles and delusions he causes as Pentheus tries to bind him echoes of a series of transformations to bull, fire, water, and air.[92] In Nonnus, finally, he undergoes an enormous series of transformations to overcome Deriades.[93]

These transformations raise one obvious preliminary objection to the approach I have been adopting. It might be supposed that Dionysos is an animal-god, in particular a bull-god, and that this is the origin and explanation of his transformations. We find, as well as the invocation in the *Bacchae*, a regular cult hymn of the Eleans which concludes by addressing the god as 'noble bull'.[94] In so far as his transformations are a narrative reflection of this animal nature he is closer to, for instance, Achelous than to Proteus or Thetis.

Dionysos is perhaps the closest figure in Greek religion to the animal-god, and his connection with a bull does seem to have similar associations of fertility to those of Achelous or Poseidon. But this is only one side of him. Some at least of his transformations are prompted by a binding in what is essentially a narrative pattern

[88] Cf. the descriptions of Proteus or Periclymenus which call their different forms apparitions or deceits: e.g. Nonn. 43. 249.

[89] On Dionysos and the pirates see Cat. 5*c* (pirates turned to dolphins).

[90] AL 10. [91] 1017 ff. [92] See Ninck, 142–3.

[93] 40. 38 ff.: panther, lion, snake, bear, fire, bull, tree, and water.

[94] Plut. *GQ* 36.

rather than the pattern of the cult epiphany. The transformations form a series in which many other animals and even elements feature as well as the bull. The function of this series seems to be to baffle the mortal observer rather than to indicate the god's affinity with any particular animal. In fact the emphasis on delusion and magical apparitions in his stories seems to bring him closer to the 'magician' Proteus than to the animal forms of Zeus and Poseidon.

Perhaps the most striking feature of Dionysos, and one which seems particularly relevant to his role as a shape-shifter, is that although he becomes one of the greatest of all the gods he retains in his myths and many of his cults a marginal character. He is above all the god of the weak and oppressed, especially women, and an opponent of the established order. Nearly all his myths show this, and it is hardly necessary to develop this point here. One may perhaps simply refer to the *Bacchae* of Euripides where we have an explicit opposition of women (and, interestingly, of the old men Cadmus and Teiresias) and the young male ruler and his soldiers. Dionysos himself appears here as effeminate and in women's clothes, an object of contempt to Pentheus. As with the other shape-shifters we find in these stories a pattern of apparent weakness leading to a frightening display of magical power.[95]

Unlike the other shape-shifters Dionysos does not live or have parents in the sea; nevertheless the sea plays an important part in his cult and myths. He is sometimes imagined as a god who arrives from the sea, and many cults have a procession in which the god is carried in a boat;[96] this is parallel perhaps to the way that he is usually presented, probably quite unhistorically,[97] as a foreigner and a god who introduces his cult from the East. In either case he is imagined as someone who comes from the outside. But the sea is also a place of refuge in the story of Lycurgus when the god is pursued by the king and takes refuge with Thetis. It is interesting that it is Dionysos who descends into the sea to fetch back to

[95] He also appears in women's dress in Aesch. *Edomoi* fr. 61; in the story of the Minyades he first appears as a woman, see AL 10; in Homer's story of Lycurgus he is a defenceless child, see *Il.* 6. 133 ff.; and in the *Homeric Hymn* he is a young boy.

[96] See Burkert, *HN* 223–4.

[97] See Burkert, *GR* 162.

Olympus that other exile, Hephaistos. He himself is never quite at home on Olympus and is almost completely ignored in the picture of the Olympians given in the *Iliad* and the *Odyssey*. Among the gods as well as among men he is an outsider. It is in this light that we should see his transformations. The fact that in his case the subversive outsider is actually successful in overthrowing the established order does not alter the fact that it is to this character that he owes his unusual gifts.

To summarize very briefly, therefore, I would argue that the series of transformations in these stories is not to be explained merely as a divine power, but that it reflects a basic difference in nature of these figures from the Olympians and the heroes on whom they are modelled. These are marginal figures: they are opposed to the Olympians in their weakness as old men or women, in their home in the sea, in their antiquity, and in their magical powers and knowledge, and their characteristic story tells how they are subdued by an Olympian or one of their favourites.

Conclusion

It is, I hope, obvious by now that there can be no one conclusion, no single explanation of metamorphosis. All along I have tried to argue that any attempt to seek the meaning of a myth in some external entity, whether this is a belief in animal-gods, some ritual feature, or some curious phenomenon of nature is a misguided one. Myths are stories, and their meaning must lie in their appeal as such. Furthermore they are traditional stories, which survive only in so far as they can appeal to successive generations of listeners: their meaning cannot consist in something apparent only to the original audience. Every now and then one comes across anomalous motifs in a myth which appear to have retained their place simply through the authority of tradition, and where it does seem more plausible to look for an origin outside the story itself: I hope I have shown that, usually at least, metamorphosis is not such a motif. For the most part the transformation makes sense within the structure of these stories, in that the imaginative function it performs within them can be tested against the patterns that are found in other Greek myths and the fantasies that are found more generally in Greek poetry and Greek beliefs about the natural world.

But also it is clear that we cannot speak of a single structure. Stories of metamorphosis offer a rich and very diverse field of fantasy and exemplify a number of quite different patterns. Within these patterns the meaning of the transformation varies, and there is no one metaphor or particular fantasy to which these stories give expression. Thus in the stories of animals transformation is associated with humiliation and madness, in those of birds it is often a form of escape, and in the stories of petrification it is usually a punishment. Neither is it a fantasy associated with a particular time of life, and thus an expression of the fear of one real physical or social change: many stories do concern boys or girls at the brink of manhood or womanhood, but we also have the transformations of Niobe, Cadmus, Lycaon, and Hecuba. Nor at the formal level is transformation a narrative motif which is interchangeable with motifs such as death (or apotheosis). The aetiological transformations are of course terminal and can therefore often be seen as a substitute for death, but this is not so of many of the changes to animals, the sex changes, or the multiple changes of the shape-shifters, which are transitional elements within a story.

There are broad themes or at least a general framework within which metamorphosis tends to be set. Transformation implies the crossing of a boundary, generally a boundary between what are seen in the rest of the story as rigid or significant categories. Prominent among such categories are the house and the wilds, the world of the living and the world of the dead, gods and men, and men and women. The hero begins in one of these worlds and through his or her transformation ends to some extent in the other; this is sometimes a metaphorical reflection or exaggeration of something that has happened in the story, and sometimes a reversal of it (it is also nearly always a form of separation and exile). However, such a broad formal analysis does not take one very far; it is the different forms such a basic structure takes on in the various types of metamorphosis myths that makes these stories interesting—their complexity rather than their uniformity.

Catalogue of Transformation Stories

I HAVE not included the transformations of the gods, or of witches and magicians, or of inanimate objects. For the sex change stories see Chapter 7.

I have referred to a number of modern discussions of the myths. It seemed unnecessary to state in each case that these stories are also discussed in the standard mythological reference books and commentaries (see especially Bömer on Ovid's *Metamorphoses* and Papathomopoulos on Antoninus Liberalis).

Under each story in the Catalogue a work will only be cited in full the first time it appears. Further references under the same story will mention only the author.

PART I. MAMMALS

a. Major Transformations

Actaeon

The story of Actaeon, the great hunter who was turned into a deer by Artemis and then torn apart by his own dogs, was popular from very early on. However, we have no complete account before Ovid. In Hesiod (see Renner, 282–7) as in the other early treatments of the story by Stesichorus (fr. 236) and Acusilaus (*FGH* 2 F 33) the reason for his punishment is that he pursued his aunt Semele as a rival to Zeus (in all our sources Actaeon is the son of Autonoe, daughter of Cadmus, and Aristaeus). The story was a common subject in Greek tragedy. We know of *Actaeon*s by Phrynichus (*TGF* 3 F 1b), Iophon (*TGF* 22 T 1a) and Cleophon (*TGF* 77 T 1), and Aeschylus treated the story in his *Toxotides* (frs. 241–6: cf. Pollux 4. 141, who mentions a tragic mask of a horned Actaeon). The title of Aeschylus' play presumably refers to the nymph companions of Artemis and therefore might suggest a plot more like the later intrusion upon the goddess and her companions than the rivalry of Actaeon and Zeus. The fragments we do have suggest that the play may have featured a characteristic opposition of the sexes (cf. *Eumenides* or *Supplices*), and it is possible that

Actaeon was here a misogynist hunter like Euripides' Hippolytus or Aristophanes' Melanion (see fr. 243).

Our earliest surviving account of the story is the brief passage in the *Bacchae* (337 ff.) where Cadmus recounts Actaeon's fate as a warning to Pentheus. Here Actaeon's crime is boasting that he is a better hunter than Artemis (but see p. 18). The comparison of Pentheus and Actaeon, two cousins who are both torn apart on Mount Cithaeron, is a common one in later literature and art (cf. Lucian *Dial. D.* 16, *Salt.* 41, *Peregr.* 2, *Deor. Conc.* 7, *Sat.* 8; Philostr. *Imag.* 1. 14; Claud. *In Rufin.* 2. 418 f.).

It is first in Callimachus, again only in a brief *exemplum*, that we find the story of how Actaeon came across the goddess bathing (*Hymn.* 5. 111 ff.). This is the version that became standard later on (see Ov. *Met.* 3. 198 ff., *Tr.* 2. 103 f.; Apollod. 3. 4. 4; Paus. 9. 2. 3; Stat. *Theb.* 3. 210 ff.; Lucian; Hyg. *Fab.* 180 and 181; Fulg. 3. 3; Nonn. 5. 287 ff.; Arn. *Adv. Nat.* 3. 34; schol. Theoc. 5. 38; Westermann, *Myth.* 360; Sen., *Oedip.* 751 ff.; Claudian). The spirit of this account is different from that of Euripides. As one might expect, Callimachus emphasizes the pathos of the story. Actaeon here is an innocent youth, the companion of Artemis, who trespasses quite accidentally; the story concludes with a description of how his mother searches for her son's body. A black-figure pyxis, which shows the dead Actaeon being carried away by Autonoe and her sisters, shows, however, that this pathetic detail is not Callimachus' own invention; see *LIMC* s.v. Aktaion (henceforth *LIMC*) no. 121. It is possible that the whole story or at least some of its details were invented to suit its context, since it is told as a comparison with the intrusion and punishment of Teiresias. But by Pausanias' time at least the story had become a local *aition*. He tells of a rock on Mount Cithaeron called κοίτη Ἀκταίωνος near which was the spring in which Actaeon saw Artemis bathing.

Our fullest source, Ovid, follows Callimachus in emphasizing the pathos of the story and the innocence of Actaeon, although he makes much more of the nightmarish aspect of the experience of the hero since Actaeon becomes a deer with a human mind (cf. Seneca or Nonnus). Other sources however make him a voyeur or even a rapist and thus come closer to the earlier conception of Actaeon (Statius, Nonnus, Fulgentius, Arnobius, Hyg. *Fab.* 180). In *Fab.* 181 Hyginus closely follows Ovid. Diodorus (4. 81) says that Actaeon assaulted Artemis in her temple when he was dedicating his hunting spoils.

It has been claimed that there was a different version of the story in which Artemis did not transform Actaeon but merely disguised him with a deer-skin. Pausanias writes:

ἐς δὲ τὴν πηγὴν ἐνιδεῖν λέγουσιν αὐτὸν λουομένης Ἀρτέμιδος ἐν τῇ πηγῇ. Στησίχορος δὲ ὁ Ἱμεραῖος ἔγραψεν ἐλάφου περιβαλεῖν δέρμα Ἀκταίωνι τὴν θεόν, παρασκευάζουσάν οἱ τὸν ἐκ τῶν κυνῶν θάνατον ἵνα δὴ μὴ γυναῖκα Σεμέλην λάβοι. (9. 2. 3)

In itself the phrase **περιβαλεῖν δέρμα** is ambiguous. But the context makes clear, I think, that a normal transformation is being referred to. This is the only reference to the conclusion of the story. Transformation is not mentioned anywhere else. It looks therefore as if what he is contrasting with the popular version is Stesichorus' motive; the transformation and death which we should expect to be mentioned somewhere are common to both versions. On this question see H. J. Rose, *Mnemosyne* 59 (1932), 431–2; G. Nagy, *HSCP* 77 (1973), 179–80.

Actaeon's dogs were a major source of interest in themselves. Some sources give lists of their names (e.g. Ov., Hyg. or the *Epyllium Actaeonis*: see Powell, *Coll. Al.* 71–2 and A. Grilli, *PP* 26 (1971), 354–67), and many writers say that his dogs were maddened by the goddess (e.g. Paus. and Apollod.; cf. two vases: *LIMC* nos. 81 and 88). After their crime the dogs feel remorse, or at least miss their master. Apollodorus tells how Cheiron made an *eidolon* of Actaeon to soothe their grief. A hexameter fragment tells how a goddess goes to Cheiron's cave and makes a prophecy that the dogs will be taken over by Dionysos (*POxy.* 2509; see Renner, 283). Armenidas had them transformed to Telchines (*FGH* 378 F 8). Nicander had them travel to India (Pollux 5. 37).

Finally, there was a Corinthian story of Actaeon, the son of Melissus, which seems to be loosely modelled on that of the Boeotian hero. Here Actaeon has been incorporated into the history of Greek colonization. The story tells how the hero was accidentally torn apart as his lover Archias and his friends struggled to take him from his family. Archias, one of the Bacchiads, the historical ruling family at Corinth, was eventually banished and went off to found Syracuse (Plut. *Amat.* 2, *Sert.* 1; cf. Parth. 14; schol. AR 4. 1212, DS 8. 10; Max. Tyr. 18. 1). See M. Broadbent, *Studies in Greek Genealogy* (Leiden, 1958), 44–51, A. Andrewes, *CQ* 43 (1949), 70–8.

The story of Actaeon was also a popular theme in ancient art (see *LIMC*; P. Jacobsthal, *Marburger Jahrbuch für Kunstwissenschaft* 5 (1929), 1–23), but the relation between the literary and the artistic traditions is not always clear. The artistic depictions of the story are concerned mainly with the end of the story, the death of Actaeon. They show Actaeon, his dogs, and usually the goddess; they are less consistent, however, in regard to Actaeon's transformation. Our earliest vases from the sixth and early fifth century do not show a transformation at all; we next find a small group of vases and a metope from Selinus which show Actaeon wearing a deerskin; after this it becomes normal to hint at the transformation by giving him horns or animal ears. The earliest of this last group of vases is about 490, but most date from the fourth century and after (*LIMC* nos. 33a ff.). It has been argued that these three types of depiction are evidence for three different versions of the story: in one Actaeon was not transformed at all, in another he had a deerskin thrown over him, as in the supposed Stesichorus version, and thirdly we have the familiar transformation story of our literary sources.

Of course the human-figured Actaeon did become an artistic type, and in this limited sense we do have different versions of the story, but we need not infer that the story of Actaeon was ever told in either of these other forms. Transformation is not a popular theme in classical art, perhaps for obvious reasons. Whereas literary treatments of the story can make much of Actaeon's human mind in an animal body a literal artistic representation of his death would simply show a deer torn apart by dogs. Classical art normally presents heroes of transformation stories in human form, and sometimes hints at the transformations indirectly. Thus Thetis on the chest of Cypselus holds a snake or in Polygnotus' underworld Callisto sits on a bearskin and Actaeon on a deerskin (see M. Davies, *JHS* 106 (1986), 182–3). It is in this light that we should see Actaeon's deerskin in the vase paintings and in the metope at Selinus. No representation shows Artemis throwing it around him, and one makes this impossible by portraying it a close-fitting tunic with sleeves (*LIMC* no. 26). It seems unlikely that the vases would be interpreted in terms of this sort of story if it were not for the supposed Stesichorus version. Even when clearer hints of the transformation do appear in the form of horns the basic artistic type remains the human figure battling with his dogs rather than the literary picture of the helpless flight of the deer. Those depictions which show neither horns nor skin are merely the simplest forms of that type.

We occasionally find hints of the rest of the story, or of some of the details of the literary versions. Two vases show Lyssa present at Actaeon's death (*LIMC* nos. 81 and 88). One of these, a fifth-century bell-crater, shows Zeus as well. This perhaps hints at the version in which Actaeon was a rival of Zeus. An Apulian amphora shows Aphrodite present at the scene, which seems to indicate the version in which Actaeon is in love with Artemis (*LIMC* no. 88). The bathing Artemis appears in several Roman representations. Another fourth-century Apulian amphora

(*LIMC* no. 110) appears to indicate a version of which we have no trace in our literary sources: a horned Actaeon is killing a deer by an altar while Artemis looks on. It seems possible that here Actaeon is, like Agamemnon, killing a sacred animal in a sacred place.

See further S. Reinach, *Cultes, mythes et religions*, iii (Paris, 1908), 24–53; L. Malten, *Kyrene* (Berlin, 1911), 16–43 and 85–93; L. Séchan, *Études sur la tragédie grecque* (Paris, 1926), 132–8; Burkert, *HN* 127–33; Fontenrose, *Orion*, ch. 2; F. Willemsen, *JDAI* 71 (1956), 29–58; B. Otis, *Ovid as an Epic Poet* (Cambridge, 1966), 367–71.

Atalanta

The story of Atalanta's transformation first appears in Palaephatus (13), who wrote, probably in the fourth century BC, a work explaining and rationalizing some of the more fantastic myths. He mentions a story that Atalanta and Melanion went into a cave while hunting and were turned into lions; but nothing is known of the cause or the circumstances of the transformation. We may assume that it had been treated by poets before this, since there would be no point in Palaephatus explaining myths that nobody had ever heard of. His other transformation stories, those of Io, Actaeon, Callisto, Kaineus, Niobe, and Mestra are the transformation stories of the classical and earlier poets rather than the typical Hellenistic ones. We know that Hesiod treated the story of the race of Atalanta, but we have no hint of the transformation in the surviving fragments (72–76; see C. Robert, *Hermes* 22 (1887), 445–64). We do know that here Atalanta's husband was not Melanion but Hippomenes (on the two husbands of Atalanta see above, ch. 3 n. 44).

The first full account of the transformation comes in Ovid's *Metamorphoses* (10. 560 ff.). Atalanta, daughter of Schoeneus, receives an oracle: 'fuge coniugis usum. | Nec tamen effugies teque ipsa viva carebis' (565–6). She takes to the wilds and sets up a race for her suitors. Eventually Hippomenes wins her with the help of Venus and the golden apples, but then earns the goddess's anger by failing to thank her. On the way home Venus inspires him with lust so that the two of them desecrate an ancient cave shrine of the Mother of the gods. The Mother decides that death is too good for them and turns them into lions: 'pro thalamis celebrant silvas aliisque timendi | dente premunt domito Cybeleia frena leones' (703–4).

We find the same story in Hyginus (*Fab.* 185), *Myth. Vat.* (1. 39 and 2. 47), and Servius (*A* 3. 113), except that in Hyginus the god is not Cybele but Zeus, and Hippomenes is sacrificing to him on Mount Parnassus when he is overcome by lust (schol. Theoc. 3. 40 speaks of an unspecified holy place). All these sources differ from Ovid also in their conclusion, that lions do not have sex (*Myth. Vat.* states that lions only mate with leopards). Apollodorus (3. 9. 2) tells how Atalanta is won in a race, though by Melanion not Hippomenes, and how the pair desecrate the *temenos* of Zeus. There are no mention of the sexlessness of lions.

Finally Nonnus says (12. 87 ff.):

> *καὶ γαμίην μετὰ νύσσαν ἀελλοπόδων Ὑμεναίων*
> *καὶ Παφίης μετὰ μῆλα λεοντείην ἐπὶ μορφὴν*
> *Ἄρτεμις οἰστρήσειεν ἀμειβομένην Ἀταλάντην.*

Here we have transformation and madness sent by Artemis, but no mention of the transformation of her husband. Since Atalanta appears to be described as a slave of Artemis in Hesiod (fr. 72), it is possible that she was the offended goddess in his story. Artemis' presence in Nonnus may therefore be a return to an earlier tradition (although Nonnus is very late he is clearly steeped in the lost works of earlier poets: see A. S. Hollis, *CQ* 26 (1976), 142–50). For the goddess's anger at Atalanta's desertion cf. schol. Eur. *Phoen.* 151; Hippo and Ethemea also provoke the goddess's anger by marrying. One might expect anyway that the introduction of Cybele into the story is a later development, since though the mother of the gods is worshipped in classical times she plays little part in myths before the Hellenistic period. Also she appears only in the aetiological conclusion to the story, and has no part in the main plot.

There are no known artistic representations of the transformation of Atalanta.

See further W. Immerwahr, *De Atalanta* (diss. Berlin, 1885); Fontenrose, *Orion*, 175–81; Detienne, *Dionysos Slain*, ch. 2.

Callisto

The story of Callisto was told by Hesiod, perhaps in two different versions (see fr. 163; Sale, *RhM* 105 (1962), 122–41). Various later adaptations of Eratosthenes' *Katasterismoi* tell how Callisto became the constellation of the Great Bear and cite Hesiod as their authority (see Robert, *Eratosth.* 50–2). Callisto, a daughter of Lycaon and a companion of Artemis, was raped by Zeus; her pregnancy was discovered when Artemis and her nymphs bathed, and Artemis in anger turned her into a bear. In this form she bore her son, Arcas, the ancestor and eponym of the Arcadians, who was discovered and taken away by goatherds. Sometime later her son, now grown up, came across his mother while hunting; he did not recognize her and pursued her into the forbidden Lycaean grove. Both mother and child were about to be put to death for their trespass when Zeus finally intervened and translated them into the stars. Even now the constellation of the Bear is not allowed to set in the sea because of Tethys' respect for Hera. If the final catasterism as well as the transformation is Hesiodic this would be the earliest, and possibly the only early, catasterism in Greek literature.

We know little of other early treatments of the story, but, as the mother of Arcas, Callisto is an important genealogical figure and was attached to various early Arcadian heroes. Eumelus (fr. 14) and Hesiod apparently made her a daughter of Lycaon (cf. a fourth-century inscription at Delphi: *FD* 3. 1 no. 3), Asius made her a daughter of Nykteus (fr. 9), and Pherecydes a daughter of Keteus (*FGH* 3 F 157). Ariaithos, a fourth-century Arcadian historian, told Hesiod's story of Megisto, daughter of Keteus (*FGH* 316 F 2). Istros made Arcas the son of Arcas and Themisto (*FGH* 334 F 75).

The story was the subject of a play by Aeschylus, but almost nothing of this survives (fr. 98). It is also referred to in a brief passage of Euripides (*Helen* 375 ff.):

> ὦ μάκαρ Ἀρκαδίᾳ ποτὲ παρθένε
> Καλλιστοῖ, Διὸς ἃ λεχέων ἀπέ-
> βας τετραβάμοσι γυίοις·
> ὡς πολὺ μητρὸς ἐμᾶς ἔλαχες πλέον
> ἁ μορφᾶ θηρῶν λαχνογυίων
> ὄμματι λάβρῳ σχῆμα λεαίνης
> ἐξαλλάξασ᾽ ἄχθεα λύπας.

This is confusing: Callisto seems here to be transformed before her seduction, in what would be a unique version of the story, and she seems also to become a lioness rather than a bear (but see ch. 3 n. 48). Rather than assuming a reference to a different tradition one may perhaps suppose that the story is being recounted very impressionistically. The account of the seduction and transformation is compressed and the time sequence distorted to give an incongruous picture of a bear entering Zeus' bed; the earlier mention of θηρῶν λαχνογυίων shows that it is literally a bear rather than a lion that is meant. In fact the whole passage is deliberately paradoxical since it is clearly perverse to call Callisto blessed and to regard her transformation as a release rather than an intensification of suffering.

The details of the seduction offered comic scope. Amphis (fr. 47) told how Zeus took the form of Artemis to seduce Callisto; when Callisto was questioned about her pregnancy she said that Artemis was responsible, and so the goddess turned her into a bear (Apollodorus mentions a story that Zeus took the form of Apollo).

Callimachus (fr. 632) told how Hera changed Callisto to a bear and persuaded Artemis to shoot her; Zeus then put the bear in the stars. Variations of this become the standard version of the story in later mythographers and poets (cf. Ovid; Hyg. *Fab.* 177; Serv. *G* 1. 138; *Myth. Vat.* 1. 17 and 2. 58; Hyg. *PA* 2. 1) and the transformation by Artemis drops out. Pausanias (8. 3. 6) tells this story as 'the current story among the Greeks'. In 1. 25. 1, commenting on statues of Callisto and Io, he notes that their stories are very similar: each suffers the love of Zeus, the anger of Hera, and metamorphosis. It is perhaps the influence of the more popular story of Io that introduced Hera into the story. In the account of Apollodorus (3. 8. 2) we find the other motif of the Io story: Zeus himself transforms Callisto to hide her from Hera. Hera, however, tricks Artemis into shooting her as a wild beast (just as Apollo tricks Artemis into shooting Orion), and Hermes takes the baby to be nursed by his own mother, Maia, on Mount Cyllene (cf. schol. Lyc. 480). In Hyginus, *PA* 2. 1, Artemis realizes her mistake afterwards and herself puts Callisto among the stars.

The longest, and in fact our only extended, accounts of the story come in Ovid's *Metamorphoses* and *Fasti* (2. 401 ff. and 2. 153 ff.). As with the story of Io, the combination of divine comedy and the human nightmare of an animal with a human mind clearly appealed to him ('mens antiqua tamen facta quoque mansit in ursa': *Met.* 2. 485). Ovid merges the different elements of the other versions of the story. He follows Amphis in having Zeus seduce Callisto in the form of Artemis. Callisto is discovered as in Pseudo-Eratosthenes/Hesiod when the nymphs bathe, and she is expelled from the band of Artemis. However, Ovid has her transformed not by Artemis but by Hera, and—unlike any of our other sources—he has this after the birth of her child. Having used the Callimachean motif of a transformation by Hera he returns to the 'Hesiodic' ending, in which Arcas pursues his mother and Zeus intervenes at the last moment to place them both in the sky.

It seems possible finally that there was a quite different version of the story in which Callisto was not transformed at all (see W. Sale, *RhM* 108 (1965), 11–35). Apollodorus, after recounting the story that Hera persuaded Artemis to shoot the transformed Callisto, says that some say that Artemis shot her because she did not preserve her virginity. We may compare in the *Certamen* (117–18):

Hesiod: αὐτὰρ ἐπεὶ δμήθη γάμῳ Ἄρτεμις ἰοχέαιρα—
Homer: Καλλιστὼ κατέπεφνεν ἀπ' ἀργυρέοιο βιοῖο

There are fourth-century coins from Orchomenus which show a human-figured Callisto shot by Artemis (*CGCBM* Pelop. Orch. 1, 190). Finally Pausanias mentions a tomb of Callisto near Cruni in Arcadia. However, it seems perfectly possible that the passage in the *Certamen* is an abbreviated version of the story (not all the brief reports of Actaeon's story mention that he was transformed even when we may assume that it is implied). The passage of Apollodorus perhaps simply suggests an alternative version of Artemis' motive in shooting Callisto: she was not tricked by Hera, but deliberately shot her (see Fontenrose, *Orion*, 72).

See also Serv. *G* 1. 246; Ps.-Clem. *Homiliae* 5. 13, *Recognitiones* 10. 22.

Callisto is not a popular figure in Greek art. Pausanias mentions statues of her on the Acropolis and at Delphi (1. 25 and 10. 9. 5). Polygnotus represented her in his underworld sitting on a bearskin (Paus. 10. 31. 10). The coins from Orchomenus were mentioned above. She also appears on several fourth-century Apulian vases (see A. D. Trendall, *AK* 20 (1977), 99–101). A calyx-crater shows her in human form together with Lyssa, Artemis, and Apollo; to one side Hermes is carrying off the baby Arcas. On an oinochoe she is shown with the hand and ears of a bear while Hermes picks up her child. This need not suggest, as Trendall argues, that she is in mid-transformation. Such mixed figures are a regular way of depicting a fully transformed character in Greek art (see M. Davies, *JHS* 106 (1986), 182–3).

See further R. Franz, *De Callistus Fabula* (Leipzig, 1890); Borgeaud, 51–5; Otis, 350–60; Fontenrose, *Orion*, ch. 4; A. Henrichs, in Bremmer, 254–67.

Galinthias

Nicander apparently told how on Hera's instructions the Fates and Eilithuia sat holding their hands entwined and thus preventing Alcmena from giving birth to Heracles (the story perhaps takes its starting-point from the passage in Homer describing how Hera delayed the birth of Heracles, *Il.* 19. 11). Galinthias, a friend of Alcmena, ran up and told them that the child had already been born. Shocked, they released their hands, and Heracles was born. In their anger at being deceived by a mortal the Fates turned her into a weasel and gave her a life in the innermost part of the house; they also gave her a disorderly method of reproduction: the weasel conceives through its ears and gives birth through its mouth. Hekate, however, pitied her and made her her attendant. Heracles remembered her service and set a statue of her by his house, to which he offered sacrifice, and the Thebans still sacrifice to Galinthias before the festival of Heracles. We thus have two different *aitia*, for an animal and a cult (AL 29).

The main change in Ovid's account (*Met.* 9. 281 ff.) is that he misses out the cult *aition* and considerably develops the animal one. The heroine (here called Galanthis) is a servant of Alcmena whose *strenuitas* is carried on in the nimbleness of the animal, and who continues living in the house in which she served. In particular the peculiar reproductive habits of the weasel now have an explicit moral relevance to the crime of the human heroine: 'quia mendaci parientem iuverat ore, | ore parit.' Our third source for this story is Libanius (*Narr.* 3), who calls the heroine Akalanthis and has Hera in person preventing the birth.

There are also two different versions of the story. Istros apparently told how the Fates released their grip when a weasel ran past and how afterwards it was thought that a weasel was Heracles' nurse (*FGH* 334 F 72; cf. Aelian 12. 5, who adds that the Thebans worship the weasel). The account of Pausanias does not mention weasels at all: the Pharmakides, women sent by Hero to prevent Alcmena giving birth, went away deceived when Historis the daughter of Teiresias uttered a cry of joy (9. 11. 3).

The relation of these different versions has been disputed (see Bömer's note on Ovid; *RE* s.v. Galinthias; M. Renard, *Latomus* 12 (1953), 137–54; Robert, *Heldensage*, 615–19; E. K. Borthwick, *CQ* 18 (1968), 200–6). Was the story of the transformation a development of an animal story? It seems more likely that both the wholly animal version and the wholly human version are rationalizations of the transformation story. If we can assume that Nicander is not inventing his report of the worship of a heroine called Galinthias, we may also assume that she was imagined in human form; it may be, therefore, that the story of her transformation into a weasel was prompted by her name (γαλέη means 'weasel'). Aelian's statement that the Thebans worship a weasel looks like a confused report of her human cult.

Whether the modern Greek folk-belief that weasels are protectors of young brides is relevant to the story is difficult to say (see *RE* loc. cit.). There is no ancient evidence for this belief. Our ancient sources emphasize the weasel's associations with magic and trickery, and one story tells how the weasel was once a human witch. The heroine of our story is not a witch, but her cleverness is her essential characteristic (this is especially clear in the version of Pausanias, where she is the daughter of Teiresias). Nicander says that she becomes an attendant of Hekate, the goddess of magic, who has no other part in the story. But it also seems likely that the beliefs about the perverse reproductive habits of the weasel—which appear well before the first report of this story (see Anaxagoras fr. 114) and were also attached to the weasel's aquatic double the dog-fish, γαλεός—were important in prompting this tale of a mythical 'midwife'.

Hecuba

The first datable reference to the story of the transformation of Hecuba is in the *Hecuba* of Euripides (1260 ff.). As elsewhere, he ends his play with a mysterious prophecy: the blind Polymestor tells how Hecuba will run up the mast of a ship in the form of dog with fiery eyes and then disappear into the sea. Her tomb will be called the κυνὸς σῆμα and will be a landmark for sailors on the Thracian coast. No reason is given for the transformation; as seen through the outraged Polymestor's eyes there is an implied psychological motivation in which transformation into a dog is a reflection of the savagery that Hecuba has shown in the main part of the play. The whole prophecy is made in an elliptical and allusive way which makes it probable that this story is not Euripides' own invention. In fact later geographers report that there was a headland called κυνὸς σῆμα which was known as the tomb of Hecuba (Strab. 13. 1. 28; cf. schol. Ptol. *Geog.* 5. 3. 4; DS 13. 40). In Euripides fr. 968 we perhaps have another reference to the transformation: Ἑκάτης ἄγαλμα Φωσφόρου κύων ἔσῃ (cf. Aristophanes, fr. 604 *PCG*). Here the sinister character of the dog, hinted at in the 'fiery eyes' of the description in the *Hecuba*, is brought out more explicitly through a ghostly dog.

With these passages of Euripides we may compare a lyric fragment that has been variously assigned to Simonides, Alcman, and Ibycus (*PMG* fr. 965): this has Hecuba transformed by the Erinyes and pictures her roaming the wilds, howling, rather than disappearing into the sea and drowning as in Euripides. The reference to a transformation by the Erinyes emphasizes not only the psychological motivation of anger and bitterness but the sinister aspect of the dog. Perhaps this dog is a ghost which had returned to haunt the living, and therefore this vision is not incompatible with the versions in which it is drowned.

The story is frequently mentioned in later writers, who usually elaborate the Euripidean core of the story to give some explanation of at least the circumstances of the transformation. Nicander (fr. 62) has her transformed after leaping into the sea in her grief. He apparently sets the story at Troy and presumably misses out the local *aition* for the *kynossema* on the Thracian coast (although this is uncharacteristic of Nicander).

In many later reports we find a stoning rather than a drowning; sometimes she is stoned by the Thracian followers of Polymestor, sometimes by the Greeks. There is usually some hint at the *kynossema*. (She is stoned by the Thracians in Lyc. 333; Ov. 13. 565 ff.; *Myth. Vat.* 2. 209; by the Greeks in Lyc. 1176 ff.; *Myth. Vat.* 3. 9. 8; *Suda* s.v. *kynossema*, where her body is thrown into the sea afterwards; Dictys, 5. 16; schol. Lycoph. 315; Tzetzes, *Chil.* 3. 245 ff. The last four are rationalized accounts which only have her stoned like a dog. She is drowned in Hyg. *Fab.* 111; *Suda* s.v. *kynosemon*; schol. Eur. *Troad.* 430; Serv. *A* 3. 6). Lycophron has a unique extension of the story. After her death Hecuba becomes the attendant dog of Hekate. Eventually Odysseus, who began the stoning, is instructed by dreams to build her a cenotaph at Pachynos in Sicily. Here the transformed Hecuba is in effect a ghost (Lyc. 1174 ff.). It has been argued that this story derives from Timaeus (see J. Geffcken, *Timaios' Geographie des Westens* (Berlin, 1892), 28).

Ovid combines the *kynossema* and her stoning with the continued wandering of the lyric fragment: 'veterumque diu memor illa malorum | tum quoque Sithonios ululavit maesta per agros' (*Met.* 13. 570–1). Apollodorus misses out the violent end. He says that Helenos took her over to the Chersonese, that she turned into a dog, and that he buried her there at the place now called Kynossema (*Epit.* 5. 23). Quintus Smyrnaeus has her petrified in dog form at Troy (14. 347 f.).

The story was frequently rationalized. Some, following what seems implied in Euripides, give an emotional or psychological explanation of the change: e.g. Cic. *Disp.* 3. 63 'Hecubam autem putant propter acerbitatem animi quandam et rabiem fingi in canem esse conversam' (cf. Plaut. *Men.* 714 ff.; Serv. *A* 3. 6). As noted above, other sources relate the transformation to her death and have her stoned like a dog. Dio Chrys. 11. 154 explains the transformation as due to the weight of her misfortunes, i.e. a dog's life; cf. Pompon. 2. 26.

This transformation is a particularly mysterious one, and there is no obvious simple explanation for it. Some modern scholars have identified Hecuba with Hekate in her dog form and thus see her as an animal-goddess (e.g. *RE* s.v. *Hekabe*, col. 2662). I have expressed general doubts about this sort of approach in Chapter 2; I merely note here that it is not clear what is being claimed by the suggestion that the epic heroine is really the goddess, since it means abandoning her defining role as wife of Priam and queen of Troy. It does seem possible, however, in view of Hekate's connections with dogs, that the similarity of names of two independent figures may have had some influence on the story.

One may wonder about the importance of the *aition*. Was the story invented to explain the local landmark of the *kynossema* or was an already existing story of Hecuba's transformation used to explain a local name? The main objection to the first hypothesis is that there is no obvious reason why the name of a headland on the Chersonese should give rise to a story about the Trojan queen (there are in fact other *kynossemata* which have not prompted such a story).

The ancient rationalizations are a useful starting-point. The psychological motivation that makes literal transformation a consequence of an inhumanly violent emotion is not uncommon in transformation stories. In Euripides' play Polymestor has earlier on described Hecuba and her companions as 'bloodthirsty bitches' (1173), and he has himself undergone a metaphorical transformation into an animal in his violent hunger for revenge (1070–3). Such a psychological motivation might have its starting-point in Homer: Hecuba's surprisingly grim desire in *Iliad* 24. 212 ff. to eat Achilles vividly suggests the animal in man (especially in the context of Achilles feeding Hector to the dogs). That, however, is not, I think, the whole explanation. Even in Euripides' account the transformation is an ambiguous and mysterious one, not a direct reflection of a moral degeneration into an animal, and such a motivation does not explain the probably older version of the story, where the transformation was not linked with Hecuba's revenge on Polymestor.

The pattern of this older version, in which transformation is a final episode in a sequence of unbroken suffering, is one which her story shares with those of Cadmus and Niobe. The comparison with Cadmus is particularly interesting, since this too comes in a mysterious prophecy at the end of a play. In both cases the heroes have had their home wrecked, have lost their children, and are forced to leave their country in exile. In this context transformation can be seen in two ways. First, as a reflection of external status: someone now outside human society, having lost both her city and her family (see e.g. Eur. *Hec.* 811), fittingly becomes a literal animal. Secondly, in a pattern seen also in stories of mourning birds and trees, she has had to endure more than a human being can bear: Quintus Smyrnaeus (14. 282 ff.) compares her even before her transformation to a dog howling uncontrollably.

But why a dog? It is important that from early on it is the eery quality of Hecuba's dog which is stressed. It is no ordinary dog but a ghostly one, often explicitly described as a follower of Hekate, the goddess of witches, and connected with a mysterious tomb (or else pictured wandering howling in the wilds). Dogs have anyway many darker associations in Greek folk-belief and religion (see H. Scholz, *Der Hund in der gr.-röm. Magie und Religion* (diss. Berlin, 1937), ch. iia). It is perhaps not coincidental that the other creature almost interchangeable with the dog in respect of such underworld or otherworldly connections is the snake (see Scholz, 47–8, 35–7; in AR 3. 1216–17 Hekate arrives crowned with serpents and accompanied by howling dogs). Cadmus and Hecuba both become creatures which are half in this world but also point out of it to the world beyond (for a similar ambiguity in the stone Niobe see Chapter 6). It is a feature of such stories where the transformation reflects extreme suffering and grief for the dead, combined with isolation from the living, that the transformed person belongs not merely to the animal world but in some respects to the world of the dead.

See further Phot. *Bibl.* 443[a]; Pollux 5. 45; Tryph. 401 ff.; Robert, *Heldensage*, 1279–86.

Hippo

The story of Hippo, daughter of Cheiron, first appears in Euripides' *Melanippe*:

> κείνην μὲν οὖν
> ξανθῇ κατεπτέρωσεν ἱππείᾳ τριχὶ
> Ζεύς, οὕνεχ' ὕμνους ᾗδε χρησμῳδὸς βροτοῖς
> ἄκη πόνων φράζουσα καὶ λυτήρια
> πυκνῇ θυέλλῃ δ' αἰθέρος διώκεται
> μουσεῖον ἐκλιποῦσα Κωρύκιον ὄρος.
> νύμφη δὲ θεσπιῳδὸς ἀνθρώπων ὕπο
> Ἱππὼ κέκληται σώματος δι' ἀλλαγάς.

(Page, *GLP* no. 14. 14–21; Pollux 4. 141 mentions a tragic mask of Hippo. Possibly she appeared on stage.) Whether the story is Euripides' own invention is difficult to say. The transformation itself is carefully explained, but the brief concluding reference to her new name and continuing career after her change suggests that in this role she may have been a familiar figure.

Callimachus apparently told a different story of how Artemis turned Hippo into a horse because she ceased hunting and worshipping her (fr. 569). Eratosthenes seems to have developed this into a catasterism (see *Cat.* 18; Hyg. *PA* 2. 18). In a story which he seems to have attributed to

Euripides he tells how Hippo, a huntress, is seduced by Aeolus and in her shame flees to the mountains. When her father Cheiron comes looking for her she prays to be transformed so that she should not be seen. Artemis finally sets her in the stars where she is still hidden from the constellation of the Centaur. Presumably Euripides is cited because this story, like that of Euripides, mentions her liaison with Aeolus. Finally Ovid (*Met.* 2. 635 ff.) returns to the Euripidean version and has her transformed for revealing the future to men. (This story too is mentioned by Hyg. *PA* 2. 18.) Here her previous name is Ocyrhoe. The first description of her in human form already anticipates her later change (in the reference to the 'rutili capilli' covering her shoulders). She herself points out the obvious connection between her new form and her father's: 'in equam cognataque corpora vertor' (663). Ovid differs perhaps from Euripides in that in her transformed state she is no more than a beast and loses the power of human speech. There is also no mention of a husband/lover or a daughter.

Io

The story of Io first appears in the fragments of the *Aigimios* and another Hesiodic work, presumably the *Catalogue* (see frs. 124–6 and 294–6). In this latter work Io was a daughter of Peiren. She was seduced by Zeus, who then turned her into a cow and swore to Hera that he had not touched her. As elsewhere in Hesiod (for instance in the story of Teiresias), the quarrel of the gods seems to have been treated in a light-hearted way; Zeus' oath is the precedent and reason for lovers' perjury going unpunished (fr. 124). Io was then guarded by Argos until he was killed by Hermes. We do not know whether in this version Io was pursued by a gadfly, or whether she finally ended up in Egypt, or even what the name of her child was (Danaus also appears in the *Catalogue*, but we do not know whether, as in Aeschylus, Io was his ancestress). In the *Aigimios* it seems that she went not to Egypt but to Euboea, which derived its name from her cow form (fr. 296; cf. *EM* s.v. Euboea). It is possible that the story was originally, and perhaps in the *Catalogue*, set near Argos. Sophocles mentions the Grove of Io (*El.* 5), and the grove and tree where she was kept by Argos are referred to by various later writers (Apollod. 2. 1. 3; Pliny, *NH* 16. 239). It is interesting that the hill on which the Heraeum stood is also called Euboea.

Both Io and Argos belong to a group of obscure early Argive heroes whose relationships vary considerably in our later sources. Argos in particular seems to have been an important figure and perhaps appeared in many stories as the human hero rather than the monstrous villain (see Apollod. 2. 1. 2). However, the story of Io is the only myth to emerge from this rather confused background, and in different versions it links her with most of these obscurer figures. Hesiod and Acusilaus are alone in making her father Peiren (Apollod. 2. 1. 3): later sources make him Inachus or Iasus. Peiren, Peiras, Peiranthos, or Peirasos, as he is known in various sources, is an early king of Tiryns rather than Argos, who set up the cult of Hera there (see Paus. 2. 17. 5). His normal daughter, the goddess's first priestess, was called Καλλιθόη or Καλλίθυια. She was mentioned in the *Phoronis* (fr. 4) though we do not know whether she had a story like that of Io. Possibly Hesiod combined two local traditions.

Io is a popular figure in the literature and art of the fifth century. Her myth plays an important part in the *Supplices* of Aeschylus and in the *Prometheus*. She was the subject of an ode of Bacchylides (19), a play of Sophocles, the *Inachus*, and a lost play of Chaeremon, the *Io* (*TGF* 71 F 9). Her story is also alluded to in several plays (Soph. *El.* 5; Eur. *IT* 394 ff., *Phoen.* 247 and 1116, *Supp.* 628 f.), and in Herodotus (1. 1 f., 2. 41). Her son Epaphus is mentioned in Pind. *Pyth.* 4. 14; *Nem.* 10. 5. Where her father is named he is always Inachus, and it seems that all the major sources knew of her pursuit by the gadfly and set the end of her story in Egypt. She has become the ancestress of Greek kings who arrive from Egypt and the East, Danaus in Aeschylus, and Cadmus in Bacchylides.

It is difficult to say whether the Egyptian connection is new or how it came about. Later on Io becomes identified with Isis, but there is no evidence for this before Callimachus (*Epigr.* 57). (Herodotus (2. 59 and 2. 41) implies that she was not; but see R. Seaford, *CQ* 30 (1980), 23–9.) This would suggest at least that we should not derive her metamorphosis from such an identification. Io may owe her connection with Egypt to her similarity with an Egyptian cow-goddess, or to the identification of Epaphus with the Egyptian bull-god Apis, which is early (Hdt. 2. 153). It is also possible, however, that this connection was an incidental consequence of her role as ancestress of the Danaids.

The treatment of the story in the *Supplices* and the *Prometheus* is similar (see *Supp.* 291 ff. and 535 ff., *PV* 560 ff.). A central theme in both these plays is the questioning of the gods' behaviour towards men. The divine comedy of Hesiod is completely absent, and the stress is put on the nightmarish suffering caused to the human lover of a god. These versions are discussed in Chapter 1.

The ode of Bacchylides is different in approach. Here we have neither Hesiod's comedy of the gods nor the tragedians' questioning of the gods. The bizarre and darker elements of the story are toned down. Io is a proper cow and an attractive one (she is a χρύσεα βοῦς and καλλικέρας δάμαλις). There is no list of wanderings, and though he mentions the gadfly there is no dwelling on Io's madness or sickness. The cow therefore becomes a merely decorative feature. This is quite in keeping with the function of the story which is to celebrate the ancestress of Dionysos.

We do not have enough of Sophocles' *Inachus* (frs. 269a–95) to come to any firm conclusions about it. It seems likely that it was a satyr play, though there are no definite references to satyrs in any of our fragments (see R. Carden, *The Papyrus Fragments of Sophocles* (Berlin, 1974), 54–5, Seaford, art. cit.). The taste for bizarre details makes it closer to the tragic treatments than to Bacchylides. In one fragment we find our earliest detailed description of a transformation, incongruously set in the house, which ends apparently with a comparison with the sphinx (fr. 269a. 42 γυνὴ λέαινα: see Carden, op. cit. 68; against a sphinx, A. M. Dale, *CR* 10 (1960), 194). Perhaps as in Aeschylus Io is a mixed creature rather than a pure cow. Secondly, it is possible that in this play Zeus was strikingly imagined as black (κάρβανος αἰθός, fr. 269a. 54). It has been plausibly suggested that this is prompted by the fact that Zeus will bear an Egyptian son (Epaphus is called κελαινός in *PV* 851). A final interesting feature of the *Inachus* is that there seems at some point to have been an increase in prosperity and fertility, though we do not know how this fitted into the story (see frs. 273 and 275, and Seaford, art. cit. 25–6). Was there perhaps some suggestion here of the fertility associated with the holy marriage? We may compare later reports that the earth bore flowers for Io to feed on (see Westermann, *Myth.* 374, *EM* s.v. Euboea) or the description in the *Supplices* of her eating flowers (538; cf. 42). This theme, which is only hinted at in Aeschylus' tragic treatment, seems more natural in a satyr play.

There were already in the fifth century rationalized versions of the story. Herodotus (1. 1) reports a supposedly Persian story that Phoenicians kidnapped Io and took her to Egypt, and a 'Phoenician' version that she had an affair with the captain of the ship. Here the story has been incorporated, like those of the rapes of Europa and Helen, into the history of the wars between Greece and Asia. (For later rationalizations see Palaeph. 42, schol. AR 2. 168, and Lyc. 1291 ff.)

We do not know of any full treatments of the story of Io in the Hellenistic period. (Even the lost Ἰοῦς ἄφιξις of Callimachus perhaps treated only the final episode of the story.) In particular we do not know whether it was treated by Nicander in his *Heteroioumena*. Like other Hellenistic writers he seems to have favoured transformations into trees and plants rather than animals. We do find, however, various developments of the story. Callimachus (fr. 685) possibly told how Iunx was transformed to a bird for causing Zeus to fall in love with Io. Moschus (2. 44 ff.), who has the story of Io depicted on Europa's basket, describes crowds watching the ποντόπορον βοῦν, Zeus' touch in Egypt, and finally the birth of the peacock from the blood of Argos. A third elaboration tells how Hierax was turned into a hawk for warning Argos (Apollod. 2. 1. 3). Finally, Io herself seems to have received a catasterism after her transformation (Eratosth. *Cat.* 14; cf. Hyg. *PA* 2. 21). Other Hellenistic writers continue the story. Just as Cadmus' wanderings and founding of Thebes are explained by his search for his sister Europa, so various reports tell of the cities founded by heroes who set out to search for Io (see Strab. 14. 10. 12, 16. 2. 5; Parth. 1; DS 5. 60. 4). Io's own wanderings often became local *aitia* (e.g. the Ionian sea and the Bosphorus—list in *RML* 2, col. 267). The connection with Egypt was particularly developed. It is in Callimachus that we first find Io identified with Isis (*Epigr.* 57), and this becomes standard (see e.g. Ov. *Fasti* 1. 454, *Ars. Am.* 1. 77 f., *Met.* 1. 747; there is a list of references in *RML* 2, col. 440). Diodorus (3. 74) makes his second Dionysos, the king of Egypt, a son of Zeus and Io. This sort of development finds its fullest form in the account of Apollodorus (2. 1. 3), who tells how the Curetes steal the baby Epaphus in Egypt on the order of Hera, and Io sets off on another series of wanderings before she finally finds him in Syria. She returns, marries Telegonus, king of the Egyptians, and sets up an image of Demeter, who was called Isis by the Egyptians. This story seems to depend partly on a comparison of the wanderings of Io with those of Isis in her search for Osiris and partly on the identification of Dionysos and Epaphus implied in Diodorus.

Our only extended accounts of the main story of Io come in the Roman poets. Calvus' lost *Io* possibly influenced Ovid's account in the *Metamorphoses* (1. 568 ff.; see Otis, 350–60). Io, the nymph daughter of Inachus, who is here seen as a river-god rather than an ordinary king, is pursued by Jupiter, as Daphne was pursued by Apollo a few lines earlier, and finally caught and concealed in a thick cloud. (This is perhaps a transferred rather than an invented motif. We may compare Hom. *Od.* 11. 243 f., where a dark wave conceals a god and his mortal lover.) Juno realizes what is going on and disperses the cloud, but Zeus has transformed Io into a cow, which Juno claims for herself. The comedy of the gods here is closer to the Hesiodic account than any of our classical sources. Io is then guarded by Argos, and the mood changes from comedy to nightmare. Characteristically Ovid goes further than most of our sources in imagining Io's reaction to her transformation. He describes her terror at seeing her new face reflected in the water and her attempts to reveal herself to her family by writing with her hoof. His main innovation in the rest of the story is to have Io pursued not by a gadfly but by a fury (though we may compare the way that in the *Prometheus* the gadfly was imagined by the deranged Io as the ghost of Argos). The account in the *Heroides* (14. 85 ff.) pursues the subjective and nightmarish view of the story still further. Io's flight becomes simply an expression of her terror at her new form and her attempt to escape it: 'quae tibi causa fugae? Frustra freta longa pererras; | non poteris vultus effugere ipsa tuos' (103–4).

See further Val. Fl. 4. 350 ff.; Paus. 1. 25. 1, 3. 18. 13, 2. 16. 1; Lucian, *Dial. D.* 3, *D. Mar.* 7, *Salt.* 43; Ps.-Plut. *Fluv.* 18; Nonn. 1. 334 ff., 3. 267 ff.; Prop. 2. 33; schol. Eur. *Phoen.* 1116; *Suda* s.v. Io; Eust. on Dionys. *Per.* 92.

Io in Art. Io is the one hero of a transformation story who is represented in classical art in a fully transformed form. This is in a group of sixth- and early fifth-century vases which depict the killing of Argos (R. Engelmann, *JDAI* 18 (1903), 37–58, nos. 9 ff.; cf. Paus. 3. 18. 3). Hermes, Argos, and the cow Io are shown, and sometimes Zeus and Hera appear as spectators. Perhaps Io is shown in this form because the chief interest of this scene is not the transformation in itself, but the group of god, monstrous herdsman, and cow. In one red-figure hydria a priestess and a temple altar are indicated, from which Io flees (Engelmann, no. 14). It is possible that this is a hint of her human status as a priestess (see J. C. Hoppin, *HSCP* 12 (1901), 341). Curiously, several early fifth-century vases show Io as a bull (see E. Simon, *AA* 1985, 265–80).

From about 470 a change in the vases takes place and Io appears as a horned maiden (Engelmann, nos. 18 ff.). Herodotus says that Egyptian images of a horned Isis were similar to Greek representations of Io. Perhaps there was an independent artistic influence even if the identification of Io and Isis did not become standard until much later. In one Apulian red-figure oinochoe an Io with a cow body and a human head is being led by Argos; this form corresponds more to the mixed monster of the *Supplices* (Engelmann, fig. 1).

As well as the common scenes of Io and Argos we also find several vases representing different episodes of the story. In a couple of red-figure vases the horned Io takes refuge at an altar while Zeus stands before her; to the left are Argos, Eros, Hera, and a satyr (Engelmann, nos. 1 and 2). On a third vase Zeus pursues and touches a horned Io, while on the other side Hera and Hermes talk (Engelmann, no. 3). The significance of the last scene is not clear. It does not seem to correspond to any of our literary versions.

Finally, two Pompeian wall-paintings show Io's arrival in Egypt (Engelmann, nos. 28 and 29). It is possible that this had become a popular Hellenistic *topos*, the subject perhaps of Callimachus' lost Ἰοῦς ἄφιξις (cf. Moschus 2. 44 ff.).

See further Cook, *Zeus* i. 437–57; F. Wehrli, *AK* Suppl. 4 (1967), 196–200; Burkert, *HN* 188–9; Otis, 350–60.

Lycaon

Lycaon, son of Pelasgus, the first man, is an early king of Arcadia (see Hes. fr. 161 and most later writers; in AL 31 he is earthborn, in Dion. Hal. 1. 11 the son of Azeios). His name links him with Mount Lycaeon, the most important cult centre of the Arcadians. Pausanias (8. 2. 1) says that he founded the cult of Lycaeus, the Lycaean games, and the city of Lycosura (Hyg. *Fab.* 225 says that he founded the cult of Mercury of Cyllene). He is also from our earliest sources the father of a large number of sons who found the other cities of Arcadia (see Hes. fr. 161; Paus.; Apollod. 3. 8. 1). In particular he is the grandfather of Arcas, the eponym of the Arcadians (Hes. fr. 163). In later writers some of his sons become the ancestors of the various Italian peoples (see Dion. Hal. 1. 11; AL 31).

In spite of his general character as a founder and patriarch his myth tells of a striking breakdown of order when he receives Zeus as his guest and serves him a cannibal banquet. The story seems to have been told by Hesiod (frs. 161–4). Our main source for the Hesiodic version is in later adaptations of Eratosthenes' *Katasterismoi* (see Hes. fr. 163), which tell how Lycaon in revenge for Zeus' seduction of his daughter served him up his child by her, Arcas. Zeus in anger turned over the table (a regular motif in such cannibal feasts), destroyed the house, and turned Lycaon into a wolf. He restored Arcas to life and gave him to goatherds to bring up. It seems unlikely that all this goes back to Hesiod (see W. Sale, *RhM* 105 (1962), 122–41). Perhaps the story originally included no more than the cannibal banquet and its punishment, the transformation to a wolf, and Arcas was introduced only to link the two Hesiodic stories of Callisto and Lycaon. It may be that the story of Arcas is an imitation of the death and rebirth of Pelops in the similar story of the feast of Tantalus.

We know very little of treatments of the story before the Alexandrian period. Lycaon presumably played an important part in the works of the genealogists. Pherecydes (*FGH* 3 F 156) apparently made him the son of Pelasgus and Deianeira and gave him Cyllene as a wife. On a fourth-century Arcadian inscription at Delphi (*FD* 3. 1, no. 3) he is the father of Callisto. *Lycaon* was the name of a tragedy of Xenocles (*TGF* 33 F 1), a contemporary of Euripides, and there was also possibly a *Lycaon* by Astydamas (*TGF* 60 F 4a). The story does not seem to appear in art at all.

Later on, the story was possibly treated by Eratosthenes in the version mentioned above (see Robert, *Eratosth.* 74–7). It is briefly referred to by Lycophron in his description of an Arcadian as a descendant of *λυκαινομόρφων Νυκτίμου κρεανόμων* (481). The victim is here Nyctimus, the son of Lycaon (cf. Nonn. 18. 20 ff.; Clem. *Protr.* 2. 36). It seems that there was more than one criminal and more than one transformation here; presumably, as in some later sources, it is the sons of Lycaon who commit the crime, but this and the more explicit account in the scholia on this passage are the only references to anyone other than Lycaon becoming a wolf. Perhaps we have here not so much an independent tradition as a merging of the fates of Lycaon and his sons in the interests of prophetic vagueness and obscurity.

It seems that there was in later writers a tendency to assume that Lycaon as a founder and a friend of the gods must have been a just man, and to transfer the crime and guilt to his sons. Thus Nicolaus Damascenus (*FGH* 90 F 38) in a partly rationalized version of the story told how Lycaon, in order to keep his people just, used to say that Zeus visited him. His sons, wishing to test this, killed a child and mixed its flesh with that of the sacrificial victim. Storms and lightning broke out and all the murderers perished. There is no mention of a punishment of Lycaon or of wolves (cf. *Suda* s.v. Lykaon). The account of Apollodorus (3. 8. 1) is similar, though it does not go so far. Lycaon, son of Pelasgus, had fifty sons who exceeded all men in arrogance and impiety. Zeus, to test them, visited them one day as a day-labourer. They offered him hospitality and having killed a local child, mixed its bowels with the sacrifice and set this before Zeus. Zeus overturned the table and struck Lycaon and his sons with thunderbolts until the earth, holding his right hand, persuaded him to spare the youngest, Nyctimus. This son succeeded Lycaon as king.

Some of Lycaon's sons have the names of giants. Also the earth's action in this story resembles that in artistic representations of the gigantomachy. This has led some to see a close connection between the primitive family of Lycaon and the giants (see F. Vian, *La Guerre des Géants* (Paris, 1952), 238–46; G. W. Elderkin, *AJA* 44 (1940), 231). We cannot tell, however, whether this is an original connection or whether the sons of Lycaon have been assimilated later because of their similar role as early enemies of the gods.

Ovid's Lycaon (*Met.* 1. 218 ff.) is quite different from the pious king of Nicolaus. He is an archetypal sinner, an exaggerated villain whose race is born from the blood of the giants. His crime is the cause of the great flood (cf. Apollod., where the flood as a punishment for Lycaon is an alternative to the normal story that it happened during the reign of Nyctimus; Serv. *E* 6. 41; *Myth. Vat.* 2. 60, 1. 189; schol. Pind. *Ol.* 9. 78). Ovid tells, like Apollodorus, how Zeus came to earth in human form to test mankind. The common people receive him with worship, but Lycaon merely laughs at this: 'Experiar deus hic discrimine aperto | an sit mortalis' (222 f.). He prepares to kill Zeus that night, and not content with this he kills a Molossian hostage and serves him at his table. Zeus overturns the house, and Lycaon flees into the wilds. It is in Ovid that we find our fullest animal *aition*: 'solitaeque cupidine caedis | vertitur in pecudes et nunc quoque sanguine gaudet . . .' (234–5). This is the only passage in our sources which explicitly sees the transformation into a wolf as an expression of moral depravity and savagery. It is in fact quite typical of Ovid to give a much stronger moral colouring to the story and its aetiological explanation (see Chapter 1); however, one suspects that some element of this must always underlie the transformation.

Finally, Pausanias mentions an 'ancient story of the Arcadians' that Lycaon, a founder and religious innovator, one day brought a baby to the altar of Zeus and sacrificed it; he immediately changed into a wolf. Pausanias later says that from this time on a man was supposed to change into a wolf at every sacrifice to Zeus (compare the various werewolf stories associated with Mount Lycaeon: see pp. 53–4). It has been suggested that this is the original story of Lycaon, which was only later elaborated into the story of the feast of the gods. But it would be unwise to assume that what appeared to the locals of Pausanias' day to be an ancient story is older than a story which goes back to Hesiod (see Paus. 8. 2).

See further Arn. *Adv. Nat.* 4. 24; Ov. *Ibis* 431 f.; Plut. *GQ* 39 and note in Halliday; Piccaluga; Burkert, *HN* 98–108; Borgeaud, 41–69; Jeanmaire, *Couroi*, 540–69; Nilsson, *GGR* 397–401; Cook, *Zeus*, i. 63–99.

Taygete

Taygete appears in the astronomical literature as one of the Pleiades (Hyg. *PA* 2. 21, cf. *Fab.* 192; this tradition goes back to Hellanicus, *FGH* 4 F 19, and perhaps to Hesiod, fr. 169). Here she is the daughter of Atlas and has a son Lakedaimon by Zeus (cf. Hyg. *Fab.* 155). On the throne of Bathycles (Paus. 3. 18. 10) were represented Zeus and Poseidon taking up to heaven Taygete and her sister Alcyone (who also appears in the list of the

Pleiades). In Pausanias' history of Sparta (3. 1. 2) Lakedaimon is son of Taygete, though her own parentage is not stated and we cannot therefore be sure that she is here one of the Pleiades.

The first possible hint of her transformation story comes in Pindar, *Ol.* 3, where he says, that Heracles caught the golden-horned hind . . . *ἅν ποτε Ταυγέτα | ἀντιθεῖσ' Ὀρθωσίας ἔγραψεν ἱεράν* (29–30). The scholia have a confusing explanation for this. One says that when Zeus pursued Taygete, daughter of Atlas, Artemis turned her into a deer to save her and then turned her back again. In gratitude Taygete dedicated the golden-horned hind to Artemis. The second report begins in the same way, but concludes: *ὅθεν καὶ εἰς ὑπόμνημα τοῦ πραχθέντος τὴν ἔλαφον χρυσώσασα ἀνέθηκε γαμηθεῖσα Διί.* The first report appears to imply that Taygete escaped Zeus, the second that she was caught by him. We do not know whether Pindar in fact knew of either of these stories or whether the scholia simply made them up to explain this reference (they appear nowhere else). If they are old one may wonder how the story of the successful virgin was reconciled with the tradition which makes Taygete the mother of Lakedaimon.

A quite different story seems suggested by Euripides' *Helen* (381–3):

> *ἅν τε ποτ' Ἄρτεμις ἐξεχορεύσατο*
> *χρυσοκέρατ' ἔλαφον Μέροπος Τιτανίδα κούραν*
> *καλλοσύνας ἕνεκεν.*

It is not clear, in the first place, that we have a reference to Taygete at all; even if Titanis is a description rather than a name her father is here not Atlas but Merops. Further differences are that the heroine of this story becomes the golden-horned hind rather than merely dedicates it, and that here she is expelled from Artemis' band in punishment rather than aided by her. What we seem to have here is the motif of the story of Callisto, in which Artemis expels a companion for being seduced by Zeus. Since these lines immediately follow a description of Callisto it seems possible that Euripides has distorted this story in imitation. On the other hand it may be that Pindar had deliberately avoided the transformation, making Taygete dedicate rather than become the golden-horned hind, and that the confusion of the scholia comes from trying to reconcile these Pindaric and Euripidean versions of the story.

Finally, we may note a story in Ps.-Plutarch (*Fluv.* 17) that Taygete, wife of Lakedaimon, killed herself in shame after being raped by Zeus.

Since these reports are so different it seems impossible to make out any development or even standard form of the myth. See Fontenrose, *Orion*, 131–3.

b. Minor Transformations

Arge

Hyginus (*Fab.* 205) tells how Arge while pursuing a stag said 'tu licet solis cursum aequaris, tamen te consequar'. The sun in anger turned her into a deer. Perhaps Arge's name suggest swiftness (dogs are πόδας ἀργοί in Homer). Arge was the name of one of the Hyperborean maidens buried by the shrine of Artemis on Delos. As a huntress one assumes that this Arge too was a companion of Artemis.

Cerastae

The Cerastae were horned men who lived on Cyprus. They used to sacrifice strangers on the altar of Jupiter Hospes that stood before their house until Venus decided to punish them with a fate that is 'medium mortisque fugaeque'. She turned them into savage bulls (Ov. 10. 222 ff.). This story occurs nowhere else. It presumably takes its starting point from the tradition that explained the ancient name of Cyprus, Cerastia, from its horned inhabitants (see Androcles, *FGH* 751 F 1). Nonnus says that horned centaurs sprang up in Cyprus from the seed that Zeus spilled on the ground in his unsuccessful pursuit of Aphrodite (5. 612 ff., cf. 14. 193 ff. and 32. 71 f.).

See Bömer's note on Ovid, 10. 220.

Helike and Kynosura: The Bears

Early writers mention only one constellation of the bear. This seems to have been explained in Hesiod by the story of Callisto. It is Aratus (*Phaen.* 26 ff.) who first mentions the Little Bear and says that both bears, which he calls Helike and Kynosura, were once nurses of Zeus on Crete. The age of this story is questionable. The two names do not suggest bears at all (Helike suggests a cow, and Kynosura was understood, and sometimes explained, as a dog's tail). There is no room for transformation here since these nurses seem to have been bears from the start.

In various reports that perhaps go back to Eratosthenes (see Robert, *Eratosth.* 56) we learn that Aglaosthenes in his *Naxica* said that Kynosura, the Little Bear, one of the nurses of Zeus, was an Idaean nymph (*FGH* 499 F 1). She was therefore human. She may have been trasformed before being set in the stars, though this is not stated. It is not until schol. *Od.* 5. 272 that we find an explicit version of a transformation story (though Robert, *Eratosth.* 25–6, argues this is the version of Aglaosthenes). Two nymphs, Helike and Kynosura, nursed Zeus while he was hiding in Crete. When Kronos appeared Zeus turned the nymphs into bears and himself into a snake and later set all these forms in the sky. We may compare the scholia on Apollonius (1. 940) which explain the name of a mountain near Cyzicus, ὄρος ἄρκτων, by a story that the nymphs who nursed Zeus here became bears. There is no reference here to catasterism.

It looks as if the story of the transformation and catasterism of Zeus' nurses had its starting-point in a local legend (or perhaps several local legends) that Zeus was nursed by bears (as he is nursed by various other animals). We know that on Cretan Ida there was a cave called Arkesion where the Couretes hid (*EM* s.v. Arkesion; cf. the ὄρος ἄρκτων at Cyzicus). This story of bear nurses perhaps then became one of the transformations of human nurses. Whether the transformation appears before the catasterism is difficult to say. That is not what our sources suggest.

See further *RE* s.v. Kynosura.

Other Nurses

Apart from the story of the bear nurses of Zeus there are three other stories of the transformation of nurses of holy children.

Oppian (*C* 4. 233 ff.) tells how the nurses of Dionysos become panthers to tear apart Pentheus, who becomes a bull. He rejects as impious lies stories about the wicked deeds of women and mothers on Mount Cithaeron. (This story gives literal form to the metaphors and delusions in the *Bacchae*.)

In *C* 3. 7 ff. he tells how the Couretes, who were nurses of Zeus in Crete, were turned by Kronos into lions. Zeus made them rulers of the animals, and Rhea yoked them to her chariot. (We may compare this story with that of Atalanta.)

Nonnus (14. 143 ff.) tells how the nurses of Dionysos were turned into centaurs by Hera.

Lyncus

Triptolemus, travelling around spreading the gifts of Demeter among men, was received by Lyncus, king of the Scythians. Lyncus attempted to kill him and take possession of these gifts himself, but Demeter intervened and turned Lyncus into a lynx (Ov. *Met.* 5. 645 ff.). The story is told in a very similar form in Hyg. *Fab.* 259, Serv. *A* 1. 323, and *Myth. Vat.* 1. 31.

Odysseus

Servius (*A.* 2. 44) has a brief and enigmatic report that Odysseus was turned into a horse. He tells how when Odysseus returns home after his wanderings he discovers that Penelope had given birth to Pan:

postquam biformem puerum vidit, fugisse dicitur in errores. Necatur autem vel senectute vel Telegoni filii manu aculeo marinae beluae extinctus. Dicitur enim cum continuo fugeret a Minerva in equum mutatus.

We may compare the statement of Sext. Emp. (*Math.* 267), that the scholars disagree with one another since one says that Odysseus was killed by Telegonus, another by a bird, and another that he was changed into a horse. This implies that transformation was the end of the story, whereas Servius might be thought to imply that he is transformed before he is killed by Telegonus. Finally Ptolemaeus Chennos (see Westermann, *Myth.* 190) has a quite different story that Odysseus was turned into a horse by an Etruscan witch Ἅλς, an attendant of Circe, and kept by her until he died (hence a θάνατος ἐξ ἁλός). We may assume that Ptolemaeus, a source of fantastic variations on familiar myths, and the author of an Ἀνθόμηρος and a Καινὴ or Παράδοξος Ἱστορία, invented this story himself.

Some scholars have supposed that the story of Odysseus' transformation into a horse has ancient origins and that he is closely related to Poseidon Hippios. They refer to the story in Pausanias that Odysseus set up a statue of Poseidon Hippios at Pheneios and kept a herd of horses there (8. 14. 5 f.; see Robert, *Heldensage*, 1050–4, Bubbe, 18 f., Burkert, *HN* 179). But our evidence for the story and for Odysseus' relations with horses is far too meagre to draw any conclusions. In none of our sources is the transforming god Poseidon.

Theophane

Theophane, who seems to have belonged to the Thracian tribe of the Bisaltae, was taken by Poseidon to the island of Crumissa (otherwise unknown) to hide her from her suitors. When they pursued her there he turned himself into a ram, and her and the islanders into sheep. The suitors began killing the sheep and so he turned them into wolves. As a ram he mated with Theophane and she gave birth to the golden-fleeced ram (Hyg. *Fab.* 188 and 3; cf. Ovid, *Met.* 6. 117 'aries Bisalta fallis').

One assumes that this story had its starting-point in the more famous story of the golden-fleeced ram, rather than in a local conception of

Poseidon as a ram-god. It is of course not surprising that the god should become a ram in such a story. Poseidon often takes animal forms, and the ram is, like the bull or the horse, a regular symbol of sexual potency (see Cook, *Zeus*, i. 429 n. 4). A close parallel to this story is the way that he becomes a horse to father the wonder-horse Arion.

PART 2. BIRDS

Aigypios

When Aigypios bribed and seduced Neophron's mother Timandra, Neophron tricked him into sleeping with his own mother Boulis. Boulis recognized her son and tried to blind him in his sleep, but Apollo intervened and woke Aigypios up. Realizing what had happened he prayed that they should all disappear. Zeus transformed them into birds. Aigypios and Neophron became vultures of the same names; Boulis became a πῶυγξ which eats only eyes; Timandra became an αἰγίθαλλος. These birds never appear together (AL 5, citing Boios).

This looks like one of those stories in which Boios has taken familiar motifs from the heroic myths and given them a bourgeois context. The motifs of incest and blinding borrowed from the story of Oedipus become a rather improbable climax to a melodrama of sexual intrigue. Seduction by bribery is a common theme in Hellenistic 'love' stories (Papathomopoulos, 81, compares AL 41 and Parth. 25. 1). However, transformation as a means of removing oneself from a particularly horrible crime is probably an old motif.

Aisakos

According to Apollodorus (3. 12. 5) Aisakos, son of Priam, was a prophet who interpreted Hecuba's dream about Paris (cf. Lyc. 224). At the death of his wife Asterope, daughter of the river Cebren, he mourned inconsolably and was transformed into a bird (the type is not mentioned). Ovid (11. 749 ff.) has a much fuller account in which he ignores Aisakos' role as a prophet and treats the transformation story as a pastoral tragedy. Aisakos hated the city and lived in the wilds. There he saw the nymph Hesperia sitting on the banks of her father, the river Cebren. He fell in love with her, but she ran away and in her flight was bitten and killed by a snake. In despair Aisakos threw himself from a cliff into the sea, but Tethys in pity transformed him into a bird. Saved against his will he dived repeatedly into the sea; the bird still 'aequora amat, nomenque tenet quia mergitur illo' (795; presumably it is a *mergus*). Cf. Serv. *A* 5. 128.

It is likely that Ovid's story is different from that of Apollodorus' source. In Apollodorus, Aisakos is already married and thus has no reason to pursue the nymph through the woods (Ovid perhaps derived this motif and that of the snake-bite from the story of Aristaeus in *Georgics* 4). The *aition* at the end of Ovid's story which derives *mergus* from *mergor* only makes sense in Latin. As Apollodorus says nothing about the sea it may be that Aisakos' links with the sea and his leap are Ovid's own innovation. However, Apollodorus' account is too brief to permit any firm conclusions.

The story that we find in Ovid is clearly modelled on that of Paris and Oenone. There too we find a Trojan prince living the life of a shepherd in the wilds and indulging in a pastoral romance. Oenone is also the daughter of Cebren and thus a sister of Hesperia (and of Apollodorus' Asterope). The imitation of Paris' story is perhaps prompted by the fact that it is Aisakos' prophecy that demands the exposure of Paris.

Anthos and his Family

Autonous owned herds of horses that were looked after by his wife Hippodameia and his children. Through neglect his land soon became overrun with weeds. He therefore called three of his children Akanthos, Schoineus, and Akanthis. His other two sons were called Anthos and Erodios. Erodios loved the horses and let them graze on the meadows. When Anthos tried to drive them away they became enraged and began to eat him. His father hesitated to help him; his mother fought with the horses but was too weak to prevent them killing him. Zeus and Apollo pitied the family and turned them all to birds. Autonous became an ὄκνος because he hesitated to help his son (ὤκνησεν), Hippodameia became a κόρυδος because ἐκορύσσετο πρὸς τὰς ἵππους μαχομένη. The children all became birds with the same names as they had already. The *erodios* now avoids the *anthos*. The *anthos* quite naturally avoids horses; when he hears a horse neighing he flies away imitating the sound (AL 7, citing Boios).

It has been suggested that this story is the plot of Agathon's play *Antheus* or *Anthos*, which, according to Aristotle, was a tragedy in which every character was invented (see S. M. Pitcher, *AJP* 60 (1939), 145–69). The chief argument for this identification is that the names of this narrative are so obviously, and sometimes ingeniously, invented to suit the story; for instance, the children bear the names both of plants and birds, while Hippodameia is an appropriate name for a horse-rearing woman. However, the invention of appropriate names is something we find in nearly all Boios' stories, and there are several other mythical heroes called Anthos.

The hostility of the *anthos* to horses is one of the mythical enmities that are so popular in ancient works of natural history. We find this particular hostility in Aristotle (*HA* 609^b), Aelian (*NA* 5. 48), and Pliny (*HN* 10. 52). Boios often adds episodes to his stories to explain such an enmity; this is the one case where one of these enmities appears to be the starting-point of the whole story.

Antigone

The story of Antigone appears only in Ovid and the Latin scholia. In a series of representations of impiety Minerva includes Antigone, daughter of Laomedon, who dared to compete with Juno and was turned into a stork (*Met.* 6. 93 ff.; cf. Serv. *A* 1. 27). Lactantius (*Narr.* 6. 1) adds that Antigone had slept with Jupiter. *Myth. Vat.* 1. 79 has a more complicated story: Antigone had said that she was more beautiful than Juno, and so the goddess turned her hair to snakes. The gods pitied her and turned her into a stork, which ever afterwards hated snakes.

The story is very close to Boios' story of the crane, which it immediately follows in Ovid's account. There, an exotic queen of the pygmies is transformed into a crane after competing with Hera. Here it is an oriental princess. The daughter of Laomedon is an obvious choice for such a role, since Laomedon is the type of barbarian wealth and power, and also godlessness. Storks and cranes are often classed together (see e.g. Artem. 2. 29, 4. 56). For the hostilities of different animals as a feature of Boios' transformation stories see under 'Anthos'. The snakes are presumably modelled on the snakes of Medusa or the dogs of Scylla, two beautiful women who having incurred the anger of a goddess are transformed into monsters.

Arne

Our only report of this story is one very brief passage of Ovid (7. 465 ff., in a list of islands):

> quamque impia prodidit Arne
> Sithonis: accepto, quod avara poposcerat, auro
> mutata est in avem, quae nunc quoque diligit aurum,
> nigra pedes, nigris velata monedula pennis.

The island must be one of the Cyclades, and Sithonis has been amended to Siphnon (see Bömer's note). We know nothing more of Arne. Her story belongs to a familiar type in which a girl betrays her city (cf. Tarpeia or Scylla, who is also transformed into a bird). The dishonesty and love of gold of the jackdaw is reported in Latin but not in Greek writers (Cic. *Flac.* 76; Pliny, *NH* 10. 77). In these Latin sources there is perhaps an implicit reference to the name *monedula*. It may be, therefore, that this story, or at least the transformation, is the work of a Roman poet (not Ovid perhaps, since he makes so little of it, but perhaps Aemilius Macer, a friend of Ovid's, who wrote an *Ornithogonia*).

Botres

At Thebes there lived an enthusiastic worshipper of Apollo, Eumelus son of Eugnotus. At a sacrifice one day his son Botres ate the brain of the victim before it was offered at the altar. In a fit of rage Eumelus struck him with a brand from the altar, and the boy fell to the ground in convulsions. Apollo, pitying the parents' grief, turned the boy into a bee-eater, which brings forth its young under the ground but constantly strives to fly (AL 18, citing Boios; cf. a brief reference in Ovid, *Met.* 7. 390, where apparently the child is a girl, and Bömer's note).

The theme of violence breaking out at the sacrifice is a basic one. One may compare in particular a very similar story attached to the tomb of Kallipolis at Megara (Paus. 1. 42. 6). The eating of a brain is most probably borrowed from the famous epic story of Tydeus and has been reduced from a horrible act of cannibalism by a blood-thirsty warrior to the greed of an over-impulsive boy. The description of the bird at the end, like other details in Boios' *aitia*, seems to be taken from Aristotle (*HA* 559[a]). The relevance here is not clear.

The Ciris

The story of Scylla who betrays her city by cutting off her father's magical lock of hair is first mentioned by Aeschylus (*Cho.* 614 ff.):

> *φοινίαν κόραν*
> *ἅτ' ἐχθρῶν ὕπερ φῶτ' ἀπώλεσεν φίλον, Κρητικοῖς*
> *χρυσεοκμήτοισιν ὅρ-*
> *μοις πιθήσασα, δώροισι Μίνω,*
> *Νῖσον ἀθανάτας τριχὸς*
> *νοσφίσασ' ἀπροβούλῳ*
> *πνέονθ' ἁ κυνόφρων ὕπνῳ·*

We know that it was also the subject of a tragedy (see Ov. *Trist.* 2. 393–4). There is no mention of the transformation or of the name of the heroine in Aeschylus or in any other classical writer.

Callimachus referred to the story in his *Hecale* (fr. 288), where apparently, as in our later sources, love has taken the place of greed as Scylla's motive. It is possible that in the *Aitia* he mentioned the transformation of Scylla into a bird, the *ciris* (see fr. 113 and note in R. Pfeiffer's edition (Oxford, 1949)). Thompson has plausibly concluded that this bird, which receives inconsistent or vague descriptions in our sources, is a mythical one (144, and *CQ* 19 (1925), 155–8). Although the bird is not often mentioned apart from this story it seems unlikely that it was invented for it, since it has no essential connection with the name of the heroine, Scylla. It may be that the *ciris* is a form of the semi-mythical bird, the κηρύλος (see Alcman, fr. 26). The immediate explanation of the link of Scylla and the *ciris* may perhaps be seen in the *aition* of our Latin sources, which derive *ciris* from κείρω (since the cutting of her father's lock is the central act of her story). (It is interesting that Aristophanes makes a similar pun about the κηρύλος, spelling it κειρύλος and making it a barber: *Av.* 300.)

We know that the story of the transformation was recounted by Parthenius (see schol. Dionys. *Per.* 420): Scylla was here transformed as she was dragged through the water tied to the stern of Minos' ship (a standard motif in our later sources); this dragging gave the Saronic Gulf its name (from ἐπισύρεσθαι). The name of the bird is not mentioned, nor is the transformation of her father Nisus. (On Parthenius' account see W. Ehlers, *Museum Helveticum* 11 (1954), 65–8.) Our other Greek source for the story is Dionysius (*Av.* 2. 15). Here the transformation is explicitly said to be a punishment: the *ciris* is hated by the other birds (a common *topos* in Hellenistic bird stories; cf. Euph. *SH* no. 413; Ov. *Met.* 11. 344 f.) and pursued by the sea-eagle. This pursuit seems to imply that the father was transformed too. It is perhaps modelled on the pursuit of the nightingale by Tereus. It has been suggested that this story goes back to Boios. It is certainly characteristic of him to have more than one character transformed in a story, since he needs to explain as many birds as possible, and to concentrate on *aitia* for birds rather than place-names, but on the other hand we already have an *aition* for the sea-eagle in Boios (see AL 11). It is impossible to say whether the story of the double transformation is later than that of the single one. Clearly the transformation of Nisus is dependent on that of Scylla, but this does not mean that it did not appear in the earliest version of the story.

The relative dates of the pseudo-Virgilian *Ciris* and Ovid's account in the *Metamorphoses* (8. 11 ff.) have been disputed (R. Lyne, *CQ* 21 (1971), 233–53, and *Ciris* 48–56, thinks the *Ciris* is second century AD; A. S. Hollis, in his commentary on *Met.* 8, suggests that it is earlier than Ovid). Both accounts ignore Parthenius' *aition* and have a double transformation (cf. the hint in Virg. *G* 1. 406–9). Ovid uncharacteristically deals very briefly with the transformations. He gives no explicit motive and no description of the bird: as Scylla clings to Minos' ship she is attacked by her father, who is now a sea-eagle (8. 148 ff.):

> Illa metu puppim dimisit, et aura cadentem
> sustinuisse levis, ne tangeret aequora, visa est.
> Pluma subit palmis: in avem mutata vocatur
> ciris et a tonso est hoc nomen adepta capillo.

Whereas in Dionysius and the *Ciris* the transformation of the father and his eternal pursuit turn Scylla's transformation into a punishment Ovid seems to reverse this and make it an act of mercy to escape the eagle.

The account in the *Ciris* is by far the longest. The motivation for the transformation is here rather confused, as the poet seems anxious to combine every version of the story (see Lyne, *Ciris* 9–10). It is seen as a punishment (48–50), as an act of pity by Amphitrite (481 ff.), and as an honour (204–5). We are also given two *aitia*. The poet hints at the derivation of the name *ciris* from κείρω, and also gives her a tuft of hair imitating that of her father (499 ff.).

Hyginus (*Fab.* 198) tells how Scylla became a fish which is still pursued by Nisus in the form of a sea-eagle (cf. Serv. *A* 6. 286). We do have independent evidence for the existence of the fish κίρρις, and it has been suggested that this may be the original form of the story (see Bömer on *Met.* 8. 151). Transformations into fish are very rare in Greek mythology; since the κίρρις is not a particularly special fish (in fact it is an extremely obscure one), and since the link between the κίρρις and Scylla is not a close one, it makes more sense to see this version as a learned variation of a more popular story of a transformation into a bird than to suppose that the bird story grew out of an original fish story.

See further Serv. *E* 6. 74; G. Knaack, *RhM* 57 (1902), 205–30.

The Cock

Lucian's dialogue 'The Cock' consists of a conversation between a man and his cock, which claims to have once been a man. The man recalls the story that the cock was once a companion of Ares who accompanied him on his visits to Aphrodite to warn him when the sun was coming up. When one night he went to sleep and allowed Ares to be caught out, Ares turned him into a bird, αὐτοῖς ὅπλοις, so that he still has the crest of his helmet. It is for this reason that cocks crow when the sun rises.

The age of this story is impossible to tell, but it is perhaps unlikely that it is an invention of Lucian himself since it plays only an incidental role in this dialogue. It is immediately rejected by the cock, who goes on to make the much grander claim, the main theme of the dialogue, that he is an incarnation of Pythagoras. It clearly takes its starting-point from the story of Ares and Aphrodite in the *Odyssey*, and from the popular tradition according to which cocks were seen as warriors (see Thompson, 34–6). We have no evidence that the cock was linked with Ares in cult (as it was with Asclepius, Demeter, Leto, and Athene). Since no attempt is made to give the hero a particular identity by setting him in a specific family or location it is difficult to know whether we should class this as a myth at all. In any case it is impossible to decide whether one should speak here of literary pastiche or popular fable.

Combe

Ovid has an obscure allusion to a transformation of Combe (7. 382–3):

> adiacet his Pleuron, in qua trepidantibus alis
> Ophias effugit natorum vulnera Combe.

Whether she is escaping a murderous attack from her sons or whether it is her sons who have been wounded is difficult to say. In his summary of Ovid's story Lactantius says: 'when the sons of Phasneus were killed . . . Combe was turned into a bird' (*Narr.* 7. 15); here it is the sons who are the victims, but we do not know who killed them, and Phasneus is not a figure we find anywhere else. We need not assume anyway that Lact. Plac. knows what story Ovid is referring to. Combe, also known as Chalcis, was a Euboean heroine, the mother of the Curetes and eponym of Chalcis (see *FGH* 1 F 129; cf. Euph. *SH* nos. 430 and 442). Nonnus (13. 135 ff.) tells how she and her son fled from their maddened father, Sokos. There were Curetes in Aetolia too and also a town called Chalcis near Pleuron (see Strab. 10. 2. 4). Perhaps we have here a confusion or a local variant of that story. In Hesychius we find κόμβα: κορώνη· πολυρρήνιοι (a people in Crete). It is therefore possible to get a story by combining the different local traditions, but these points of contact may be completely incidental, and it may be that Ovid knew some completely different story.

See *RE* s.v. Kombe.

The Crow

The virgin goddess Athene transformed the virgin daughter of Coroneus in Phokis into a crow, to save her from Poseidon. She was the constant companion of the goddess until she was replaced by the owl (*Met.* 2. 569 ff.). The story, which occurs nowhere else, is perhaps an invention of Ovid's; it is not an obvious animal *aition*. The crow is not normally a comparison for a beautiful woman, and its most commonly reported traits are not referred to in this story. Nor does the story have its starting-point in a historical cult relation of Athene and the crow (the crow in the hand of her statue at Korone might be merely a reference to the name of the town: Paus. 4. 34. 6). The story was clearly developed as an elaboration of the more popular story of how the crow lost the favour of Athene and was banned from the Acropolis because it reported the disobedience of the Cecropidae (Callim. fr. 260; see H. Lloyd-Jones, *HSCP* 72 (1967), 125–45; cf. Amelesagoras, *FGH* 330 F 1). This story immediately precedes the transformation story in Ovid.

The Birds of Diomedes

The story that Diomedes left Argos and settled in Italy was apparently told very early on (Mimn. fr. 22). He had cults in various cities in Italy and was particularly associated with the Adriatic, where he is supposed to have founded several cities. (On Diomedes in Italy see Strab. 5. 1. 9; R. L. Beaumont, *JHS* 56 (1936), 194–5; J. Bérard, *La Colonisation grecque de l'Italie méridionale* (Paris, 1957), 368–76; G. Giannelli, *Culti e miti della Magna Grecia*[2] (Florence, 1963), 52–61.) Off the coast of Apulia were two islands known as *Diomedeiai*, where his companions were supposed to have been transformed into birds. Our earliest known reference to this story is in a work of Lykos (see Antig. *Mir.* 172), a fourth-century writer of Italian history: on the island of Diomedeia there was a group of herons that fawned on Greek visitors and were said to be the companions of Diomedes.

Lycophron (592 ff.), without giving any reason for the transformation, provides a detailed description of the birds' life on Diomedeia. They build an elaborate city on the model of Thebes. They follow any Greeks who land but shun barbarians τῆς πρὶν διαίτης τλήμονες μεμνημένοι. Virgil (*A* 11. 271 ff.) has Diomedes himself report the fate of his companions. Here transformation is seen as a punishment for Diomedes' wounding of Aphrodite. Ovid (*Met.* 14. 484 ff.) takes this motif one step further and has some of Diomedes' companions transformed after abusing Venus for her persecution of them. In neither Virgil nor Ovid is there a reference to the island or the behaviour of the birds; they are both more concerned with the dramatic moment of the change than the continuing ornithological curiosity.

Antoninus (37) has a fuller story that probably goes back to Nicander (see R. Holland, *Heroenvögel in der gr. Mythologie* (Leipzig, 1895), 22–3). He tells how Diomedes wins land in Italy, dies, and is buried on the island of Diomedeia. The Illyrians, who are jealous of the farming skills of Diomedes' Greek followers, attack and kill them while they are offering a funeral sacrifice to the dead hero. Zeus makes their bodies disappear and changes their souls to birds. These birds approach Greeks, but when an Illyrian lands on the island they disappear. (The farming motif seems to be a variation of a different tradition that when Diomedes was cheated of his new land he cursed it with infertility until it should be farmed by Greeks: see schol. Lyc. 592 f.)

The birds and their island are refered to in a number of later prose works which seem to have a common source (see Pliny, *NH* 10. 126, who cites Juba; August. *De Civ. D.* 18. 16, who is following Varro; Arist. *Mir.* 79; Solinus, 2. 45; Ael. *NA* 1. 1). These reports tell how the birds wash and tend the tomb and temple of Diomedes. They are friendly to Greeks, but if any barbarians land on the island they attack them. Ps.-Aristotle says that they were transformed after being shipwrecked on the island and that their leader Diomedes was treacherously killed. There are further reports in Strabo (6. 3. 9), who says that the birds distinguish between good and evil men, and in schol. Lyc. (on 592 f.), which says that the companions were transformed while mourning for the hero.

This story of an element of Greekness being preserved in a strange and hostile land has a close parallel in a report about the dogs at a temple of Athene on the mainland in Daunia: these animals too fawn on Greeks but are hostile to barbarians (Ael. *NA* 11. 5; Arist. *Mir.* 109 says that the axes of Diomedes' companions were dedicated here). It is tempting to suppose that the original starting-point of the bird story too is a local temple story on the island of Diomedeia and to assume that the story of the temple birds in Pliny–Augustine–Ps.-Aristotle is the original form of the story. However, it seems questionable that there ever was a temple and worship of Diomedes on Diomedeia. Our evidence consists basically of one version of the story of the birds, another report in Pliny (12. 6) of plane trees round the shrine, and a citation of Ibycus by the scholia on Pindar (*Nem.* 10. 12, *PMG* fr. 294) for the claim that Diomedes was worshipped as a god on an island in the Adriatic. What Ibycus actually said is uncertain, but it was perhaps something more like the reports of Achilles' afterlife and worship on the mythical island of Leuke in the Black Sea. It seems that Pliny's references both to the birds of Diomedes and to the plane trees round the temple are taken from literary sources rather than personal enquiry. As A. Ernout points out (*Pliny, NH* 12 (1949), 67), the discussion of plane trees comes almost entirely from Theophrastus. In one passage Theophrastus says that plane trees grow nowhere in the Adriatic except round the ἱερόν of Diomedes (*Hist. Pl.* 4. 5. 6), but it seems more likely that this refers to Diomedes' temple at Timauon, which had a famous grove (Strab. 5. 1. 8). By far our most specific and detailed source for Diomedes' connections with the Adriatic is Strabo. He refers to various cults and foundations, including a sacrifice and a story of Diomedes' apotheosis at Timauon, and then mentions his disappearance on the deserted island of Diomedeia. He makes no reference to a temple, worship, or even a tomb here. Pliny's description of the birds purifying the tomb/temple is more or less identical to descriptions of birds caring for the temple of Achilles on Leuke and caring for the tomb of Memnon; it is a regular mythical motif rather than a unique local phenomenon. It seems possible, therefore, that the temple of Diomedes, rather than being the historical core of the story as is usually assumed, is itself an element within the developed myth.

Doves

Ktesilla. Nicander told of how Ktesilla, a girl from Ceos, was tricked by Hermochares, an Athenian, into swearing she would marry him, just as Acontius tricked Cydippe: he inscribed the oath on an apple and let her pick it up and read it aloud. Her father, having promised her to Hermochares, and having himself sworn an oath, then arranged her marriage to someone else. Through the god's will Ktesilla fell in love with Hermochares, and they ran away together and were married in Athens. Later she died in childbirth because her father had broken his oath, but when they carried out the body for burial a dove flew away and the body disappeared. The oracle told Hermochares and the Ceans to set up a shrine at Ioulis to Ktesilla, and they still sacrifice to her, the Ioulians calling her Aphrodite Ktesilla, and everyone else Ktesilla Hekaerge (AL 1; cf. the brief reference in Ov. *Met.* 7. 369–70).

The obvious question about this story concerns its relation to Callimachus' story of Acontius and Cydippe (frs. 67–75), to which it is explicitly compared in Antoninus' text. This shares the motif of the oath in the apple and the father's unsuccessful attempt to marry the heroine to someone else, and it is interesting to note that Ioulis, the home of Ktesilla, is also that of Acontius. One assumes that Nicander must have been aware of these links with the earlier work; the question is whether his story is a purely literary-inspired imitation or whether it is a genuine local variant. The fact that he refers to a specific and presumably genuine cult suggests that the immediate *aition* for this, the death, disappearance, and transformation of Ktesilla, may be a local cult story. But the motif of the apple seems out of place; it is in fact made redundant by the father's own oath, which is the important motivating element in the story. It looks therefore as if Nicander has deliberately used the earlier incidents of Callimachus' story and merged them with a real local *aition*.

It is possible that the dove in this story is to be at least partly explained by the fact that Ktesilla is to become a form of Aphrodite, a goddess who has a special connection with doves (see Thompson, 244–6). Perhaps the final merging with Aphrodite has helped to inspire the earlier motif of the apple (apples are frequently a symbol of Aphrodite and the gifts of lovers: see A. R. Littlewood, *HSCP* 72 (1967), 147–81).

With the story of Ktesilla we may compare the Near-Eastern story of Semiramis. Here too the appearance of doves following her death is the sign of apotheosis; and here too doves have a close relation with an important local goddess of whom Semiramis becomes a form (see DS 2. 4).

The Oinotropoi. The Oinotropoi—Oino, Elaia, and Spermo—were the daughters of Anius, the priest of Apollo on Delos, to whom Dionysos gave the power of producing wine, olive oil, and corn (in Apollod. *Epit.* they are called Oinotrophoi, and it is said that they could produce food from the earth). There are several different versions of their story. The *Cypria* (fr. 29) apparently told how Anius offered to let them support the Greek army for nine years on Delos, since he knew that Troy would not fall before then. Another version told how when the Greek army were oppressed by hunger at Troy they sent for the Oinotropoi from Delos, who came and saved them (Lyc. 581 and scholia; cf. Simon. fr. 537). According to a third version they refused to come, and when the Greeks captured and bound them they called upon Dionysos, who turned them into doves and released them from their chains (Ov. 13. 640 ff.; Serv. *A* 3. 80). Servius says that Anius had consecrated his daughters to Dionysos, and that from the time of their transformation it was not allowed to kill doves on Delos. Neither of these facts is in Ovid, who is clearly not Servius' source and who says that they were turned into the doves of Venus. There seems to be a reference to this transformation story in Lycophron, who says that they did feed the Greeks at Troy, but calls them *οἰνοτρόπους Ζάρηκος ἐκγόνους φάβας* (580). Here, in the context of an obscure oracular speech by Cassandra, *φάβας* can be taken as no more than a metaphor (elsewhere Helen and Iphigeneia are referred to as doves), but it seems hard to believe that there is not also a hint at the transformation.

The source of Ovid's and Servius' accounts may be Callimachus' *Aitia* (fr. 188), or perhaps Euphorion, who wrote a poem called *Anius*. (For Callimachus see G. Wentzel, *Philol.* 51 (1892), 46–64; this is attacked by F. Noack, *Hermes* 28 (1893), 146–50.) It is perhaps a genuine local *aition*. We have independent evidence that there were sacred doves at Delos in the third century BC (see *BCH* 14 (1890), 392–3).

One can only guess at the origins of this story. The magical powers of the Oinotropoi are clearly closely connected with their special relation with Dionysos. The miraculous production of food and drink is a familiar Bacchic miracle (see Eur. *Bacchae* 704 ff. or AL 10). Their father Anius has close links not only with Apollo but with Dionysos. His grandfather Staphylos was the son of Dionysos and the discoverer of wine. It has been argued that the form Oinotrophoi suggests that they were in origin the nurses of Oinos (a name of Dionysos; see *RE* s.v. Oinotropoi), but we have no further hints of such a relation with Dionysos. There is no mention of the cult of the Oinotropoi on Delos, and the doves are associated with the temple of Apollo rather than Dionysos (Dionysos himself takes on animal rather than bird forms). It is perhaps safer to assume that the starting-point for the story of their transformation was not a Dionysiac cult legend (like for instance the miraculous disappearance and apotheosis of the daughters of Staphylus), but the epic story of the offer of Anius.

It has been suggested (see *RE* article, col. 2279) that the transformation may have its origins in the fact that there is a type of dove called *οἰνάς*, but none of our sources mention this dove. Finally it is just possible that this story which makes doves in their human form the magical producers of food may be influenced by the Homeric belief that it is doves which bring the gods their ambrosia (see *Od.* 12. 63).

Pelia and Peristera. The connection of Aphrodite and doves is more central in two probably very late stories. Here the link not only helps to explain the story but is itself the subject of the *aition*. Servius tells a story in which Venus, the doves, and apples all appear. Melus is a friend of Adonis on Cyprus who marries Pelia, 'dicata et ipsa Veneri'. After Adonis is killed, first Melus and then Pelia kill themselves and are turned into an apple and a dove (*E* 8. 37). The woman who is 'dicata Veneri' naturally becomes the goddess's sacred bird.

Myth. Vat. 1. 175 tells how when Cupid and Venus compete in collecting flowers the nymph Peristera helps Venus to win. Cupid turns her into a dove, which is therefore said to be 'under Venus' protection'. Again the dove is linked with another symbol of Venus, this time not fruit but flowers. These aetiological stories are quite different from those of Nicander. The *aitia* are more obvious, and the stories lack any local or particular element (the heroines even have generic names). These look more like the inventions of a scholar creating comprehensive systems than genuine local *aitia* (see the discussion of Nicander in Chapter 1).

The Pleiades. Several stories tell how the Pleiades were women who were transformed into stars. One version says that as they were pursued by Orion they were transformed first into doves and then into stars (schol. *Il.* 18. 486). Although this appears only in the scholia, the association of the name Pleiades with doves was noted much earlier on. The Pleiades are sometimes spelt *Peleiades*, and Aeschylus takes up this ambiguity and puns on it (ἄπτεροι Πελειάδες in fr. 312). Conversely, Moero explained that the Homeric doves that carry ambrosia to Zeus are really the Pleiades (cf. the rising images used of ταὶ πελήαδες in Alcman, fr. 1. 60). Clearly, therefore, such passages as Pindar, *Nem.* 2. 11 ff. (ἔστι δ' ἐοικός | ὀρειᾶν γε Πελειάδων | μὴ τηλόθεν Ὠαρίωνα νεῖσθαι), even if they do not already imply a story of Orion chasing doves, could easily be the starting-point of such a story.

Perhaps what helps to prompt this story, in addition to the meaning of their name and the proximity of the Pleiades to the constellation of Orion, is the metaphorical use of the dove. The dove is traditionally the object of pursuit by a predator (e.g. *Il.* 22. 139), and it is also frequently a metaphor for women. These two uses may be combined: women as objects of male pursuit are often compared to doves (see e.g. Aesch. *Supp.* 223 f.). See further Calame, ii. 72–7.

Eagles

Aetos. Servius, *A* 1. 394, tells how Jupiter's companion when he was hiding in Crete was a boy called Aetos. Later Juno, in jealousy, turned him into the eagle. In reward for bringing Ganymede up to heaven Jupiter set him, as well as Ganymede, in the stars. This is one of the not very subtle aetiological stories that often appear only in Servius (see further on Pelia and Peristera). The bird that is φίλτατος οἰωνῶν to Zeus is explained as a human lover of Zeus. As often, the *aition* is added on to a better known story, in this case the carrying up to heaven of Ganymede by the eagle. Perhaps it was the association of the eagle with Ganymede that led to the eagle itself being made a boy lover of Zeus.

Merops. In *Iliad* 24. 293 the eagle is described as φίλτατος οἰωνῶν to Zeus. The scholia explain this by a story about Merops, the ancient king of Cos who mourned unceasingly for his wife and was finally transformed by Rhea because he had entertained her at his home. He now always sits beside Zeus. In Hyginus (*PA* 2. 16) it is Juno who transforms him, and she sets him in the stars. As an eagle he loses his human grief.

Meropis and the Meropes are epic names for Cos and its ancient inhabitants (see *Hymn. Hom. Ap.* 42; fragments of the *Meropis*, an anonymous epic poem, tell of their battle against Heracles: see *SH* no. 903A). Merops is the eponym of these people (Hsch. s.v. μέροπες; Steph. Byz. s.v. Μέροψ), and thus like Periphas he is seen as an ancient figure. He is earthborn according to one account (Steph. Byz. s.v. Κῶς); another report makes his family earth-worshippers (see AL 15). It is possibly also this Merops whom Clement refers to as one of the first worshippers of the gods (*Protr.* 3. 44). He is therefore quite naturally the friend of Rhea. His entertaining of Rhea suggests an age when gods and men ate together, and this perhaps explains why he sits beside Zeus. As in the case of Periphas, there is no evidence that he played a part in older cults (see S. Sherwin-White, *Ancient Cos* (Göttingen, 1978), 334).

Possibly the original story told of a transformation into a bee-eater, μέροψ (see Cook, *Zeus*, ii. 1132; P. Chantraine, in *Mélanges Fr. Cumont*, i (Paris, 1936), 121–8). Perhaps an eagle may have been felt to be a more appropriate bird for a king. What is clear is that he is not primarily a bird hero in the sense of someone invented to explain a particular bird (since his name is clearly derived from his people, the Meropes). It would therefore be possible for one bird to be substituted for another or even for the apparent meaning of his name to be ignored altogether. Heroes with bird names do not necessarily acquire stories of transformations into birds (e.g. Aerops, Dryops, Koronis, Penelope, Alkyone the Pleiad, or Epopeus).

Periphas. Periphas was a just and pious earthborn king of Athens before the time of Cecrops. He was held in such high respect that men decided to transfer to him the honours they paid to Zeus and called him Zeus Soter and Ἐπόψιος and Μειλίχιος. Zeus' first reaction was to destroy him with a thunderbolt, but on Apollo's request not to destroy him totally he went down to the house of Periphas, and seizing hold of him as he was making love to his wife he transformed him into an eagle. Because of Periphas' holiness the bird still has special honours. He is the king of the birds, he guards Zeus' sceptre, and he is allowed to approach Zeus' throne. His wife prayed to be turned into a bird too so that she might continue to live with him , and she became a φήνη, a form of vulture that is a good omen for men (AL 6; cf. Ov. 7. 399–400). (It may be relevant that according to Aristotle (*HA* 619[b]) the φήνη was supposed to bring up the eagle's young.)

No source is cited, but the transformation of the hero's wife, the fact that transformation is a direct punishment, the interest in augury, and the absence of local *aition* all point to Boios rather than Nicander.

It has been suggested that this story has its roots in old religious beliefs. H. Usener (*Kleine Schriften* (Leipzig, 1913), iv. 66–7) argued that Periphas was in origin Zeus himself and that the story has been euhemerized. Cook (*Zeus*, ii. 1122–37) argued that it recalls an age when kings were regarded as gods; at their death their souls took the form of eagles, and the royal power was thus transmitted to their successors in the form of eagle-tipped sceptres. A later age regarded these pretensions of earlier kings as impiety and invented stories of punishment.

Neither of these views is very convincing. There is no suggestion at all in the *aition* for our story that Periphas continued to receive worship or that he became any form of Zeus (the story thus differs from some of Nicander's religious *aitia* such as the story of Ktesilla). There is no real evidence that *Periphas* was an epithet of Zeus (in the story he is worshipped under quite conventional and irrelevant epithets). There is no independent evidence for an ancient king of Athens called Periphas, and it looks as if he has been invented for this story. There is finally no evidence for the belief that the king's sceptre contained the soul of his predecessor in bird form (see J. R. T. Pollard, *AJP* 69 (1948), 353–76).

The story should perhaps be taken at its face value as an aetiological bird story which has its starting-point in the close relation of Zeus and the eagle and the special position of the eagle among birds. Periphas is not an actual bird name, but if it is connected with περιφανής it is an appropriate name for an eagle (cf. Nyctimene, who becomes an owl). That the special bird of a god was the rival or enemy of the god during its human life is a familiar pattern (cf. Meropis in AL 15). We need not adopt Cook's hypothesis of god-kings to suppose that the story also depends on a special relation of kings and eagles. The king of the birds must naturally have been a human king.

The Emathides

The story of the Emathides was apparently told by Nicander (AL 9). Pieros, earthborn king of Emathia, fathered nine daughters at the same time as Zeus fathered the Muses in Pieria. These held a contest with the Muses on Mount Helicon. When the daughters of Pieros sang everything grew dark, but when the Muses sang stars, rivers, and sea stood still, and Mount Helicon rose up into the sky in pleasure until, on the orders of Poseidon, Pegasus stopped it with a blow from his hoof. In punishment for competing with the gods the Muses turned the sisters into nine different birds.

Instead of giving extravagant descriptions of the response of nature to the songs Ovid (5. 293 ff.) makes the contest little more than a frame for various other stories. The Muses win the contest, and when the Pierides reply by insulting them the Muses transform them. They all become magpies and thus retain their 'garrulitas studiumque immane loquendi'. Ovid's and Nicander's treatments of this story are discussed in Chapter 1. Antoninus has probably given us an abbreviated account of Nicander's story. He does not say, for instance, that Pegasus' blow produced the Hippocrene spring (see Ov. 5. 256 ff.), which one assumes was the chief aetiological point of this story. As it stands, this account is unusual among Nicander's stories in not offering a local *aition*.

The story clearly has its starting-point in the use of 'Pierides' as an epithet of the Muses themselves (first in Hes. *Scut.* 206; in *Theog.* 53 they are born in Pieria). Indeed, Epicharmus (fr. 41) makes a Pieros the father of the Muses. Pausanias has a rationalized account according to which a mortal king Pieros had nine daughters who shared the names of the Muses, and those who were known as the sons of the Muses were actually the sons of these women (9. 29. 4). In Nicander's story we find the familiar pattern of an epithet, hero, or animal associated with the cult of a god being projected back in myth as a rival or enemy. Sometimes the name or epithet may go back to some older figure which the god has replaced (e.g. Hyakinthos), but in this case we have no evidence at all that the Pierides have an existence independent of the Muses. The distinction may perhaps be prompted by the fact that the Muses are associated with two quite different places, Pieria in northern Greece, and Mount Helicon.

There are possibly some older features within this story (see ch. 1 n. 17 and text), but since the epithet *Pierides* does not appear in Homer and Hesiod and the classical explanation of it is different it seems probable that this story is a Hellenistic invention. Singing contests are an obvious way of having a story within a story, a favourite device of the Hellenistic poets (including perhaps Nicander: see AL 17), and it is possible that this was the attraction of the story for Nicander as well as Ovid. One may note finally that a singing contest is an appropriate theme in a story of transformation into birds. Comparisons between birds and singers are a regular *topos* of classical and Hellenistic poetry, and Ovid's transformation of mortal pretenders into magpies recalls such passages as Pindar, *Ol.* 2. 86 ff.

Halcyons

Alcyone and Ceyx. We have two main versions of this story. The first, which appears to go back to Hesiod, tells how Ceyx and Alcyone called themselves Zeus and Hera and were in punishment turned into the birds of the same name (see Hes. frs. 15 and 16, *Papyri in honour of E. G. Turner* (London, 1981), 8–9, and Renner, 291; cf. similar accounts in Apollod. 1. 7. 4, schol. *Il.* 9. 562). The second, for which Nicander is cited, and which is the version of the later poets, tells how Ceyx is accidentally drowned in a shipwreck and Alcyone mourns inconsolably until she is turned into a halcyon (for Nicander see Probus *G* 1. 399; cf. Ov. 11. 410 ff.; Lucian, *Halc.* 2; Dionys. *Av.* 2. 8; Serv. *G* 1. 399; Hyg. *Fab.* 65).

On the face of it we have a characteristic change from a tale of the punishment of blasphemers to a pathetic Alexandrian story of a random accident and the separation of two innocent lovers. (We may compare the story of Hero and Leander, another favourite of the Hellenistic poets; M. Pohlenz (*Hermes* 48 (1913), 7–10) shows that Ovid's treatment of the story of Alcyone is closely modelled on it.) But the situation is perhaps more complicated. As Otis (392–4) points out, the Hesiodic account ignores the fact that they are sea-birds: we should expect the sea to feature in the *aition*, as it does in the *aitia* for all other sea-birds. Also the brief hints of the story in Homer and Euripides suit the Nicandrean story better than the Hesiodic one. In the *Iliad* (9. 562 ff.) a comparison is drawn between the grieving Marpessa and the halcyon (like the bird heroine Marpessa has been separated from her husband). In Euripides (*IT* 1091–2) there is again a comparison with the mourning halcyon. In both cases the emphasis is on the bereft halcyon, whereas the Hesiodic story tells of the transformation of both husband and wife. Schol. *Il.* 9. 562 tries to reconcile the Hesiodic and Homeric accounts by saying that the two birds were separated at their transformation, but this is unconvincing since they are closely related sea-birds. Otis supposes that the version which combines the two stories (schol. Ar. *Av.* 250) and has Ceyx punished for his arrogance by being drowned in a shipwreck is the original one, but this looks too much like a contamination of the two versions. Possibly, therefore, the original was a simpler version of Nicander's story, and merely told how Alcyone wept for an unnamed husband. Ceyx, who is an important figure in the epic sagas, may have been introduced because his wife was called Alcyone (see the Hesiodic *Marriage of Ceyx and Alcyone*, frs. 263–9; R. Merkelbach and M. L. West, *RhM* 108 (1965), 300–17), and because his name resembled that of another sea-bird (the *κήξ* is mentioned by Homer; *κῆυξ* does not seem to be a popular bird name outside this story).

The later poets follow the Nicandrean version, with a number of variations. All make the story an *aition* for the halcyon days, a period of calm in the middle of winter. (The tradition of the halcyon days goes back as far as Simonides (see Arist. *HA* 542^{b}4), but we do not know whether these were connected with Alcyone before the Hellenistic period.) There is a special appropriateness in Ovid's version, where Alcyone is the daughter of Aeolus, king of winds. Ovid characteristically gives the story a positive and romantic ending in which, because of Alcyone's love, Ceyx is reanimated and husband and wife are reunited as birds. In the reports of Ovid and Dionysius, which speak of the love of the halcyon for her husband, there is perhaps a hint at a further tradition about the halcyon which told how the halcyons carry their husbands, *κηρύλοι*, on their back when they are too old to fly. Schol. Ar. *Av.* 250 says that Ceyx was turned into a *κηρύλος*.

See further E. Fantham, *Phoenix* 33 (1979), 330–45; W. K. Kraak, *Mnemosyne* 7 (1939), 142–7; A. F. Griffin, *CQ* 31 (1981), 147–54.

Alcyone, Daughter of Sciron. According to Probus' commentary on the *Georgics* (1. 399) Theodorus' *Metamorphoses* told how Alcyone daughter of Sciron was thrown by her father into the sea in punishment for her promiscuity after she misunderstood his orders to seek a husband (*SH* no. 750; cf. Ov. 7. 401). Hardly anything is known of Theodorus or his *Metamorphoses*. He is presumably earlier than Ovid, since Probus says that Ovid followed him. Lafaye (36) suggests that he was forced to think up this bizarre story because Nicander had already made popular the pathetic story of Alcyone wife of Ceyx. It does look like a pastiche in which the familiar motifs of Greek myths are put incongruously together. Sciron, one of the famous villains of Greek heroic stories, who used to throw strangers down a cliff, is here seen resorting to the same means to settle a domestic dispute. It is possible (see *RE* s.v. Alkyone) that his presence in this story was partly prompted by the desire to offer a local *aition*. Bordering the Isthmus of Corinth (the home of Sciron) was a sea known as the ἀλκυονὶς θάλασσα (see Strab. 8. 2. 3, 9. 1. 8).

The Daughters of Alkyoneus. Pausanias told in his lexicon how the daughters of the giant Alkyoneus threw themselves into the sea from Cape Canastron after their father was killed by Heracles. Aphrodite transformed them into halcyons (see Eust. *Il.* 9. 563). This story is of a familiar type in which the name of the dead hero is interchangeable. Here the similarity of Alkyoneus and halcyon gives a special point to the choice of hero.

The Daughters of Kinyras. According to Eustathius (*Il.* 11. 20) the daughters of Kinyras threw themselves into the sea and became halcyons after their father was defeated in a musical contest and killed by Apollo. We have here a story of a similar type to the last one. There is no special point in the names here, but it is perhaps appropriate that the daughters of a singer become singing birds. More specifically the story may have played upon the meaning of Kinyras' name: κινυρός means 'mournful', and halcyons were birds which were famous for their plaintive song. This story is a variation on the more general tradition that Kinyras was a protégé or son of Apollo (see Pind. *Pyth.* 2. 15). This ambiguous relation between a craftsman and the god of his craft is a regular one. See further *RML* s.v. Kinyras, col. 1191.

Hawks

Daidalion. Ovid has Ceyx tell his guest Peleus the sad fate of his brother Daidalion (11. 291 ff.). Unlike Ceyx, Daidalion had a violent nature and was a lover of war. He had a daughter Chione who, having borne sons to both Apollo and Hermes, boasted that she was more beautiful than Diana. The goddess killed her in punishment, and Daidalion gave way to a terrible grief. He finally ran into the wilds and threw himself from a cliff. Apollo made him a bird but let him keep his warlike character: 'et nunc accipiter, nullis satis aequus, in omnes | saevit aves aliisque dolens fit causa dolendi.' Here the savage character of the hawk is a continuation rather than a reversal of the human hero's nature and state of mind (this is typical of Ovid; see Chapter 1). It is interesting that, unlike eagles, whose predatory nature is, in transformation stories at least, outweighed by their connection with Zeus and with kings, hawks are always seen as evil and greedy birds (cf. also Tereus).

This story appears nowhere else except in Hyginus (*Fab.* 200), who is clearly following Ovid. It is possible that Ovid is himself following Nicander (the other transformations within the epyllion of Ceyx and Alcyone both seem to be derived from Nicander). The striking contrast, however, between the natures of the two brothers and of the birds they become may be Ovid's own (see A. F. Griffin, *CQ* 31 (1981), 147–54). The story that the twins Philammon and Autolykos were born after their mother had slept in one night with both Apollo and Hermes is an old one (see Hes. fr. 64 and Jacoby on *FGH* 3 F 120; according to the older tradition she was called Philonis). But it is only in Ovid that her father is called Daidalion and that we find the story of her death and his mourning. It is not obvious why Daidalion was introduced. His name neither means nor suggests a bird, nor is it a familiar heroic name. It is possible that Daidalion and the story of his mourning have a more interesting history than we have evidence of.

See further F. Frontisi-Ducroux, *Dédale* (Paris, 1975), 160–8 for a structuralist view of the story.

Hierax. Hierax was a special favourite of Demeter who made the mistake of giving food to the starving Trojans. These had not given offerings to Poseidon, and so he had destroyed their crops and sent a sea-monster against them. When he learnt what Hierax had done Poseidon turned him into a bird whose name he bore and reversed his *ethos*: from being loved by men he is now hated by the birds, and instead of helping men he now kills his fellow birds (AL 3, citing Boios).

This story is discussed in Chapter 4. For the characteristic features of a story of Boios see Chapter 1. The punishment of the Trojans by a sea-monster seems to be taken from the more famous story of Laomedon and Hesione. The motif is perhaps not very well incorporated here: whereas Hierax's help enables the Trojans to deal with the failure of their crops nothing is said about what happens to the sea-monster. The theme of the bird hated by its fellow birds is a common one in transformation stories (see below under owls). What is unusual here is that Hierax's *ethos* is reversed; normally this fate follows some outrageous crime.

Iktinos

The story of the kite appears only in Dionys. *Av.* 1. 7. After the death of his wife Iktinos developed a passion for, and pursued, their daughter Side. She killed herself on the grave of her mother, and from her blood there arose a pomegranate tree (σίδη). Her father was transformed into a kite (ἴκτινος), which will never sit on or even look at a pomegranate tree.

Though we have no other reference to the kite's dislike of pomegranates we may assume that this was not invented for the sake of the story but is an independent example of the popular theme of (usually mythical) antipathies of animals and plants. The theme of the transformation of incestuous rapists into birds of prey is discussed in Chapter 4. We know nothing more of this family and we are not told where the story is set. Iktinos has clearly been invented for this story, and it may be that Side has too. The pomegranate is sometimes a symbol of Aphrodite and fertility, but more obviously relevant here, apart from the connection with the kite, is that its colour was thought to resemble blood: see page 280.

Ismenides

The recently discovered papyrus dictionary of metamorphoses had the following entry (Renner, 289):

Αἴθυιαι Ἁλιάκμονος τοῦ Ἁλιάρτου θυγατέρες ἑπτὰ τὸν ἀριθμὸν θρηνοῦσαι τὴν Ἰνὼ μετεμορφώθησαν ὑπὸ Ἥρας εἰς [....] παρ' Αἰσχύλωι καλοῦνται μισοκόρωνοι.

Ovid recounts this story in *Met.* 4. 543 ff.: here Ino's attendants, the Ismenides, blame Juno for their mistress's death, and as they prepare to leap into the sea after her the goddess turns some of them into sea-birds and some into rocks. Even before the discovery of the papyrus Eitrem had suggested that Ovid's sea-birds were **αἴθυιαι**, the bird into which Leucothea transformed herself in the *Odyssey* (*RE* s.v. Leukothea). The transformation may, however, be a purely literary reminiscence and we must not assume that *aithuiai* were sacred birds of Leucothea. (According to AL 15 it is the **βύσσα** which is her sacred bird.) Whether Aeschylus knew the story is impossible to say. We also do not know if the cult of Athene Aithuia at Megara is relevant. (In one version the site of Leucothea's leap into the sea was near Megara.) Athene and her other birds, the owls, were supposed to hate the crows. But the transforming goddess in this story is not Athene but Hera.

Haliakmon is not mentioned elsewhere, and his name may have been understood to mean sea-eagle (see Renner, 291).

Iunx

Callimachus apparently told how Iunx, daughter of Echo or Peitho, bewitched Zeus into sleeping with her or with Io, and Hera in punishment turned her into a bird and made her **συνεργεῖν ταῖς φαρμακείαις** (Callim. fr. 685). The *Suda* and Photius say that she was turned to stone.

The *iunx* was the name of a bird and a magic wheel which was supposed to have the power to induce love: see note on Theoc. 2. 17 in A. S. F. Gow's commentary (Cambridge, 1950). The earliest description of the device, that in Pind. *Pyth.* 4. 214 ff., gives an alternative version of its origin, saying that Aphrodite fastened the bird to a wheel. This is one of several Hellenistic transformation stories which were inspired by the story of Io (see Cat. 1*a* s.v.). It seems to be a straightforward *aition*: a magical bird is naturally assumed to have been a human magician (cf. one story of the magical animal, the weasel, p. 206). The petrification is presumably a secondary development (since it lacks any obvious aetiological point): it is easy to see why a stone should be considerd a suitable alternative to the magical bird (see ch. 6 n. 28 and text).

Kleinis

In Babylon there lived a rich and pious man called Kleinis. He was especially devoted to Apollo and Artemis and often accompanied these gods to the land of the Hyperboreans and saw their famous ass-sacrifices. He wanted to perform the same sacrifice back at home, but Apollo refused to allow it: he was prepared to accept this sacrifice only from the Hyperboreans. Kleinis wished to obey the god, but his sons, Lykios and Harpasos, freed the asses and they began to eat Kleinis and his family. The gods pitied them. Poseidon turned his wife, Harpe, and his son, Harpasos, into birds of the same name. As a favour to Artemis and Leto, Apollo transformed Kleinis and two other children, Artemiche and Ortygios, who had wanted to obey the god: Kleinis became a form of eagle, the ὑπαίετος, Artemiche became a πίφιγξ, a bird loved by gods and men, and Ortygios an αἰγίθαλλος because he had tried to persuade his father to sacrifice goats (αἶγας) instead of asses. Lykios became a white raven, which later turned black because it informed Apollo of the marriage of Koronis with Alkyoneus.

This story appears only in AL 20 where Boios and the *Apollo* of Simmias the Rhodian are cited (on Simmias, a scholar and poet who lived about 300 BC, see H. Fränkel *De Simia Rhodio* (diss. Göttingen, 1915)). We have one fragment of the *Apollo*, in which someone, presumably Kleinis, describes his journey to the land of the Hyperboreans. The story is in many ways typical of Boios (see Chapter 1): we have the exotic location and the invented family who all have generic or significant names. (Harpasos and Lykios are the disobedient sons; Lykios, Ortygios, and Artemiche are all names which stem from the cult of Apollo and Artemis.) As often, the story has its starting-point in the story of an older poet. The ass-sacrifices of the Hyperboreans are mentioned by Pindar (*Pyth.* 10. 33; cf. Callim. fr. 186. 10). The story of the raven and Koronis had already been told by Hesiod (see fr. 60).

Meleagrides

The mourning of the Meleagrides for Meleager was apparently mentioned by Sophocles. Pliny says that according to Sophocles '(electrum) ultra Indiam fieri e lacrimis meleagridum avium Meleagrum deflentium' (*NH* 37. 40). Whether this mourning was part of a transformation story is uncertain (Bömer on Ov. 8. 533 thinks it was not). It is difficult to imagine, however, why these birds should mourn for the hero if they are not his transformed relatives. This story may well have been modelled on that of the mourning sisters of Phaethon, who wept tears of amber after they had been transformed into trees. That story had been treated by Aeschylus and perhaps by Hesiod. *Meleagris* is the name of a real species of bird, the guinea-fowl, and this name perhaps invited a connection with the hero Meleager. One cannot be certain, however, that the name of the species is independent of the story, because we have no reference to the species before Sophocles' reference to this story and it may have been introduced to Greece later. It seems likely that even if Sophocles had heard of birds called *meleagrides* these were not at that time a familiar household bird but fabulous and mythical creatures (perhaps already connected with amber: see Mnaseas cited by Pliny, 37. 40), whose magical and exotic character as well as their name made them suitable for his story.

The story of the transformation was told by Nicander (AL 2). After Meleager's death his sisters wept inconsolably at his tomb until finally Artemis turned them into birds and moved them to the island of Leros, calling them *meleagrides*. Every year λέγονται πένθος ἐπὶ Μελεάγρῳ φέρειν. It is uncertain whether this last comment implies that they flew to Meleager's tomb in Aetolia as the birds of Memnon flew to the tomb of that hero. Pliny (10. 74) reports that the birds of Meleager fight in Boeotia, presumably round a tomb. (He adds that the tomb of Meleager had made guinea-fowl famous.) These details may be, however, simply an imitation of the story of the birds of Memnon (with which the report is explicitly compared) rather than a local *aition*.

Characteristically Nicander has changed a fabulous ending to a local *aition*. The temple birds on Leros (see Ath. 655 C, who cites Klytios the Milesian, a pupil of Aristotle; Aelian *NA* 4. 42 and 5. 27; *Suda* s.v. Meleagrides) were looked after by the priests and not allowed to be eaten. The *Suda*, as an alternative to the story of Meleager's sisters, says that some say the birds were τὰς συνήθεις Ἰοκαλλίδος τῆς ἐν Λέρνῃ παρθένου. Whether this implies another transformation story is difficult to say. There is no reason to believe anyway that the practice of keeping guinea-fowl at Leros goes back beyond Sophocles and that therefore a local *aition* is the original form of the story.

Nicander's story is briefly recounted in a number of later writers with a few small changes (Apollod. 1. 8. 3; Ov. 8. 526 ff.; Ael. 4. 42; Hyg. *Fab.* 174; Stat. *Theb.* 4. 103; *Myth. Vat.* 1. 198, 2. 144). None of them follow Nicander in having the birds moved to Leros, and only Ovid follows him in specifying Artemis as the transforming god. Apollodorus describes the women simply as mourners rather than as sisters of Meleager. Aelian says that they were οἰκεῖαι and adds that they call out their name. Finally Strabo (5. 1. 9) speaks sceptically of a report that the Ἠλεκτρίδες νῆσοι (cf. Pliny, 4. 103) were at the mouth of the Po, and that there were *meleagrides* on them. This looks like some later writer's attempt to give a more specific setting to the story of Sophocles.

The Birds of Memnon

The story of the birds of Memnon first appears in Ovid. Aurora, mourning for the death of her son, asked Jupiter for an honour for him, some 'solacia mortis'. From the ashes of his funeral pyre came forth birds which divided into two groups and fought a battle. Finally they fell back into the ashes as *inferiae*. They were named Memnonides, and every year they renew their battle and die again (13. 600 ff.).

In later accounts the birds are the transformed companions of the hero (QS 2. 549 ff.; Lact. Plac. *Narr.* 13. 3; Serv. *A* 1. 751; Dionys. *Av.* 1. 8). Quintus tells how the winds carry the corpse of Memnon to the river Asopus. His companions too are mysteriously carried there, and they bury him. As they mourn they are transformed into birds which are still called Memnonides. They fly about the tomb, scatter dust on the grave, and kill each other in battle, thus bringing pleasure to their master in Hades or Elysium. (Lactantius says that it was his sisters who were transformed, perhaps confusing this story with that of the Meleagrides.) Dionysius says merely that the behaviour of the birds shows that they must be transformed men. He is more interested in describing their continuing strange habits. He says that they are Aethiopian birds which fly to Memnon's tomb at Troy. There they fight battles, wash themselves in the river, and sprinkle dust on the tomb in honour of the king. The behaviour of the birds is a *topos* in itself, and a number of writers describe this natural wonder without referring to the story of their origin at all (see Pliny, 10. 74; Ael. 5. 1; Paus. 10. 31. 6).

The story of the Memnonides must be older than Ovid. Polygnotus' underworld at Delphi showed Memnon birds on the cloak of the hero (see Paus. 10. 31. 6). The story of the hero had been treated by the *Aethiopis*, Hesiod (possibly; see fr. 353), Simonides (fr. 539), Aeschylus (frs. 127–30), and Sophocles (frs. 28–33). Which of these first told the story of the birds and whether this story mentioned their transformation is uncertain. (The *Aethiopis* had made him immortal (see *PEG* p. 69), but this is incompatible with a tomb.) Moschus refers briefly to the mourning of the birds in 'eastern glens beside the tomb of Memnon' (3. 41–2). His reference to 'eastern glens' suggests that, like the Meleagrides, they were originally fabulous birds mourning in the East. It may have been some Hellenistic poet such as Nicander who first linked this story with the local tradition that Memnon was buried by the Asopus (just as he links the Meleagrides with the temple birds on Leros). On the other hand it may be that the local story is the origin of the poetic tradition.

Mounichos

This story appears only in AL 14, where no authority is cited, and in a very brief passage of Ovid (13. 717–18). Mounichos the son of Dryas, a seer and a just man, was king of the Molossians. He and his family were loved by the gods. One night robbers attacked their house and set fire to it. To save them Zeus turned the whole family into different birds: τριόρχης, ὄρχιλος, αἴθυια, ἰχνευμών, κύων, and πιπώ. All these birds live together in the forest, except his daughter Hyperippe, who was turned into an *aithuia* because she leapt from the fire into water.

It has been plausibly suggested that the story comes from Boios (see Papathomopoulos, 103). Especially characteristic is the way that the whole family is transformed into different birds and these each receive a description. The story is in fact little more than an excuse for a list of transformations, though it is surprising in view of this that the whole family are given non-bird names.

A. B. Cook (*CR* 18 (1904), 81) bases upon this story a theory of woodpecker priest-kings. This seems very implausible. At most one might suggest that the special favour which the seer-king enjoyed with Zeus, and the name of his father Dryas, may owe something to the fact that the most famous cult of the Molossians was that of Zeus and his holy oaks at Dodona.

The Nightingale

Our oldest source is Homer (*Od.* 19. 518 ff.):

> ὡς δ' ὅτε Πανδαρέου κούρη, χλωρηῒς ἀηδών,
> καλὸν ἀείδῃσιν ἔαρος νέον ἱσταμένοιο,
> . . . . .
> . . . . .
> παῖδ' ὀλοφυρομένη Ἴτυλον φίλον, ὅν ποτε χαλκῷ
> κτεῖνε δι' ἀφραδίας, κοῦρον Ζήθοιο ἄνακτος

The scholia explain this in terms of a story that appears to go back at least to Pherecydes (*FGH* 3 F 124). Aedon, married to Zethus, is envious of her sister-in-law Niobe's abundance of children. She attempts to kill the eldest, but ends up accidentally killing her own child. In one version she becomes a bird directly, in another she is first pursued by her husband; a third source speaks of her killing Niobe's sons, but then killing her own in fear of Niobe's revenge. Whether this was Homer's story, an independent tradition, or simply made up to explain the Homeric passage seems difficult to say; compared with the more popular story of Procne it seems a little lacking in invention, and the variations do look rather like weak and arbitrary permutations of the details of the Homeric core. However, it is at least clear that in Homer's daughter of Pandareos, the wife of Zethus, we have a different figure from the two daughters of Pandion.

The daughters of Pandion, Procne and Philomela, are the main characters of the Attic version, the most familiar story of the nightingale (for which see p. 99). The first traces of this story are early. Already in Hesiod (*Op.* 568) and Sappho (fr. 135) the swallow is called Pandionis; this suggests that they knew a transformation story about the swallow, and that this concerned the family of Pandion, not Pandareos. In fact Hesiod is cited as authority for a fully developed version of the cannibal banquet story as an *aition* for the sleeplessness of the nightingale (see fr. 312). We may compare a seventh-century metope which shows two women bending over something; one is called 'Chelidon', and the other's name begins with A (it is presumably Aedon: see K. Schefold, *Frühgriechische Sagenbilder* (1964), 33–4, pl. 20). It is interesting that at this stage the characters retain their bird names. It seems possible that the nightingale is still called Aedon in Aeschylus, who is the first source to mention Tereus (*Supp.* 60 f.).

It is generally agreed that the story received its definitive form in the *Tereus* of Sophocles (frs. 581–95). Here the characters receive their familiar names; we have the marriage to a Thracian king, the rape, the mutilation, the recognition, and the vengeance of the sisters. One change from Aeschylus is the transformation of Tereus into a hoopoe rather than a hawk, possibly because of the belief that the immature hoopoe is a hawk (fr. 581). Word-play on the Greek for hoopoe, ἔποψ, which may have been understood to mean the same as *Tereus*, seems likely to have played a part.

Later variations in this story are minor. Tereus is usually a king of Thrace (see Thuc. 2. 29; Apollod. 3. 14. 8; Ov. 6. 424 ff.), but Pausanias sets the story in Daulis (1. 5. 4); Thucydides reconciles the two traditions by making Daulis inhabited by Thracians, and Apollodorus has Tereus catch up with the sisters at Daulis. In another local version he becomes a Megarian king who commits suicide when he cannot catch the sisters (Paus. 1. 41. 8). Roman writers usually change round the transformations, making Philomela the nightingale (e.g. Serv. *E* 78; Hyg. *Fab.* 45; *Myth. Vat.* 1. 4 and 2. 17; and probably Ovid), and thus miss the *aition* we find in some Greek writers for the tuneless twittering of the mutilated swallow as opposed to the melodious voice of the nightingale (see e.g. Eust. *Od.* 19. 518). In some late sources even the dead child becomes a bird (in *Myth. Vat.* 1. 4 a *phasianus*; in Servius a *fassa*).

Ovid makes the Thracian setting an excuse for giving a Dionysiac colouring to the story; Procne simulates a Bacchic frenzy as she goes to find her sister in the mountains. It seems possible that this was in Accius too (Ribbeck, *TRF* 1. 642), and therefore perhaps even in Sophocles. In Hyginus, Tereus reports that Procne was dead; having thus tricked Pandion into letting him marry his other daughter he then gives Philomela to a neighbouring king as a slave (there are incoherent hints of this tradition in Apollodorus too).

Apart from the Pherecydes and Sophocles stories there are in later sources two more stories of the nightingale. One is that of Boios, who, with a number of important additions, tells the Attic story of the daughter of Pandareos and gives it an Ionian setting (see ch. 4 n. 9). Helladius tells a story of Aedon, daughter of Pandareos of Dulichium and her husband, Zetes, son of Boreas. Suspecting that her husband is having an affair with a hamadryad and that her son Aetylus is helping him, she kills her son as he returns one day from hunting (see Photius, *Bibl.* 531; cf. Eust. loc. cit.).

The story is discussed at length in Chapter 4. See further I. Cazzaniga, *La Saga di Itys* (Varese, 1950–1); G. Mihaelov, *Annuaire de l'Université de Sofia* 50. 2 (1955), 77–208; M. Mayer, *Hermes* 27 (1892), 489–99; J. E. Harrison, *JHS* 8 (1887), 439–45; J. R. T. Pollard, *AJP* 69 (1948), 353–76; J. Fontenrose, *TAPA* 79 (1948), 125–67; and for ritual explanations of the story O. Schroeder, *Hermes* 61 (1926), 423–6, and Burkert, *HN* 201–7.

Oinoe

See p. 21.

Owls

Ascalaphus. Ovid tells a story of how Ascalaphus, son of Orphne and Acheron, saw and reported that Persephone had eaten in Hades, and thus prevented her from returning permanently to her mother. Persephone sprinkled him with water from the Phlegethon, and he was turned into a bird (5. 538 ff.):

> foedaque fit volucris, venturi nuntia luctus,
> ignavus bubo, dirum mortalibus omen.

We find brief reports of this story in the Latin scholia; a few differences in detail make it probable that Ovid is not the only source (see Serv. *A* 4. 462, *G* 1. 39; schol. Stat. *Theb.* 3. 511; *Myth. Vat.* 1. 7, 2. 100). A possibly older version of the story appears in Apollodorus (1. 5. 3 and 2. 5. 12); when Ascalaphus, son of Acheron and Gorgyra, informed on Persephone, Demeter laid a heavy rock on him in Hades. When Heracles, having freed Theseus from Hades, rolled away the stone of Ascalaphus Demeter transformed him into an ὦτος (cf. Renner, 293; the first part at least of the story is referred to by Euphorion, fr. 9. 13–15). Becoming a bird of the night is perhaps an equivalent fate to being buried under a stone: in both cases Ascalaphus is cut off from the light (i.e. he suffers a form of death, since 'seeing the light' is a traditional way to express being alive), just as the goddess is herself.

It seems likely that this story is connected with the use of ἀσκάλαφος as a bird name (see Arist. *HA* 509[a]). One assumes that this bird was an owl, but we know almost nothing about it. It is not mentioned by any of our sources. It is usually supposed that there is an important connection between Ascalaphus and Askalabos, who in a story of Nicander's is turned into a lizard (ἀσκάλαβος) for mocking Demeter when she drinks. Both stories are elaborations of incidents in the *Homeric Hymn to Demeter*. Ovid's account of the story of Ascalaphus is very close in some of its details to Nicander's story of Askalabos. In both cases the criminal is sprinkled with water, and in both cases he becomes a hated creature. As the owl lives in darkness, so the lizard hides in ditches.

Harpalyke. The story of Harpalyke first appears in complete form in Parthenius (13), where Euphorion and Dectadas (otherwise unknown) are cited as authorities. Her father Klymenos raped her, married her off to Alastor son of Neleus, and then took her back again and lived with her openly in Argos. In revenge she cut up their child and served his flesh to her father at a public festival. She then prayed to be removed from men and became a bird, the χαλκίς; Klymenos committed suicide (cf. schol. *Il.* 14. 291). We have a fragment of Euphorion's *Thrax* in which the first part of this story is recounted. We are told here that the bird was hated by its fellow birds and that it became the attendant of Athene (*SH* no. 413; cf. K. Latte, *Philol.* 90 (1935), 133). It seems that the *chalkis* is a large predatory night bird which is rather more formidable than the γλαῦξ (see Thompson under κύμινδις). This perhaps suits the name of the heroine.

A different version of the story is recounted by Hyginus (*Fab.* 204; cf. 238, 246, 255). Here she is the daughter of Schoineus, king of Arcadia. Hyginus tells of the rape and cannibal meal without referring to the marriage, and instead of being transformed Harpalyke is killed by her father. This version seems to make her a double of Atalanta, who is the daughter of Schoineus (in Apollod. 3. 9. 2 her mother is Klymene); this perhaps depends on a merging of this Harpalyke with the Thracian Harpalyke, the daughter of Harpalykos, who is, like Atalanta, a wild huntress (see Hyg. *Fab.* 193, and Serv. *A* 1. 317). It is possible that the Harpalyke of the transformation story grew out of the other one (see *RML* article). The name, for instance, which is not a bird name, better suits the wild Thracian woman, and the cannibal feast reminds one of the story of the Thracian Tereus.

Meropis and her Family. Eumelos, the son of Merops, lived on Cos, τὴν Μεροπίδα νῆσον, and had three arrogant children, Meropis, Byssa, and Agron. Their land was very productive because they worshipped only the earth. They never mixed with other men nor went to the city to celebrate the festivals of the gods, but rejected all invitations and abused the gods. One night Hermes, Athene, and Artemis visited them and when they received only insults transformed them into birds. Meropis was transformed by Athene into an owl. Byssa became a bird of the same name and is called the bird of Leucothea. Agron was transformed by Hermes into a *charadrios*, and when Eumelos reproached Hermes he too was transformed into a νυκτικόραξ κακάγγελος. These all seem to be night birds (AL 15, citing Boios; the story occurs nowhere else).

The only transformation which has a special relevance to the god concerned is Athene's change of Meropis into an owl. Since she also bears the name of the island it is possible that her change is the starting-point of the story and the model for the others. The connection of this family with Merops has produced a rather incongruous mixture. On the one hand these are the grandchildren of a king of Cos and a heroic figure: on the other the description of this family who spend all their time on the farm and refuse to visit the city suggests the bourgeois world of new comedy (e.g. the *Dyskolos* of Menander). Boios' story had perhaps something of the same tone as Callimachus' treatment of the legend of Erysichthon.

There are echoes here of the story of the Minyades (AL 10) in the nocturnal visit of the gods and its magical consequences. The Minyades too refuse to leave their house to join in the festival that everyone else is celebrating.

See further S. Sherwin-White, *Ancient Cos* (Göttingen, 1978), 290–2.

The Minyades. Leukippe, Arsippe, and Alkathoe were the daughters of Minyas, king of Orchomenos. They were *ἐκτόπως φιλεργοί* and refused to join the other women of the city as maenads in the mountains. Dionysos came to them in the form of a young girl and tried to persuade them not to neglect his rites. When they still refused he transformed himself into a lion, a leopard, and a bull, and nectar and milk ran from the ceiling. The sisters were terrified and tearing apart Leukippe's son they took to the mountains as maenads. They lived there on ivy, laurel, and bindweed, until Hermes turned them into birds, *νυκτερίς*, *γλαῦξ*, and *βύξα* all of which avoid the light of the sun (AL 10). Corinna (fr. 665) and Nicander are cited as sources; we may assume that Nicander is here the immediate source as he is for so many of Antoninus' other stories (whereas no reference is given for Corinna, a particular book of a particular work of Nicander's is named).

The story is told with a number of differences of detail in Aelian (*VH* 3. 42). The reason given here for the Minyades' rejection of the god is that they wanted husbands (though this conflicts with the fact that Leukippe has a child). They stayed at home weaving until suddenly ivy, vines, and snakes wrapped themselves round their looms, and wine and milk dripped from the ceiling. When even this did not persuade them they were inspired to perform an act as bad as the horror that was performed on Mount Cithaeron (i.e. the killing of Pentheus), and they tore apart the young child of Leucippe as maenads tear apart a fawn. They then joined the real maenads, but when these rejected and pursued them because of their crime they were turned into birds.

Ovid (4. 32 ff. and 388 ff.) has a fairly free adaptation of the story which avoids the horrific climax, perhaps because he has just treated the story of Pentheus at length. The Minyades, who here lived at Thebes, stayed at home weaving and telling each other stories. Suddenly they heard the sounds of strange instruments, their looms turned to vines, the house shook, and the sounds of wild beasts were heard. The sisters hid in their house and all became bats. Even now they live in houses and, hating the light, live in darkness. Whereas in Nicander we probably have another example of birds of the night feeling shame after an outrageous crime, Ovid merely has the perpetuation of their fear and of their love of the home.

Finally Plutarch (*GQ* 38) mentions the crime, though not its cause or the transformation, as the *aition* for a rite at Orchomenos. He says that the guilty women of the story were called Αἰολεῖαι (or ὀλεῖαι: see Halliday, 167–8; A. Schachter, *Cults of Boiotia* (London, 1981), i. 180–1), and their husbands who wore clothes of mourning were called Ψολόεις. Even now the descendants of these women received the same name and once a year at the Agrionia they were pursued by the priest of Dinysos carrying a sword and if he caught any of them he was entitled to kill them.

If we accept the traditional view that Corinna was a contemporary of Pindar (see K. Latte, *Eranos* 54 (1956), 56–67; M. L. West, *CQ* 20 (1970), 277–87, thinks she is late), then some form of this story is quite old. It has been argued that it was the subject of the *Xantriai* of Aeschylus (see H. J. Mette, *Der verlorene Aeschylos* (Berlin, 1963), 146–7). We do not know, however, whether the transformation is an older part of the story. It seems to form no part of Plutarch's aetiological story.

It is usually supposed that this story has a ritual origin: either it preserves the original form of the rite, i.e. a *sparagmos* of a human victim (see Halliday on *Plut. GQ* 38, or Burkert, *HN* 195–9) or else it arose as an *aition* for a ritual chase and was then turned into a bird story (i.e. Plutarch's story is the oldest). With regard to the first view there is very little evidence to suggest that the *sparagmos* of a human being was ever part of the Bacchic rites. (For doubts about any form of the *sparagmos* as a maenad ritual see A. Henrichs, *HSCP* 82 (1978), 121–60.) It may be that the story is in origin an *aition*, but it is interesting to note that Plutarch's account of the ritual does not suit even his version of the myth. The husbands, the Ψολόεις, though they are clearly important in the ritual, have no part in any version of the story. It is perhaps more likely that an independent story has been taken up and attached to this rite (compare the way that the story of the nightingale becomes attached to the ritual stoning at the tomb of Tereus in Megara). The story belongs to a familiar type which tells of resistance to Dionysos followed by madness and punishment (cf. the stories of Pentheus, Lycurgus, Boutes, the Proitides). These stories are not obvious *aitia*, and it is not clear that any ritual will explain them.

Nyctimene. In Ov. 2. 590 ff. the crow refers to the story of the owl of Athene. This was once a woman from Lesbos called Nyctimene who is supposed to have 'defiled her father's bed'. Now 'conscia culpae | conspectum lucemque fugit tenebrisque pudorem | celat et a cunctis expellitur aethere toto' (just like Euphorion's *chalkis*: *SH* no. 413). Ovid is too allusive here to be inventing his own variant on the story of the *chalkis*. It is possible that this story was told by Callimachus (see frs. 326, 519, 608, 803). It seems unlikely that Ovid is following Boios, who explained the owl of Athene by a different story (see AL 15). Nicander explains the γλαῦξ by the story of the Minyades. In the mythographers and scholia we find further accounts of the story of Nyctimene but with differences of detail which suggest that it received several treatments in the poets. Hyginus (*Fab.* 204), like Ovid, sets the story in Lesbos; he names the father Epopeus and says that he raped her. In schol. Stat. *Theb.* 3. 507 and *Myth. Vat.* 2. 39 Nycteus, the king of the Aethiopians, is seduced by his daughter Nyctaea with the help of her nurse. When he realises who his seducer is he tries to kill her and she is transformed (though still into the sacred bird of Athene). This version is perhaps modelled on the almost identical story of Myrrha. It is in imitation of this perhaps that it takes on its exotic Eastern location. Schol. Stat. adds that according to some Nyctaea was the daughter of Proitos and was transformed into a bird to avoid her father. See further: Serv. *G* 1. 403.

One assumes that this story and Euphorion's story of the *chalkis* are closely related. But it is not obvious which was the model for which or whether they are independent local versions. It is interesting that neither is set at Athens where the owl's association with Athene is most famous. This and the fact that Athene seems to play no part in either story suggest that these stories were not invented specifically to explain the cult relations of the bird.

Polyphonte. The story of Polyphonte appears only in AL 21, where Boios is cited. Polyphonte, daughter of Thrassa, daughter of Ares, scorned Aphrodite and, taking to the wilds, became a companion of Artemis. In revenge Aphrodite maddened her and made her fall in love with and mate with a bear. Artemis rejected her and turned all the animals against her, and so Polyphonte fled back to her father's house where she gave birth to two monstrous children, Agrios and Oreios. These made a practice of bringing home strangers and eating them, and thus earned the hatred of Zeus, who sent Hermes to punish them. Hermes wanted to cut off their hands and feet, but Ares, since they were his descendants, saved them from this fate and with Hermes turned the family into birds. Polyphonte became a στύξ, a night bird which neither eats nor drinks, and is a sign of war and strife for men. Oreios became a λαγῶς, an ill-omened bird. Agrios became a vulture, the most hateful of all birds to gods and men. The gods inspire him with an insatiable lust for human blood. Their servant they made an ἴπνη (woodpecker).

It has been suggested that Polyphonte, like Callisto and Taygete, is a double of Artemis and that her story was originally told of Artemis herself (see Papathomopoulos, 116). I have suggested that this is implausible in the other cases, and there is much less reason to believe it here. As a companion of Artemis she clearly has something in common with the goddess, but that is no reason to suppose that we have here a survival of a bestial marriage of Artemis. The story has obvious echoes of, and was perhaps modelled on, the more shocking plays of Euripides, most obviously the *Hippolytus* and the story of Pasiphae in the *Cretans*. The Thracian setting is appropriate for such barbarous crimes (cf. the story of Tereus).

See also G. Oliphant, *TAPA* 44 (1913), 133–49, who argues that the στύξ like the Latin *strix* is a bat, and that Polyphonte is in origin a vampire witch.

Peacocks

Argos. The story of Argos should not perhaps really be classed as a transformation story at all. Moschus, our earliest source, says that the peacock arose from the blood of the dead Argos (2. 58 f.). Such a birth is common in the case of flowers, which are often little more than a memorial of the dead man, but unusual in bird stories. Ovid, as usual making the *aition* more explicit, says that Juno put the eyes of her human servant into the tail of her bid (1. 722 ff.—here the bird already exists). Several reports in later writers refer to a full transformation, or at least say that the peacock was once Argos (Dionys. *Av.* 1. 28; Martial, 14. 85; Nonn. 12. 70 f.; *Myth. Vat.* 1. 18, 2. 5; schol. Ar. *Av.* 102). The story is unlike our other bird stories in that the animal form is not a reflection of the character, feelings, or experiences of the human hero, but preserves an entirely external characteristic, his eyes.

This is one of a number of bird stories which have been attracted to the story of Io in the Hellenistic period (see Cat. 1*a* s.v.). This story has perhaps been prompted by the fact that peacocks were Hera's sacred birds on Samos (see Antiphanes, fr. 175).

See W. Bühler, *Die Europa des Moschos* (Wiesbaden, 1960), 104–5.

Erinona. An alternative story of Adonis tells how he raped Erinona who was loved by Zeus. Adonis fled to Mount Casium, where Zeus struck him with a thunderbolt, while Erinona was turned into a peacock. Later Adonis was restored to life, and Erinona was returned to her human form; they lived together in the woods and had a son Taleus (Serv. *E* 10. 18).

The story perhaps depends for its details on a local background (see *RE* s.v. Erinona: e.g. Zeus was worshipped as *κεραύνιος* on Mount Casium). But we do not know if the peacock had any particular local significance. In its main themes the story has echoes of two stories of other hunters, Actaeon (also a rival of Zeus) and Hippolytus (also restored to life through a goddess's favour).

Perdix

The story that Daedalus killed his nephew out of jealousy of his skill appears to go back to Sophocles and Hellanicus (fr. 323 and *FGH* 4 F 169). Daedalus threw him down from the Acropolis and then fled from Athens to Crete. Our reports of this nephew are extremely confusing. In some sources he is called Perdix (Sophocles; Ov. 8. 236 ff.; Hyg. *Fab.* 39), in some Talos (Hellanicus; DS 4. 76; Apollod. 3. 15. 9; Lucian, *Pisc.* 42) or Kalos (Paus. 1. 21. 4). According to the *Suda* and Photius (s.v. *Πέρδικος ἱερόν*) it was his mother who was called Perdix. It is only in Ovid that we find the story that he was transformed by Athene into a partridge. The bird retains his 'vigor animi' and his name, but avoids high places.

Much has been written about the origin of this character and his possible relation to the Cretan bronze giant Talos (see e.g. Cook, *Zeus*, i. 724–8; F. Frontisi-Ducroux, *Dédale* (1975), 121–34; *RML* s.v. Perdix). But from our point of view all that is relevant is that one of his names, together with his dramatic death in falling from a rock, made him an obvious subject for a transformation story (Soph. fr. 323, *ὄρνιθος . . . ἐπώνυμος Πέρδικος* suggests that the name Perdix was prior to and not invented for the transformation story). Leaping or falling from a rock is a common prelude to transformation into a bird (cf. e.g. Daidalion, Kyknos, Aesacus). It is perhaps in keeping with the more pathetic character of the transformation story that in Ovid Perdix is a child. There is no suggestion of this in our other sources.

H. J. Rose (*JHS* 48 (1928), 9–10) sees the transformed Perdix on a fifth-century vase. This seems doubtful.

Swans

Kyknos, Son of Apollo. Kyknos, son of Apollo and Thyrie, who lived near Calydon and Pleuron, was *εὐσχήμων τὴν ὄψιν, τὸ δὲ ἦθος ἄχαρις καὶ ἄγροικος*. When he was finally abandoned by his suitor Phylios, whose patience he had exhausted by making him undertake a series of formidable tasks, he threw himself into Lake Conope and disappeared. His mother threw herself into the same lake, and Apollo turned them both into birds. The lake was called Kykneia, and many swans still collect there. Nearby is the tomb of Phylios (AL 12, citing Nicander and Areus). Although no mention is made here of the relation between Apollo and swans one assumes that it is this relation which explains Apollo's role in the story. This story looks like a combination of the popular Hellenistic *topos* of the cold-hearted lover (see AL 39) with the folk-tale pattern of the tasks of the suitor: in this case the relation of Kyknos and Phylios is obviously closely modelled on Heracles' service under Eurystheus (see M. P. Nilsson, *The Mycenaean Origin of Greek Mythology* (Cambridge, 1932), 212), and in fact Heracles himself appears briefly in this story as Phylios' helper. Characteristically for Nicander the story ends with a local *aition* in addition to the transformation.

Ovid's brief account has a different ending. He calls the mother Hyrie, and instead of having her also transformed into a bird he says that her tears formed a lake called Hyrie (7. 371 ff.). Since we have independent evidence that the lake near Conope used to be called something like Hyrie (Hydra, in Strab. 10. 2. 22) it seems that either Ovid was using Areus' account or that in this instance Ovid is closer than Antoninus to Nicander's version. (It seems unlikely that Ovid would have had the knowledge to correct Nicander's account.)

Kyknos, Son of Ares. Kyknos, son of Ares, is one of the most famous opponents of Heracles (see Fontenrose, *Python*, ch. 2). His story was told in the pseudo-Hesiodic *Scutum*, and apparently by Stesichorus and a cyclic poet (see Stesich. fr. 207; schol. *Il.* 23. 346). It was a very popular theme in ancient art (see Brommer, *Vasenlisten*, 102–8). The story normally ends with his death and burial, but Boios apparently told of his transformation: . . . *ὑπὸ Ἄρεως τὸν Κύκνον ὀρνιθωθῆναι καὶ παραγενόμενον ἐπὶ τὸν Σύβαριν πόταμον πλησιάσαι γέρανῳ* (Ath. 393 E; it must be the son of Ares that is meant here, although Athenaeus has just been talking about the son of Poseidon).

Since swans appear to play no part at all in other accounts or representations of the story one's first reaction is to suppose that Boios' version is a late addition prompted by the meaning of the hero's name. But Kyknos is an odd name for a hero who has nothing to do with swans. It is not a normal heroic name, nor is it the name of a relevant city or people. Some may have supposed that Kyknos was in origin a warrior priest of Apollo (see Farnell, *Cults*, iv. 273; F. M. Ahl, *AJP* 103 (1982), 373–411). But although Kyknos has an ambivalent relation with Apollo (in Stesichorus he apparently built an altar to him out of skulls: usually it is Apollo who sends Heracles against him), the chief god of this story and the one who transforms him is Ares, who has no apparent relation with swans. An alternative would be to suppose that Kyknos was in origin a bird monster (see Fontenrose, *Python*, 101–4). The swan is not just a symbol of love and song, but may be seen as a fierce and warlike creature (see Ath. 393 A). It is impossible to come to any conclusion on the available evidence.

Kyknos, Son of Poseidon. Kyknos, son of Poseidon, is also an epic figure. The *Cypria* apparently told how this invulnerable warrior was killed by Achilles at Troy (*PEG*, p. 42; cf. Hes. fr. 237). His transformation comes only in Ovid (12. 143 ff.):

> victum spoliare parabat:
> arma relicta videt: corpus deus aequoris albam
> contulit in volucrem, cuius modo nomen habebat.

It immediately follows and is compared with the transformation of the invulnerable Kaineus, which also appears only here; one or both of these may be Ovid's own invention.

The swan nature of this hero was apparently suggested fairly early on: Hesiod said he had a white head (fr. 237; cf. Hellanicus, *FGH* 4 F 148). Another story has him nursed by swans as a baby (Ath. 393 E). Whether these descriptions follow simply from his name (which has then an independent origin) or reflect a swan character that is the source of his name seems difficult to say. One should at least not assume that his parentage suggests an original aquatic nature. Poseidon is the father of magical and invincible heroes in general rather than of specifically water-creatures.

Kyknos the Ligurian. There appear to be two stories of the Ligurian Kyknos. One told how he was turned into a swan in his grief for the death of his friend and lover Phaethon. In his new form he still sings mournfully. Hyginus (*Fab.* 154) ascribes this story to Hesiod, but this seems doubtful (see Diggle, *Phaethon*, 15–26). It was apparently treated by Phanocles, a perhaps third-century writer of a work called Ἔρωτες ἢ Καλοί which recounted the homosexual affairs of gods and heroes (see fr. 6). Compare Ovid (2. 367 ff.); Virgil (*A* 10. 189 ff.) who implies a catasterism; Claudian (*VI Cons. Hon.* 173 ff.); and Servius (*A* 10. 189), where the catasterism is explicit.

Pausanias (1. 30. 3) says that the swan is a musical bird because it was once the king of the Ligurians and a favourite of Apollo. Lucian (*Electr.* 4) mocks the story that swans were once musicians, πάρεδροι of Apollo. It is impossible to say which story is the original one. A Ligurian king might easily be imagined as a musician (since Ligurian could be derived from λιγύς). It might be that Phanocles decided to give a homosexual twist to an already familiar story. On the other hand Ligurians are known from early on as inhabitants of the Far West, the mythical location of the Eridanus, Phaethon's fall, and the mourning of the Heliades (see e.g. Eur. *Tro.* 437).

For Kyknos' appearance on Roman sarcophagi in depictions of the death of Phaethon see *RML* iii. 2198; Diggle, 213.

The Thieves

There was in Crete a sacred cave in which Rhea gave birth to Zeus, and which no mortal or god was allowed to approach. Every year the cave blazed with fire when the blood of Zeus boiled. In this cave lived the holy bees, the nurses of Zeus. Laios, Keleos, Kerberos, and Aigolios dared to enter this cave in order to steal honey, having first covered themselves with bronze. But when they drew off the honey and saw the swaddling clothes of Zeus their bronze armour shattered; Zeus was about to destroy them with a thunderbolt, but Moira and Themis prevented him because dying was not allowed in such a holy place. Instead he turned them to birds of the same name. These birds are good omens because they saw the blood of Zeus (AL 19, citing Boios).

This story is made up of a number of strange details which may be survivals of old beliefs and rites (see Papathomopoulos, 111–13). (For the birth-cave of Zeus see P. Faure, *Fonctions des cavernes crétoises* (Paris, 1964), 94–120; for the annual boiling of Zeus' bood, Nilsson, *MMR* 543; for bees as nurses of Zeus, Cook, *Zeus*, ii. 927–8, and *JHS* 15 (1895), 1–15; for the connection of bronze with Zeus' birthplace, Strab. 10. 3. 11.) But whether the story as a whole or the transformation is old is uncertain. The pattern in which intrusion upon a god or a holy place is followed by transformation is a fairly ageless one.

This story should not be used as evidence for Cretan bird-gods, as was argued by H. A. Krappe, *Mnemosyne* 9 (1941), 241–57; see J. R. T. Pollard, *AJP* 69 (1948), 353–76 (cf. W. R. Halliday, *CR* 36 (1922), 110–12).

PART 3. PLANTS

In addition to the references given here, see further Murr and Boetticher, who discuss most of these stories.

a. Trees and Shrubs

The Cypress Tree

According to Ovid the cypress was once a beautiful boy who lived on Ceos and was loved by Apollo. One day he accidently killed his pet deer, and in his grief he asked to be able to mourn for ever. He was turned into a cypress, a tree of mourning, the god concludes: 'lugebere nobis, | lugebisque alios, aderisque dolentibus' (10. 106 f.). Lactantius (*Narr.* 10. 3/4) adds that the boy's father was Amycleus (presumably in imitation of the similar story of Hyakinthos). Servius (*A* 3. 680) says that his father was Telephus (perhaps because Telephus was himself suckled by a deer) and that his lover was Apollo or Silvanus (cf. Serv. *G* 1. 20; Probus, *G* 2. 84; *Myth. Vat.* 2. 177 and 1. 6). The story is the subject of a number of Pompeian wall-paintings (see W. Helbig, *Wandgemälde* (Leipzig, 1868), nos. 218–19; K. Schefold, *Vergessenes Pompeji* (Berne, 1962), pl. 54. 3).

Servius also tells a different story about Kyparissos. In this he was a beautiful and chaste Cretan boy who was loved by Apollo or Zephyrus. In order to preserve his chastity he went to Mount Casium in Syria where he was turned into a cypress. We may compare the report in Philostratus (*VA* 1. 16) that in the grove of Apollo Daphnaios near Mount Casium was the cypress which the earth sent up in honour of the Syrian youth Kyparissos. The story is clearly modelled on that of Daphne, whose story was also set in this grove and whose tree stood near the cypress. In this form the story must be fairly late since the shrine and grove were dedicated by Seleucus Nicetor, one of Alexander's generals, but like the story of Daphne it may have been transferred from elsewhere (cf. Nonn. 11. 362 ff. where no location is specified).

There is no reason to believe that the story of Apollo's mourning lover is any older than Ovid. The story of the deer looks like an imitation of the shooting of Sylvia's deer in the *Aeneid*. Ovid's *aition* too looks like his own invention: the cypress seems to have been a Roman tree of mourning, and there is little evidence that it had this function in Greece (see Bömer on 10. 106). Cypresses stood by the grave of Alcmaeon (Paus. 8. 24. 7), but many other trees stood beside dead heroes, while all sorts of gods had groves of cypresses (see e.g. Paus. 2. 24. 5; 2. 2. 4; 2. 13. 3; 10. 38. 9).

It is possible, of course, that Ovid's Greek original had a different form, which told of the death or flight of Kyparissos and which perhaps explained a special relation between Apollo and the cypress like that between Apollo and Hyakinthos. However, there is no evidence that Kyparissos was, like Hyakinthos, an independent figure associated with the cult of Apollo, nor does Apollo have an exclusive relation with the tree. It seems that there was a cypress grove of Apollo Kyparissios on Cos (see *LSCG* 150), but there were other gods whose associations with cypresses were stronger (see Boetticher, 492–4).

The oldest attested story of the cypress is different. Probus (*G* 2. 84) cites Asclepiades (*FGH* 12 F 19) for a story that Boreas, king of the Celts, planted this new tree in honour of his dead daughter Kyparissia (again we have a wind appearing in the story of a plant; cf. Boreas in the story of Hyakinthos or Pitys, or Zephyrus in the story of the cypress).

Finally *Geop.* 11. 4 tells a story of how the daughters of Eteocles, while performing a dance in honour of the Graces, fell into a well. The earth in pity sent up cypress trees as a memorial to them (cf. Westermann, *Myth.* 387).

Daphne

According to Parthenius, our oldest extant source, Daphne was a daughter of Amyclas who became a follower of Artemis and hunted all over the Peloponnese. She was loved by Leucippus, son of Oinomaos, who disguised himself as a woman to be near her. Apollo, who also loved the girl, inspired a desire to bathe in Daphne and her companions, and Leucippus was discovered and killed. When Apollo then pursued Daphne himself she begged Zeus ἐξ ἀνθρώπων ἀπαλλαγῆναι and so became a tree (Parth. 15; cf. Probus, *E* 3. 62). As sources for this story are cited Phylarchus (*FGH* 81 F 32) and a Diodorus (*SH* no. 380) who is otherwise unknown. We have an independent report of Phylarchus' story: according to Plutarch he identified Pasiphae, who had an oracle at Thalamai, with Daphne, daughter of Amyclas, and said that she fled from Apollo, was transformed into a plant, and received the power of prophecy (*Ages.* 9).

Ovid (1. 452 ff.) makes Daphne the daughter of Peneios and sets the story in Thessaly. Here too she is a huntress nymph pursued by Apollo, but neither here, nor in any later account of the story of the transformation is there any mention of his human rival Leucippus. As Apollo is about to catch her she appeals to her father (or perhaps to the earth: there are textual problems here; see Bömer on 1. 544) to destroy the beauty that has ruined her. Apollo embraces the tree that she becomes: 'at quoniam coniunx mea non potes esse | arbor eris certe dixit mea.' It has been plausibly suggested (see Bömer on 1. 452) that the change of setting was introduced to explain the laurel of Tempe which was brought to Delphi in a regular festival (see Callim. fr. 194; cf. Nic. *Alex.* 197 ff.).

In the Roman period the story became very popular. It was a theme in wall-paintings, mosaics, and sculptures (see C. Müller, *Röm. Mitt.* 44 (1929), 59–86). The flight of Daphne was the subject of mimes (Lucian, *Salt.* 48). The story is frequently mentioned in later writers and the scholia; not only was it a particularly pathetic story, but it offered scope for allegory and symbolism. (For the laurel as a symbol see A. Kambylis, *Die Dichterweihe und ihre Symbolik* (Vienna, 1965), 18–23.) The standard story in most of these later writers is slightly different from that of Phylarchus and Ovid and does not speak of a proper transformation at all (schol. Lyc. 6; Liban. *Narr.* 11; Paus. 10. 7. 8; Nonn. 42. 387 ff.; schol. *Il.* 1. 14; Palaeph. 49; Serv. *A* 2. 513; *Myth. Vat.* 1. 116; *Geop.* 11. 2—but Fulg. 1. 14, Hyg. *Fab.* 203, and *Myth. Vat.* 3. 8. 4 appear to follow Ovid). Daphne is here the daughter of the river Ladon in Arcadia and of the earth. Apollo sees, desires, and chases her. She appeals to the earth which swallows her up and then, to comfort Apollo, sends up a plant. He calls this Daphne and makes garlands from it.

Daphne and the river named Ladon were transferred to Daphne, a suburb of Antioch in Syria. There Seleucus Nicetor founded a shrine to Apollo Daphnaios and to Artemis on a spot where he found an arrow marked Φοίβου (see Lib. *Or.* 11. 94; cf. Strab. 16. 2. 6). The story according to Libanius was that Apollo was upset over the girl's transformation and fired off all his arrows.

Finally, Pausanias tells the story of Leucippus that we find in Parthenius, without reference to the final transformation. But he describes it as a story of the Arcadians and Eleans and sets it by the spring of the river Ladon, whose daughter he says Daphne was (Paus. 8. 20).

It is difficult to say how the story developed. Phylarchus'/Parthenius' 'Laconian' story is our oldest version of the myth. But it seems likely that this was already a blending of different local traditions; Pausanias says that the story of Leucippus and Daphne was an Arcadian one, and even Parthenius/Phylarchus makes Leucippus a son of Oinomaos, a king of Pisa. It seems unlikely also that the 'Laconian' version which concludes with the local *aition* for the cult of Pasiphae was the original form of the story. There is no essential link between Pasiphae and Daphne, and it is difficult to see how her cult could have in itself prompted the story of Daphne. Whether, therefore, the story of Daphne began as an elaboration of the story of Daphne and Leucippus, which perhaps originally had no transformation (as in Pausanias), or whether it was an independent story that became attached to an Arcadian heroine of the same name is impossible to say.

There were two mythical priestesses at Delphi called Daphne and Daphnis (see Paus. 10. 5. 5 and DS 4. 66). Both seem to be projections of the famous laurel at Delphi, which was supposed to be a part of the shrine even before Apollo's conquest (Eur. *IT* 1246 f.). It is interesting, however, that none of our stories identifies the Daphne of the transformation stories with one of these, or links the human heroine (as opposed to the plant) with Delphi. So it is unlikely that Daphne arose from one of these figures or that her story began as a Delphic temple story. The story clearly springs from a general association of laurel with the god (though of course the associations of the laurel and the priestesses at Delphi may colour later versions of the story).

Fontenrose (*Orion*, ch. 3) argues that Daphne is in origin Artemis, in the form of Artemis Daphnia (at Olympia: Strab. 8. 3. 12), and that the story was originally told of the goddess herself. This is particularly clear, he argues, in the story of Leucippus, where Daphne is, like Artemis, accompanied by a band of companions. However, it is difficult to see what it would mean to say that the story of Daphne originally concerned Artemis: its essence consists in the transformation and the love of Apollo. Neither of these seems relevant to Artemis: gods never transform themselves into trees as they do into animals and birds.

Dryope

Dryope was the only daughter of Dryas, king of Oeta. While looking after her father's sheep she became a companion of the nymphs and was raped by Apollo. When their son, Amphissos, grew up she was taken off by the nymphs to become one of them; in her place they made a poplar appear from the earth, and by the poplar a spring. Amphissos founded a shrine of the nymphs here and instituted a ritual race. Women were not allowed to attend this because two girls had revealed the place of Dryope's disappearance; they were transformed by the nymphs into pines (AL 32, citing Nicander).

Ovid is our only other source for the story (9. 331 ff.). Here Dryope is the daughter of Eurytus and sister of Iole. (This is clearly a means of linking the transformations of Dryope and Alcmena's servant Galanthis.) One day she broke off a lotus flower for her baby son; the tree bled, and she began to turn into a tree herself. The bleeding tree was in fact the transformed Lotis, and Dryope had unintentionally committed a crime by picking its flowers. The details of this story and its tone are different from Nicander's. Nicander is interested in cult *aitia*, while Ovid tells the sentimental story of the separation of mother and child. Thus Nicander's adult Amphissos, a king and founder, has been changed to a baby. The transformation is no longer an apotheosis but a pathetic punishment. On the bleeding tree in Ovid's version see page 131. Nicander's choice of a disappearance rather than a proper transformation is typical of his cult *aitia* (see Chapter 1).

It is interesting that Dryope becomes not an oak (δρῦς) but a poplar. In fact none of the heroes of Nicander's tree stories bear the names of the trees they became. These are not *aitia* for species of trees (see Chapter 5). The name Dryope perhaps suggested trees in general (see schol. *Il.* 11. 86) and also the ancient inhabitants of the land, the Dryopes. Murr (18–19) notes that the poplar is a common tree in groves of the nymphs.

Karya

Karya and her sisters, Lyko and Orphe, were daughters of the Laconian king, Dion. Apollo granted his daughters special powers of perception and prophecy, but instructed them not to use these powers against the gods. Dionysos fell in love with Karya, and when her sisters discovered this through their special skills and tried to keep her away from him he sent them into the mountains in a frenzy and turned them into stones. He then turned Karya into a tree of the same name. When Artemis told the Laconians what had happened they set up a temple to Artemis Karyatis (for the cult of Artemis at Karyai see Paus. 3. 10. 7). (For a different *aition* for this see schol. Stat. *Theb.* 4. 225.)

The story appears only in Servius (*E* 8. 29), and this account is not completely clear. It appears to belong to a familiar type in which jealous sisters interfere with a god's love affair, or prophets misuse their powers and are punished. (Compare the stories of Aglauros, Klytie, Teiresias, Phineus, or Hippo.) We are not told why Karya is herself transformed. (We should expect her to die first, or to resist the god's advances.) As Servius tells the story, it is an *aition* for the cult of Artemis Karyatis and no natural *aition* is given, but Artemis has nothing to do with the story. There is no reason to believe that Karya is Artemis herself (see above under Daphne). It is possible that cult links of Artemis and Dionysos are relevant (see H. Jeanmaire, *Dionysos* (Paris, 1957), 70–1); but against see Calame (i. 264–76), who argues that the story has its origins in young girls' initiations and that the metamorphosis is an initiatory death. For general doubts about such an approach see Chapter 2: in particular it takes no account of the difference in fate of the sisters. The story illustrates a regular difference between transformation into trees (usually of lovers of gods) and petrifications (usually of their enemies): see Chapter 5.

Leuke

The story of the white poplar appears only in Servius, commenting on *E* 7. 61 'populus Alcidae gratissima': Leuke was a daughter of Ocean, a beautiful nymph who was carried off to Hades by Pluto. When she died Pluto, 'in memoriae solacium', ordered the λεύκη to grow in the Elysian Fields. When Heracles was in the underworld he made himself a crown from its leaves. Homer therefore called it ἀχερωίς.

The legend that Heracles brought the poplar from the underworld is found in other sources without reference to the transformation, and this may have been the immediate starting-point of our story (see Paus. 5. 14. 3; Serv. *A* 5. 134). Servius and the *Suda* claim that the white poplar was generally regarded as an underworld plant (*Suda* s.v. λεύκη). This is accepted by most modern scholars (see e.g. Murr, 21–3). The main evidence for this is the Homeric name of the tree, but possibly ἀχερωίς means no more than 'river tree': Acheron like Achelous, is a general name for rivers, and neither of the references in Homer suggests an underworld character (*Il.* 13. 389, 16. 482). Homer mentions groves of Persephone in the underworld (*Od.* 10. 509 f.), but the trees here are αἴγειροι and ἰτέαι. It seems likely that the Homeric name was the starting-point of both stories, and the underworld associations. Possibly too the later name *leuke* may have encouraged such associations; one thinks of the λευκὴ πέτρη in the *Odyssey* that marks the entrance to the underworld, and the mysterious island of Achilles which was also called Λευκή. There is also the λευκὴ κυπάρισσος at the entrance to Hades in the Orphic gold leaves (see G. Zuntz, *Persephone* (Oxford, 1971), 355–93).

Leukothoe and Klytie

Leukothoe was the daughter of Eurynome, the most beautiful woman in the land of spices. Her father was Orchamos, king of Persia. One night Helios visited Leukothoe disguised as her mother and seduced her. Klytie, a previous lover of the sun who was jealous of Leukothoe, informed her father, and in his anger he buried Leukothoe alive. Helios scattered the earth with his rays, but Leukothoe had already died. He sprinkled the body and the ground with nectar, the body melted, and a spice plant rose from her grave towards him. Klytie, now rejected by the sun, sat grieving on the ground, eating and drinking nothing. Eventually she became a bloodless plant that always turns towards the sun (Ov. 4. 190 ff.). Lactantius (*Narr.* 4. 5) implausibly cites Hesiod (fr. 351). The story is also found in an anonymous Greek source (see Westermann, *Myth.* 348), which says that the father was called Orchomenos and that Klytie was the sister of Leukothoe; the plant she becomes is identified as the heliotrope.

It seems likely that Ovid had a Greek source for the story, and that it was not his own invention; the story of the heliotrope clearly has its origins in the meaning of its Greek name. We have a further and independent reference to Leukothoe and her relation with the sun: Hyginus (*Fab.* 14) lists among the Argonauts the child of Sol and Leukothoe, Thersanon (otherwise unknown), and says that he came from Andros.

P. Perdrizet (*RHR* 105 (1932), 207–17) argues that the story is an original Babylonian one which was taken up by the Greeks. This is possible, but it seems significant that all the characters have familiar Greek names. Orchamos and Eurynome are transparent names of rulers (ὄρχαμος ἀνδρῶν is a Homeric phrase: see e.g. *Il.* 2. 837). The spice plant belongs in the East, and it would be natural, therefore, for a story to be created of how it was once an Eastern princess. The story certainly has an exotic and magical character, but this may owe more to the Greek and Roman imagination than to Eastern historical reality. Orchamos' cruelty, for instance, may be seen as the projection on to an Eastern tyrant of a more familiar custom or fantasy: Ovid himself mentions the traditional Roman custom of burying alive unchaste vestal virgins (*Fasti* 6. 458; see Bömer on *Met.* 4. 420). The unusual motif of the body disappearing after being soaked in nectar perhaps has its starting-point in the Homeric description of Thetis' using nectar to preserve Patroclus' body (*Il.* 19. 38 f.). After being mixed with nectar Adonis' body gives birth to the anemone (Ov. 10. 732, and cf. 14. 605 ff.; see Bömer on 4. 25). The dissolving of the body into the earth is itself a variation of the familiar motif of a body being swallowed up by the earth prior to the appearance of a plant. The idea that the rising of the plant from the earth gives the hero a qualified immortality is a familiar one. But this is taken a little further and has a special relevance here. When the sun says that though he cannot bring her to life 'tanges tamen aethera' (4. 251), he appears to be hinting at the role of incense at sacrifices to the gods.

See further Detienne, *Gardens of Adonis*, 37–8.

With the story of Leukothoe we may compare that of Libanos, an Assyrian boy loved by the gods whose body grew into an incense tree (*Geop.* 11. 17).

Lotis

In *Met.* 9. 342 ff. Ovid tells how a lotus tree bled when Dryope picked its flowers. He continues (346 ff.):

> scilicet, ut referunt tardi nunc denique agrestes
> Lotis in hanc nymphe, fugiens obscena Priapi
> contulerat versos, servato nomine, vultus.

The story is elsewhere mentioned only by Servius, who adds nothing to Ovid's brief report (*G* 2. 84; this is identical with *Myth. Vat.* 1. 26, 2. 179, and 3. 6. 26). A different form of the story, without a transformation, is found in two passages of the *Fasti*. In 1. 415 ff. Ovid explains the sacrifice of asses to Priapus by the story that a donkey woke up the sleeping Lotis as Priapus attempted to rape her. She thus escaped and the god was ridiculed. In 6. 319 ff. this same story is told with Vesta taking the place of Lotis. Here it is an *aition* not only for the sacrifice of asses at Lampsacus but for the Roman custom of giving donkeys wreaths of leaves in honour of Vesta.

It is normally thought that these three passages show Ovid's development of a local *aition*. The original story is the *aition* for the ass sacrifice in *Fasti* 1. In *Fasti* 6 Ovid has developed this Greek story to give a Latin cult *aition*. In the *Metamorphoses*, where his interest is different, he has turned it into a transformation story. Not only is the transformation not mentioned in the *Fasti* story, but it could have no place in it, since that story tells of the successful escape of Lotis. This is plausible; on the other hand we have no other reports of the Lampsacus *aition* or the ass sacrifice, and a heroine named Lotis fits the transformation story better than the local *aition*.

The Messapian Shepherds

Near the 'sacred rocks' in the land of the Messapians ἐπιμηλίδες νύμφαι were seen dancing by some boys who were looking after the flocks. These boys boasted that they were better dancers than the nymphs and challenged them to a contest. When the nymphs won they turned the boys into trees on the spot. Even now the trees produce a sound of human mourning in the night and the place is called *Νυμφῶν τε καὶ Παίδων* [*τόπος*] (AL 31, citing Nicander).

Ovid (14. 512 ff.) briefly tells how the nymphs transformed a shepherd who mocked and mimicked their dancing. He became a wild olive, and the bitterness of its fruit continues the sharpness and bitterness of his words. Characteristically Nicander's local *aition* for particular trees has become an *aition* for a species (see Chapter 1). The local curiosity of the speaking tree seems a subject that Nicander is fond of quite apart from the opportunity it represents for a transformation story. (We may compare the tree of Marsyas in *Alex.* 303 f.) Whether we have here a real local Messapian story (as is suggested in *RE* 9, col. 743) or an imitation of a local *aition* by Nicander is impossible to say. We find that all his tree stories tend to be set in wild places among primitive people and to concern shepherds and nymphs.

Minthe

In 10. 728 ff. Ovid hints at the transformation of a woman into the mint plant: 'an tibi quondam | femineos artus in olentes vertere mentas | Persephone, licuit . . .' Our fullest account of this story is in Oppian (*H* 3. 486 ff.). Minthe was once a nymph of the underworld and Hades' mistress. When the god carried off Persephone, Minthe arrogantly boasted that she was more beautiful than Persephone and that Hades would soon return to her. Demeter in anger trampled her into the earth and destroyed her. From the ground there sprang up a *ποίη οὐτίδανος* that bore her name. In schol. Nic. *Alex.* 375, Photius s.v. *Μίνθα*, and Strabo, 8. 3. 14, she is said to have been transformed by Persephone. Photius and Strabo also say that Mount Mintha near Elis was named after her, and Strabo adds that near the mountain were a precinct of Hades and a grove consecrated to Demeter. One assumes that the myth began as a local story at the shrine of Hades near Mount Mintha. It is possible that there was some special relation between the god and the plant.

Detienne (*Gardens of Adonis*, ch. 4) offers a structural interpretation of the myth according to which the opposition of the mint to cereals in the world of plants corresponds to the opposition of the concubine to the wife in the social code. He suggests that mint is a plant that was seen both as an aphrodisiac and as a cause of barrenness, and he cites in support of his approach a report that identifies Minthe with Iunx, the daughter of Peitho

(Photius s.v. Μίνθα; Iunx interferes with that other divine marriage, that of Zeus and Hera). It may be that the role of the plant as an aphrodisiac, or at least its sweet smell, is relevant to Minthe's character as a lover: our sources specify that she becomes the type of mint known as ἡδύοσμον. But Detienne's wider scheme and the opposition of mint to Demeter, corn, and marriage seems less convincing. Far from being an exotic and disreputable plant like the spices, mint is best known for its simple healthy qualities, and it was a major component of the drink of Demeter at Eleusis, the *kykeon*. Detienne takes up only certain qualities of mint, and ones that are not obviously relevant to our story. It is true, of course, that the relation of Hades and Minthe is a barren one, but so is that of Hades and Persephone. Detienne ignores the fact that Hades is not only a husband but the god of death.

The Sisters of Phaethon

According to Pliny (*NH* 37. 31) the story of how, after their brother's death, the sisters of Phaethon were transformed into trees and wept tears of amber was first told by Aeschylus, presumably in his *Heliades*. Some sources claim that it was told by Hesiod (fr. 311: see Hyg. *Fab.* 154; Lact. Plac. *Narr.* 2. 2–3). It seems that Hesiod did speak of amber on the banks of the Eridanus (fr. 150), but whether this was connected with the story of Phaethon and the Heliades is uncertain (see Diggle, 10–27; J. Schwartz, *Pseudo-Hesiodeia* (Leiden, 1960), 301–6). We know almost nothing of Aeschylus' play (frs. 68–73a) other than that the Heliades were set by the Eridanus and that the death of Phaethon may have given rise to a permanent mourning of women in the Adriatic (see fr. 71; cf. Polyb. 2. 16; Plut. *Mor.* 557). It may be that its plot was the ἱστορία παρὰ τοῖς τραγικοῖς given by the Homeric scholia (on *Od.* 17. 208). As well as their son Phaethon, Helios and Rhode had daughters—Phaethusa, Lampetie, and Aigle. When Phaethon fell into the Eridanus in the Far West, Zeus made an ἀνάμνησιν τῶν κακῶν and turned the sisters into poplars. From their weeping comes amber, the fruit of the tree. On the other hand the fact that the play was called the *Heliades* may suggest that the sisters played a larger part: one may compare Hyginus' unique report that the sisters of Phaethon were transformed after they had yoked Phaethon's chariot (Hyg. *Fab.* 152a; see Diggle, 30).

One can only guess at the origins of the story. Phaethusa and Lampetie were already daughters of the sun in Homer (*Od.* 12. 132), who herded his cattle on the island of Thrinacia (perhaps in the Far West). The Greek word for amber, ἤλεκτρον, is closely connected with and perhaps derived from ἠλέκτωρ, a name of the sun (see Pliny, *NH* 37. 31), and the daughters who also take their names from the sun's epithets might seem appropriate figures to produce it. We also know that amber was linked with the Eridanus and the Far West or North very early on, perhaps in a tradition independent of and prior to this story (see Hes. fr. 150 and Hdt. 3. 115). Finally, it may be that the legend of the mourning of the women of the Adriatic is earlier than, and helps to suggest, the story of the mourning sisters.

Our earliest surviving reference to the story is a passage of the *Hippolytus* (738 ff.):

> ἔνθα πορφύρεον σταλάσ-
>   σουσ' ἐς οἶδμα τάλαιναι
> κόραι Φαέθοντος οἴκτῳ δακρύων
> τὰς ἠλεκτροφαεῖς αὐγάς.

Here the description forms part of an escape fantasy in which the remote, peaceful, and beautiful grief of the sisters of Phaethon is contrasted with the chorus' present misfortunes: the chorus wish to fly on past these trees to the gardens of the gods in the Far West. (For the association of the trees with the garden of the Hesperides, compare the account of Theomenes in which the Hesperides pick up the amber that falls from the trees, see Pliny, 37. 38; in Ovid the Hesperiae bury Phaethon.)

We do not know whether the story was treated in Euripides' *Phaethon*. But it seems that in this play the body of Phaethon was brought back to his home in Ethiopia; so there can have been no mention of trees beside the Eridanus. But one fragment (782) runs: ψυκτήρια | δένδρη φίλαισιν ὠλέναισι δέξεται. Clearly this description would be appropriate to the transformed sisters, though it may be simply a hint at the Aeschylean version he has not used.

In the Hellenistic period the story was apparently treated by Nicander (see Pliny, 37. 31) and it is hinted at by Aratus (360). There are also fragments of an Alexandrian description of the trees beside the Eridanus in *PTeb.* 3. Our only surviving account is the description of the trees in Apollonius (4. 613 ff.). This picture is quite different from Euripides' peaceful scene. The trees here are set beside another famous natural marvel, the smoking and foul-smelling lake into which Phaethon fell and which no bird can fly over (cf. Arist. *Mir.* 81). The sisters are here incongruously mixed creatures whose sinister shrieking keeps the Argonauts awake throughout the night (wailing trees are a favourite Alexandrian *topos*: cf. Nic. *Alex.* 303 f., or AL 31).

The story is very frequently, though usually briefly, referred to in the Roman period. There are few new elements. Occasionally the sisters of Phaethon become synonyms for poplars in general (see Catull. 64. 290; *Culex* 127–30). Usually it is the special amber-producing trees by the Eridanus that are referred to (Cic. *Arat.* 146 f.; DS 5. 23; Strab. 5. 1. 9; Virg. *E* 6. 62 f., *A* 10. 189 ff.; Ov. 2. 319 ff.; Lucian, *Electr.*; Hyg. *Fab.* 152 and 154; Serv. *A* 10. 189; Heraclit. *Incred.* 36; Nonn. 2. 152 ff., 11. 32 ff., 38. 432 ff.; Hsch. s.v. ἤλεκτρος). Virgil calls the trees 'Phaethontiades' (cf. Sen. *Herc. Oet.* 188), perhaps on the analogy of 'Meleagrides', the sisters of Meleager, and says that they were 'alni' (*E* 6. 62 f.; in *A* 10. 189 ff. they are poplars). The Heliades also perhaps appear in depictions of the fall of Phaethon on Roman sarcophagi (see Diggle, *Phaethon*, 210–20), and a picture, perhaps imaginary, is described in Philostr. *Imag.* 1. 11. There are, however, apparently no early depictions of the story.

Philemon and Baucis

Philemon and Baucis were an old couple who received Zeus and Hermes in their humble cottage and were therefore saved from the great flood with which the gods destroyed the people of Phrygia. Their house became a temple, and the old couple, after serving as priests, were turned into trees. Local peasants still point out an oak and a lime tree which grow from the same trunk. The narrator of the story says that he saw votive wreaths hanging from the branches and he concludes: 'cura deum di sint et qui coluere colantur' (Ov. 8. 620 ff.).

An enormous amount has been written about this story and its origins, and so I can be brief here. (See esp. Bömer's and Hollis's commentaries on this passage; L. Malten, *Hermes* 74 (1939), 176–206; J. Fontenrose, *CPCP* 13 (1945), 93–119.) It is generally agreed that the story is a combination of a favourite Greek literary *topos* and local Phrygian traditions. Homer (*Od.* 17. 485 ff.) describes how the gods visit men in human form, and there are a number of Hellenistic poems that describe the reception of a god or hero in a humble home (compare e.g. Callimachus' *Hecale*). (For Phrygian traditions of the flood see Bömer on Ov. 8. 616; for the popularity of tree cults in Asia Minor, Malten, art. cit. 197–201.) The *aition* at the end with its reference to tree worship is quite different from any of our other stories of transformation into trees.

Philyra

Hyginus (*Fab.* 138) tells how Philyra was raped by Saturn in the form of a horse in Thrace and gave birth to the centaur Cheiron. When she saw that she had produced a monster she begged Jupiter to turn her into another species. He turned her into the tree of the same name. Other sources tell of the rape of Philyra, but none mentions this last transformation; so it is probably a fairly late addition to the story, presumably prompted by the meaning of her name. (It is perhaps modelled on the transformation of Smyrna, who begs to be removed from the living and the dead out of shame for her outrageous crime.) On the other hand many primitive figures were imagined as having been born from trees or tree nymphs (cf. the centaur Pholos whose mother is Melia). Perhaps Cheiron originally belonged to this type (see Murr, 16; Preller, 481).

Phyllis

Phyllis was a Thracian princess who committed suicide when her husband or lover, the Athenian prince Demophon or Akamas, did not return to her from Athens as he had promised. The story may have its origins in Athenian interest in this area in the fifth and fourth centuries (see Aeschines, 2. 31 and scholia, which say that Athenian disasters in this area were due to Phyllis' curse). But the connections of Akamas and Thrace are older (see U. Kron, *Die zehn attischen Phylenheroen* (Berlin, 1976), [illegible]).

No account of the story survives before the Roman period, but then it seems to have become very popular (Ov. *Rem. Am.* 591 ff., *Her.* 5. 2, *Ars Am.* 3. 37 f.; *Culex* 131 ff.; *AP* 7. 705; Apollod. *Epit.* 6. 16). Ovid's contemporary Tuscus wrote a *Phyllis* (see *Pont.* 4. 16. 20; Persius 1. 34 mentions its popularity). We may assume that these accounts stem from the lost treatment of the story by Callimachus (fr. 556). Ovid hints at a story of trees mourning for her: '. . . non flesset positis Phyllida silva comis' (*Rem. Am.* 606; cf. *Culex* 131 ff.). Pliny cites Cremutius for a report that the tree from which Phyllis hanged herself is never green (16. 108). Hyginus (*Fab.* 59) says that trees grow at Phyllis' tomb which at certain times weep for her death. It is only in Servius that we find an explicit transformation story (*E* 5. 10). He tells how she was transformed into an almond tree 'sine foliis'. Demophon returns too late and embraces the tree, which then sprouts leaves. This is the *aition* for the Greek word φύλλα. Servius claims, wrongly, that the story was told in Ovid's *Metamorphoses*.

Since we have no early account of the story we can only guess at its development. It is possible that the transformation only appeared at a late stage. Phyllis' name is clearly not derived from φύλλα or from any sort of tree, but from the Thracian district Phyllis by the river Strymon (though the associations of the name may perhaps have helped to prompt the transformation story); the *aition* for φύλλα looks like a desperate attempt to find an etymological link between tree and heroine. Perhaps the story of the grave-trees which seems to be already hinted at in Ovid gave rise to the story of the transformation. We learn from Antipater (*AP* 7. 705) that the tomb of Phyllis was a local landmark near Amphipolis. We may assume that these grave-trees were almonds, and that Servius thus preserves one element of the older story, since the almond has no obvious aetiological point in his account.

The idea that trees shed their leaves in mourning is a type of metaphor that is particularly popular in the Hellenistic poets. (It is an example of the wider *topos* of the sympathy of nature.) We may compare the trees of Protesilaus which wither away when they become big enough to see Troy, or those of Phaethon or Smyrna which weep tears of amber and myrrh, or the tree of Marsyas which moans in the wind, or the flowers of Ajax and Hyakinthos which have a cry of grief inscribed on their petals.

Pitys

The love of Pan for the nymph Pitys is mentioned fairly frequently in ancient sources (Theoc. *Syrinx*; Prop. 1. 18. 20; Lucian, *Dial. D.* 22. 4; *Daphnis and Chloe* 2. 39; Nonn. 2. 108). But it is only the very late sources that explicitly refer to a transformation. Nonnus (42. 259 ff.) says that Pitys φυγόδεμνος was pursued by Pan, and implies that she was swallowed up by the earth. Libanius (*Narr.* 27 and 28) tells how Pan's unsuccessful rival Boreas killed Pitys and the earth in pity sent up a tree. Her leaves still crown Pan, but she sighs when Boreas blows. The first story is clearly modelled on that of Daphne, and the second on that of Hyakinthos. The starting-point of Pitys' story is Pan's pine-crown (see *AP* 6. 253; Ov. 1. 699) just as the starting-point of that of Daphne is Apollo's laurel wreath.

Platanos and Elate

The stories of Elate and Platanos, which appear only in one very late source, are almost identical (Elate: Lib. *Narr.* 34; Platanos: Westermann, *Myth.* 381). They are sisters of the Aloades, the giant twins who threatened and were destroyed by the gods, and after their brothers' deaths they mourned until they were turned into trees. They still retain their great size. The story belongs to the general type of the transformed mourner; the particular link, however, of large tree and large woman is unusual (usually size is an irrelevant issue in transformations: huge men may become tiny birds and flowers). As well as their size it is perhaps the giants' wild and primitive nature that is relevant to their transformation (see Murr, 120); early savage men were thought to have been born from trees, and many of them bear tree names (e.g. Dryas, Elatos, Dryops, Peukas).

Smyrna

Apollodorus gives three reports of Adonis' birth: he was the son of Metharme, daughter of Pygmalion and of Kinyras, who founded Paphos after emigrating from Syria; according to Hesiod, he was the son of Alphesiboia and Phoinix; and, according to Panyassis, the son of Theias, king of Assyria. In this last account Theias had a daughter Smyrna who because she did not honour Aphrodite was inspired with a passion for her father. With the aid of her nurse she slept with him for twelve nights. When he discovered who she was he pursued her with a sword and she prayed to be made ἀφανής. She was turned into a tree from which Adonis was born (for the question of how much of this goes back to Panyassis see V. J. Matthews, *Mnemosyne* Suppl. 33 (1974), 120–5): Apollod. 3. 14. 3 f.

Smyrna does not appear again until the Hellenistic period. Lycophron refers allusively to her story (828 ff.):

ὄψεται δὲ τλήμονος
Μύρρας ἐρυμνὸν ἄστυ, τῆς μογοστόκους
ὠδῖνας ἐξέλυσε δενδρώδης κλάδος

(*Μύρρα*, according to Athenaeus, is the Aeolic form of *Σμύρνα*; the scholia to Lycophron say the city he refers to is Byblos in Phoenicia.) Antoninus (34) tells a full version of the story which perhaps goes back to Nicander. Theias is again the father and he lives by Mount Libanos. There is no mention of Aphrodite's anger here; we are told simply that Smyrna rejected all her suitors because of her monstrous love for her father. The story unfolds as in Panyassis. Smyrna is revealed when her father brings in a light. In her shock she gives birth on the spot and prays to be removed from both the living and the dead. Zeus turns her into a tree that once a year weeps a fruit of myrrh from its wood. Her father commits suicide. The main difference from Panyassis, therefore, and from other, later versions, is that Adonis' miraculous birth from a tree has been replaced by a familiar type of aetiological *aition*. (It is perhaps an imitation of the amber-weeping trees of Phaethon.) This is perhaps in keeping with the entirely human motivation of Smyrna's crime.

According to Pseudo-Plutarch (*Mor.* 310 F–311 A) the story was treated by Theodorus in his *Metamorphoses* (*SH* no. 749; on Theodorus see p. 240).

We do not know whether Pseudo-Plutarch is reproducing Theodorus' particular version of the story; he gives the version that later became standard in the scholia, in which the father is Kinyras and Smyrna is transformed by Aphrodite. Philostephanus is cited by Probus (*E* 10. 18) for a unique version of the story, in which Adonis was 'ex Iove sine ullius feminae accubitu procreatus'. One assumes that this was an unusual way of describing Adonis' birth from a tree, but the reference to Zeus is strange. The story of Adonis seems to have been assimilated here to the stories of the miraculous births of Dionysos or Athene from Zeus.

The story was the subject of a famous lost poem by the neoteric poet Cinna (frs. 6–7 *FPL*; Lyne (note on 206) argues that there are fragments in the *Ciris*). Ovid's elaborate treatment (10. 298 ff.) must have been influenced by this (see Otis, 392–3, and Lyne, loc. cit.) although the tone is perhaps different. Instead of the sentimental treatment of the heroine (suggested by Cinna, fr. 6), we have the mock solemn condemnation of a monstrous crime ('procul hinc natae, procul este parentes', 300). In 311 ff. he says that her love was inspired not by Cupid but by a fury. Ovid's main differences from Antoninus are that the father is Kinyras, king of Cyprus (although in his version the location seems to waver between Cyprus and the East: see e.g. 316 or 475 ff.) and that Smyrna brings forth her child in tree form, but only after she has wandered all the way to Arabia (the home of the spice tree). The Naiads take the child away and anoint him with his mother's tears. Cf. *Ars Am.* 1. 285 ff.

The other sources show minor differences (see Prop. 3. 19. 15; Hyg. *Fab.* 58; schol. Theoc. 1. 107; schol. Lyc. 829; Lucian, *Salt.* 58; Opp. *H* 3. 402; *Ciris* 237 ff.; Fulg. 3. 8; Serv. *E* 10. 18, *A* 5. 72). A first-century fresco shows 'Mirra' in flight (see W. Atallah, *Adonis dans la littérature et l'art grec* (Paris, 1966), 41). Most sources, like Ovid, make Smyrna's father Kinyras. (In Hyg. *Fab.* 58 the Cypriot and Asian traditions are reconciled by making Kinryas king of Assyria; elsewhere in Hyginus he belongs in Cyprus.) Usually Smyrna's love is caused by Aphrodite, and sometimes a motive is given for her enmity. (In Hyginus her mother claims she is more beautiful than the goddess; the scholia to Theoc. say that she boasted about her hair.) Servius says that the anger of the sun was responsible for her incestuous love; this perhaps reflects the role of the sun in the production of myrrh (cf. Fulgentius' explanation of the story). Most sources have Adonis born from the tree. Some give a reason for the splitting of the tree that frees him. (Servius says it follows a blow from a boar, presumably an anticipation of his death, or a blow from his father's axe.) In explanation of *A* 5. 72, 'materna myrtus', Servius tells the familiar story but ends it with a transformation into a myrtle, the plant of Venus, rather than a myrrh tree. Another version (see Hsch. s.v. μυρίκη) says that the tamarisk (μυρίκη) derived its name from the daughter of Kinyras' mourning (μύρεσθαι).

Much has been written about the origins of this story (most fully by Atallah, *Adonis*; but cf. J. G. Frazer, *The Golden Bough: A Study in Comparative Religion*[4] (London, 1911–12), Pt. 4; Bömer on Ov. 10. 298; Detienne, *The Gardens of Adonis*; S. Ribichini, *Adonis: Aspetti 'orientali' di un mito greco* (Rome, 1981)). Frazer saw Smyrna's incest as a distorted record of a historical custom of kings marrying their daughters, but this does not explain the suicide of her father or Smyrna's flight and transformation, which are at the heart of the story. Ribichini adopts a more sophisticated approach and sees the oriental motifs of the story (particularly the incest, but also the magical tree) as a projection of Greek beliefs about the Orient which help to characterize a world opposed to that of normal Greek behaviour (cf. A. M. G. Capomacchia, in *Adonis: Relazioni del colloquio in Roma 22–3 maggio 1981* (Rome, 1984), 95–103). There may be something in this, but again it must be stressed that it is the unusual nature of Smyrna's behaviour even in an Eastern context which is crucial in this story.

Atallah suggests that the incest is a late motif inspired by the fact that Kinyras was himself a lover of Aphrodite. But Kinyras' place in the incest story is also late (not definitely until Ovid). Although he appears early as the father of Adonis on Cyprus (in the comic poet Plato, fr. 3) the transformation story is set in the East in our earliest version and the father is Theias.

Detienne sees myrrh as the plant of seduction and argues that it corresponds in the vegetable code to Adonis, the human seducer: the story of Smyrna is not just a causal preliminary to Adonis' career, but a parallel myth of seduction. There are problems in arguing that the stories are closely parallel. Smyrna's behaviour is a perverse and criminal act, whereas Adonis is much more the passive victim of the love of goddesses. It is also true that our sources do not tend to characterize Adonis as a perfumed hero. However, it does seem likely that the connection of spices with Aphrodite and love is one of the factors that have influenced the story. There are also other relevant considerations: the eastern and exotic associations of the spice plant are appropriate to a hero who is always seen as a foreigner. Looking backwards to Smyrna rather than forward to Adonis, one can recognize in the story familiar patterns in which transformation follows an outrageous crime, particularly incest, and in which trees are thought to weep. Finally, what is perhaps just as important as the kind of tree is the fact that Adonis is born from a tree at all (in Hes. fr. 139 his father is Phoinix). This is an example of the unusual and even miraculous birth that characterizes certain types of hero, particularly the primitive hunters who become lovers of the gods (e.g. Orion who is born from an ox-hide, or Attis whose father is an almond, or Agdistis who is born from a rock).

Syrinx

Ovid tells how the reed-pipe was once a beautiful hamadryad called Syrinx. She lived in Arcadia and was a virgin huntress. One day she was pursued by Pan, and reaching the river Ladon in her flight she begged her 'liquidas sorores' to change her form. She was transformed into reeds which Pan made into a pipe: 'hoc mihi colloquium tecum . . . manebit' (1. 689 ff.; cf. the similar account in the anonymous mythographer in Westermann, *Myth.* 347).

The story seems to be a popular one in the Greek romances. Longus (2. 34) gives it to one of his shepherds who claims to have heard it in Sicily. To suit the pastoral context Syrinx was here a human goatherd and friend of the nymphs whose voice was pleasing then as it is now in her new form. She scorned the love of Pan, and when chased hid in the woods and disappeared. Pan cut down the reeds in anger, but did not find the girl. He made a pipe which has unequal reeds just as their love was unequal. Achilles Tatius (8. 6) gives the same story the form of a local *aition*, and sets it near Ephesus: Pan puts the pipe in a cave which was dedicated to Artemis, and there it still plays a part in a test of virginity. See also Serv. *E* 2. 31. In all these later reports a disappearance has replaced a transformation (see above under Daphne for a similar development). Finally, Nonnus briefly refers to the story of Syrinx on a number of occasions in his lists of φυγόδεμνοι (2. 118, 16. 332 ff., 42. 383 ff.). The story is perhaps illustrated on coins of Thelpusa (a city on the river Ladon) of the Roman period, which show Pan holding a tall reed (see *RML* iii. 1467, fig. 25).

The story has a familiar pattern; it is almost identical with those of Daphne, Pitys, and Lotis (and in Nonnus it is compared with the first two of these). It combines the type of the *aition* for a god's favourite plant with another popular Hellenistic subject, an account of the inventors of various artefacts and skills (see Papathomopoulos, 118 n. 6). We have a number of reports about the invention of the *syrinx* (see Bömer on Ov. 1. 691). It is ascribed to Hermes, Silenos, Marsyas (see Ath. 184 A). Theocritus is the first writer to ascribe it to Pan (in his *Syrinx*); we may compare Virg. *E* 2. 32 f. These reports do not obviously imply a transformation story. On the other hand it seems unlikely that Ovid invented it; the versions of the Greek romances and Servius do not seem to be dependent on his account.

The Thracian Women

The story of how the Thracian maenads who tore Orpheus apart were transformed by Dionysos into trees is told only by Ovid (11. 68 ff.). The type of tree is not specified. We may compare with this the report that the Thracians still tattoo their women in punishment for this crime (Phanocles, 1. 23 ff.). The death of a special hero frequently collects local *aitia*. (We may compare the way that the death of Phaethon gives rise both to the weeping poplars and to the fact that the women of the Adriatic wear mourning.) Whether this was a real local *aition* or Ovid's own invention is impossible to say.

Minor Transformations

There is a group of very similar stories of dying favourites of a god which only appear in very late writers.

Amaracus. Amaracus, son of Kinyras, was a perfume maker of Aphrodite who died and was transformed to the herb *amaracus* (Serv. *A.* 1. 693). For the connection of Kinyras and perfume see Alcman, fr. 3. 71 f.

Ampelos. Ovid in the *Fasti* (3. 409 ff.) tells how Ampelos, a young lover of Dionysos, is set in the stars as the constellation Vindemitor after he has fallen off a tree. Nonnus (10. 175 ff.) has him transformed after falling off a bull. It has been claimed that the transformation is represented in a third-century BC statue which shows a small female figure holding out a cluster of grapes to Dionysos, but this seems questionable (see *LIMC* s.v. Ampelos no. 1).

Elaia. The olive, a plant that is loved by Athene and whose fruit and leaves are prizes for athletes, was once a female athlete, a favourite of Athene, who was killed by jealous rivals (see Westermann, *Myth.* 369). *Geop.* 11. 6 tells an identical story of Myrsine who becomes a myrtle; this is also said to be a favoured plant of Athene. In other sources, however, Athene has no particular connection with the plant, which is usually a plant of Aphrodite (although see Murr, 90–1).

Karpos and Kalamos. Karpos, son of Zephyrus and Hora, was loved by Kalamos, son of the Maeander river. When Karpos was drowned in the

Maeander Kalamos asked that he might join his lover in death, and so Jupiter turned him into the reeds on the river bank and turned Karpos into the fruit of all things 'ut semper renasceretur' (Serv. *E* 5. 48). Nonnus adds that Karpos was drowned when the wind drove a wave into his face, and the story is thus assimilated to that of Hyakinthos (which Kalamos mentions in his complaint: Nonn. 11. 370 ff.).

Kissos. Kissos was a young dancer of Dionysos who fell off a tree. Earth in pity sent up a plant which winds round the tree like the dancing boy (*Geop.* 11. 29; Nonn. 12. 97 f. and 12. 190 ff.).

Melus. Melus was a companion of Adonis on Cyprus, who after Adonis' death hanged himself from an apple tree and was turned by Aphrodite into the fruit of the tree (Serv. *E* 8. 37).

Myrtle. Servius (*A* 3. 23) tells how the myrtle, the plant that is sacred to Venus, was once her human priestess. For a different story see under 'Elaia'.

b. Flowers

These are in a separate category since usually it is only Servius who speaks of a full transformation.

Adonis

Nicander apparently told how the anemone was born from the blood of Adonis (see schol. Theoc. 5. 92). One assumes that, as in Ovid (10. 728 ff.; cf. *Fasti* 5. 227 f.), this story explained the blood-red colour of the flower. Ovid describes how Aphrodite sprinkled his blood with nectar; the blood bubbled and within an hour a flower had appeared. He has the further *aition* that the flower is only a short-lived one since it is destroyed by the winds. (Though Ovid does not name the flower this detail must depend on the meaning of the word *anemone*.) Servius (*A* 5. 72) says that the flower is specially protected from the winds, while Pliny, though he does not mention the story of Adonis, says that the anemone derives its name from the fact that the flower will only open if the wind blows. These explanations clearly go back to Greek sources, but whether Nicander made use of the same *aition* as we find in Ovid or Servius seems impossible to say (Nonnus hints at a similar *aition* to Ovid's when he calls the flower μινυνθαδίη: 15. 355; cf. 2. 88).

Bion's lament for Adonis mentions different connections with flowers. He says that anemones were born from the tears of Aphrodite and roses from the blood of Adonis (but Paus. 6. 24. 7 says that roses are sacred to Aphrodite and linked with the legend of Adonis). Schol. Lyc. 831 says that anemones were made red by the blood of Adonis and roses by the blood of Aphrodite (cf. *Geop.* 11. 17). Finally, another passage of Servius (*A* 10. 18) goes one step further and says that Adonis was transformed into a rose.

The reason for the appearance of a rose in the story of the death of Aphrodite's lover is quite obviously that it is the flower of Aphrodite and love. The colour of the anemone makes it a generally suitable flower to be connected with a dead hero. (It is a regular *topos* that a hero's blood gives a plant its red colour; see e.g. Paus. 9. 25. 1 or Ov. 4. 158 ff.) Detienne has argued that the relevant quality of the plant is its odourlessness and that this makes its creation an appropriate conclusion to the career of Adonis, the perfumed hero (see *Dionysos Slain*, 50). This seems dubious. No source gives this aetiological conclusion to the story, and this reference to its lack of smell comes only in one special context (in the scholia on Theoc. 5. 92 explaining Theocritus' dismissive comparison of the anemone with a rose). Ovid cannot have been aware of this characteristic of the flower since he has Adonis' blood sprinkled with 'odorato nectare' (10. 732). Nor can Bion, who says that anemones were born from the tears of Aphrodite.

Ajax

See Hyakinthos.

Anethus

'Papaver, Narcissus, Anethus pulcherrimi pueri fuerunt quique in flores suorum nominum versi sunt' (Serv. *E* 2. 47).

Hyakinthos

It is in Ovid that we find our first full account of the transformation of Hyakinthos. He is a boy-lover of Apollo whom the god accidentally kills in a discus contest. The god announces (10. 204 and 206):

> Semper eris mecum memorique haerebis in ore
>
> . . . . .
>
> flosque novus scripto gemitus imitabere nostros

From the bloodstained ground there arose a flower on which the god inscribed 'AIAI'. At Sparta he was commemorated in an annual festival. (In

Fasti 5. 223 ff. it is Hyakinthos', not Apollo's, grief that is inscribed on the petals.)

The killing of Hyakinthos by Apollo with a discus is a story known to Euripides (*Helen* 1469 ff.), but there is no reference here to a transformation. Euphorion wrote a *Hyakinthos*, but the inscribed flower in fr. 40 is the flower of Ajax, not Hyakinthos (cf. Theoc. 10. 28, Ov. 10. 207 and 13. 395; no source speaks of Ajax being transformed into this flower). A transformation story is first hinted at in Nicander (*Ther.* 902 ff.). The story is a popular one in later writers and the scholia. (See Lucian, *Dial. D.* 14; Palaeph. 46, not thought to be a part of the original work; Nonn. 3. 153 ff., 10. 253 ff., 11. 364 ff., 19. 104, 29. 97; schol. Nic. *Ther.* 903; Westermann, *Myth.* 387; Philostr. *Imag.* 1. 24; Serv. *E* 3. 63; 3. 106; Philargyrius, *E* 3. 63; schol. Stat. *Theb.* 4. 223; *Myth. Vat.* 1. 117, 2. 181; and, without a transformation, Apollod. 1. 3. 3). Sometimes the accident is caused by the jealous Zephyrus (Palaeph.; Nonn.; schol. Stat.), or by Boreas (Serv.; *Myth. Vat.*). One assumes that Zephyrus owes his place to his traditional association with spring flowers (see Callim. *Ap.* 81 ff.). But the winds are anyway often depicted as violent lovers. Sometimes, as in Ovid, the plant is born from Hyakinthos' blood (Lucian; Philostr.; schol. Stat.; schol. Nic.), sometimes from his ashes (Philargyrius, who adds that a spring was produced by the tears of the mourning nymphs). In one source he is actually transformed (Serv. *E* 3. 63).

How much this story owes to the historical cult of Hyakinthos at Amyclae is disputed. Rohde (*Psyche*, i. 137–41) argued that the story is a late invention that merely uses the hero's name. Pausanias (3. 19. 4) says that on the throne of Bathycles at Amyclae he was shown as a bearded figure being taken up to heaven with his sister Polyboia. For a tradition of Hyakinthos as a father of daughters see Apollod. 3. 15. 8 and Hyg. *Fab.* 238. M. J. Mellink, however, sees Hyakinthos as a symbol of the vegetation, a dying child-god (*Hyakinthos* (Utrecht, 1943)). One should not perhaps read too much into the bearded figure on the throne of Bathycles; there was a similar shift in the representations of a number of other gods and heroes in the classical period (e.g. Dionysos or Actaeon). On the other hand the only certain link of cult and myth seems to be the death of Hyakinthos and his link with Apollo. We know of no role of the flower in the Hyakinthia, and there is no link of god or flower-hero with vegetation in general. The idea of the child-god (in the sense of a baby needing a nurse, like the child Zeus or Sosipolis) seems to have no support either in the cult of Hyakinthos or in the myth (in which, like Apollo himself, he is a young athlete). On the cult of Hyakinthos see further Brelich, *Paides*, 177–9; Burkert, *GR* 19.

Mecon

Mecon was an Athenian youth loved by Demeter and transformed into a poppy (Serv. *G* 1. 212; cf. Serv. *E* 2. 47).

Narcissus

Narcissus, the son of Cephisus and Leiriope, was a beautiful boy, who, cursed by a rejected lover, fell in love with his own reflection. He wasted away and disappeared, and in his place there appeared a flower (Ov. 3. 339 ff.). In the account of Conon (24) the story becomes an *aition* not only for the flower, which here springs from his blood, but for the worship of Eros at Thespiai. (For the setting at Thespiai cf. Stat. *Theb.* 7. 340 ff.; Eust. *Il.* 2. 498; Paus. 9. 31. 7.) Pausanias tells a rationalized version of the story in which when his twin sister died Narcissus used to look into a spring, imagining he was seeing her reflection. Nonnus has him born on Latmos to Endymion and Selene (48. 582 ff.). Servius (*E* 2. 47) and schol. Stat. *Theb.* (7. 340) say that he was actually transformed. See further Hyg. *Fab.* 271; Philostr. *Imag.* 1. 23; Westermann, *Myth.* 323; *Geop.* 11. 24. Narcissus is a very popular figure in Pompeian wall-paintings (see W. Helbig, *Wandgemälde* (Leipzig, 1868), 297–303); these usually show him sitting beside a spring; sometimes Eros or the nymphs appear. (For statues and gems see *RML* article.)

It is difficult to drawn any firm conclusions about the origin and development of this story. It is not clear, for instance, whether the story was invented to explain the flower or whether the flower is a later addition to a story about an independent local hero. Narcissus had a tomb at Oropus, but here his story seems to be a different one (see Strab. 9. 2. 10 and Probus on *E* 2. 48), and there is no evidence in our sources that he was a cult hero at Thespiai. The cult of Eros at Thespiai is not enough in itself to have given rise to the story, and it is not suggested anywhere that the flower had a special role in this cult. No source develops the story much as a natural *aition* or gives any connection between plant and hero apart from the name (it is not, for instance, a bloodstained plant, or one with markings of grief), but it is easy to imagine why the story might be considered appropriate (see the discussion of flower-heroes in Chapter 5). The narcissus is the prime example of the beautiful alluring plant. It is a narcisuss that entices and traps Persephone in *Hymn. Hom. Cer.* 8 ff.; it is a δόλος and is *θαυμαστὸν γανόωv*.

Smilax and Krokos

This story is mentioned by various writers, but nowhere do we find a full account. Ovid says 'Crocon in parvos versum cum Smilace flores | praetereo' (4. 283 f.). Pliny (*NH* 16. 154) says that the *smilax* is a 'lugubris' plant because the girl Smilax turned into a plant out of love for Krokos; not realizing this, people use the plant in sacred rites of the gods and pollute them. Galen (ed. C. G. Kühn (Leipzig, 1821–3), vol. 13, p. 269), citing Philo, sets the story in Lydia: Krokos was a boy who was accidentally killed when he was throwing the discus with Hermes (the story is presumably an imitation of that of Hyakinthos); cf. Servius *G* 4. 182. These sources make no reference to Smilax. Nonnus refers to the story several times. (One passage, 12. 86, suggests a story in which it was Krokos who desired Smilax.)

PART 4. STONES

a. People

Aglauros

Ovid (2. 708 ff.) tells how when Hermes attempts to seduce the Athenian princess Herse, her envious sister, Aglauros, blocks his way (her envy is a punishment sent by Athene for opening the casket of Erichthonius). Hermes therefore turns her into stone where she stands.

Until recently this was one of the few metamorphoses in Ovid which appear in no other source. Now a papyrus reveals that it was mentioned by Callimachus, but with Pandrosos, not Aglauros, as the envious sister, thus helping to confirm, if confirmation was needed, that Ovid was not inclined to invent whole stories (see A. Henrichs, *Cronache Ercolanesi* 13 (1983), 33–43).

The three sisters, Aglauros, Pandrosos, and Herse, are important figures in Attic cult and genealogy. Apollodorus (3. 14. 3) mentions the union of Hermes and Herse and says that their son was Cephalus, but tells no story about this. H. Fränkel (*Ovid* (Berkeley, 1945), 209) supposed that the petrification story is an *aition* for a real statue on the Acropolis, W. Wimmel (*Hermes* 90 (1962), 326–33) more plausibly suggests that its origins lie in the story of the punishment of the two sisters for opening the casket of Erichthonius. In other accounts they are driven mad by Athene and throw themselves off the Acropolis. In Ovid the punishment is separated from the account of their crime and combined with the story of Hermes, but it is nevertheless made a consequence of the earlier and more famous crime while the intrusion into the god's romance is several times linked with her earlier criminal curiosity or intrusion (e.g. 2. 748 f.). (For the pattern of petrification for intruding upon a god see p. 141, and more specifically of petrification following an attempt to come between the god and his lover, compare the story of Karya and her sisters: Cat. 3*a*.)

Alcmena

Antoninus tells how when Alcmena, the mother of Heracles, dies at Thebes Zeus sends Hermes to take her to Elysium as a wife for Rhadamanthys. When the children of Heracles carry out her coffin for burial they discover a stone inside instead of her body. They place this in a grove, which is the site of the *heroon* of Alcmena at Thebes (AL 33, citing Pherecydes). Plutarch (*Rom.* 28) compares the story with the disappearance and heroization of Cleomedes, Aristeas, and Romulus; Pausanias (9. 16. 7) reports a Theban story that Alcmena was transformed, but does not mention a *heroon* or cult; DS (4. 58) speaks of τιμαὶ ἰσόθεαι after her disappearance, but does not mention the stone. Also relevant is a Hellenistic relief at Cyzicus which apparently showed Heracles leading his mother to Elysium to marry Rhadamanthys (see *AP* 3. 13).

This story has the same form as Nicander's local cult *aitia*, and it is possible that he rather than Pherecydes is Antoninus' direct source. The stone appearing instead of the body in a coffin is perhaps a mythical reflection of certain customs in which a stone can act as a double or a replacement for a corpse (see J. P. Vernant, *Mythe et pensée chez les grecs* (Paris, 1965), 251–64).

The development of the story may be disputed. There was a tradition in Boeotia that the living Alcmena married Rhadamanthys after he had fled from Crete and after Amphitryon had died (see Apollod. 2. 4. 11; Plut. *Lys.* 28 has been thought to state that he had a tomb by her side at Haliartus, but see A. Schachter, *Cults of Boiotia* (London, 1981), i. 9). One might argue that an independent association of Alcmena with Rhadamanthys, who presides over the Elysian Fields in Pindar *Ol.* 2. 75, has prompted the story that she was translated to Elysium and married him there. On the other hand translation to Elysium is a regular fate for heroes and their families, and we often hear that a hero is given as a bride someone with whom he had no connection in his life (Achilles' brides include Medea and Helen, and his mortal loves Briseis or Deidamia are forgotten). Perhaps Rhadamanthys is to be seen simply as the most revered figure and thus the best husband in Elysium. The story of the translation is older than any report of the marriage of Alcmena and Rhadamanthys in their lifetime, and it would be equally plausible to suppose that this was a rationalization of an older story. See further Schachter, op. cit. 15.

Arkeophon and Arsinoe

Arkeophon loved Arsinoe, daughter of Nikokreon king of Cyprus. When she and her family rejected him he starved himself to death. Arsinoe, πρὸς ὕβριν, looked out at his funeral, but Aphrodite, μισήσασα τὸ ἦθος, changed her to stone (AL 39, citing Hermesianax).

Nikokreon was a real king of Cyprus who lived only shortly before Hermesianax's own time. Unusually, therefore, this myth has a historical, and a recent historical, setting. The main story of the misfortunes of the lover of a hard-hearted woman or boy is a very common Hellenistic type. Plutarch (*Mor.* 766 c) refers to this story and compares it with the Cretan story of Gorgo (cf. also Antoninus' own story of Kyknos). Plutarch calls the hero Euxynthetos and the woman Leukomantis. (Or else he compares the Cyprian story with that of Euxynthetos: the text may be corrupt. See E. Rohde, *Der griechische Roman und seine Vorläufer*[3] (Leipzig, 1914), 86 n. 1.)

Ovid tells a similar story to Antoninus', but he calls his lovers Iphis and Anaxarete (14. 698 ff.). The symbolism of the story is much more explicit here: 'paulatimque occupat artus | quod fuit in duro iam pridem pectore, saxum (757–8). Unusually Ovid gives a cult *aition* where Antoninus has none: the transformed Anaxarete becomes a cult statue of Venus Prospiciens. Since such *aitia* are not a favourite motif of Ovid it is possible that this is not his own invention, but was in his source. On the other hand we have no other reference to this statue.

Aspalis

Aspalis was a young girl who hanged herself to avoid being raped by Tartarus, the brutal tyrant of Melite in Pthia. Her brother then disguised himself as her and killed the tyrant. Tartarus was thrown into the river, but they could not find Aspalis' body anywhere: it had disappeared κατὰ θεόν and in its place there appeared a statue standing beside that of Artemis. It was named Aspalis Ameilete Hekaerge, and every year the virgins of the city hang up a young goat because Aspalis, a virgin, had hanged herself (AL 13, citing Nicander).

For the characteristic Nicandrean pattern of disappearance of a hero and appearance of a cult object see Chapter 1. More specifically the name

Hekaerge suggests that this figure was seen as a form of Artemis herself. The story thus belongs to a regular type in wich a human heroine becomes the epithet of a god (we may compare Nicander's story of Ktesilla who becomes *Κτήσυλλα Ἑκαέργη*: AL 1). In this case the *aition* takes the form of the familiar pattern of the killing of a monster. We may compare Nicander's own story of Lamia, and the story of the hero of Temesa (cf. Pausanias' story of Menestratos: 9. 26. 7). Common features are the predatory monster who has to be appeased by young girls or boys, the monster-killer who disguises himself as a victim, and the disappearance of the monster's body in water. Here the motifs of the story have been rationalized and reduced to a human level, though the name of the tyrant Tartarus hints at his monstrous prototypes.

Battos

Antoninus (23) tells how Battos, who lived in the *Βάττου Σκοπιαί* in Arcadia, saw Hermes leading away the cattle he had stolen from Apollo and demanded a reward for keeping silent. Hermes promised this to him, and after hiding his cattle he returned to test him. When the disguised god offered him a cloak Battos told him what he had seen. Hermes struck him with his staff and turned him to stone. Now cold and heat never leave him, and the place is still called *Βάττου Σκοπιαί*.

Ovid (2. 676 ff.) tells the story with a few more details. Battos is here an old man, a shepherd who looks after the mares of Neleus. Hermes offers him a cow, and in return Battos promises 'lapis iste prius tua furta loquetur' (696). When he yields to the disguised Hermes' offer of a bull and a cow, the god laughs: me mihi, perfide, prodis? | . . . ait periuraque pectora vertit | in durum silicem, qui nunc quoque dicitur index' (cf. *Ibis* 586 'laesus lingua Battus ab ipse sua').

The sources cited for Antoninus' story are Nicander, Hesiod, Didymarchus' and Antigonus' *Metamorphoses*, and Apollonius in his epigrams, ὥς φησι Πάμφιλος ἐν α'. One assumes that Nicander, who is mentioned first and is the main source for most of Antoninus' stories, is the main source here. We have no independent evidence for any of these versions. *The Homeric Hymn to Hermes*, which tells the story of Hermes' theft of cattle, does not mention Battos, but it does mention an old man in a vineyard at Onchestos. Hermes offers him a reward if he keeps silent, but when Apollo arrives the old man tells what he knows without being offered anything. There is an obvious resemblance between this character and Battos, particularly in the account which makes Battos an old man. It is possible that the episode of the Homeric hymn is the starting-point of the Hellenistic story. On the other hand the account in the Homeric hymn leaves one with the impression that there is more to the story (the character is given some importance through the account of Hermes' bribe, but his reasons for rejecting this and the consequences of his action are not referred to). Perhaps, therefore, it is this account which is a variation on a familiar story.

The motif of speech and silence which is central in both Ovid's accounts is not emphasized in Antoninus. This motif is, however, perhaps not Ovid's own invention but is bound up with the meaning of Battos' name (Hsch. s.v. βαττολογία: ἀργολογία, ἀκαιρολογία; we may compare the closely parallel story of the talkative Cyprian woman: see below). There seems no reason to suppose with R. Holland (*RhM* 75 (1926), 160) that the silence of the stone is connected with the Roman formula for oaths: 'si sciens fallo, tum me Diespiter . . . eiciat uti ego hunc lapidem.' It is possible, finally, that Antoninus preserves in a confused form a different *aition*. Battos is bribed by a cloak, and we are told that in his stone state neither cold nor heat leave him. Had there been simply a reference to cold there would be a special appropriateness in the punishment, but the reference to heat rather blurs this point.

Britomartis

Antoninus (40) tells how Britomartis, after escaping Minos in the nets of some fishermen and thus receiving the name Dictynna, came to Aegina in a fishing boat. When the fishermen too attempted to rape her she fled to a grove and disappeared. A statue of her appeared in the temple of Artemis, but in the place where she disappeared a temple was built for her, she was called Aphaia, and was worshipped as a god.

No source is given, but the story has the familiar form of one of Nicander's cult *aitia*, in which a human hero vanishes, an object miraculously appears, and a cult is established. Here the pattern is given a special relevance because the name Aphaia suggests a disappearance. We do not know how old the identification is of Aphaia with the Cretan goddess Britomartis/Dictynna (see J. P. Harland, *Prehistoric Aegina* (Paris, 1925), 92–100, who thinks it is late; Papathomopoulos, 163). The *aition* for Dictynna's cult in Crete, which tells how she leapt into the fishermen's nets to escape the pursuit of Minos, appears in Callimachus' *Hymn to Artemis* (195 ff.; cf. Paus. 2. 30. 3; *Ciris* 294 ff.).

See also R. Holland, *Hermes* 60 (1925), 59–65, who thinks that the whole of Nicander's story is modelled on Callimachus' account of Artemis' career in the hymn.

The Man who saw Cerberus

Ovid compares Orpheus to a man petrified by fear on seeing Cerberus 'with chains on his middle neck' (10. 6. 64 ff.). Nothing more is known of this story. It may be an amplification of a detail in the story of Heracles' capture of Cerberus. (Euphorion fr. 51 describes how women and children hid as Heracles brought the monster to Mycenae; metamorphoses are frequently added on to the heroic stories in this way.) This man is of the same type as, and perhaps identical with, the subject of the proverbial expression δειλότερος τοῦ παρακύπτοντος. Zenobius (3. 32) explains this by a story that a man who had hidden in a cave in terror of Heracles was petrified as he peeped out. Such stories are perhaps modelled on the story of the Gorgon.

The Cyprian Old Woman

Lycophron (826) refers enigmatically to the petrification of an old woman: πέμπελον γραῦν μαρμαρουμένην δέμας. The scholia tell a story that is closely parallel to that of Battos. Aphrodite, angry with the gods, went away and hid on Cyprus. When the gods came in search for her an old woman showed them where she was. Aphrodite petrified her, and a στήλη still stands there (Hesychius explains πέμπελος as στωμύλος, λάλος).

Daphnis

Ovid refers allusively to a story of the petrification of Daphnis (4. 276 ff.):

> 'Vulgatos taceo' dixit 'pastoris amores
> Daphnidis Idaei, quem nymphe paelicis ira
> contulit in saxum.'

According to Servius (*E* 8. 68) Daphnis was loved by a nymph Nomia. When he scorned her and pursued Chimaera the nymph blinded him and then turned him into a stone. At Cephaloeditanum (a town in Sicily) there was said to be still a stone in the shape of a man.

The constant feature in many versions of the story of Daphnis and the nymph is his blinding (e.g. Ael. *VH* 10. 18, for which Stesichorus is cited, probably spuriously: see M. L. West, *CQ* 20 (1970), 206). In one later version this is followed by his falling down a cliff (schol. Theoc. 8. 92), in another by his being taken up to heaven and a spring appearing (Serv. *E* 5. 20), and here by petrification. There is perhaps a similarity between the punishments of blinding and petrification. Stones may be seen as eyeless or blind (see Aesch. *Ag.* 418): blinding and petrification tend to be parallel punishments (e.g. Teiresias is blinded and Kalydon petrified for intruding on a bathing goddess). The fact that Ovid and Servius have such completely different locations perhaps suggests that a local landmark was not the origin of this story.

The Victims of the Gorgon's Head

It is generally considered that the Gorgon's head began as a motif in art and only later acquired a body and a story (see T. P. Howe, *AJA* 58 (1954), 209–21; C. Hopkins, *AJA* 38 (1934), 341–58). Homer refers several times to the Gorgon's head as an object of terror (e.g. *Il.* 5. 741 f., 8. 349, 11. 36; *Od.* 11. 634 f.): it decorates the *aegis* of Athene, and it is also one of the horrors of the underworld. There is no hint of a story about it. In the *Theogony* (270 ff.) we find the story that Medusa, one of the three Gorgon sisters, was killed by Perseus. The *Catalogue* seems to have told the story of Perseus (see fr. 135), and one fragment mentions Polydectes (8). It is not until the fifth century that we find a definite reference to the petrifying power of the Gorgon's head. Pindar (*Pyth.* 10. 48) describes Perseus as 'bearing a stony death to the islanders' (presumably Polydectes and the people of Seriphos are meant; cf. *Pyth.* 12. 12). In Pherecydes (*FGH* 3 F 11) the quarrel of Polydectes and Perseus springs from Polydectes' designs on Perseus' mother Danae. (Cf. Apollod. 2. 4. 2; Strab. 10. 5. 10; Paus. 1. 22. 7. Ov. 5. 242 ff. and Serv. *A* 6. 289 say that Polydectes refused to believe that Perseus killed the Gorgon, and so Perseus showed him the head. In Hyg. *Fab.* 64 he plots against Perseus' life.) It seems likely that Aeschylus treated the story in his *Polydectes* (T78, 15b).

One assumes that the Gorgon's power to turn to stone has its origins in the same sort of idea as the English metaphorical sense of 'petrification'. The state of helpless shock and immobility produced by extreme fear became a literal petrification. For a metaphorical petrification as a result of extreme fear we may compare the description of Teiresias after his intrusion on Athene (Callim. 5. 83–4):

> ἑστάκη δ' ἄφθογγος, ἐκόλλασαν γὰρ ἀνῖαι
> γώνατα καὶ φωνὰν ἔσχεν ἀμηχανία.

or Conon's rationalized account of the effect of the Gorgon (40); and for a literal petrification that of the Man who saw Cerberus (see Cat. 4*a* s.v.). Our early sources emphasize that it was not merely the king but his people who were petrified, and their petrification is not demanded by the story of Perseus. Other factors may be relevant here: Pindar perhaps implies a pun on λαός/λᾶας (*Pyth.* 12. 12). Strabo apparently makes their petrification an explanation of the rockiness of the island (and cites the comic poets in support of this). This rockiness is mentioned by other sources independently of the story (see *AP* 13. 12. 6: τρηχεῖα).

Like many other famous heroic myths the story of Perseus later acquired a further series of transformations. One told how Perseus petrified Phineus, a rival for the hand of Andromeda (Ov. 5. 230 ff.; Apollod. 2. 4. 3; schol. Lyc. 838). (The rival is Agenor in Hyg. *Fab.* 64, and Phoinix in Conon 40; Phineus was first mentioned apparently in Euripides: see Apollod. 2. 1. 4.) Polyidos told how Perseus petrified Atlas, here a Libyan shepherd who tried to block his way, and turned him into the mountain (see schol. Lyc. 879; cf. Ov. 4. 631 ff.). The strory is presumably inspired by the identification of the mountain in Africa with the mythical Titan. We find a blending of the two already in Herodotus (4. 185). Ovid (5. 237 ff.) says that he transformed his grandfather's enemy Proitos. One tradition said that he petrified the sea-monster that was threatening Andromeda (see Lyc. 836 and scholia; Pompon. 1. 64). Howe (art. cit.) argues that vase paintings show a story that Perseus used the head against satyrs in his battle with Dionysos; but see K. Schauenburg, *Perseus in der Kunst des Altertums* (Munich, 1960), 102–3. Nonnus has Perseus using the head against the maenads in this battle (47. 664 ff.), but like the other details of his account this may be his own fantasy. The *Suda* (s.v. Medusa) has a story that Perseus accidentally petrified himself. For the petrification of coral by the Gorgon's head see Ov. 4. 740 ff.

See further J. P. Vernant, *La Mort dans les yeux* (Paris, 1985).

Haemon and Rhodope

Haemon and Rhodope were an arrogant pair of lovers who called themselves Zeus and Hera and were therefore turned into mountains (see Ov. 6. 87 ff.; Ps.-Plut. *Fluv.* 11. 3; cf. Lucian, *Salt.* 51 and 2; Serv. *A* 1. 317; schol. *Ibis* 561). Ps.-Plutarch says that they were an incestuous brother and sister, and schol. *Ibis* that they were father and daughter. Lucian mentions Rhodope alongside Phaedra as one of the μαχλότατaι women of the past. The story has a similar form to that of Ceyx and Alcyone. That explained the relation of two sea-birds: this that of two neighbouring mountains which are frequently mentioned by the poets as a pair. On lovers and stones see p. 144.

Iodama

Pausanias (9. 34. 2) says that Iodama was a priestess of Itonian Athene near Koroneia. One night when she entered the temple precinct Athene appeared to her wearing the head of the Gorgon on her tunic, and she was turned to stone. Because of this a woman still lights a fire on Iodama's altar saying: 'Iodama lives and asks for fire'.

One assumes that the transformed Iodama becomes a cult statue (though Pausanias does not explicitly say this). It is usually thought that Iodama is a local god replaced by or rather absorbed into the cult of Athene. One report says that Athene and Iodama were both daughters of king Itonios and that Athene killed her sister in a fight (schol. Lyc. 355). Simonides the genealogist made her the mother of Thebe and the bride of Zeus and thus gave her a central role in Boeotian genealogy (*FGH* 8 F 1). Her story is a combination of the type in which a miraculous escape or disappearance is followed by the appearance of a cult statue (cf. the stories of Aspalis or Dictynna) and of the type in which some intrusion upon a god is punished by petrification.

Kelmis

Ovid (4. 282 f.) refers briefly to the story of the transformation of Kelmis: 'tu quoque, nunc adamas, quondam fidissime parvo | Celmi Iovi.' It is possible that he is referring to a story which appears in Zenobius (4. 80) explaining the proverb Κέλμις ἐν σιδήρῳ and which is attributed to Sophocles (fr. 365):

αὕτη τάττεται ἐπὶ τῶν σφόδρα ἑαυτοῖς πιστευσάντων, ὅτι ἰσχυροὶ καὶ δυσχείρωτοι πεφύκασι. Κέλμις γὰρ εἷς τῶν Ἰδαίων Δακτύλων, τὴν μητέρα Ῥέαν ὑβρίσας . . . (text uncertain) . . . *ἀφ' οὗ ὁ στερεώτατος ἐγένετο σίδηρος.*

The Idaean Dactyls are mentioned in a fragment of the *Phoronis* (fr. 2), where they are described as magicians who lived on Phrygian Ida. They were companions of the mountain mother and the craftsmen who first discovered iron. Another tradition connected them with Crete (see e.g. AR 1. 1129); it seems that here they were identified with the Couretes and, like them, seen as guardians of the baby Zeus (see Paus. 5. 7. 6). This must be what Ovid is referring to by 'fidissimus Iovi'. This story shows that, like the Telchines, the Dactyls are ambiguous figures, specially favoured and skilful creatures who sometimes go too far. (In fact in Nonn. 14. 36 ff. Kelmis as Skelmis is one of the Telchines. Nonnus may be following Callimachus: see fr. 100, and C. Gallavotti, *Riv. Fil.* 40 (1962), 294–6.)

Kerkopes

The Kerkopes were a famous pair of cheats and liars who were the subject of a comic poem ascribed to Homer (see E. Kinkel, *Epicorum Graecorum Fragmenta* (Leipzig, 1877), 69–70). They are frequently mentioned in the comic poets, and their name seems to have become a general name for rogues (see I. Bekker, *Anecdota Graeca* (Berlin, 1814–21), i. 271. 13 and 22). The most famous story associated with them is that of their capture by Heracles μελάμπυγος. They were also the subject of two transformation stories. Pherecydes is cited for a story that Zeus turned them into stone for lying to him, or lying to men in general (*FGH* 3 F 77; cf. *Suda*, Photius s.v. κέρκωπες; Zenobius, 4. 50, 1. 5). Xenagoras, a third-century BC historian and geographer, said that they were transformed into apes and placed on the island of Pithecusae, to which they gave its name (*FGH* 240 F 28). Ovid is a little more specific in his *aition*: he describes how Zeus 'abstulit usum | verborum et natae dira in periuria linguae; | posse queri tantum rauco stridore reliquit' (14. 97 ff.).

It seems possible that the story of the petrification had its starting point in some stones known as Κερκώπων Ἕδραι at Thermopylae (Hdt. 7. 216, although Zenobius, 4. 50, sets the story in Lydia). The other transformation may be partly prompted by the meaning of their name, as W. C. McDermott suggests (*The Ape in Antiquity* (Baltimore, 1938), 61): κέρκος means a tail. More generally the ape is itself a symbol of deceit, trickery, and ugliness and is used as a term of insult very much as 'Kerkops' is (see Ar. *Ach.* 907, *Av.* 441, *Ran.* 708). The ape too is proverbially contrasted with Heracles (Lucian, *Pisc.* 37 and schol.). It may be that even in their normal state they were seen as dwarfs and scarcely human creatures (see *EAA* s.v. Cercopi; McDermott, op. cit. 231). What role the island of Pithecusae played in the development of the story is uncertain. Their location there may be a secondary development of an already existing transformation story, or it may be that the appropriateness of the island's name was one of the factors that prompted the story in the first place. Lycophron (688 ff.) hints at a different story in which the apes on the island were the transformations of those who had made war on the Olympians. Perhaps our story grew out of this one.

Kragaleus

Kragaleus, son of Dryops, was an old man who lived in Dryopis, where he had a reputation for justice and wisdom. He was asked by Apollo, Artemis, and Heracles to settle their dispute as to which of them should have the city of Ambracia in Epirus. When he decided in favour of Heracles, Apollo turned him into stone. The Ambraciotes still consider that their city belongs to Heracles and his children, and after the festival of Heracles they offer funeral sacrifices to Kragaleus (AL 4, citing Nicander and the *Ambrakika* of Athanadas: *FGH* 303 F 1; cf. Ov. 13. 712 ff.).

This story mixes history and mythology and explains a link between Epirus and a hero located in Phocis or Thessaly. Kragaleus is normally assumed to be an eponym of the Kragalidai, a tribe of southern Phocis who until the sixth century ruled Delphi in alliance with Krisa (Aeschin. 3. 107). Another report says that the Kragalidai were kings of Krisa (Hsch. s.v. Κραγάλιδαι). The Dryopians were regarded as primitive inhabitants of Greece and were usually set in Phocis and Thessaly. Apollo's speech in this story, however, tells how Melaneus, the king of the Dryopes, conquered Epirus and had a daughter, Ambracia. The cult of Kragaleus, therefore, and this story, commemorate the pre-history of Ambracia and link the contemporary city founded by Corinthian colonists with the more primitive past. One assumes that this story was not prompted by a real local landmark since that would not be anywhere near Ambracia (although Ovid does appear to set the story there).

See further E. Oberhummer, *Akarnanien, Ambrakia, Amphilochien im Altertum* (Munich, 1887), 61–4.

Lethaia and Olenos

The only reference to this story is in a list of petrifications in Ovid (10. 67 ff.):

> quique in se crimen traxit voluitque videri
> Olenos esse nocens, tuque o confisa figurae
> infelix Lethaea tuae, iunctissima quondam
> pectora, nunc lapides quos umida sustinet Ide . . .

One assumes that Lethaia was one of those women who boast that they are more beautiful than a goddess (cf. Oinoe or Antigone). She was presumably transformed in punishment, and her husband Olenos shared her fate. (The motif of two related objects or animals having once been a human husband and wife is a common one: cf. Haemon and Rhodope or Alcyone and Ceyx.) Ovid's account seems to imply a contrast between stones and human love (on this theme see Ch. 6).

Lichas

Ovid (9. 211 ff.) tells how Heracles picks up Lichas, the herald who has unknowingly brought him the poisoned robe and throws him out to sea. As he flies through the air he is drained of blood in fear and becomes a rock. He still has human shape, and sailors avoid stepping on him as if he were able to feel. Hyginus (*Fab.* 36) has a rock appearing after Lichas disappears in the sea (cf. *Myth. Vat.* 2. 165).

The story of Lichas' death is an old one. Aeschylus refers to the τύμβος ἀθλίου Λίχα (fr. 25e, 12), by a headland of Euboea. Sophocles tells how Heracles throws him against a rock out in the sea (*Trach.* 772 ff.). Strabo (9. 4. 4) speaks of three islands off the coast of Euboea called the Lichades, supposedly named after Lichas. It is normally supposed that it was the name of these islands that gave rise to the story of Lichas' rock-tomb and then of his petrification. This is plausible, but since the first mention of the Lichades is so much later than the earliest reference to the rock of Lichas we cannot be certain.

See further *RE* s.v. Lichas; F. Stoessl, *Der Tod des Herakles* (Zürich, 1945), 83.

Niobe

The story of Niobe is one of the most popular of all transformation stories. (Its development is discussed in a very full *RE* article by A. Lesky.) It first appears as an *exemplum* in *Il.* 24. 602 ff.: on the Homeric treatment see Chapter 1. This account does not mention the names of Niobe's family, and we do not know whether she is here the wife of Amphion, the king of Thebes. Since Homer sets the transformed Niobe on Mount Sipylus it might be argued that her story began as a local Lydian *aition* and that her connection with Thebes came later. Lesky plausibly argues, however, that the connection with Greece is original and that her location on Mount Sipylus is possibly a secondary development: the Homeric story, in our later accounts, is always told of Niobe, wife of Amphion, and the Lydian story mentioned by some writers is quite distinct from it (see below). The Homeric scholia say that she was known to the Lydians not as Niobe but Elymen. Finally, Niobe is an important figure not only in Thebes but in Argive genealogy (she is the daughter of the first man Phoroneus and the first mortal bride of Zeus: see Apollod. 2. 1. 1).

The story was apparently treated or mentioned by Hesiod (see Ael. *VH* 12. 36), Sappho (fr. 142), Alcman, Lasos, Mimnermus, Pindar (see Ael. loc. cit.), and Bacchylides (see Aul. Gell. 20. 7), but we know almost nothing of these accounts except for the number of children they gave her. (The discrepancies in the poets over the number of Niobe's children seem to have become a regular *topos* in literary discussions: see Ael., Aul. Gell. loc. cit.) Sappho is supposed to have said that Leto and Niobe were once friends (fr. 142; cf. a wall-painting from Herculaneum which shows them quarrelling as children, in anticipation of their later more serious quarrel: R. M. Cook *Niobe and her children* (inaugural lecture, Cambridge (1964), no. 12). Pindar spoke of her wedding to Amphion (fr. 64). Telesilla said that Amphion was killed too, and that two of her children were saved (see Apollod. 3. 5. 6). Timotheus apparently had her descending to Hades (see Ath. 341 C).

There are lost plays of Aeschylus (frs. 154a–167b) and Sophocles (frs. 442–451) called *Niobe*. Aeschylus had Niobe sitting veiled and silent at the tomb of her children (see Ar. *Ran.* 911 ff.). The one extended fragment (154a) shows that the story had acquired a characteristic Aeschylean framework. It is the disaster to the house that is stressed, it may be that Amphion, the head of the house, had incurred Apollo's anger in some way and that Niobe's boasting is an element in a more complex plan of divine punishment (see lines 12 f.—but their interpretation is disputed).

All we know of Sophocles' play is that he had Niobe punished in Thebes but then return to Lydia (cf. Pherecydes, *FGH* 3 F 38, Apollod. 3. 5. 6; Hellanicus, *FGH* 4 F 21, mentions Sipylus). There are two brief mentions of the story in other plays. In the *Antigone* we have, as in Homer, an ambiguous description of the weeping rock/woman. Antigone, about to be buried alive in a cave, compares herself with Niobe imprisoned in a rock (823 ff.). The chorus reply that Niobe is *θεός τε καὶ θεογενὴς* and that Antigone is privileged to share her fate. In *Electra* 150 ff. the heroine says:

ἰὼ παντλά-
μων Νιόβα, σὲ δ' ἔγωγε νέμω θεόν,
ἅτ' ἐν τάφῳ πετραίῳ,
αἰαῖ, δακρύεις.

There seems no reason to count these passages as evidence for an actual cult of Niobe, since they can be explained entirely in terms of their context. In both cases a contrast is drawn between a specially privileged and divinely born heroine of the distant past and the present reality. Nor is there any reason to believe with Lesky that Niobe is in origin an earth-mother goddess. Argive tradition makes her the first woman, but that is a different conception.

Euripides only briefly mentions the story (see frs. 34a and 453; and

Phoen. 159 f., where he mentions the tomb of Niobe's children outside Thebes).

We also have reports of a different story of Niobe in Xanthos' *Lydiaka* (*FGH* 765 F 20). After quarrelling with Leto Niobe suffered a series of misfortunes. Her husband Assaon was killed while hunting and her father then demanded that she marry him. When she refused he invited her children to a feast and burnt the house down with them inside. Niobe herself was transformed to stone (or to ice), or else threw herself off a cliff. Lesky suggests that the heroine of this story was originally not Niobe but Elymen (which the Homeric scholia say was Niobe's Lydian name). He compares the other famous incest stories set in Asia Minor, those of Byblis and Kaunos, and Smyrna. These are much more likely, however, to be Greek fantasies than independent local stories (see p. 300).

As with the story of Io, which was also very popular in the classical period, straight accounts of the story of Niobe seem to be rarer in the Hellenistic writers. But it was apparently told by Euphorion (fr. 102); and Simmias the Rhodian (fr. 5) and Neanthes (*FGH* 84 F 6) told Xanthos' version of the story (see Parth. 33). It was a popular subject of rationalization. Philemon said that Niobe was called a stone because her sufferings had rendered her speechless (fr. 101; cf. Cic. *Tusc.* 3. 63). Palaephatus (8) said that she was confused with a statue on the tomb of her children. There are a number of epigrams on statues of her (see *AP* 16. 129 and 134).

Our only long account of the story in any period is that of Ovid (6. 146 ff.). Instead of the irresponsible chatterer of the epigrams we find here a god-defier on a grand scale. Borrowing a motif from the Dionysos stories he describes how Niobe bans the newly introduced cult of Leto, complaining that it is she who should be worshipped. As often, the final transformation becomes a continuation of the character's human condition; Ovid's account has similarities with some of the explanations of the rationalizers as he describes how Niobe sits silent and still among the corpses of her children. Because he has set the transformation on the spot of the disaster Ovid then introduces a miraculous whirlwind which carries off the stone figure to its present site on Mount Sipylus, where tears still run down its face.

See further Stat. *Theb.* 3. 191 ff., 6. 124 f.; Sen. *Agam.* 394 ff.; Hyg. *Fab.* 9; Paus. 1. 21. 3, 8. 2. 7; QS 1. 294 ff.; Nonn. 2. 159 ff., 14. 271 ff., 12. 79 ff., 15. 374 f., 48. 406 ff.; Tzetzes, *Chil.* 4. 419. Pausanias claims to have actually seen her stone. He says that from close up it looks like an ordinary rock but from a distance like a woman (cf. QS). For Niobe as a subject of dramas in the Roman period see *AP* 11. 246, Suet. *Nero* ch. 21; for Niobe as a subject of mime see *AP* 11. 253, 255, Lucian, *Salt.* 41. Artemidorus says that the story is πολύθρηνος (4. 47). The Νιόβης πάθη were proverbial (Apostol. 12. 11).

For representations of Niobe in ancient art see R. M. Cook, op. cit. The death of Niobe's children was a very common subject. None of these representations add much to our knowledge of the myth of Niobe (usually the mother does not appear at all). One Apulian vase of the fourth century (Cook, op. cit. no. 14) shows Niobe sitting on her children's tomb, several gods including Zeus and Hermes, and perhaps Tantalus. It is generally thought that this was inspired by Aeschylus' play.

Pandareos

Antoninus (36) tells how Pandareos stole the golden dog of Zeus from the god's shrine in Crete and gave it to Tantalus to look after. When after a time Pandareos asked for it back Tantalus swore that he had never received it. Zeus petrified Pandareos on the spot and, for his perjury, struck Tantalus with a thunderbolt and set Mount Sipylus on his head.

The story is also mentioned in the Homeric scholia (on *Od.* 19. 518; cf. on 20. 66 and schol. Pind. *Ol.* 1. 91a). Homer himself merely says that the daughters of Pandareos were left as orphans and does not mention the fate of their father (*Od.* 20. 66 ff.). The scholia mostly say that he stole a ἡφαιστότευκτος dog from Zeus and gave it to Tantalus. When Zeus sent Hermes to fetch it Tantalus swore that he did not have it. Zeus put a mountain on Tantalus and retrieved the dog; Pandareos fled to Athens and Sicily where he died. One of the scholia (B) says that it was Tantalus who stole the dog and Pandareos who committed the perjury (Paus. 10. 30. 2 says that they were both involved in the theft and the perjury. Two early vases also show Pandareos as the keeper of the dog, and it looks therefore as if Tantalus may have been introduced only later on (see L. D. Barnett, *Hermes* 33 (1898), 638–43; cf. *RE* s.v. Pandareos). Whether this story ended with Pandareos' petrification is uncertain.

Pausanias says that Pandareos came from Crete (not as elsewhere Miletus). M. Guarducci (*SMSR* 16 (1940), 1–8) supposes that the story of the dog is an old Cretan story. She compares both a Cretan story in which Euxynthetos is sent to fetch the dog of Praisos (see Strab. 10. 4. 12) just as Heracles is sent to fetch Cerberus, and also the tradition that Procris received her wonder-dog from Minos. It is uncertain, however, whether we have echoes here of forgotten Cretan legends or a pastiche of the legend of Heracles and Cerberus. (In the story as we have it the golden dog made by Hephaistos seems to be modelled on the golden dogs made by Hephaistos for Alcinous in the *Odyssey*.)

The Propoitides

The story of the Propoitides is mentioned only in Ovid. These were women of Cyprus who denied that Aphrodite was a god. In anger the goddess made them first prostitutes (10. 238 ff.),

> utque pudor cessit, sanguisque induruit oris,
> in rigidum parvo silicem discrimine versae.

The moral symbolism of this transformation is characteristic of Ovid: the story acts as a prelude and contrast to the story of Pygmalion, which describes the opposite process as a statue comes to life through the power of love.

This story possibly has its origins in a tradition that the daughters of Kinyras, Aphrodite's priest on Cyprus, were the first prostitutes, a tradition that is itself thought to depend on the institution of temple prostitution on Cyprus (see Plut. *Mor.* 777 D and Apollod. 3. 14. 3). One can perhaps see a development of the story here. Plutarch says that Aphrodite was angry with the daughters of her *propolos* because they first took money from young men, and Apollodorus that the daughters of Kinyras gave themselves to strangers because of Aphrodite's anger. Finally in Ovid we have a petrification (Ovid is of course the earliest of these writers, but Plutarch and Apollodorus may have followed earlier sources). Possibly another passage of Ovid is relevant (6. 99 f.):

> [Kinyras] gradus templi, natarum membra suarum
> amplectens saxoque iacens lacrimare videtur.

Perhaps this story told how his daughters were turned into the steps of the temple they had desecrated. Where the name *Propoitides* was derived from is impossible to say. Since it is such an unusual one it seems unlikely that Ovid invented it.

It is important to stress finally that though this story may have a starting-point in cult practice it belongs in its developed form to a familiar type. One thinks particularly of the daughters of Proitos, who take to the wilds and promiscuity through a goddess's anger.

Pyrrhos

Nonnus refers to a transformed figure which stands near the rock of Niobe on Mount Sipylus (12. 81 ff.):

καὶ ἔσσεται αὐτόθι γείτων
Πύρρος ἐρωμανέων Φρύγιος λίθος, εἰσέτι Ῥείης
οἶστρον ἔχων ἀθέμιστον ἀνυμφεύτων ὑμεναίων.

This story seems to belong to the familiar type in which a favourite of a goddess abuses their special relationship and attempts to rape her. (Cf. Orion or—a closer parallel—Kelmis.) It is possible that this is the same Pyrrhos as that mentioned in Paus. 7. 5. 11.

b. *Petrified Animals and Objects*

The Teumessian fox and the dog of Cephalus: *Epigonoi* fr. 5; Aristodemus, *FGH* 383 F 2; Istros, *FGH* 334 F 65; Ov. 7. 763 ff.; Apollod. 2. 4. 7; Ps.-Eratosth. *Cat.* 33; AL 41.
The wolf which was sent by Psamathe to attack Peleus' cattle: Lyc. 901 f. (and the scholia on these lines and 175); AL 38; Ov. 11. 266 ff.
The snake which attacked Orpheus' head: Ov. 11. 56 ff. (cf. 7. 358); Ps.-Plut. *Fluv.* 3. 4.
Sciron's bones: Ov. 7. 443 ff.
The altar of Midas: Plut. *Par.* 5.
The snake at Aulis, and the Phaeacian ship: above, ch. 1. n. 3.
Pompilos' ship: Cat. 5*c* s.v.
Cadmus and Harmonia in snake form: Cat. 5*c* s.v.
Hecuba in dog form: Cat. 1*a* s.v.

PART 5. MINOR CATEGORIES OF TRANSFORMATIONS

a. *Springs and Rivers*

We know that works on rivers which mixed history, geography, and mythology were common from the Hellenistic period (see e.g. Callim. frs. 457–9, and for a list of such works O. Schneider, *Callimachea* (Leipzig, 1870), 325–7). Transformation stories were one way, and not the most popular one, of explaining the names of these rivers. Our only extant example of such a work, the Pseudo-Plutarch *De Fluviis* explains how various rivers were called after the heroes who drowned in them.

I shall be fairly brief with these transformation stories since they are all very late. (Our main source is Ovid, and it is possible that he has invented several of the proper transformations.) In most cases transformation is a secondary development of some older motif; very often for instance the heroes of these stories have an earlier history as spring-nymphs or river-gods. The stories conform to two fairly standard narrative types.

i. Springs, Lakes, or Rivers Formed Through Weeping

This type is a further example of the pathetic fallacy in which nature is seen to feel human grief. It may be compared with, and was presumably derived from, the type of the mourning stone, tree, or bird. Rose, pointing out that many of these stories are set in Asia Minor, suggested that the type may have its origin in Eastern folk-tale. But we have no examples of the type in indisputably non-Greek myths (see H. J. Rose, *CR* 42 (1928), 171, and 43 (1929), 61).

Byblis

Nicander apparently told how Byblis, in despair over her love for her brother Kaunos, tried to throw herself off a cliff, but was saved by the nymphs and turned into a hamadryad. In her place there appeared a spring which is still called 'The Tears of Byblis' at Miletus (AL 30). Ovid tells how she is rejected by her brother and dissolves into a spring through endless weeping (9. 447 ff.). Other sources say that a spring arose from her tears after she hanged herself (see Apollonius, fr. 5; Aristokritos, *FGH* 493 F 1; Ov. *Ars Am.* 1. 283; Conon, 2; Paus. 7. 5. 10; Hyg. *Fab.* 243; Nonn. 13. 548 f.; schol. Theoc. 7. 115; schol. Dionys. Per. 533; the oldest story apparently told of Kaunos' love for Byblis (see Arist. *Rh.* 1402^{b}; cf. Nikainetos fr. 1)). Ovid is therefore the only source who recounts a proper transformation. We may compare the spring known as 'The Tears of Manto', which apparently never acquired a transformation story (schol. AR 1. 308).

There is some evidence to suggest that brother–sister marriage was a custom among Carian royalty (see S. Hornblower, *Mausolus* (Oxford, 1982), App. 2). Our story is not a direct reflection of this, since the plot depends on the inevitable separation of the lovers, but the custom may have encouraged such fantasies among the Greeks (for the same reason the existence of this custom would not suggest that the story is a local non-Greek one).

Hyrie

See under Kyknos. Only Ovid has her transformed into a lake.

Kleite

The spring Kleite was supposed to commemorate Kleite, the wife of Cyzicus, who killed herself in grief after her husband's death. In Apollonius (1. 1063 ff.) the spring is formed from the tears of the nymphs who mourned her; according to the mythographers cited by the scholia it was formed from her own tears. The Orphic *Argonautica* (593 ff.) amplifies this by saying that the earth sent up the spring after receiving her tears. No source has a full transformation.

Kyane

Cicero (Verr. 4. 107) and Diodorus (5. 4. 2) tell how a spring appeared on the spot where Hades descended to the underworld with Persephone. Ovid develops this into a transformation story in which the nymph of the already existing spring Kyane attempts to block Hades' path, and when he passes straight through her spring she melts away in grief and becomes the water she once ruled over. Here Ovid plays on a conventional ambiguity of water and water-god. Normally the god has ambiguously both human and elemental form: here the two are opposed for the sake of allowing a transformation. In Claudian (*Rapt. Pers.* 3. 246 ff.) Kyane is one of Persephone's companions who dissolves into water after her mistress vanishes.

Marsyas

In a characteristic variation of the normal story, in which the river is formed from the blood of the defeated and skinned Marsyas, Ovid has it formed from the tears of the nymphs and satyrs who mourned for him (6. 392 ff.; cf. *Myth. Vat.* 1. 125). Perhaps Apollonius' story of Kleite is Ovid's model here.

Peirene

Pausanias (2. 3. 3) says that Peirene, the famous Corinthian spring, was once a woman who was transformed weeping for her son Kenchrias. The heroine, Peirene, presumably a spring-nymph, is an early figure (see Hes. fr. 258); as in many of these stories, a spring- or river-spirit is later seen in a rationalized way as a mortal who becomes a spring through transformation.

ii. Stories in which a Hero's Dead Body is Turned into a Spring or River

As a pathetic conclusion in which there is usually no continuity of consciousness or emotion, this type of transformation is close to that of the flower-hero. I include only those stories in which a full transformation is implied in at least one source. Several other stories merely say that the hero's blood began a stream.

Acis

Ovid tells how Galatea's lover, Acis, is crushed by his jealous rival, Polyphemus, with a stone. Through Galatea's powers the trickle of blood changes to water, and Acis emerges as a horned river-god (Ov. 13. 876 ff.; cf. Serv. *E* 9. 39, 7. 37; Sil. 14. 221 ff.; *Anth. Lat.* 151, 886). The story of Polyphemus' wooing of Galatea goes back to Philoxenos, but Acis first appears here, and the story may have been invented by Ovid himself. (None of the later sources adds much to Ovid, and their accounts may have been derived from his.) The story appears to belong to the type in which a river is created from a hero's blood (this is the form of the story in Servius), but Ovid speaks of a full transformation. An ambiguity between human and elemental forms in descriptions of river-gods is the starting-point of several transformation stories: here Ovid produces confusion by referring to the anthropomorphic conception actually within a transformation story. The setting of the story, Galatea's continuing grief, and her regret at being unable to save her lover suggest that the transformation should be seen, as such transformations usually are, as a pathetic compromise rather than a positive rebirth, but Ovid's actual description of Acis as an anthropomorphic river-god makes it hard to see why the lovers are now separated.

Alope

Hyginus (*Fab.* 187; cf. 238 and 252) tells how Alope, the daughter of Kerkyon, was seduced by Poseidon. Their son Hippothoon was exposed, suckled by a mare, and later became the eponym of one of the Athenian tribes, but she herself was killed by her father and then transformed by Poseidon into a spring called Alope near Eleusis (cf. Hsch. s.v. Ἀλόπη, which says that the spring was also known as Φιλότης). The story of Hippothoon's birth seems to have been a popular one in classical Athens; we hear of *Alope*s by Choirilos (*TGF* 2 F 1), Euripides (frs. 105–113), and Karkinos (*TGF* 70 F 1b); cf. Pherecydes, *FGH* 3 F 147 and Demosthenes

60. 31. We do not know whether the transformation formed part of these earlier stories. Hyginus' account is an incoherent mixture of accounts, and Pausanias mentions a grave of Alope near Eleusis, which suggests a different tradition (1. 39. 3). We may assume perhaps that, as often, the local ancestral hero (here Hippothoon) was the son of a local spring or river deity, and that the name of his mother prompted the story of transformation later on. See U. Kron, *Die zehn attischen Phylenheroen* (Berlin, 1976), 177–80.

Aura

Aura is a huntress companion of Artemis. When she is raped by Dionysos she goes mad, eats her own child, and leaps into the river Sangarios. Zeus turns her into a spring (see Nonnus 48. 238 ff.). The spring is not named, and one assumes that this is not a local *aition*. Perhaps the transformation is Nonnus' own addition to the story (our only other account of it, the slightly different story of Aura in *EM* s.v. *Δίνδυμον* makes no reference to it). The story conforms to a common pattern in which a suicidal leap into water precedes transformation (normally to a sea-bird or a rock); such a suicidal leap is the regular means of giving a river a name in the Pseudo-Plutarch *De Fluviis*. But also it may be relevant that being thrown into a river or being transformed into a spring is a common end for monsters (such as Aura has become; see further under Lamia).

Dirke

See under Lamia.

Lamia or Sybaris

Nicander is cited for a story that the monster Lamia or Sybaris lived in a cave at the foot of Mount Parnassus and terrorized the local people until it was destroyed by Eurybatos who had fallen in love with one of its victims. He dragged the monster out of its cave and threw it down a rock: it disappeared, and from the rock there appeared a spring which the local people still call Sybaris (AL 8).

The story corresponds closely in its details with the story of the hero of Temesa (Paus. 6. 6. 7; Strab. 6. 1. 5; Ael. *VH* 8. 18; Callim. frs. 98–9—see Rohde, *Psyche*, i. 154; Fontenrose, *Python*, 101–4) and with that of Aspalis (AL 13). What is particularly relevant from our point of view is that in all three cases the monster finally disappears in water. Lamia is transformed into a spring, the hero of Temesa disappears into the sea, and the body of Aspalis' persecutor Tartarus is thrown into the river that bears his name. It is possible that underlying this motif is the same sort of feeling that led people to throw polluted objects into sea or rivers (see Papathomopoulos, 102). It may have been thought that mere death was not enough for these monsters and that they would not have been satisfactorily disposed of unless they disappeared in this way. We may compare the story of Dirke, the evil queen of Thebes who persecuted Antiope. After her savage punishment (she is either dragged to death behind a bull or stoned by her people) she is thrown into the spring which bears her name (see Eur. in Page, *GLP* 61 f.; Nic. Dam. *FGH* 90 F 7; Apollod. 3. 5. 5). Later sources say that her body or her blood was transformed into a stream (Stat. *Theb.* 3. 204 f. and schol.; Hyg. *Fab.* 7; *Myth. Vat.* 1. 97). It seems significant also that a large proportion of the heroes in the *De Fluviis* leap into a river after committing incest or family murder (i.e. an especially polluting crime). After telling the story of the incestuous Hydaspes, Pseudo-Plutarch (1) reports that the Indians throw virgins who prove unchaste into the river in which he was drowned.

Marsyas

It was noted above that Ovid is unusual in having the river Marsyas created from the tears of Marsyas' mourners. More common is the version which has the river born from his blood (Alex. Polyh. *FGH* 273 F 76; Palaeph. 47; schol. Plat. *Symp.* 215 B, *Minos* 318 B; Hyg. *Fab.* 165). Nonnus (19. 317 ff.) implies a full transformation, and Pausanias' account (10. 30. 9) suggests that he was seen as a local river-god. Eustathius (on Dionys. Per. 321) says that his skin was thrown into the river and washed down to the sea. Our reports of the river go back earlier. Xenophon (*An.* 1. 2. 8) says that at Kelainai, the source of the river, the skin of Marsyas was shown in a cave, and that this gave the river its name. To what extent the Greek legend of Marsyas contains a local element is impossible to say; one assumes at least that Marsyas was connected with Kelainai and its river before the origin of the transformation story, and that this story was a later elaboration of this connection.

Pyramus and Thisbe

In several late Greek authors we find references to a story of Pyramus and Thisbe which is quite different from that of Ovid. Nicolaus (see Westermann, *Myth.* 384) says that Thisbe, the lover of Pyramus, committed suicide after becoming pregnant, and Pyramus then killed himself too. Pyramus became the river of that name in Cilicia, and Thisbe became a spring that comes out beside him. (Cf. Nonn. 12. 81 ff., 6. 344 ff.;

Himerios, *Or.* 1. 11; Them. *Or.* 11. 151.) It is possible that this was the Hellenistic aetiological story from which Ovid derived his own story, but it is perhaps equally possible that Ovid's own story was the starting-point of this one. It appears to be closely modelled on the story of the love of the river Alpheios for the spring Arethusa (and Nonnus 6. 344 ff. has the two rivers meeting underground in their search for their beloved springs).

Selemnos

Pausanias reports a local story about the river Selemnos in Achaea. This river was once a shepherd who died of love for the nymph Argyra. In pity Aphrodite turned him into a river. Since he still loved her, just as the river Alpheios loves Arethusa, Aphrodite granted him forgetfulness. The water of the river still cures men and women of love. This is one of the few spring or river stories which are specifically said to be local stories, and even here the more famous story of Alpheios and Arethusa seems to have been its model (7. 23. 1–3).

iii. *Direct Transformations*

There are two other stories which do not fit either of our two categories, and where we have a direct transformation of the living hero.

Arethusa and Alpheios

It seems that the original story of Alpheios merely told how the river crossed from Elis to appear at the spring Arethusa at Syracuse (see Ibyc. fr. 42; cf. Pind. *Nem.* 1. 1 where Ortygia is called ἄμπνευμα σέμνον Ἀλφεοῦ; Timaeus is cited in Polyb. 12. 4d, the Delphic oracle by Paus. 5. 7. 3). It is not until the late Hellenistic period that we find the story that he came out of love for the Sicilian spring-nymph Arethusa (see Mosch. 6; Virg. *A* 3. 694 ff., *E* 10. 4 and Servius; Ov. *Am.* 3. 6. 29 f.; Stat. *Silv.* 1. 2. 203 ff., *Theb.* 1. 271 f.; Lucian, *D. Mar.* 3, *Salt.* 48; Nonn. 6. 340 ff., 13. 324, 37. 171 ff., 40. 560 f., 42. 104 ff.; Westermann, *Myth.* 361; *AP* 9. 362, 683; Ach. Tat. 1. 18). One late tradition says that he pursued Artemis herself across the sea (schol. Pind. *Nem.* 1. 1, and *Pyth.* 2. 7; there is no reason to believe, as is argued by Fontenrose, *Orion*, 57–60, or *RML* s.v. Alpheios, that this is the original form of the story). Only Ovid and Pausanias tell a transformation story. Ovid says that Arethusa was an Elean huntress who was transformed by Artemis into a stream to escape the amorous river-god. When he too transformed himself to water Artemis opened up the earth and let Arethusa escape to Sicily (5. 573 ff. and 5. 487 ff.). Here it would seem that Arethusa does escape and that, unusually, it is Arethusa who crosses the sea and not Alpheios (although the summary of the story in Lact. Plac. *Narr.* 5. 8 has Alpheios cross with her). Pausanias (5. 7. 2) in a partly rationalized account tells how Arethusa and Alpheios were once a hunter and huntress. She did not want to marry him and crossed over to Sicily where she was transformed into a spring; out of love Alpheios too was changed into a river.

As with most of our spring stories, transformation seems to be a secondary and later motif; here it is the elaboration of a different sort of miracle, the journey of a river across the sea. The transformation is perhaps prompted by an ambiguous view of rivers as human beings as well as natural forces that is inherent in the very common stories of rivers' amorous adventures (cf. Achelous' wooing of Deianeira and Perimele). It is the role of rivers as figures of fertility and ancestors that is perhaps the starting-point of such stories of river-lovers, but part of their attraction for later writers at least is the paradoxical picture it allows them to draw of the river in love: e.g. Moschus says *καὶ ποταμὸν διὰ φίλτρον ἔρως ἐδίδαξε κολυμβῆν* (6. 8).

Several accounts play upon aquatic metaphors to produce incongruous pictures (e.g. Nonn. 42. 108 *οὐ φύγε θερμὸν ἔρωτα καὶ εἰ πέλεν ὑγρὸς ὁδίτης*; cf. Ov. 5. 638). As in the type of the mourning stone, human feeling has transcended the limitations of apparently inanimate nature.

See further A. Tomsin, *Antiquité classique* 9 (1940), 53–6; R. Stoneman, *Maia* 28 (1976), 227–9.

Rhodopis

Having sworn that she will never submit to Aphrodite, the huntress Rhodopis falls in love, and breaks her oath in a cave near Ephesus. She is transformed into a spring called Styx, which now acts as a test of virginity (Ach. Tat. 8. 12).

As in the case of Selemnos, the peculiar properties of a spring are explained in terms of a story that it was once a human being. The story is closely parallel to Achilles' version of the Syrinx story, which has Syrinx too becoming a virginity test near Ephesus. Whether this is a real local *aition* or whether Achilles Tatius has invented spring and story to suit the romance's preoccupation with virginity is difficult to say. One can only suggest that if he was inventing both story and magical spring we should expect the spring to bear the name of the heroine. Perhaps the story of the huntress Rhodopis is in origin an independent one.

iv. Fragmentary or Unknown Transformations

Arethusa, Daughter of Hyperos

The fragment of a papyrus dictionary of metamorphoses (see Renner, 287) mentions a story that Arethusa was transformed into a spring in Euboea after some encounter with Poseidon. Hesiod is cited as the source. Arethusa, daughter of Hyperos, is mentioned in Eustathius (on *Il.* 2. 542) who says that she gave her name to the spring. This might seem to be another example of a heroine who derives her name from a local spring and later prompts a transformation story, but the citation of Hesiod, if reliable, would mean that the transformation appears before any independent mention of the heroine. This is a uniquely early date for a spring story; perhaps Hesiod merely mentioned the heroine and her encounter with the god.

The Lover of the River Kydnos

A fragment of Parthenius tells of how a nymph loved the river Kydnos and Aphrodite turned her into a spring (see Eust. *Il.* 2. 712; cf. Nonn. 40. 141 ff., and 2. 143 f. where the heroine is called Komaitho). It is not clear why she was transformed. This seems to be the earliest example of a full transformation into a river or spring. As in later versions of the story of Alpheios and Arethusa, we have a contrast of the fire of love and of water.

Sangas

Rhea turned Sangas into the river Sangarios for some unspecified impious behaviour (schol. AR 2. 722; *EM* s.v. Σαγγάριος).

b. Islands

Aegina

The scholia to *Il.* 1. 180 tell how Zeus turned Aegina, the mother of Aeacus, into an island and himself into a stone to deceive her father, the river Asopus. One assumes that this is an elaboration of the normal story that Aegina was brought by Zeus to the deserted island of Aegina to which she gave her name (see Paus. 2. 29. 2; Ov. 7. 616). Like rivers and springs, islands and cities are often personified as nymphs and ancestors, and it seems to be this ambiguity that is the starting-point of this transformation. Whereas transformation into a stone is a barren fate, the islands Aegina, Perimele, and Asteria are, like the heroines of the plant stories, lovers of the gods.

The Echinades and Perimele

Our only source for these stories is Ovid (8. 577 ff.). In explanation of a group of islands called the Echinades at the mouth of his river, Achelous tells his guests how he punished some nymphs who forgot to honour him by sweeping them out to sea. One is left to assume that the nymphs were transformed into islands. Beyond the others, he continues, is an island that he loves, called Perimele. She was once a human lover of his whom her father threw off a cliff in punishment. Achelous supported her with his waters and begged Poseidon to transform her. Both stories use standard narrative motifs; these motifs derive further point in each case from the ambiguity between the anthropomorphic god and his natural element. Whether the stories are older than Ovid is difficult to say. The story of the Echinades is perhaps told in too abbreviated a manner to have been invented by Ovid. Apollodorus (1. 7. 3) reports that Perimele was a wife of Achelous who bore him Hippomedon. Perhaps this is an older tradition and the starting-point of the transformation story.

c. *Insects, Reptiles, and Sea Creatures*

Arachne

Ovid tells how the famous Lydian weaver, Arachne, challenged Athene to a contest of weaving. Athene depicted the punishment of sinners by the gods, Arachne the disreputable love-affairs of the gods. Unable to find fault in her work Athene strikes Arachne and drives her to hang herself. In a mixture of pity and desire to punish her further Athene turns her into a spider, and in this form she and her descendants still practise her skill (6. 1 ff.). The story seems already hinted at by Virgil, who describes the spider as 'invisa Minervae' (*G* 4. 246). Pliny (*NH* 7. 196) says that Closter ('spindle') son of Arachne invented the spindle.

It is unnecessary to conclude with *RML* that the story arises from a conflict of Greek and Asian cults in Lydia. The story is an unusually obvious *aition* which sets out to explain the distinctive trait of an animal (it is closer in this sense to the animal fables than many transformation stories). The comparison between the spider's web and the work of human spinners is found already in Aeschylus (*Ag.* 1492).

According to the scholia to Nicander (*Ther.* 11) Theophilus, a pupil or follower of Zenodotus, told a different story about the spider. Arachne and Phalanx were a brother and sister at Athens who were specially favoured by Athene (she taught Phalanx fighting and Arachne weaving).

The pair committed incest and were transformed by Athene into spiders, which are eaten by their children (φάλαγξ is a type of spider). We find the weaving motif here too, but the important *aition* explains the popular belief, already found in Aristotle, that spiders eat their mothers (*HA* 555). For the correspondence of eating one's family and incest see Chapter 4.

Askalabos

In the course of her wanderings Demeter was received by an Attic woman called Misme and given a κυκεών to quench her thirst. Misme's son, Askalabos, mocked her for her eager drinking, and Demeter threw the remains at him. He became an ἀσκάλαβος, a gecko, which is hated by gods and men and has a life in ditches; whoever kills it wins the goddess's favour (AL 24, citing Nicander; cf. Ov. 5. 446 ff.). The story is referred to in Nicander's *Theriaca* too (486 ff.), but here the incident is set not in a humble peasant's home (as it is explicitly in Ovid's account, and implicitly in that of Antoninus), but in the palace of Keleus and Metaneira, who in the *Homeric Hymn to Demeter* are the king and queen of Eleusis. One assumes that the story has its starting-point in the episode of the *Homeric Hymn* which tells how Demeter breaks her fast and takes the *kykeon* when she is made to smile by the jokes of Iambe (an episode which is thought to be a reflection of ritual: see Richardson's commentary, 213–15). In Nicander's story too the *kykeon* and joking are associated, but the joking becomes a mockery of, and an offence against, Demeter herself. The story is an example of a familiar Hellenistic type in which a god or hero is received in a humble home. A. Delatte (*Le Cycéon* (Paris, 1955), 27–36) argues, however, that this change is not a Hellenistic innovation but the older form of the story; he suggests that the *kykeon* was a humble rustic drink and therefore more appropriate to Antoninus' rustic setting than to the palace of the hymn or the *Theriaca*. But, as Richardson (App. 4) points out, the *kykeon* is a heroic drink in the *Iliad* and the *Odyssey*. Unusually for one of Nicander's stories there seems no obvious cult *aition*, and we hear nothing anywhere else of a special relation between Demeter and the gecko. Also there does not seem to be any specific aetiological appropriateness in the transformation. The story perhaps belongs to a more general pattern. The gecko is a creature of night and an ill-omen. (It appears as an animal of ill-omen on a vase showing the setting out of Amphiaraus. See *LIMC* s.v. Amphiaraus no. 7.) The story thus belongs to a series in which animals or plants with an association with the underworld or with darkness are said to have been cursed by Demeter or her daughter (cf. the stories of Ascalaphus or Mint).

Cadmus and Harmonia

At the end of the *Bacchae* (1330 ff.) Cadmus receives a mysterious prophecy:

> *δράκων γενήσει μεταβαλών, δάμαρ τε σὴ*
> *ἐκθηριωθεῖς' ὄφεος ἀλλάξει τύπον*
>
> . . . . .
>
> *ὄχον δὲ μόσχων, χρησμὸς ὡς λέγει Διός,*
> *ἐλᾷς μετ' ἀλόχου, βαρβάρων ἡγούμενος.*
>
> . . . . .
>
> *. . . ὅταν δὲ Λοξίου χρηστήριον*
> *διαρπάσωσι, νόστον ἄθλιον πάλιν*
> *σχήσουσι· σὲ δ' Ἄρης Ἁρμονίαν τε ῥύσεται*
> *μακάρων τ' ἐς αἶαν σὸν καθιδρύσει βίον.*

The barbarian army is presumably the Illyrian tribe of Encheleis. Herodotus mentions an oracle that they would be destroyed after sacking Delphi (9. 43 f.). Euripides wrote a *Cadmus* of which almost nothing is known (see fr. 448). Fr. 930 which describes a transformation into a snake is sometimes attributed to this play. This is the only early reference to the transformation, but since his account is so allusive it seems unlikely that Euripides invented it. Pindar says merely that Cadmus was removed to the Islands of the Blest (*Ol.* 2. 78).

The next hint of the transformation comes in Callimachus, who speaks of the stones of Harmonia ὄφις (fr. 11) by the Illyrian Gulf. Nicander (*Ther.* 607 f.) refers to the area round Drilos as 'the abode of Cadmus and Harmonia, where they creep as a pair of fearsome snakes'. Ovid (4. 563 ff.; cf. 3. 6 ff.), in our fullest account, tells how Cadmus leaves his city after Pentheus' death, weighed down by sorrows, and when he reaches Illyria prays to be turned into a snake himself if it was his killing of a sacred snake that was responsible for his family's disasters. Both he and Harmonia are transformed and become 'placidi dracones' which remember what they were before. In Hyginus (*Fab.* 6) and Nonnus (2. 671 ff., 4. 420, 5. 121 ff., 44. 107 ff., 46. 360 ff.) transformation is a punishment for the snake-killing; in *Myth. Vat.* 1. 150 it is a release from suffering; in Stat. *Theb.* 2. 289 ff. it is the work of the necklace of Eriphyle. Apollodorus (3. 5. 4) tells how Cadmus leads the Encheleis to victory over the Illyrians, and after ruling them for a period is turned into a snake and sent by Zeus to the Elysian Fields. Lucan (3. 189) derives the name Encheleis from Cadmus' snake form. See also Hor. *Ars P.* 187; Philostr. *Imag.* 1. 18; Dionys. Per. 390 ff. The transformation into a snake is nearly always set in Illyria and at the end of his wanderings, and is in fact part of a series of connections with several places in Illyria (see R. L. Beaumont, *JHS* 56 (1936), 163 and 196–7). One famous landmark is the tomb and the magical stones of Cadmus (see Callim. fr. 11, cited above; AR 4. 517; Phylarchus, *FGH* 81 F 39; Dionys. Per. 390 ff.; Steph. Byz. s.v. Dyrrachium; Ps.-Scylax, 24). Nonnus combines this landmark with the transformation and says that Cadmus and Harmonia were transformed into snakes and then petrified (however, this should not be seen as evidence for two real snake-shaped stones but as an imitation of the miracle of the petrification of the snake in *Iliad* 2. 319).

The transformation is a mysterious one, and none of the narrative reasons offered in the various versions of the story are entirely satisfactory. If, for instance, it was a punishment for the killing of the snake why did it happen so late? One is tempted therefore to look for external factors to explain this story. The most common view (see F. Vian, *Les Origines de Thèbes* (Paris, 1963), 122–4; Dodds on *Bacchae* 1330) is that Cadmus is in origin an οἰκουρὸς ὄφις, a founder who lives on in his palace in snake form as a guardian deity, like Erichthonius at Athens or Kychreus at Salamis. The latter has a similar ambivalent relation with snakes: he is described sometimes as the killer of a snake, and sometimes as the snake itself or its protector (see Hes. fr. 226; DS 4. 72; Apollod. 3. 12. 7; schol. Lyc. 451; Paus. 1. 36. 1; Steph. Byz. s.v. Κυχρεῖος). Another approach is to start with the Illyrian connection and to suppose that it was the identification of Cadmus with a local snake-hero that explains his transformation, or helps to explain his departure from Thebes (see U. von Wilamowitz, *Pindaros* (Berlin, 1922), 36–7; Beaumont, art. cit.; Dodds on *Bacchae* 1330).

These are all possible explanations, though in each case there are problems. The major objection to the theory of the οἰκουρὸς ὄφις is that Cadmus' transformation is always connected with his departure from Thebes. No source has him living on at Thebes as a snake. Furthermore, unlike Erichthonius or Kychreus, Cadmus is an outsider and a foreigner and not an earthborn founder. (In this respect he is distinguished from the Spartoi, his fellow founders of Thebes.) Whereas the kings of Athens progressively grow out of their snakiness and their connections with the earth (see R. Parker, in Bremmer, 193) Cadmus develops these connections only at the end of his life.

Dodds supposes that his exile is explained by the historical expulsion of the Cadmeians and their cults (he cites Hdt. 5. 61), but it is interesting that in historical times most of the important Theban cults were supposed to have been founded by Cadmus and the site of his house on the Acropolis was still a holy place (Paus. 9. 12. 3). We do not have enough evidence to come to any conclusion about the theory of an Illyrian snake-god. A Roman inscription in Illyria refers to a god called Drakon (see Wilamowitz, op. cit. 37), but there is no reason to connect this with Cadmus. Also there is no reason to believe that the famous stones of Cadmus were snake-shaped.

Whether or not one accepts such explanations one should perhaps look more closely at the function of transformation in this story. Presumably part of its point, particularly in Euripides' account, is its mysterious nature and the fact that it does not seem to have been caused directly or deservedly by anything that Cadmus has done. Snakes are generally signs and messengers of the otherworld and particularly of the underworld, and there is an appropriateness in the fact that Cadmus and Harmonia pass on in this form. (One source has them taken to Elysium in a chariot drawn by snakes: schol. Pind. *Pyth.* 3. 153b.) More specifically this transformation belongs in the class of those where the change is the final episode in a series of misfortunes and may be seen either as a release or as an expression of the fact that they are more than a human being can bear. One may compare Niobe or Hecuba. Like Cadmus both these heroines are transformed for no apparent reason on leaving their cities in despair.

Chelone

Servius tells a story of how when all gods, men, and animals are invited to the wedding of Juno and Jupiter, Chelone alone refuses to go. Her house is thrown into the river and she is turned into a tortoise that must always carry its home about with it (Serv. *A* 1. 505; cf. *Myth. Vat.* 1. 101, 2. 67).

This story seems to be derived from a fable of Aesop. Fable 108 (ed. A. Hausrath[2], 1957) tells how, when all the animals were invited to the divine wedding, the tortoise alone refused to come and Zeus therefore compelled her to carry her house on her back. This story is much more coherent than Servius' account and was therefore probably the original version. This is the one case where we can see how a myth has developed from an animal fable. Although several others, particularly the stories of the smaller and humbler animals, are of a similar type, these are not typical of transformation stories as a whole.

The Grandson of Kephisos

Ovid refers allusively to an unknown story that the grandson of Kephisos was turned into seal by Apollo (7. 388). Kephisos was a river-god in Attica, Boeotia/Phocis, and Argos. Perhaps the Phocian Kephisos is most relevant to Apollo; he had a grandson called Delphos who gave his name to Apollo's shrine (Paus. 10. 6. 4). One might expect him to become a dolphin rather than a seal (as Apollo himself becomes a dolphin to lead his servants to Delphi in the *Homeric Hymn to Apollo*).

Herdsmen Turned to Frogs

Antoninus (35) tells how Leto tried to wash her new-born children at the spring Melite, but was driven away by some cowherds who wanted to bathe their cattle. She was led by wolves to the river Xanthos, where she drank and bathed her children; she consecrated the Xanthos to Apollo, and called the land Lycia because of the wolves. Returning to Melite she turned the herdsmen to frogs, drove them into the spring, and gave them a life καθ' ὕδατος. As frogs they still live in rivers and marshes. The story is attributed to Nicander, and to Menecrates the Xanthian in his *Lykiaka* (*FGH* 769 F 2).

Ovid (6. 339 ff.) tells the same story without the aetiological details (cf. Serv. and Probus, *G* 1. 378). He has Leto transforming the herdsmen immediately and does not mention any further journey. It has been suggested (see Papathomopoulos, 148) in view of this that Antoninus' account is a mixture of two sources: Menecrates, it is argued, told of the journey to the Xanthos, and Nicander told of the transformation. This is possible, but such aetiological details are normally a feature of Nicander's stories and are commonly missed out in Ovid's adaptations of them. It is objected that Leto's failure to punish the herdsmen immediately is strange, but this is quite in keeping with her helpless state during her persecution by Hera. The story is in a sense a continuation, on a more mundane level, of the epic story of her rejection by one land after the other when she wanted to give birth. One suspects that Antoninus' motive of wanting to bathe her children is older than Ovid's motive of simple thirst: this is a regular motif in stories of mythical heroines' secret births (one may compare, for instance, Rhea's search for a spring in Callimachus' *Hymn to Zeus*). We may note finally that the story is very similar in form to Nicander's story of Askalabos' encounter with and mockery of Demeter, again a goddess in exile, and it is therefore no surprise to find that Servius substitutes Demeter for Leto in his version of the story. See further E. Romisch, *Gymn.* 69 (1962), 350–65.

Ptolemaeus Chennos (4) told how the nymphs who buried Euphorion, a victim of Zeus' thunderbolt, were turned into frogs. For Ptolemaeus see p. 222. This pastiche looks back on the one hand to the mourning trees of Phaethon or the popular myths of tuneful mourning birds, and on the other to the comic tradition that gives frogs absurd pretensions to song.

Kerambos

Kerambos (or Terambos as he is called in the manuscript of Antoninus) was a shepherd who lived on Mount Othrys. He was a great musician and a friend of Pan and the nymphs. But when he ignored Pan's advice to take his flock down from the mountains and told scandalous stories about the nymphs, his flocks died and the nymphs turned him into a beetle (*κεράμβυξ*). Children break off its head and carry it about as a toy; it resembles a lyre with its horns (AL 22, citing Nicander). Ovid briefly refers to a story of Cerambus on Mount Othrys (7. 353 ff.). But he tells how with the help of the nymphs he rises above and thus escapes the flood on wings.

It is impossible to draw any conclusions about the relation of Ovid's to Nicander's story. Ovid's winged figure might be a beetle, but a bird would be more appropriate (it is difficult to imagine that anyone could be turned into a beetle as a favour). Possibly Kerambos was not invented for Nicander's transformation story but was a local shepherd hero like Daphnis, of whom various stories were told about his relations with Pan and the nymphs. One element at least of Antoninus' story, the hero's lyre-playing, looks like an alien element introduced to give the transformation more aetiological point: the lyre seems the wrong instrument for this bucolic musician.

Melissa

Columella speaks of a story that a beautiful woman called Melissa was turned by Jupiter into a bee (9. 2. 3). There seems to have been a tradition that Zeus was nursed by bees on Crete (see e.g. AL 19). In one source this is rationalized in a story that he was nursed by a nymph called Melissa (Lactant. *Div. Inst.* 1. 22). Perhaps this story went one stage further and supposed that Melissa was Zeus' lover (we may compare the stories about the eagle, which in one source fed Zeus as a child and in another was a lover).

Muia

In his encomium of the fly (*Musc. Enc.* 10) Lucian tells a story that Muia was a rival of Semele for Endymion. She was a beautiful woman, but one who was too fond of talking and singing. When she attempted to rouse Endymion from his magical sleep by her singing Semele turned her into a fly. In this form she disturbs the sleep of all, particularly of the young and delicate, and sucks their blood, not from savagery but from love.

Like Lucian's story of the cock it is a transparent *aition*, which, since its hero is not given a particular family or place can hardly be described as a myth at all. Like that story it has its starting-point in a more famous myth rather than any cult relation of the animal, but whether it is an example of literary pastiche by Lucian or a popular animal fable is impossible to say.

Myrmex

Myrmex, a favourite of Athene and renowned for her cleverness, revealed to men and claimed the credit for Athene's invention of the plough. The goddess turned her into an ant, and she became the enemy of the corn she had helped men to produce. Zeus later turns the ants back into human beings for Aeacus (Serv. *A* 4. 402). The latter story, which seems to be very old, is presumably quite independent in origin from the initial transformation although it may have helped to prompt it. The ant is a traditional stealer of corn. Its proverbial industriousness perhaps helps to make the human Myrmex a follower of Athene. Athene possibly had connections with the plough in Thessaly and Boeotia, where she was known as Βούδεια (Lyc. 359) and Βοαρμία (Lyc. 520): see Detienne–Vernant, 178–9.

Nerites

Aelian says that the θαλάσσιοι λόγοι told two stories about the *nerites*, which is now the most beautiful of sea snails but was once the beautiful son of Nereus. According to one he was the companion of Aphrodite while she lived in the sea, and when he refused to accompany her to heaven she transformed him and gave the wings she had been offering him to Eros. According to the other he was the lover of Poseidon and used to drive his chariot across the waves; the sun transformed him in anger at his speed. Perhaps, Aelian suggests, the sun was Poseidon's rival for his love (*NA* 14. 28).

There seems no reason to believe that this shellfish had a cult relation with any of the gods of these stories. Both stories appear to have their starting-points in famous passages of epic (*Il.* 13. 21 ff. describes how Poseidon drives his chariot through the waves, and *Theogony* 191 ff. tells how Aphrodite emerged from the sea). It is interesting that in each case the framework of the story is an opposition between the sea and the heavens.

Pirates Turned to Dolphins

Our oldest source for the story of Dionysos and the pirates is the *Homeric Hymn to Dionysos* (of uncertain date but probably pre-Hellenistic: see O. Crusius, *Philol.* 48 (1889), 193–228, and the commentaries by T. W. Allen, W. R. Halliday, and E. E. Sykes[2] (Oxford, 1936) and F. Cassola (Milan, 1975)). This tells how Tyrrhenian pirates seized him after he appeared on the sea-shore in the form of a young man (no setting for the story is given). They tried to tie him up, but the bonds miraculously fell off him. The helmsman realized that they had captured a god, but the others ignored him. There then followed a series of θαύματα ἔργα: vine and ivy appeared on the mast, Dionysos became a lion, and he made a bear appear. He seized the leader of the pirates, and the others leapt into the sea and became dolphins. The helmsman alone remained and was reassured by the god. We may compare this with a passage of Euripides' *Cyclops* in which Silenos says that when Hera aroused the Tyrrhenian pirates against Dionysos Silenos and the satyrs set sail to rescue him (11 ff.). The motif of the rescue is, one assumes, prompted by the special context of the plot of the *Cyclops*. Pindar apparently treated the story, though we know nothing of his account (fr. 236).

In the Hellenistic period we find a slightly different version of the story. Aglaosthenes in his *Naxica* apparently told how Dionysos and his companions asked to be taken to Naxos. (See Hyg. *PA* 2. 17; Naxos is always his destination in later sources.) When the ship went a different way his companions began to sing. Carried away by the music the pirates danced out of the ship, leapt into the sea, and became dolphins. In memory of this the god placed an effigy of one of them in the sky. No doubt this story was supposed to explain the dolphins' love of music (which was also illustrated in the story of their rescue of Arion). We may compare with this version our one representation of the story in art, a fourth-century monument at Athens (see *LIMC* s.v. Dionysos no. 792). This showed Dionysos sitting on a rock playing with a panther while the pirates are being punished by the satyrs. Some are being beaten, and others have leapt into the sea and are half turned into dolphins. In some later sources this motif of Dionysos' helpers is carried a stage further, and the story is assimilated to the stories of the god's military conquests. Philostratus (*Imag.* 1. 18) describes a sea-battle between two different ships, and Lucian (*Salt.* 22) says that, as well as the Indians and the Lydians, Dionysos conquered the Tyrrhenians.

Most of our other sources are closer to the story of the *Homeric Hymn*. Ovid takes up and elaborates the motif of the good helmsman, whom he calls Acoetes (3. 582 ff.; cf. Pacuvius cited in Serv. *A* 4. 469). No later source speaks of a transformation of Dionysos himself, although Nonnus has him assuming giant form like Demeter in the epiphany of Callimachus' hymn, but they all develop the description of the miracles and delusions worked by the god (see Nonn. 45. 105 ff., 47. 630; Apollod. 3. 5. 3; Hyg. *Fab.* 134; Sen. *Odeip.* 449 ff.; Serv. *A* 1. 67; *Myth. Vat.* 2. 171, 1. 222). Some later writers identify the Tyrrhenian pirates with the Etruscans, so that the story becomes an *aition* for the name of the Tyrrhenian Sea (see Servius, Ovid, Hyginus, Nonnus). There are further hints of the story in *AP* 9. 82, 524 and Lucian, *D. Mar.* 8.

Some scholars have attempted to explain the story as an *aition* for a cult of Dionysos Delphinios (see *RML* 1. 1083, and for another religious interpretation Crusius, art. cit. 217). But we have no evidence for such a cult, or any other link of Dionysos and dolphins. Allen, Halliday, and Sykes, on the other hand, see the story as a simple animal *aition*. They cite several late authors who explain the friendliness of dolphins to men on the grounds that they were once men themselves (Lucian, *D. Mar.* 8; Oppian, *H* 1.648; Porph. *Abst.* 3. 16). But it is difficult to see how the story could have arisen in such a context, since these men are evil pirates who show only aggression to their fellow men. (Philostratus, loc. cit., gets round this by saying that Dionysos changes their character as well as their form.) In fact most of our sources do not derive any animal characteristics from the story of the transformation. (One assumes that the possible *aition* for their love of music in Aglaosthenes' version is a later development.) The truth is perhaps that dolphins are not the starting-point and chief interest of this story. What is important is that the pattern of the god's miraculous epiphany demanded some transformation (we may compare the similar story of Dionysos' epiphany to the Minyades), and that, since this is an epiphany at sea, dolphins are an obvious choice; they are symbols of the sea in ancient art (for instance in a depiction of Dionysos' epiphany at sea: *LIMC* s.v. Dionysos no. 788), they were felt to have human qualities, and they do play a part in stories of pirates. The question of why Dionysos should be given an epiphany at sea is a more complicated one (see e.g. Burkert, *HN* 218–26).

Pompilos and his Ship

Okyrrhoe was the beautiful daughter of Chesia and the river Imbrasos on Samos. Pursued by Apollo, she flees to Miletus and asks Pompilos, a ferryman and friend of her father, to take her on his ship. He does so, but Apollo appears, seizes the girl, petrifies the ship, and turns Pompilos into the fish of the same name, making him the ὠκυάλων νηῶν παιήονα δοῦλον (Apollonius, frs. 7–9; cf. Aelian, *NA* 15. 23).

Pompilos' transformation is a straightforward aetiological one. A man who is described as δυσκελάδου δεδαὼς θοὰ βένθεα πόντου naturally becomes a fish that guides ships across the sea (for the character of the *pompilos* see Ath. 283 D). The story is an unusual mixture of myth and the themes of the Greek romance. The heroine's father is a river, and her pursuit by Apollo recalls the story of Daphne. The petrification of the ship is an echo of Poseidon's petrification of the ship of the Phaeacians in the *Odyssey* (the Phaeacians too are punished for transporting someone against the will of a god), and the transformation of Pompilos himself recalls the transformation of the sailors into dolphins in the *Homeric Hymn to Dionysos*. But the flight of the persecuted heroine in a ship, and the location of the story in Miletus and Samos, take us into the world of the Greek romance.

Tithonus

The story of Eos' unsuccessful attempt to win immortality for her lover Tithonus is first told in the *Homeric Hymn to Aphrodite* (218 ff.). The poet makes no reference to a transformation, but says that as he became older and older Eos finally placed him in a room and closed the doors:

> τοῦ δ' ἤ τοι φωνὴ ῥεῖ ἄσπετος, οὐδ' ἔτι κῖκυς
> ἔσθ' οἵη πάρος ἔσκεν ἐνὶ γναμπτοῖσι μέλεσσιν.

A story ascribed to Hellanicus (see schol. *Il.* 3. 151) says that when he was consumed by old age he was turned into a cicada (cf. schol. Lyc. 18; Serv. *G* 3. 328; *Suda*/Photius s.v. Τιθωνοῦ γῆρας). Schol. *Il.* 11. 1 says that since it was not possible for Tithonus to die Eos turned him into the cicada, the most musical of creatures, so that she could hear him sing. In one source the story is assimilated to the type of the mourning bird, and Tithonus is transformed 'dum ille longae vitae fata defleret' (schol. Stat. *Theb.* 5. 751; in Virg. *G* 3. 328 the song of the cicada is described as 'querelae').

J. T. Kakridis (*Wien. Stud.* 48 (1930), 25–38) has argued that the transformation story is older than the *Homeric Hymn*. He suggests that some of the details of the hymn's account suit the transformation story much better than the context in which they appear. The ἄσπετος φωνή suggests not the quavering voice of an old man, but the loud song of the cicada. (He compares the Homeric expression ἄσπετος κλαγγή.) Also he points out that the hymn seems to imply that Eos stopped feeding Tithonus when he was locked in his room, and he compares this with the popular legend that the cicada fed on nothing but dew (see Plat. *Phaedr.* 259 B, where it is told how the cicadas were once men who in their love of music forgot to eat and drink). However, the contrast of vigour of speech and bodily weakness is characteristic of descriptions of the old (cf. *Il.* 3. 151). Also what is actually said in the hymn about food is that before locking him up Eos tried to delay Tithonus' ageing by feeding him on ambrosia; if it is implied that she stopped feeding him this makes perfect sense in the context of the hymn: she has now abandoned him to his fate. It is more plausible to imagine that the suggestive details of the hymn, and also the simile of the *Iliad* which compares old men talking to cicadas, were the starting-point of the transformation story (*Il.* 3. 151). Perhaps also the legend that they fed on dew makes them suitable lovers of the dawn.

See further Davies and Kathiramby, 126–7.

Index

In general only the main character in any transformation story is included in the index.